Deregulation or Re-re

Deregulation or Re-regulation?
Regulatory Reform in Europe and the United States

Edited by Giandomenico Majone

Pinter Publishers, London
Distributed exclusively in the USA and Canada by ST. MARTIN'S PRESS

First Published in Great Britain in 1990 by
Pinter Publishers, 25 Floral Street, London WC2E 9DS

Paperback edition first published in 1992

Distributed exclusively in the USA and Canada by St. Martin's Press, Inc.,
175 Fifth Avenue, New York, NY 10010, USA.

British Library Cataloguing in Publication Data
A CIP catalogue record for this book is available from
the British Library.

ISBN 0-86187-834-5 (Hbk)
ISBN 0-312-04183-7 (Hbk - St. Martin's Press)
ISBN 1-85567-088-7 (Pbk)

First Published in the United States of America in 1990

ISBN 0–312–04183–7

Library of Congress Cataloging-in-Publication Data

Deregulation or reregulation? : regulatory reform in Europe and in the United States
/ edited by Giandomenico Majone.
    p.   cm.
  ISBN 0–312–04188–7
  1. Deregulation. 2. Deregulation—Europe. 3. Deregulation–
–United States. I. Majone, Giandomenico.
HD3612.D48 1990   89–29482
338.94—dc20   CIP

Typeset by Selectmove Ltd
Printed and bound in Great Britain by Biddles Ltd.

Contents

List of Contributors

Charles B. Blankart,	Technische Universität, Berlin
Stephen Breyer,	Judge, US Court of Appeals for the First Circuit, Lecturer in Law, Harvard University Law School
Robert W. Crandall,	The Brookings Institution, Washington, DC.
Christian Joerges,	Universität Bremen and European University Institute, Florence
Erich Kaufer,	Universität Innsbruck
John Kay,	London Business School
Gunther Knieps,	Rijksuniversiteit Groningen
Philippe Koebel,	Ministry of Finance, Paris
Giandomenico Majone,	European Policy Unit, European University Institute, Florence
Anibal Santos,	Universidade Catolica Portuguesa.
Matthias-Wolfgang Stoetzer,	Technische Universität, Berlin
John Vickers,	Nuffield College, Oxford
Ernst Ulrich Von Weiszäcker,	Institute for European Environmental Policy, Bonn

Acknowledgements

The authors wish to thank the *California Law Review* for permission to reproduce the article 'Antitrust, Deregulation, and the Newly Liberated Marketplace', by Stephen Breyer.

List of Figures

List of Tables

Introduction

Giandomenico Majone

This volume brings together the main results of a conference organized by the European Policy Unit of the European University Institute in late November 1988. The purpose of the conference was three-fold: to assess recent developments in key areas of regulation in America and in Europe; to explore the implications for national policies of the growing body of European Community regulation, especially in view of the completion of the internal market; last, but certainly not least, to stimulate interest in an area of research – the political economy of regulation – which until recently has been largely neglected by European scholars.

What is Regulation?

As every student of the subject knows, in America regulation is a distinct type of policy-making that has spawned a distinct theoretical and empirical literature; indeed, in economics and political science the study of regulation has been elevated to the status of a subdiscipline (Noll, 1985). The situation is different in Europe. Here, despite the intensity of the current debate about deregulation at the national and Community levels, research on the economics and politics of public regulation is still a relatively new area of scholarship. Paradoxically, the study of deregulation has preceded the theory, if not the practice, of regulation.

There are several reasons why European social scientists have not developed anything comparable to the American theories of regulation. To begin with, the term itself is often used differently on the two sides of the Atlantic. In Europe there is a tendency to identify regulation with the whole realm of legislation, governance and social control. This broad use of the term makes the study of regulation coextensive with law, economics, political science and sociology, and thus impedes the development of a theory of regulation as a distinct kind of policy-making.

By contrast, within the framework of American public policy and administration, regulation has acquired a more specific meaning. It refers to sustained and focused control exercised by a public agency over activities that are generally regarded as desirable to society (Selznick, 1985: 363–4). This characterization makes explicit the two distinguishing features of American-style regulation. The reference to socially desirable activities excludes, for example, most of what goes on in the criminal justice system: the detection and punishment of illegal behaviour is not, in this sense, regulation. At the same time, it suggests that market activities are 'regulated' only in societies that consider such activities worthwhile in themselves and hence in need of protection as well as control.

The second characteristic – sustained and focused control by a public agency – implies that regulation is not achieved simply by passing a law, but requires detailed knowledge of, and intimate involvement with, the regulated activity. As one of the most distinguished students and practitioners of regulation in the New Deal era put it, 'the art of regulating an industry requires knowledge of details of its operations, ability to shift requirements as the condition of the industry may dictate, the pursuit of energetic measures upon the appearance of an emergency, and the power through enforcement to realize conclusions as to policy' (Landis, 1966: 25–6). It follows that regulatory policy-making requires, not bureaucratic generalists, but specialized agencies or commissions capable of fact-finding, rule-making, and enforcement.

In turn, these differences in meaning reflect significant ideological and institutional differences between the American and the European approach to the political control of market processes. The long tradition of regulation in the United States – which at the federal level goes back to the 1887 Interstate Commerce Act regulating the railroads, and setting up the corresponding regulatory commission – expresses a widely held belief that the market works well under normal circumstances, and should be interfered with only in specific cases of 'market failure' such as monopoly power, negative externalities, or inadequate information.

In Europe, popular acceptance of the market ideology is a more recent phenomenon. For most of the period between the great deflation of 1873–96 and World War II, large segments of political opinion were openly hostile to the market economy, and sceptical about the capacity of the system to survive its recurrent crises. Hence in industry after industry the response of most European governments to perceived cases of market failure was not regulation, but nationalization, industrial reorganization and planning, and other forms of corporate intervention (see the chapter by Blankart for German examples).

Moreover, even when regulatory instruments like price controls, standard setting or licensing have been used, there has been a general reluctance to rely on specialized, single-purpose agencies. Instead, regulatory functions have been assigned to traditional ministries or inter-ministerial committees. The absence of independent regulatory bodies, the confusion of operation and regulation, the preponderance of informal procedures for rule-making, and the diffuseness of various corporatist arrangements of self-regulation, are all factors that explain the low visibility of regulatory policy-making in Europe, and the consequent lack of sustained scholarly attention.

Meaning of Regulatory Reform

The absence of a significant body of theoretical and empirical literature on regulation explains a certain confusion about the meaning of deregulation in the European context, and its relations to other measures of liberalization or to privatization. In Europe, as in the United States, traditional structures of regulation and control are breaking down under the pressure of powerful ideological, technological and economic forces, and are being dismantled or radically transformed. This is often called 'deregulation', but as several contributors to this volume point out, that is a misleading term.

Neither in the United States nor in Europe has deregulation meant an end to all regulation. As Breyer points out, airlines have not been deregulated with respect to safety, and newly deregulated industries have lost their pre-existing statutory immunity from the American anti-trust laws. Despite major changes in the United States telecommunications sector, important segments of the industry remain regulated. In fact, Robert Crandall writes, all of the regulatory institutions that controlled telephone rates twenty-five years ago are alive and well. In Europe, especially in Great Britain, privatization of natural monopolies has been followed by price regulation (see the chapter by Santos).

Deregulation may also mean less restrictive or rigid regulation. Thus, the rationale for public intervention has seldom been challenged in the increasingly important area of 'social' regulation – environment, health, safety, consumer protection. Here the important issue is not deregulation but rather, as Ernst von Weiszäcker argues, how to achieve the relevant regulatory objectives by less burdensome methods of governmental intervention. In sum, what is observed in practice is never total deregulation, but a combination of deregulation and reregulation. This apparently paradoxical combination is what is meant by 'regulation reform' (see, in particular, the chapter by Kay and Vickers).

Regulatory Reform in the European Community

A particularly important example of regulatory reform, which is discussed by Christian Joerges and by other contributors to this volume, is the 'new approach' to Community-wide regulation developed by the Commission in the wake of the *Cassis de Dijon* judgment of the European Court of Justice. The main objective of the Community in its first twenty-five years has been the harmonization, rather than the unification, of national regulations. Harmonization is the adjustment of national rules to the requirements of a common market. Its characteristic instrument is the 'directive', since this instrument of Community legislation only specifies the regulatory objectives to be achieved, leaving the choice of methods to the Member States.

Substantial progress has been made in this way in the creation of harmonized rules on a Community-wide basis. However, by 1985 the Commission had to acknowledge that the amount of work that remained to be done was such that the goal of completing the internal market by 1993 could not be achieved by relying exclusively on the harmonization approach. In the words of the Commission (1985: 18), 'experience has shown that the alternative of relying on a strategy based totally on harmonization would be over-regulatory, would take a long time to implement, would be inflexible and could stifle innovation'.

The new approach has three key elements: regulation at Community level is to be replaced, whenever possible, by mutual recognition of national regulations and standards; harmonization is to be confined to laying down 'essential health and safety requirements' which will be binding on all Member States; technical specification of these requirements is to be left to European and national standardization organizations (the so-called reference technique).

The obvious advantage of the new approach is that it greatly reduces the regulatory workload of the policy-making organs of the Community. In particular, the principle of mutual recognition – which rests on the assumption that the health and safety objectives of the Member States are equally valid in principle, even if they are pursued by different methods – eliminates the need of drafting directives suitable to the substantive needs and legal tradition of twelve national actors. In a system as varied as the European Community it makes very good sense to apply the old subsidiarity principle of federalism according to which the higher level of government should intervene only to provide public goods that lower levels cannot supply (Dehousse, 1988). Also, as Kay and Vickers suggest, the replacement of harmonization by mutual recognition and by the delegation of standard setting to technical bodies introduces a principle of competition between rules and between regulators that may stimulate flexibility and policy innovation.

However, the chapters by Joerges and by Kaufer point out the limits of the new approach, as well as the difficulties of implementing it. The emphasis on mutual recognition and on the delegation of standard setting leaves open regulatory gaps that will have to be closed eventually. For example, mutual recognition cannot handle negative externalities that transcend national boundaries; nor can it solve problems which have proved too difficult even for the traditional approach through harmonization, as in the case of pre-market testing of new medical drugs. As Kaufer argues, differences among the national schools of medicine, different attitudes toward the evaluation of risks and benefits, and differently perceived needs for new drugs will lead to divergent interpretations of new-drug approvals, despite the fact that they have been prepared according to a standardized European format. The most likely result, in Kaufer's opinion, is that the Commission will feel compelled to push for a centralized European Drug Agency to replace the cumbersome and ineffective multi-state application procedure now in use.

Institutional Implications

The issue of European regulatory agencies or inspectorates is receiving increasing attention, not only by academics but also by policy-makers. Thus, in January 1989 the President of the European Commission, addressing the European Parliament, proposed the creation of a European Environmental

Agency in order to support, coordinate and complement national efforts in implementing Community regulation. President Delors' proposal has been well received, on the whole, at the meeting of the ministers of the environment held in Caceres, Spain, at the beginning of May 1989. In another significant recent development, the European Parliament has called for a centralized air traffic control (ATC) system for the European Community. The new European ATC organization would have responsibility for centralized equipment procurement, operation of certain ATC facilities, collection of user charges, enforcement of common ATC standards, and research and development.

It is important to note that these moves toward independent regulatory agencies, like analogous developments at the national level (see, for example, Koebel's discussion of recent changes in the regulatory framework for telecommunications in France) represent a natural evolution of the regulatory approach. To repeat a point already made, regulation is not achieved simply by passing a law, but requires detailed and continuous attention to the regulated activity. Hence, regardless of the initial institutional arrangements, something looking very much like a regulatory agency or commission, capable of detailed assessment and rule-making and having an appropriate staff and field offices, is bound to emerge sooner or later.

Also in this respect, the American experience is very instructive, without in the least implying that the US regulatory agencies are appropriate models for European bodies. On the contrary, there are good reasons to believe that quite different organizational designs should be adopted in Europe (see Kaufer's discussion of possible models for a European Drug Agency).

The Uses of International Comparisons

Judge Breyer reminds us that it is always debatable to what extent one can transfer the experience of one country to other societies with different political and administrative traditions. Yet the papers in this volume show that in today's interdependent world knowledge of international policy developments is absolutely indispensable. For example, it is clear that the regulatory changes that have taken place in the US telecommunications sector are having major repercussions in virtually all European telecommunications industries. As Knieps argues, the experience of the United States, and also of Japan and Great Britain, casts doubts on the wisdom of the strategy of partial deregulation adopted by the European Commission (see the chapter by Ungerer).

According to Knieps, a more promising approach for a European telecommunications policy would be to allow free entry into all subparts, including public networks and basic telephone services. The socially desired objective of universal service should be achieved, not by the traditional method of cross-subsidization but by a universal service fund financed by the new entrants and existing firms (the point is further developed by Blankart). Comparative analysis also permits evaluation of the differential impact of similar policies in different systems. Thus, in his chapter on airline deregulation Stoetzer shows that deregulating the prices of scheduled flights will have a smaller effect in Europe than in the United States. This is because most air traffic in the United States is on scheduled flights, while a large part of European air traffic is carried by chartered flights, the prices of which are not regulated.

These are only two examples. The reader of this volume will find many other instances of the heuristic value of comparative policy analysis. This conference and the resulting book will have served a very useful function if they increase the awareness of policy-makers, businessmen and analysts, in Europe and in the United States, toward the international dimensions of regulatory reform.

Acknowledgements

It is a great pleasure to acknowledge the superb assistance provided by the staff of the European Policy Unit – Mr Peter van den Bossche, Dr Renaud Dehousse, Ms Annette Merlan and Ms Evelyne Dourel, both in the organization of the conference on regulatory reform and in the preparation of this volume. As editor, I am especially grateful to Professor Charles B. Blankart whose advice has been invaluable in all stages of this enterprise.

References

Commission of the European Communities, (1985), *Completing the Internal Market*, Luxembourg, Office for Official Publications of the European Communities.

Dehousse, Renaud, (1988), 'Completing the Internal Market: Institutional Constraints and Challenges', in Roland Bieber, Renaud Dehousse, John Pinder, Joseph H. Weiler (eds), *1992: One European Market?*, Baden-Baden, Nomos.

Landis, James M. (1966), *The Administrative Process*, New Haven, (CT., Yale University Press (1st edn 1938).

Noll, Roger G. (1985), 'Government Regulatory Behaviour', in *idem* (ed.), *Regulatory Policy and the Social Sciences*, Berkeley and Los Angeles, University of California Press, pp. 3–63.

Selznick, Philip (1985), 'Focusing Organizational Research on Regulation', in *Regulatory Policy and the Social Sciences, op. cit.*, pp. 363–7.

1. Regulation and Deregulation in the United States: Airlines, Telecommunications and Antitrust

Stephen Breyer

The object of this paper is to help explain American regulation and deregulation to a European reader. It will do so in two ways. **Part I** will present an elementary overview of American regulatory systems. It is aimed, in part, to help the reader see how American legal, political, and administrative institutions – different from those of Europe – have created several different kinds of 'regulatory systems', each of which calls itself 'regulation'. The term 'deregulation', too, has different meanings, depending upon the particular kind of regulation at issue.

Part II will discuss, with greater sophistication and in greater depth, recent experience with two important examples of deregulation: airlines and telecommunications. It will make the reader aware of how 'deregulation' of such industries requires them to cope with the American antitrust laws, laws that some describe as but another form of 'regulation' but which may be better understood as a necessary effort to make deregulated markets function competitively.

The paper will draw no general conclusion, for the extent to which one can transfer American experience to communities with different institutional histories is still a matter for speculation.

Part I   An Elementary Overview

Regulation[1]

Regulation, particularly in the United States – at least 'economic regulation' broadly conceived – typically refers to governmental efforts to control individual price, output, or product quality decisions of private firms, in an avowed effort to prevent purely private decision-making that would take inadequate account of the 'public interest'. Congress established the first modern regulatory agency (the Interstate Commerce Commission) in 1887 to control railroad rates. By the 1960s government regulation of 'prices' or 'entry' was commonplace in the transportation, communications, and utility industries. Federal or state regulatory bodies exercised control over trucking, airlines, telephone services, electricity, radio, television and natural gas. The federal government regulated the safety of products or production methods in the transportation, food, and drug industries; it also regulated banks and issuers of securities to protect depositors and investors. In the 1960s and 1970s, the scope of regulatory activity expanded still further, when the federal government began to regulate oil prices, imposed controls on environmental pollution, and regulated the safety of the workplace, on the highway, and of consumer products. It also increased regulatory efforts to protect investors, including pension holders and commodities traders. To understand these diverse regulatory efforts, it may help to consider (1) the legal and administrative framework in which they arise; (2) the reasons for regulating; and (3) the resulting 'regulatory' systems that have emerged.

THE INSTITUTIONAL CONTEXT

It is important to keep in mind several special characteristics about American legal, administrative, and political institutions, the institutional framework in which American regulatory systems have arisen. First, the federal judiciary has played a major role in shaping the content of particular regulatory systems. Federal judges, however, unlike many of their continental European counterparts, are not specialists in administrative law or in government bureaucracy. Nor are they (in the European sense) 'professional' judges. That is to say, they do not choose to become judges early in their careers, but the government appoints them (as in England) typically aged 40 and 50, often out of a career as practising lawyers. Many of them will more readily sympathize with problems facing the courtroom litigator than with those facing a bureaucratic administrator. At the same time (unlike England) federal courts review all significant administrative action, setting aside not only agency action that violates a statute, but also action that the court decides is unreasonable. Moreover, court review takes time, months and sometimes years. Thus, virtually all significant administrative action must meet a standard of 'reasonableness' applied by nonspecialist judges. And (because of the time needed for review) it is difficult to change administrative policies quickly or often.

Second, American 'separation of powers' principles have created a federal political system that, to European eyes, may seem surprisingly fragmented. Regulators exercise legal powers that Congress delegates to them in sometimes detailed, individual statutes. The President, whether or not he is of the same political party as a majority of Congress, cannot easily change these statutes, regardless of his own political programme. Nor can the President easily tell his own Executive Branch regulators just what to do. The statutes, as just mentioned, typically delegate legal power to the regulators (to 'the

Secretary', 'the Administrator', the 'Board') not to the President; sometimes they delegate power to an 'independent' board or commission, the membership of which the President can change only slowly, over time; and in any event, direct intervention by the President into the details of regulatory decision-making may well produce a political reaction by affected interest groups (in part using the claim that the intervention is 'inappropriate') that would impose a political price Presidents may not willingly pay. These facts tend to make regulatory programmes less flexible, resisting major changes of direction; and they also mean that different regulatory programmes can work at cross purposes, suffering through lack of strong, central (White House) coordination.

Third, the United States (perhaps because it lacks an historical tradition of centralized bureaucratic administration) relies less, in setting administrative policies, upon the judgement of highly trained 'professional' civil servants, than upon the use of legalistic, adversary, court-type procedures. That is to say, the regulatory agencies themselves typically obtain written submissions from interested persons, hold hearings, obtain replies, and then embody their decision in a regulatory 'rule' that a court will later review. Some describe the regulatory agencies as acting like 'little courts' and like 'little legislatures'. Of course, European government decision-makers will also hear from interested parties, but the degree to which American administrative decision-making proceedings are adversary; the degree to which they resemble court proceedings; the extent to which they are open; and the extent to which the administrators are themselves bound by rule and regulation, all may surprise the European observer.

The net result of these institutional characteristics and tendencies is economic regulation that (1) tends to operate in an adversary relation with industry; (2) tends to be created and applied by a subject-matter-specific governmental administrative bureaucracy working somewhat independent of central control; (3) to a degree is developed through legal, courtroom type procedures, and (4) is embodied in legal rules that may seem somewhat inflexible and rather resistant to change. These institutional characteristics mean that regulatory systems cannot easily be 'fine tuned'; regulatory actions are cannons, not rifles. These characteristics also mean that different regulatory programmes have sufficient stability and common characteristics to warrant consideration as several distinct 'systems'. They have led some to characterize 'regulation' in general as a 'middle way' of relating government to industry, somewhere between 'nationalization' and complete 'laissez faire'.

REASONS FOR REGULATION

One can best begin to understand different systems of economic regulation by classifying the 'reasons' asserted as justifying them. Advocates of individual regulatory programmes assert many different reasons in support of each. Yet, a small number of important economic reasons appear and reappear as 'justification' for particular kinds of regulation. Those economic reasons assume that an unregulated marketplace is the norm. Regulation is then 'justified' in so far as it is needed to overcome one or more market 'defects' that might otherwise prevent purely free markets from serving the 'public interest'. The market 'defects' that have most often led to a demand for regulation can be classified as follows:

1   *The need to control monopoly power*   When economies of scale in a particular industry (say, electricity production or local telephone service) are so great as to make it inefficient for more than one firm to operate in that industry, that firm – a 'natural monopolist' – can increase its profits by restricting output and charging higher than competitive prices. Regulation of such an industry aims to improve 'allocative efficiency' by holding prices down closer to costs. In principle, by doing so, regulation will help provide a set of price signals that, considered from the point of view of the economy as a whole, will guide raw materials towards products that consumers want more, and away from those they want less. The extent to which regulation can help to achieve this economic objective of 'allocative efficiency' is much debated. In any event, regulation of the 'natural monopolies' also rests upon other, less technically economic objectives such as fairer income distribution, avoiding discrimination in price or service among customers, and distrust of the social and political (as well as the economic) power of an unregulated monopolist.

2   *The need to control windfall profits*   'Economic rents' in the form of 'windfall profits' may occur as the result of a sudden increase in a commodity's price, benefiting any firm that has a pre-existing stock in the commodity or controls a specially low cost source of its supply. Those who owned large stocks of oil in the 1970s, for example, could obtain windfall profits when OPEC raised the price of new oil; owners of old, cheap natural gas, if free to raise prices, would obtain a windfall when the costs of finding new natural gas rose; and those who own existing housing can obtain windfalls if construction costs rise suddenly and faster than other costs. Since windfall profits or 'rents' commonly exist to some degree in many highly competitive industries, they are typically not thought to call for regulation. But, when they are unusually large in amount and seem not to reflect any particular talent or skill on the part of producers, there may be a demand for regulation that seeks to transfer allegedly huge and undeserved profits from (say, oil or gas) producers (or owners) of the scarce resource to consumers. This type of justification underlay, for example, the regulation of natural gas in the 1960s and oil in the 1970s, and it underlies rent control in housing today.

3   *The need to correct for spillover costs*   Regulation is often demanded on the ground that a product's price does not reflect certain major costs that its production imposes on society. Thus, the price of steel may not have reflected the 'spillover' cost (the 'externality') that its production imposed in the form of air pollution. Demand for steel was therefore greater than it would have been had its buyers had to pay the cost of these adverse side effects. Of course, the harmful effects of pollution result both from the steel company's production process and the fact that people live near the plant. In theory, steel users and pollution sufferers might agree to share the cost of antipollution devices – if they could bargain among themselves. Such bargaining typically is impractical, however. And, regulation, particularly environmental regulation, as a way to correct for the presence of important

spillover costs, reflects that fact. Regulation has not taken the form of 'price' controls, but, rather, has consisted of a societal effort to control products or production process defects through the use of standards.

4 *The need to compensate for inadequate information* Consumers need adequate information for competitive markets to function well. Government regulation sometimes aims at lowering the costs of obtaining adequate information. In particular, government action has been called for when (1) suppliers mislead consumers whose available legal remedies, such as private court actions, are expensive or impractical; (2) consumers cannot readily evaluate the information available, such as the potential effectiveness of a drug; or (3) the market on the supply side fails (for some special reason) to furnish the information needed or demanded. In the former instance, the government has created special consumer protection commissions; in the latter two instances, the government may seek to provide more, or better, information or to require producers to supply the information, as in the case of financial or securities disclosures.

5 *The need to eliminate 'excessive' competition* The 'price and entry' regulation of airlines, trucking, and ocean shipping was often justified by the asserted need to control 'excessive' competition – competition that allegedly would lead to unreasonably low prices, bankruptcies, and the survival of one or two firms, which would then set unreasonably high prices. In historical context, some airlines advanced this argument fearing competition from government-subsidized rivals. Regulated railroads also advanced the argument in an effort to extend regulation to encompass the prices set by their competitive rivals, the trucking companies. The argument sometimes amounted to a fear of 'predatory' pricing. A dominant firm might set prices below its variable costs, with the object of driving its rivals out of business, later raising its prices and recouping lost profits before new firms, enticed by the higher prices, enter the industry. Most economists doubt that firms can readily set predatory prices in the transportation industries.

6 *The need to alleviate scarcity* Sometimes regulation has been demanded as a method for allocating items in short supply. Sudden and dramatic price increases or sudden supply failures (such as an oil boycott) lead to the claim that allocation through the unregulated marketplace will cause too severe hardship for too many users. A shortage may result from outside forces (such as a boycott by producers), from the operation of a different regulatory programme (as low regulated prices arguably led to a natural gas shortage) or from a specific decision to abandon the market to achieve (often vaguely specified) 'public interest' objectives (as in allocating radio and television licenses).

7 *Other justifications* Other justifications occasionally advanced in support of a regulatory programme include the following. A person other than the one who pays may make a purchasing decision, leading to a larger purchase than if the buyer had to pay himself. Medical care is often cited as an example, for the patient's insurance company, or the government, not the patient, pays the bill. And government regulation of medical service costs is sometimes advocated, in part for this reason.

Unequal bargaining power is sometimes used as a rationale for regulation that would protect small firms, or suppliers, or customers, from the power of the large firms or buyers with whom they must deal. State regulators, for example, prescribe standard forms for insurance contracts. Federal regulators administer labour laws that exempt labour unions from the antitrust laws that at one time prohibited their operation.

Occasionally, regulatory agencies have sought to engage in 'planning' on the ground that individual firms, because of various institutional rigidities, would fail on their own to produce on an efficient scale. Also, occasionally regulators have acknowledged a degree of 'paternalism' in their regulations, as, for example, when ordering motorcyclists to wear crash helmets.

Some regulatory programmes rest primarily upon one single economic justification; other regulatory programmes rest upon combinations of these justifications; in such a case not all need be accepted as valid by those who continue to support the programme. In the case of regulation of workplace safety, for example, some argue that workers do not know enough about accident risks to insist upon adequate safety expenditures. This is an 'information inadequacy' rationale. Others may claim that too few workers are organized well enough to bargain for the health and safety they need. This is an 'unequal bargaining power' rationale. Still others may say that any worker/employer bargain over safety leaves out of account the needs of others, the worker's family or the government, who suffer or pay the bill in case of accident. This is basically a 'spillover' rationale. Finally, workers may overlook the likely effects of health or safety hazards. In so far as regulation seeks to give them what they *ought* to want (but do not want in fact) the rationale is paternalistic.

A regulatory programme's rationale does not always provide a basis for determining whether, to what extent, or what type of, regulation is appropriate. It offers a place to begin criticism and analysis. One can reach evaluative conclusions only after examining the system actually used to regulate and comparing it with proposals for modification or deregulation.

METHODS OF REGULATION

Although all regulation involves a governmental bureaucracy that 'commands and controls' individual action by private industry, one can distinguish among different sorts of regulatory programmes according to specific methods used to effectuate that 'control'. The classical regulatory methods that have been used to attain specific regulatory ends include the following:
1 *Cost of service ratemaking* This system is commonly used to set prices in a wide variety of individual industries, ranging from electricity, to local telephone service and (historically speaking) including airlines, trucks, and railroads. In principle, the regulator determines a revenue requirement based upon the regulated firm's costs during a 'test year'. These costs include operating costs, taxes, an allowance for depreciation, and a 'reasonable profit' defined as a 'reasonable rate of return' times a 'rate base' which, roughly speaking, amounts to the remaining undepreciated portion of investments valued historically. Once the revenue requirement is determined, the regulator sets rates designed to recover, during the coming period, the amount of the

revenue requirement. A host of practical and theoretical economic problems arise in seeking to translate this abstract formula into a set of bureaucratic practices administerable through adversary hearings.

2   *Historically based price setting*   This system, the only practical administrative price-setting alternative to cost of service ratemaking, has been used during wartime and other emergencies for administering economy wide price controls. It has also been used to control oil prices, and it has sometimes been suggested for use in controlling hospital prices. It consists of holding prices at their level as of a certain past date (say, 'last August 1') and then allowing each producer to raise his price above that level, but only in so far as the increase can be justified by certain allowable cost increases (say, by increases in the price of raw materials, the price of which was not controlled). The system requires continuous administrative adjustment as administrators must, for example, cope with pricing new products, adjust for changes in demand, deal with numerous 'special cases', provide ways to deal with resulting shortages, and enforce a system where evasion is relatively easy. Over time, the need for individualized consideration of a firm's costs and prices, has led the system to evolve towards 'cost of service ratemaking'. A variation of this system ('current prices plus a general inflation adjustment') has been proposed for use in respect to electricity and telephone services.

3   *Allocation under a public interest standard*   Agencies charged with allocating a valuable commodity in short supply, such as television licences, or transportation routes, have developed a system that allows them to choose among 'qualified' applicants after a lengthy public hearing at which each applicant sets forth qualifications and argues that it is 'best'. The system requires the agency first to define the precise commodity awarded, i.e. the specific characteristics of the broadcast licence or route. It then sets and applies minimum criteria in the form of standards that weed out those not minimally qualified. Finally, it selects among competing applicants, subjectively deciding which will best serve the 'public interest' on the basis of their presentations at the hearing.

This system embodies a basic conflict between the business manager's need to select the 'best applicant' according to his subjective judgement and the legal system's preference for selection based upon objective criteria that can be used to demonstrate the rationality and fairness of a particular choice – of, say, a licensee for a television channel worth many millions of dollars. It often proved difficult or impossible to find any meaningful set of coherent criteria that will choose among qualified applicants (hence, the tendency to use the general term 'public interest'). Yet, in the absence of any such set, the system tends to spawn long complex hearing procedures (for all characteristics are relevant) and it is open to charges of inconsistency, or worse.

4   *Standard setting*   Regulators set vast numbers of standards, particularly in respect to product quality or production methods, forbidding, for example, methods or products that are unsafe or spread pollution. Setting standards typically requires the regulator to obtain information and advice from a wide range of interested parties; the industry, consumer groups, suppliers, customers, employees, other government bodies, and so forth. The regulator typically must decide such questions as: (1) Should it aim the standard directly at the relevant evil (say, pollution) or at a surrogate (biological

oxygen demand, in the case of water pollution)? (2) How specific should the standard be? (3) To what extent should the standard embody a requirement for performance ('brakes must stop the car within 'x' feet') and to what extent should it insist upon a particular design? (3) Should it adopt standards requiring industry to create new technology not yet in existence?

The regulator will likely promulgate a standard as a proposal before modifying and finally adopting it. The agency will receive comments from different parties; and then to a degree it will often 'negotiate' a final compromise standard among interested groups – a compromise aimed at minimizing opposition that could take the form of court suits or a refusal to comply voluntarily. The difficulties of developing adequate information, coordination among agencies, enforcement, and surviving judicial review are such that important standards, once adopted, tend to stay in place, unmodified for many years, controlling in important ways how the industry produces or what it sells.

5 *Historically based allocation* Just as history can provide a price-setting standard that temporarily circumvents cost of service ratemaking, so it can provide an allocation standard that temporarily circumvents the complexities of public interest allocation and standard setting. Goods temporarily in short supply – such as oil in 1973, California water in 1976, and natural gas in 1977 – can be allocated provisionally according to historical usage in a given preceding year. That is to say, each claimant will receive the same amount used during that year minus, say, 'x' per cent. This system works only temporarily, however, for the regulator has to set priorities (some uses are more important than others), the regulator must take account of special and changing circumstances (e.g. new users), and the regulator typically must modify the rule to minimize the threat to competitive processes in secondary markets. In practice, regulators using this system have tended to make *ad hoc* exceptions (cf. 'public interest' allocation) and also to develop more detailed sets of standards, with the result that this type of system has not maintained separate, historical identity for any significant period of time.

6 *Individualized screening* Sometimes regulators, unable to develop precise standards, must screen out, on an individualized, case-by-case basis, unacceptable persons or products, such as unfit airline pilots, unsafe food additives, ineffective drugs, or unreasonably toxic substances. Typically, the regulator delegates the screening task to a group of experts, who listen to the applicant, and make a recommendation to the administrator. This type of regulatory system faces its greatest challenge when called upon to screen out substances with very small risks of great harm, for example, carcinogens. Then the regulator must deal with the fact that tests for small carcinogenic risks are often inconclusive; experts may disagree or refuse to provide meaningful judgements (particularly if all proceedings must be public); the effort of weigh 'risks' versus 'benefits' is time-consuming and filled with subjective judgement; and inevitably it is easier politically to ban new products than to remove existing products from the market.

The administration of each of these classical regulatory systems has proved controversial – with lengthy argument about whether or not the regulatory 'cure' is worse than the 'disease' (a matter requiring analysis of the reasons for regulation in a particular case and an examination of alternatives). As a result, a consensus about the desirability of regulation tends to exist only where the 'market defect' thought to call for regulation is obvious and serious.

Regulatory Reform

Beginning in the mid-1970s public dissatisfaction with many of the burdens that regulation imposed combined with economists' criticism of many specific regulatory programmes to create a strong political movement bent upon ending many particular regulatory programs, and reforming others.

DEREGULATION

The major reforms, enacted in the mid and later 1970s and early 1980s, amounted to 'deregulation' of structurally competitive industries, industries which, critics argued, should never have been subject to regulation in the first place. They included the following.

1 *Airlines* Economists had long criticized this economic regulation of domestic air transport. They claimed that regulation's rationale – 'excessive competition' – was a chimera, without application to the structurally competitive airline industry. They argued that regulation simply prevented firms from competing in price, thereby leading them to compete instead by scheduling an excessive number of flights with excessively empty airplanes while charging higher fares. In the early 1970s, the Senate Judiciary Committee, together with the Department of Transportation and the White house, examined the industry in detail and basically accepted the critics' arguments. They found that regulation had worked to suppress price competition, keeping prices high. It had led airlines to substitute service for price competition, with the result that there were frequent, uncrowded flights. Regulation had protected existing carriers by refusing permission to enter the industry to new firms that wished to charge lower prices. (Between 1950 and 1974, for example, the Civil Aeronautics Board received 79 applications from firms wishing to enter the domestic industry, some of them offering significantly lower prices. It granted none. In the 10 years preceding 1974, it granted fewer than 10 per cent of the applications by existing firms to serve new routes; in the 5 years preceding 1974, it granted fewer than 4 per cent.) Regulators kept the market share of existing firms relatively stable. (In 1938 the 4 largest domestic carriers accounted for about 82 per cent of all domestic travel; by 1972, their share fell to about 60 per cent, though in the meantime, the industry expanded by 23,800 per cent.) Regulators would not allow the more efficient firms to pass on to consumers the benefit of that efficiency by cutting prices. At the same time, the government investigatory bodies found little evidence suggesting a need to impose *economic* price-and-entry regulation upon the industry; there was no 'market defect' requiring major government intervention.

In 1976 and 1977 the Civil Aeronautics Board itself studied the matter. Its Chairman introduced a policy of 'administrative deregulation', while he supported legislation that would end regulation. This legislation became law in 1978; and a few years thereafter, the Civil Aeronautics Board went out of existence. The result is that any carrier 'fit, willing, and able' to fly, may enter the industry and charge, roughly speaking, whatever prices it pleases. It is regulated in terms of its safety, but not in respect to the prices that it seeks to charge. And, the results so far (discussed in Part II, below), are about what the reformers predicted: prices have fallen, travel has increased, and the industry's major problems consist of crowding and delays, not high fares.

2   *Trucks*   The industry is structurally similar, in relevant respects, to airlines, though it is considerably larger. Deregulation has taken the form of the agency (the Interstate Commerce Commission) relaxing the rules on new entry, permitting individual truckers to set prices of their choice, and abolishing 'rate bureaus' (informal truck owner cartels that previously fixed rates submitted to the ICC for approval). Most observers believe that, as a result, prices have fallen significantly (but wages, too, have fallen to a degree). The Federal Trade Commission has recently estimated the total benefits of trucking deregulation 'to be between $39 and $63 billion per year, or between $160 and $260 for every American'.[2] A new statute enacted in the late 1970s permitted (indeed, encouraged) the ICC to adopt these new policies. Unlike airlines, 'deregulation' of trucks could take place as a result of administrative (agency) decisions; it would not require new statutory (congressional) action.

3   *Railroad deregulation*   A statute enacted in 1980 required the Interstate Commerce Commission to permit railroads to abandon unprofitable lines more easily and to set prices more freely than was permissible in the past. As a result, nearly two-thirds of the industry has been freed from detailed economic supervision. There is a special problem in respect to railroads, however; namely, that they arguably possess significant market power in respect to certain of their shippers, in particular shippers of coal. The statute seeks to maintain traditional regulatory pricing rules where monopoly power is present, but to rely more upon competitive pricing where it is not. Defining the demarcation, a regulatory matter, has proved difficult; and it has left the railroads to struggle with a mixture of regulatory, and free market, price regimes. So far, the result seems to be falling costs, falling real rates in respect to some but not all commodities, roughly constant coal shipping rates, roughly constant real wages, and significantly increased productivity.[3]

4   *Natural gas*   From the late 1950s through the early 1970s the Federal Power Commission regulated the field price of natural gas, the prices charged by the many producers who dug wells, discovered gas, and sold the gas to pipelines which would transport it to consumers. Most economists came to believe that the natural gas production industry was structurally competitive; they recognized that prices has risen in the late 1950s, but they believed that the price rise reflected rising costs, or perhaps increased competition by new pipelines wishing to *buy* gas in the field, not monopoly selling power by producers. They came to see regulation as reflecting a desire by gas customers to impose a form of 'rent control'.

The result of the Commission's efforts to hold down field prices in the 1960s was a serious natural gas shortage in the winters during the early 1970s. Efforts by the Commission to raise interstate rates did not cure the problem, in part because the new rates were not high enough to entice producers away from making sales in unregulated, *intra*-state markets. Eventually, the misallocations became sufficiently serious to produce a political demand for change. In the mid-1970s, Congress enacted a new law, which both permitted prices to rise on previously discovered gas and effectively deregulated the prices of new gas. As more and more 'old' gas has been consumed and new gas found, the production of gas has become less and less regulated. Prices have not gone up significantly in the 1980s.

5 *Telecommunications* Deregulation has taken place in this industry primarily as a result of court decree. The industry previously consisted of three parts: (1) *long distance service* (provided by AT & T); (2) *local service* (provided by local AT & T subsidiaries); (3) *equipment manufacturing* (provided by Western Electric owned by AT & T). As a result of a consent decree entered in a government antitrust suit, Western Electric has been split from AT & T, AT & T (long distance) has been split from the local operating companies, and most of the local operating companies (local service) have been split from each other, each forming a separate business. At the same time, the regulators have encouraged the entry of new competition into both manufacturing and long distance service. (The local companies are considered 'natural monopolies'.) The results of lessened regulation and increased competition in long-distance service so far are controversial. Part II, below, will discuss problems and controversies in detail.

6 *Other deregulatory efforts* The deregulation of stockbrokers' fixed commissions began, with regulatory commission decisions, in the late 1960s. Subsequently, this issue became part of a broader campaign to deregulate financial institutions, involving a set of issues related to 'customer safety', still in the process of being decided.[4] There is also discussion about the advisability of deregulating the production of electricity[5] and the transport of oil and gas by pipeline.[6]

It should be noted that 'pure deregulation' still involves application of antitrust laws. This matter will also be discussed in Part II.

LESS RESTRICTIVE REGULATION

The deregulatory movement has found it more difficult to achieve significant change in classical regulatory programmes governing health, safety and the environment, areas where the economic rationale for government intervention is stronger, and the free market alternatives to classical regulation less obviously superior. In these latter areas, 'regulatory reform pressure' has taken the form of advocating, not total deregulation, but rather less restrictive or less burdensome methods of governmental intervention aimed at achieving the relevant regulatory end.

1 *Disclosure* Regulation that requires only disclosure does not dictate the

type of product that must be sold or the process that must be used to produce
it. Thus, it is typically less restrictive than standards that would constrain
consumer product choice or screening that would ban certain products (say,
drugs or food additives) from the market. Developing effecting rules for
disclosure, however, can itself prove difficult. Moreover, disclosure is likely
to prove effective only where the public can understand the information
disclosed, where it is free to choose on the basis of that information, and
where it believes the information is materially relevant to the choice. That
is to say, a label that simply announces 'this food risks cancer with a chance
of one in 50,000' may mean virtually nothing to a buyer because it does not
suggest what to do.

2   *Taxes*   Taxes have been advocated specifically as substitutes for regulation in two instances. First, classical regulation as a means for controlling
'rents' is highly inefficient, for, to the extent that it holds down price, *ipso facto*,
it creates a shortage (as in the case of natural gas regulation). In principle, a
windfall profits tax will (at least sometimes) accomplish similar redistributive
ends without risking similar inefficiencies.

Second, taxes arguably offer a more efficient way to deal with spillover
problems. Even a small tax on polluting materials (such as sulphur dioxide),
it has been argued, will prove more efficient than 'standard setting' at controlling pollution, for it will encourage producers to shift to more pollution-free
production processes without at the same time forbidding the continued use
of polluting processes where such a change is inordinately expensive. Once
the tax level is determined (a difficult matter), government officials need
not decide upon precise pollution-control levels for each source; there is no
discrimination against new sources.

European nations have required water pollution treatment charges. The
Netherlands and Japan have imposed taxes on air polluters. Furthermore,
China is introducing a pollution-tax system. But experience with taxes, while
favourable, is nonetheless limited. In the United States, industry has opposed
taxes because they require payment for all discharges. Environmental advocates have also opposed them on the theory that, when paid, they provide a
licence to pollute. They have also expressed concern that monitoring techniques are not adequate to prevent cheating.[7]

3   *Marketable rights*   Economists have suggested that the government create a limited number of saleable rights to engage in a limited amount of
undesirable conduct, such as polluting. Their holders would sell them, and
they would ultimately end up in the hands of those firms that would find it
most costly to stop polluting (and consequently to whom the right to pollute
is worth the most). The main differences between this type of system and
taxes as a method for dealing with 'spillover' problems is the following: a tax
allows firms to know the *price* of using a polluting product, but one cannot say
in advance *how much pollution* there will be (how many firms will choose to stop
polluting rather than pay the tax). A system of marketable rights allows one
to know in advance the *amount of pollution* (which will equal the sum of rights
issued), but one cannot know in advance the *price* of continuing to use a process that emits pollutants (the price set by the 'right's' marketable value).

The environmental regulatory agencies have begun to experiment with 'marketable rights' by allowing firms to trade 'grandfather' authorizations to continue polluting and by allowing individual firms freedom to choose *how* to reduce pollution to a level equal to that which the authorities fix in terms of the content of an imaginary bubble placed over a factory. Plant can use reduction of emissions from existing units to add new ones. Students of the subject believe these emissions programmes have saved costs and encouraged new investment.[8]

The use of 'marketable rights' has also been advocated as a substitute for regulation in other regulated areas, such as the allocation of landing rights at crowded airports.

4 *Bargaining* Reformers have advocated the use of bargaining among interested parties as an alternative to classical standard setting, say, in the area of safety regulation. Bargaining allows the parties to trade less desired, for more desired, features; it permits decentralized decision-making allowing individualized practices to reflect local conditions; and it minimizes enforcement problems. On the other hand, results reached through bargaining may harm persons not represented at the bargaining table; regardless, bargaining will not work unless interested parties can organize sufficiently to appoint a representative with power to make those he represents stick to their agreement. There have recently been several instances of successful use of bargaining to create governmental regulatory standards, standards that would otherwise have been promulgated after adversarial 'notice and comment' rulemaking procedures.[9]

At the present time, significant progress has been made in 'deregulating' those industries where the economic case for 'free markets' is strong and that for regulation weak. The extent to which 'reform' will go further and encompass 'less restrictive alternatives' to classical regulation remains to be seen.[10]

Part II   Airlines and Telecommunications[11]

As Part I of this article pointed out, the major changes brought about so far by American 'regulatory reform' consist of deregulating industries that are structurally competitive. Deregulation has not meant an end to *all* regulation; it has typically meant removing or significantly limiting the government's power to control prices and entry, while (in the case of transport) leaving intact the government's power to maintain safety. It has also meant that the newly deregulated industries have lost their pre-existing statutory immunity from the American antitrust laws; now those laws apply to them as they do to other unregulated industries.

Nonetheless, in the context of 'public policy', the newly deregulated industries are not quite like industries that were never regulated at all. There remain special risks to the public that may call for special policies. Part II will analyze some of those special risks, by focusing upon two recently deregulated industries – airlines and telecommunications. First, it describes the classical relationship between antitrust and economic regulation and how that relationship applies in the context of the airline and telecommunications industries. Next, it analyzes the difficulties of applying antitrust policy to airline mergers – difficulties that illustrate the risk that general antitrust policy will fail to take account of the special characteristics of individual deregulated industries. Then, it discusses the risk that government policy-makers, in an era of deregulation, will protect competitors instead of protecting competition, thus confusing antitrust's ends with its means. It goes on to analyze the risk that local regulators will not follow sound economic principles when defining the relationship between newly competitive and still-regulated industries. Finally, it examines the risk that residual areas of potential monopoly power, often called 'bottlenecks', will cause anticompetitive harm in newly deregulated industries.

Antitrust, Regulation, and the Deregulatory Experience

THE CLASSICAL THEORY: ANTITRUST AND ECONOMIC REGULATION

To understand the risks that deregulation poses, one must understand the classical theoretical relationship between antitrust and economic regulation. In classical theory, both institutions aim to achieve similar economic objectives. One might describe these goals as the 'benefits' that can flow from workable competition, namely (1) prices close to incremental costs, leading to buying and production decisions that minimize economic waste; (2) efficient production processes; and (3) innovation as to both product and production process.

Economic regulation bypasses the competitive process and seeks to obtain these benefits *directly*. Regulation typically involves an administrative body that deals with private firms through an adversarial process. Regulators create a vast network of rules and orders that determine the regulated firms' prices while, in principle, spurring those firms toward innovation and production efficiency.

Antitrust, on the other hand, tries to achieve these benefits *indirectly*. The antitrust laws set forth a few negatively phrased directives, which are enforced by the courts or the Federal Trade Commission. They prohibit both anti-competitive market behaviour, such as price fixing, and behaviour that may lead to or help maintain anti-competitive market structures. Sometimes, as in the case of unjustified monopoly, they may require restructuring a market. In essence, they promote competition so that competition itself can bring us its economic benefits.[12]

From a classical perspective, these economic benefits, perhaps like happiness or reputation, are best secured when one does not aim at them directly. Decentralized individual decisions made in a workably competitive marketplace or more likely to prove economically efficient, to bring about efficient production processes, and to encourage desirable innovation than are the centralized, bureaucratic decisions of the economic regulator. Classical theory emphasizes the many systematic institutional features of regulatory system that prevent them from ever coming close to replicating the effects of well-functioning competitive markets.

The classicist nonetheless finds reasons for regulating. He points to 'defects' in certain markets that prevent competition from working properly.[13] For example, he may point to the natural monopoly, where economies of scale are so large that a single firm can produce an industry's entire output at lowest cost. He may claim that competitively set prices take inadequate account of 'spillover costs', such as environmental pollution. He may express concern about inadequate consumer information or exorbitant rents, which for one reason or another may require direct governmental intervention. For present purposes, it is important to see that regardless of the merits of these reasons in any particular case, the classicist embraces regulation *faute de mieux*. Competition is more desirable, and antitrust may help maintain competition. Yet for one reason or another, in these special markets, competition cannot work or by itself is inadequate. Thus, one must turn to regulation as a supplement or substitute.

On this view, antitrust is not another form of regulation. Antitrust is an *alternative* to regulation and, where feasible, a better alternative.[14] To be more specific, the classicist first looks to the marketplace to protect the consumer; he relies upon the antitrust laws to sustain market competition. He turns to regulation only where free markets policed by antitrust laws will not work – where he finds significant market 'defects' that antitrust laws cannot cure. Only then is it worth gearing up the cumbersome, highly imperfect bureaucratic apparatus of classical regulation. Regulation is viewed as a substitute for competition, to be used only as a weapon of last resort – as a heroic cure reserved for a serious disease.

THE MODERN EXPERIENCE: AIRLINE AND TELEPHONE DEREGULATION

This view of antitrust and regulation may be inadequate, inaccurate, incomplete, or all three, but it is important to understand because it helps to explain much of the economic deregulation we have seen in the past fifteen years. Airline deregulation, for example, reflects the reformers' belief that airline markets are workably competitive. Even markets with only one or two carriers typically are considered 'contestable'. If entry by other firms is easy enough to keep carriers serving the market from raising their fares too high, then regulation is unnecessary.

The reformers also argued that the 'market defect' that allegedly necessitated airline regulation did not exist. The regulators could not explain what they meant when they raised the spectre of 'excessive competition'. Antitrust enforcement could prevent 'predatory pricing', if that is what they feared. The structure of the airline industry foreclosed any risk of plant closure during a recession, if they were worried about wasteful investment. Even Colonel Gorell, the industry spokesman who appealed for protectionist regulation in 1938, admitted that he had never actually witnessed excessive competition among airlines – though he claimed to 'have been shaking in [his] boots' because it had come so close.[15] If no defect could be demonstrated in the

1930s – after several years' experience without economic regulation – then one might question whether it would materialize with deregulation in the 1970s.

The strength of the arguments that the industry could support competition and the weakness of the regulatory justification led reformers to present their claims to Congress. After entertaining extensive debate and considering vast amounts of empirical evidence, including practical regulatory experiments in California and Texas and the initial results of Alfred Kahn's first experiments with deregulation at the Civil Aeronautics Board (CAB), Congress enacted legislation deregulating the industry.[16]

Deregulation of the telephone industry was similar, at least in theory. Reformers became convinced that both telephone equipment manufacturing and long-distance telecommunications service could become workably competitive industries. They lost confidence that 'natural monopoly' – the market defect that allegedly required regulation – in fact existed in these markets. They thought that both the telephone equipment manufacturing industry and the long-distance telecommunications service industry were large enough to support not just one, but several, competing firms of efficient size.[17]

Despite their similarities, airline deregulation and telephone deregulation differed in several respects. First, the rationale for telephone regulation ('natural monopoly') was different from that for airline regulation ('excessive competition'). Second, the arguments that long-distance telecommunications could not support several competitors were stronger than similar arguments concerning airlines.[18] Third, there were no practical experiments with long-distance telecommunications, as there were with airlines, that could provide empirical support for the feasibility of competition.[19] Fourth, the income effects of telecommunications deregulation probably favoured the business community[20]-whereas airline deregulation probably favoured the ordinary traveller or consumer. Fifth, Congress found serious problems with the way in which the relevant administrative agency, the CAB, regulated the airlines,[21] it did not find comparable problems with existing telephone service regulation by the FCC. Finally, Congress was the institution that implemented airline deregulation, whereas the courts and the FCC implemented telephone deregulation.[22]

From the classical perspective, however, the similarities between airline and telephone deregulation are more important than the differences. These similarities suggest that antitrust can adequately replace regulatory efforts to provide economic protection for the public. They also suggest that the most obvious risk to the public is that the reformers were wrong in thinking that the newly deregulated markets would be structurally competitive.

There are three reasons to resist the temptation to rehearse here the standard arguments about structural competition. First, those arguments have been made many times before.[23] Second, telephone deregulation is not yet complete, and thus the evidence concerning its advisability is not clear. Since the basic legal changes are in place and are unlikely to be reversed, any discussion of the wisdom of telephone deregulation is likely to prove more academic than useful.

Third, in the airline industry, the evidence so far suggests that the reformers were right: Competition has yielded benefits to consumers. Many new firms have entered the industry,[24] and more markets are being served by competing airlines.[25] Since 1974, the year before the CAB abandoned classical rate regulation and began to let new firms enter the industry, average real fares have fallen 25 per cent.[26] Had real fares stayed constant since 1973, travellers would have had to play $9.7 billion more to fly the 270 billion passenger miles they flew in 1985.[27] Most recently, Professor Alfred Kahn has stated that airfares since 1976 reflect an average 'price decline of almost 30 per cent in real terms as of July 1988'. He adds that if average fares 'had merely remained constant in real terms' since 1976, travellers in 1987 'would have paid $20 billion more for their tickets – in which event, of course, many fewer of them would have travelled.'[28] Overall, seat availability, flight frequency, and mileage flown have increased.[29]

The Air Transport Association reports that the number of passengers flying per year increased from 173 million in 1971 to 457 million in 1987. The percentage of all Americans who have flown commercially also increased from 49 per cent in 1971 to 72 per cent in 1987. The domestic industry flew 400 billion seat miles in 1987 compared with 163 billion in 1975. The distribution of the 'increased service' was broad, with hardly any communities actually losing service.[30] Employment and certain real wages in the airline industry rose through 1983, though more recently real wages trends may have changed.[31] Admittedly, comfort and service quality have declined, but the more crowded conditions and reduced amenities in large part reflect the buying public's preference for lower prices.[32] Competition has forced a better match between supply and demand, leading to greater efficiency and increased satisfaction of consumer preferences.[33]

At the same time, there is little reason to believe that these benefits have been achieved at the cost of airline safety. Airlines have not been deregulated with respect to safety. Critics correctly point out that the number of airline fatalities in 1985 – about 2,000 – was unusually large.[34] For the most part, however, the deaths occurred in crashes of chartered aircraft, whose fares have never been regulated, and foreign carriers.[35] The single major accident involving a newly deregulated carrier was the 'downdraft' crash of a Delta L-1011 in New Orleans, which resulted in 134 fatalities – only 7 per cent of the death total for 1985. Overall, statistics kept since the advent of complete deregulation in 1978 suggest that the airline safety record has improved.[36] Recently, the National Transportation Safety Board reported that scheduled major air carriers suffered 300 accidents, including 45 fatal accidents between 1970 and 1978. Between 1979 and 1987, the numbers fell to 180 accidents, including 25 fatal accidents. The accident rate fell from 0.675 accidents (0.101 fatal accidents) per 100,000 departures to 0.355 accidents (0.049 fatal accidents) per 100,000 departures. On the other hand, the rate of 'near mid-air collisions' (per 100,000 flight hours) rose from 1.19 in 1983 (when figures were first compiled) to 2.45 in 1986.[37]

Accepting the proposition that deregulation was well conceived in the first place, the classical view would now look to traditional antitrust policy to protect the public. But this view overlooks some important concerns. There are certain *special* risks and policy problems that arise in these newly deregulated industries.

Risk One: General Antitrust Policy Will Overlook the Special Features of Particular Industries

ANTITRUST POLICY AND AIRLINE MERGERS

Broadly stated, the first of these special risks is that general antitrust policy will not take account of the special characteristics of deregulated industries. This abstract concern is made sensible with a contemporary example: the risk that antitrust policy will fail to deal appropriately or adequately with airline mergers. Antitrust policy may prove too lenient on the airlines, allowing mergers that unnecessarily concentrate the industry, thereby reducing competition to the point where fares unnecessarily increase. Alternatively, it may prove too strict, failing adequately to recognize potential gains in efficiency that would lead to savings that competition would pass on to the public.

One might initially ask why this is a special problem for airline deregulation. After all, the antitrust laws apply to nearly every industry. The risk of an inappropriately lenient, harsh, or indiscriminate antimerger law is always present. Moreover, it is not clear that airline mergers warrant special concern. Proponents of deregulation did not rest their case on likely deconcentration. They argued instead that competition, including potential competition, would force prices down and increase traveller choice, irrespective of whether the industry became more, or less, concentrated.[38] Given the static market shares and artificial price and service patterns that thirty-eight years of regulation created,[39] it is hardly surprising that sudden freedom to compete produced radical changes in market shares, leading to some bankruptcies and cost pressures to merge. Finally, despite the many recent mergers and merger proposals, the airline industry is no more concentrated today than it was under regulation, and it will be only marginally more concentrated even if all the currently proposed mergers are approved.[40] With respect to merger policy, then, airlines would appear on the surface to be no different from other industries.

Airline mergers do warrant unusual scrutiny, however, because empirical generalizations that support current merger policy do not necessarily reflect the special circumstances of the deregulated carriers. By administrative necessity, merger policy deals with *typical* relations between market structure and competitive behaviour. Antitrust rules designed to deal with industry in general may not reflect properly the special features of the airline industry. Some of these features recommend a more stringent policy; others counsel us toward a more lenient one.

THE ARGUMENT FOR A MORE STRINGENT AIRLINE MERGER POLICY

Four factors contribute to the argument that present antitrust policy will not prove sufficiently strict in dealing with proposed airline mergers.

1   *Recent changes in antitrust enforcement policy*   Although the antitrust community has focused considerable attention upon changes in both the method for calculating market concentration and the substantive standards that define levels of concentration that the Department of Justice will tolerate,[41] the change in the Department's attitude toward the role of potential competition is, for present purposes more significant.[42] One can understand this change in attitude by focusing upon two hypothetical mergers.

First, imagine a proposed merger of two firms, each with a 15 per cent share of a market presently consisting of six large firms and ten small ones. A merger optimist, realizing that market share figures reflect only rough generalizations drawn from behaviour in many different industries, will look for other indicators of likely future industry behaviour. If there are three potential competitors that might enter the market should prices rise, s/he will hesitate to condemn the merger. S/he sees the presence of potential competitors as a safety valve, available to keep anti-competitive behaviour, such as tacit price collusion under control.

The merger pessimist, however, will not shade the market figures of the two merging firms to reflect the presence of potential competitors on the edge of the market. In his/her view, 'potential competition is no substitute for actual competition'. Of course, she admits that in extreme cases this generalization fails. For example, in the 1960s, the Department of Justice thought it might have found an envelope paper monopolist in a single firm that accounted for 100 per cent of the envelope paper business. Many firms not then producing envelope paper could have started doing so quite easily, however, simply by turning a dial on their machines to change the paper's thickness. Where entry barriers are so low that a 'monopolist' has no power to raise prices, even the pessimist will not worry about proposed mergers. In the ordinary case, however, the pessimist will hesitate to discount the loss of actual competition. S/he knows that mergers within a market increase the risk that firms will raise prices from competitive levels *up to* the height of the entry barrier, up to the point where potential competitors will step in.

Now imagine that instead of the proposed merger of actual competitors in the aforementioned market, two of the three potential competitors propose to merge. The optimist will not worry very much about this potential merger either. S/he will note that after the merger, two potential competitors will still remain, and the market will continue to support many actually competing firms. S/he will defend the merger by arguing that as long as actual competition exists, potential competition will not be an important force for keeping prices low.

The pessimist also has a different attitude towards this proposed merger. S/he fears the removal of even a potential competitor, for s/he suspects that the potential competitor's threat of entry may have had a present, perhaps unmeasurable, effect in keeping prices low. The pessimist fears

that the elimination of a potential competitor will increase the probability
of anticompetitive behaviour.

The recent change in attitude regarding antitrust enforcement can only be
described as a shift from the views of the pessimist to those of the optimist.
The enforcers believe they have scientific support for such a shift because
many economists argue that antitrust merger policy in the 1960s was too
stringent.[43] Critics respond that the enforcers are over-reacting by using
more lenient concentration numbers, shading those numbers to reflect potential competitors, and treating less seriously horizontal mergers that remove
potential competitors. They are double- or triple-counting – or non-counting
– the number of competitors or potential competitors. The resolution of the
argument depends upon matters that are notoriously difficult to determine
empirically, such as the height of entry barriers and the tendency of firms to
raise prices when faced with potential competitors. Here we need note only
the change in enforcement attitude.

2 *The importance of potential competition in the airline industry* Advocates of
deregulation did not argue that each airline would find itself battling hosts
of actual competitors. They claimed only that the threat of entry into a
particular market by airlines not currently serving that market would hold
prices down.[44] The relevant market for the traveller is usually a 'city pair',
the two cities between which the traveller wishes to fly.[45] The extent to
which a threat of entry into this market can hold down prices is a matter
of degree. An airline that serves City *A* and City *B*, but does not fly between
them, can enter the *A-B* market at very low cost, and there are several such
airlines serving most major routes.[46] For carriers that serve only one end
point, *A or B*, the cost of entering the *A-B* market is higher. For airlines
in the general region, but not serving either *A* or *B*, the cost is higher
still. Entry costs rise continually as one considers competition from firms
elsewhere in the nation, charter carriers, firms with extra planes elsewhere
in the world, and firms that would enter the industry from scratch. Congress, as early as 1975, believed that there were enough potential entrants
at the low end of the entry cost continuum to keep prices low in particular
markets.[47]

One cannot easily determine the 'correct' number of potential entrants
necessary to keep prices close to competitive levels. One can only say
qualitatively that the nearer the potential competitor and the easier it is to
enter a particular city pair, the greater the threat of entry and the closer
to the competitive level prices are likely to be. Given the importance of
potential competition, every *unnecessary* removal of a significant carrier as
an independent entry-threatening entity gratuitously raises the probability
of unwarranted price increases.

3 *The political significance of airline deregulation* Airline deregulation is a great
experiment in the power of the free market to help the consumer. Yet, it needs
friends Business travellers, who are less sensitive to price than other travellers,
dislike crowded planes and airports. Unions are understandably unhappy
about wage cuts and freezes. Towns that have lost service are keenly aware
of their losses.[48] Under these circumstances, savings in economic efficiency
must be translated into lower prices. The ordinary traveller must understand

that fares are significantly lower, or deregulation will lose effective political support.

4   *The Department of Transportation's authority over airline mergers*   In 1984, amendments to the Airline Deregulation Act transferred responsibility for determining the legality of a proposed merger to the Department of Transportation.[49] given its institutional history, however, that department may be less sensitive than the Department of Justice to potential anti-competitive problems. The Department of Transportation's relative inexperience in enforcing antitrust law suggests that it should scrutinize with special care the airline mergers opposed by the Antitrust Division.

THE ARGUMENT FOR A MORE LENIENT AIRLINE MERGER POLICY

The primary reason for fearing that ordinary antimerger policy will prove too strict derives from the fact that antimerger enforcers rarely confront industries that are emerging from nearly forty years of regulation. The enforcers must bear in mind that the CAB artificially stabilized airline market structure. Between 1938 and 1972, for example, the airline industry grew by 23,800 per cent, but the market shares of the major carriers changed very little.[50] The leading carrier, United, accounted for just over 20 per cent of industry sales in 1938 and roughly the same in the early 1970s.[51] The market share of the four largest firms fell from more than 80 per cent in 1938 to roughly 60 per cent in 1972, but the CAB permitted no significant new firm to enter the industry.[52] The CAB also carefully controlled the airlines' routes and services. The industry's route structure reflected to a considerable degree the CAB's 'handicapping' system of awarding more profitable, less competitive routes to weaker carriers. The fare structure reflected neither costs nor traveller demand so much as a bureaucratic rule of 'equal fares for equal miles'.[53]

Deregulation of the airlines has upset these longstanding patterns of operation. Free competition has meant experimentation with fares and service. It has meant radical change as firms discover that they must respond to cost and demand. It has meant potential failures as firms guess wrong or become the victims of competitive circumstances beyond their control.[54] These changes create pressures to merge, for merger offers a way to help employees, customers, and owners avoid the ill effects of bankruptcy. Merger also allows the acquiring firm to obtain airplanes or other resources that it may use more efficiently. It may turn out, for example, that Carrier A can use Carrier B's physical plant or other resources more effectively – B's fleet may consist of aircraft ideal for A's operation. Taken together, these considerations mean a lengthy period of industry 'shakedown'. Antitrust enforcers should take these circumstances into account.

In my view, these facts suggest a need for leniency with respect to 'failing company' and 'efficiency' defences in merger cases. Antitrust policy usually insists on fairly clear proof of imminent bankruptcy before accepting a 'failing company' defence to an otherwise unlawful merger. It has also long viewed with suspicion claims that a merger is justified by 'efficiency'.[55] Greater

willingness to accept these defences may be warranted in the airline industry
because of the greater likelihood that such claims will be well founded in the
facts and important to the success of deregulation.

RESOLUTION: OUTLINES FOR A PRO-COMPETITIVE AIRLINE MERGER POLICY

These two sets of considerations – one arguing for a more stringent merger
policy and the other for greater leniency – are not inconsistent. They suggest a
policy that – compared to present attitudes – is more hostile to and suspicious
about likely anti-competitive consequences, particularly the loss of potential
competitors. But they also suggest a policy that is more receptive to possible
justifications for approving an acquisition, such as efficiency and imminent
failure. Antitrust enforcers would look for the most pro-competitive ways
to achieve the benefits asserted in these defences. For example, antitrust
enforcers would allow Carrier A to acquire failing Carrier B only if there
were no 'alternative purchaser' whose acquisition of B would risk fewer
anti-competitive consequences.[56] Further, they would insist that acquisi-
tions be structured so as to maximize their pro-competitive impact. This
would require airlines to divest themselves of routes in direct competition
with those of the companies they propose to acquire.[57] Enforcement efforts
that are sensitive to these concerns may resolve some of the apparent tensions
in antitrust policy regarding airline mergers. Overall they would prove more
hostile to airline mergers than are present efforts.
    The object here is not to offer specific recommendations, however, but only
to highlight the risk that merger policy will not pay adequate attention to the
special circumstances of the airline industry. Those circumstances recommend what some might see as a shift away from present antitrust attitudes.
Legal authority for any such shift can be found in the statute governing the
Department of Transportation, which establishes a 'public interest' test to be
applied in merger approval decisions.[58] Since economists continue to believe
that the airline industry is not, structurally speaking, a 'natural monopoly'
or even a 'natural tight oligopoly', competition in a free market policed by a
strong antimerger policy should provide sufficient protection for the public.

Risk Two: Antitrust Policy Will Protect Competitors to the Detriment of Competition

A second special policy risk of deregulation is that government policy-makers
will protect competitors instead of protecting competition. This is a problem
familiar to students of antitrust.[59] It arises when regulators or antitrust
enforcers confuse means with ends by thinking that the object of the law
is to protect individual firms from business risks rather than to bring
consumers the price and production benefits that typically arise from the
competitive process. Where deregulation is at issue, the consequence of
misdirecting protection is to threaten to deprive the consumer of the very
benefits deregulation seeks.

THE EXPERIENCE WITH TELECOMMUNICATIONS

The most obvious 'deregulatory' example of this risk arises in telecommunications. In order to come to the point where the problem is obvious, one must understand a set of complex changes in both the economic perceptions and the legal structure of the industry.

1 *Changing economic perceptions* Ten or fifteen years ago, most economists would have thought the following analogy described long-distance service.[60] Imagine a river spanned by a bridge that costs $50 million per year to maintain. The bridge, a natural monopoly, is regulated. A classical problem in regulation is what price the regulator should charge for crossing the bridge. Imagine that a 50c. toll is sufficient to raise the money necessary for maintenance, but a $1.50 toll would be needed to raise maintenance money and *also* provide a fair return to investors. Principles of regulation would seem to require the latter toll. Unless investors earn a fair return, their investment has been confiscated, and as a practical matter, future investors probably would not be so foolish as to provide money for projects in regulated industries.[61]

Yet the $1.50 toll can have unfortunate consequences. Imagine a person who wants to cross the bridge, who would pay $1.00 for the trip, but who cannot afford $1.50. The result is a sad one, for the economy could provide this person with what s/he wants – a bridge crossing – at far less than what s/he is willing to pay, at a cost of no more than 50c. worth of real resources. But because the toll is $1.50, s/he must remain on the river bank without crossing. Still worse, a ferryboat might offer to take him/her and others across the river for $1.00. If this $1.00 fare represents the real resources used in running the ferryboat, the result is very wasteful. Society will have used up $1.00 worth of resources to provide by ferry boat what it could have provided by the bridge for only 50c. An extra 50c. of resources has been used unnecessarily.

There are two classical regulatory solutions to this problem. If the regulator is certain that the incremental cost of providing crossings by bridge is less than by ferry, s/he might simply forbid the ferryboat to enter the crossings market. Suppose, however, that the regulator cannot reliably determine the ferry's incremental costs; these costs may be $1.00, but may be only 40c. In that case, the solution may be to allow the bridge to cut its prices to the level of its incremental costs, particularly if the bridge can do so selectively, by charging a lower price to those most likely otherwise to use ferryboats. As a practical matter, the bridge might lower its toll for pedestrians, charge a lower toll per person for those who cross as bus passengers, or charge a higher toll for trucks, which cannot use the ferryboat. Though persons discriminated against may complain, the regulator will reply that, in the absence of discrimination, the low-toll bridge-crossers would desert the bridge for the ferryboat. They would then contribute nothing toward covering the fixed investment costs of the bridge. And since fewer bridge crossers would now have to cover the same fixed costs, the price of a crossing would rise still higher. As long as the low-toll crossers are covering at least a portion of fixed costs (by paying a toll of at least 51c.), the discriminatory pricing system – a form of what is called Ramsey pricing[62] benefits everyone.

This famous bridge example was thought to have described the AT & T longlines circumstance before 1975. AT & T was the bridge. It had a large investment sunk into the provision of long-distance service;[63] its incremental (or marginal) costs of providing that service were lower than its total average costs. The new entrants, such as MCI, were ferry-boats that offered customers lower prices.[64] AT & T might claim that they did so only because they did not have to recover the costs of the sunk investment; they were $1.00 ferry-boats. MCI might claim, however, that it was simply more efficient than AT & T; it was a 40c. ferry-boat. Thus, it should be allowed to compete.[65]

This argument has shifted considerably in the last decade. Because many of AT & Ts sunk costs have been recovered through depreciation, commentators seldom argue that AT & T's unrecovered depreciation represents a major reason for charging prices higher than those of its long-distance competitors. Also, there is now considerable agreement that longlines telecommunications does not possess the characteristics of a natural monopoly. Natural monopoly rests upon substantial economies of scale. According to recent cost break-downs, however, 60 per cent of the present costs of long-distance telecom-munications represent 'access costs' – payments that long-distance companies make to local telephone companies to use their lines in order to reach local customers who make or receive long distance calls. Thirty per cent represent marketing costs. And only 10 per cent represent the cost of the physical long-distance plant – the portion of costs that can most plausibly be argued to exhibit economies of scale.[66] Moreover, MCI, Sprint, and other companies have invested nearly as much money in fiberoptic communications equipment and other forms of transmission equipment as has AT & T, suggesting that they do not believe themselves beset by insurmountable handicaps of scale.[67] All in all, there is considerable empirical evidence suggesting that AT & T probably enjoys no significant cost advantage in supplying service. Thus, there is no bridge; all the companies are ferry boats.

2 *Changing industry structures* In part as a result of changed perceptions of the long-distance market, two separate but related legal developments have radically changed the structure of the industry. First, the entry of MCI and other carriers into the industry – an entry brought about not by Congress but by the FCC and the courts[68] – made it possible for customers to avoid higher priced AT & T service and choose lower priced alternatives. The ready availability of these alternatives, facilitated considerably by technological advances,[69] forced the regulators to allow AT & T to reduce its prices to some degree,[70] irrespective of any structural change in the AT & T system. Moreover, new technology allowed large long-distance customers to build their *own* long-distance systems and to *bypass* AT & T.[71] Thus, even if MCI had not entered the long-distance market, this threat of bypass would have forced regulators to permit AT & T to lower its prices.

The AT & T consent decree[72] complemented the changes brought about by new entry, separating those portions of AT & T that, at least argu-ably, constitute part of competitively structured industries (manufacturing and long-distance communication) from those portions of the industry that remained natural monopolies (local operations). The Bell Operating Compa-nies (BOCs), which operate local service, remain regulated by local utility commissions. The object of the decree is to produce a 'level playing field' for competition between AT & T and other carriers and manufacturers in the competitive sections of the industry.[73]

'Deregulation' of the 'telephone industry' thus involves two separate industries: manufacturing and long-distance service. The consent decree involved *both* of these industries, splitting both manufacturing and long-distance service from local service. Long-distance service deregulation involves two sets of governmental actions – one 'regulatory set' allowing new firms to compete, and one 'antitrust set' (the consent decree) splitting local from long-distance service. And there are two separate justifications for these actions with respect to longline service. One justification views AT & T as the bridge, and MCI as a potentially lower-incremental-cost ferry-boat; the other, more current justification regards all long-distance carriers, including AT & T, as ferry-boats. Finally, it is notable that new technology, with its bypass problem, effectively compelled many of the FCC's deregulatory actions entirely independent of the consent decree.

THE TROUBLE WITH COMPETITIVE HANDICAPPING

With all this background in mind, one can understand the major policy risk presently inherent in long-distance deregulation. That risk is that AT & T will not be allowed to compete effectively by cutting its prices. Either the regulatory system or the antitrust laws may be used to protect new competitors rather than to serve the ends of competition. Indeed, the FCC has thus far acted as a regulatory 'handicapper' in three ways.

First, it requires AT & T to pay far more money to local telephone companies for the right to use local networks to connect with long-distance customers (the access charge) than it requires AT & T's competitors to pay for the same service.[74] It does so, arguably, because the connection that AT & T typically obtains is more desirable to consumers (to reach AT & T longlines the customer need dial only 1; to reach other companies, the customer must dial four figures). In the short run, this differential access charge is economically inefficient.[75] The public is generally best served if it is allowed to select its most preferred option at actual cost. There is no more reason, in the short run, to prevent AT & T from taking advantage of its better connections than to handicap a bridge because the road connecting it to town is better than the road from town to the ferry. But one can argue that in the long run the public will benefit if AT & T's superior access to local exchanges – an artifact of its past control over local service – is eliminated. The consent decree has therefore required the local telephone companies to provide equally good connections to AT & T's competitors by converting their equipment so that customers can choose which longlines firm to connect with 1 + dialing.[76] In the mean time, the differential access charge will protect the new companies from short-term losses.[77] The current differential charges can be viewed as a kind of tax, levied to upgrade the highway and pier to allow cars to board the ferries as easily as they can drive to the bridge. When 'equal access' is complete, there will no longer be any good economic reason for charging AT & T more for access than its competitors.

Second, the FCC for some time deliberately maintained a 'price umbrella' over AT & T's competitors. It refused to allow AT & T to cut its prices to the level of its incremental costs, a refusal that allowed the ferry-boats to offer lower priced, though higher cost, service.[78]

Third, the FCC imposes on AT & T a set of administrative requirements that do not apply to AT & T's competitors. When AT & T wishes to change its rates, it must file a proposed tariff. AT & T's competitors may then complain, the matter will be set for a hearing and there is likely to be considerable delay before the rate takes effect. AT & T thus loses the benefit of its new tariff for several months, and its competitors gain the opportunity for anticipatory response.[79]

Two arguments have been advanced in favour of handicapping AT & T. First is the fear of predatory pricing.[80] The argument is that if regulators do not keep AT & T's prices high, AT & T will price below its incremental costs in order to drive its competitors from the market and then raise prices high enough (and long enough) to recoup its losses (and more) before new firms attracted by the higher prices, enter the market. This scenario is analogous to one in which the bridge, despite facing incremental costs of 50c. per crossing, were to react to the ferry's 40c. charge by charging 30c. tolls for long enough to drive the ferry out of business. Furthermore, proponents of handicapping argue, the difficulty of determining whether a particular price is below marginal cost requires a preventive handicap.[81]

Yet one might ask why, in the post-divestiture world, regulation is necessary to prevent predatory pricing, particularly if AT & T and its competitors are all ferryboats. AT & T could not easily fund below-cost pricing in long-distance service for an extended period by raising prices in its monopoly markets; to the extent that AT & T retains any monopoly markets, they are small.[82] Beyond this question, however, is a more fundamental one: does AT & T have a strong enough incentive to drive competitors from the market? To do so would likely invite either reregulation or an antitrust suit under section 2 of the Sherman Act,[83] with the predatory pricing advanced as an 'exclusionary practice' leading to monopoly power. But, if AT & T did not drive its competitors from the field how could it ever recoup what it lost by charging below-cost prices? When it raised its prices later in an effort to recoup, its competitors – still in the industry – would simply undersell it.[84] In any event, why should regulators, rather than antitrust enforcers, decide whether predatory pricing exists? Of course, if AT & T is a bridge, one might find cost complexities that argue for having regulators look for predatory pricing; but then one would face the countervailing risk that the regulators, by preventing the bridge from cutting prices to incremental costs, would destroy the whole point of allowing new competition, namely, creating a marketplace test for low-cost long-distance service.

A second, and better, justification for handicapping AT & T is an 'infant industry' argument. AT & T, it is claimed, has considerable name recognition and other historical advantages. If its competitors are protected for a while, they will eventually become strong enough to compete effectively.

This argument, while logical, is subject to the traditional attacks on 'infant industry' protectionism. Given their growth and investment, do AT & T's competitors, really need protection?[85] Protection may discourage these 'infants' from developing the efficient practices needed to make them viable future competitors.[86] Why can't they find investors who will sustain them in the short term, given the prospect of efficiency and profits in the long run?[87] Finally, how long should we tolerate higher prices today in the hope of lower prices and better products tomorrow? Will our telecommunications infants ever grow up?

It is also interesting to note that long-term handicapping is wasteful even if deregulation itself was wrongly conceived – even if (contrary to this chapter's basis assumption) long-distance service is a natural monopoly. In that case, forbidding AT & T from cutting its prices would deprive consumers of the benefits of lower costs. Such a prohibition would support inefficient ferry-boats in the presence of a bridge that could carry the traffic at lower social cost. Of course, if, as we have assumed, the long-distance industry is not a natural monopoly – if it is structurally competitive – then once AT & T's competitors become reasonably established, handicapping AT & T simply interferes with the competitive process. It discourages the very price cutting that deregulation seeks to bring about.

This is not to say that it makes no difference whether AT & T is a bridge or another ferry-boat. It does make a difference, but not a difference that public policy can do much about now. Suppose, after all, that the 'bridge-and-ferry-boat' characterization of the problem is correct. Suppose that AT & T's fixed costs consist not of steel or cables or rights-of-way, long since depreciated and written off, but of such hard-to-measure intangibles as 'systems' costs or 'experience', or a research group like Bell Laboratories, or other related advantages that make AT & T a potentially lower-cost carrier than *any* of its competitors. Given existing deregulation, could we ever find this out? Would AT & T be likely to prove its cost advantages by dropping its prices and driving all others from the market? As aforementioned, this would invite a monopoly suit under section 2 or reregulation through congressional legislation. Why would AT & T not tolerate a few competitors, keeping its prices high enough to earn extra profits for itself while keeping its competitors in business? General Motors was often accused of pursuing just such a strategy.

It would indeed be ironic were AT & T to become, in this sense, a hypothetical General Motors. It would also cast an interesting light on institutional methods of carrying out deregulation. In both the airline and telephone industries, economists argued that economic evidence revealed structural competition. The evidence seemed stronger, however, in the case of airlines. The airlines presented Congress with practical examples of deregulation – in California and in Texas. Airline deregulation was introduced by legislation after congressional study and empirical agency experimentation. In contrast, telephone deregulators produced no comparable history of agency failure. Telephone deregulation was introduced by courts acting on complaints by regulators and private parties. In a sense, telecommunications deregulation is deregulation of, by, and (perhaps) for the mandarins.[88]

Whether or not deregulation was initially a good idea, it is now an accomplished fact. Although new competitors may need some period of direct protection, it is difficult to find any theoretical or practical reason to continue that protection indefinitely. Thus, it is fair to count a policy of protecting competitors, rather than competition, as one of the policy risks facing the newly deregulated world.

Risk Three: Regulatory Policy Will Fail in Treating Regulated Segments of Otherwise Deregulated Industries

A third risk inherent in deregulation arises out of the relationship between newly competitive firms and other still regulated parts of the industry. America may be seeing a variation on the old 'regulatory scenario', where regulated railroads urged the regulation of trucking and barge lines to prevent their own rates from being undercut by unregulated free competition. The problem that has arisen in telephone industry is that deregulated competition for long-distance calls will force local regulators to respond with changes in the structure of local and long-distance calling prices. The policy risk is that regulators will not base their response upon economically sound principles of regulation.

THE PROBLEM OF BYPASSING

The problem arises not from the breakup of AT & T, but rather from the initial decision of courts and regulators to allow new firms into the long-distance business. The deregulatory vision was that competing carriers would continue to connect customers to their long-distance lines through the established local exchanges.[89] However, new technological developments, especially microwave, have made it feasible for these companies, as well as AT & T, to bypass the local companies in connecting certain large customers.[90] Firms can offer, and major customers can buy, long-distance telephone service that does not use the existing lines and switching belonging to the (former) Bell system.

Returning to the bridge example will help to illustrate this problem. Whether or not the bridge offers a good analogy for long-distance service, it does provide a local service analogy. The scenario, again, is that the bridge has high fixed sunk costs. The possibility of using ferry-boats to bypass the bridge is real. The ferry boat has total costs that may well be greater than the incremental costs, but less than the average costs, of using the bridge. But only a few special kinds of users – say trucks – can use the ferry-boat. The analogy to local telephone service is a good one. The local systems have large sunk costs. Certain large businesses can bypass the system on certain kinds of calls by using technology that involves lower average costs than the average costs of going through the local system. But if the incremental costs of bypassing are higher than the incremental costs of traditional routing, then the lower price of bypassing encourages economic waste.

In so far as this description fits current circumstances, the stage is set for a kind of tragedy.[91] How can business customers be prevented from deserting the present local system when they make long-distance calls? The. obvious economic answer is by lowering the price of their existing service. Just as trucks can be kept on the bridge by cutting truck tolls, so businesses can be convinced to use the local network for long-distance dialing by lowering the charge. Moreover, there is a logical answer for any other customer who objects: If the bridge does *not* lower the truck toll, trucks will desert it for the ferry, and fewer customers will remain to share the cost of the bridge. Each of these customers will then have to pay even more than if the bridge had cut the truck toll. How far the bridge must cut the truck toll to prevent truck desertion is, however, a difficult empirical question, particularly in the telephone context, where tolls must cover *categories* of users. In so far as a toll is cut more than necessary to prevent desertion, the cut burdens other users with unnecessarily high tolls.

The strategy of reducing telephone rates in order to prevent bypassing by long-distance callers is further complicated by certain special features that have until now characterized telecommunications pricing. First, long-distance calls traditionally have been priced so that the contribution each long-distance call makes to the cost of the local service needed to connect it is far higher than the contribution each purely local call makes to the same cost.[92] The purpose of this difference in contribution has been to ensure the nearly universal availability of local service to the American public.[93] Second, commercial callers have paid proportionately more for telephone service in order to secure lower rates for residential users.[94] Finally, urban users have paid prices above cost so that the high costs involved in serving rural areas would not result in prohibitive prices there.[95] The net effect of these three sets of price differences has been a substantial excess charge on large commercial callers. It is as if the bridge, prior to ferry-boat entry, charged trucks far more for crossing than it charged other vehicles. This difference did not matter (at least for our purposes) so long as AT & T had a monopoly on long-distance service. The result today, however, is that the local price cuts that are necessary to retain the large customers are far greater than they might otherwise have been, thus producing greater political resistance from those who will be burdened with higher rates.[96] In addition, any solution to the bypassing problem must be sensitive to the need to maintain universal service as mandated both by law[97] and by social considerations.

The problem, then, is that the price cuts to large businesses necessary to prevent bypassing, with its attendant economic waste and harm to consumers, are likely to encounter political resistance and to compromise the goal of universal service.

PREVENTING BYPASSING

Three possible approaches to the problem are apparent. First, one might try to restore the pre-regulation status quo.[98] To do this, the local companies would have to assess a heavier access charge on *all* long-distance carriers. This charge – which the carriers would then pass on to consumers in the form of higher rates – would prove the equivalent of the effectively higher contribution that the unified AT & T once provided to local service by charging more for long distance. At the same time, the regulator would impose some kind of tax on carriers not connected to any local system, the proceeds from which would support the local carriers. This tax would raise the price of bypass service to the level of traditional service so that bypassing would not pay.

This type of solution amounts to the banning of ferry-boats by taxing them out of existence. Such an approach is subject to both practical and theoretical objections. On the practical level, the tax on bypassing carriers is likely to be extremely difficult both to devise and to enforce. The principal difficulty in devising the tax would be setting it at a level high enough to discourage uneconomic bypassing and yet low enough not to obstruct the introduction of systems that in fact involve lower incremental costs than traditional routing.[99] Other problems would arise from the inevitable pressures to provide exemptions from the tax to certain users, such as government.[100] On the enforcement level, it is often difficult to identify which calls made on non-traditional media are long-distance, even with current technology[101] – and technologies making detection even more difficult would undoubtedly arise were a tax system to provide an incentive for their development.

On the theoretical level, the solution of imposing access charges and bypass taxes, even if properly enforced, would create economic waste. The most serious problem is that it discourages long-distance calling where the user is willing to pay more than the incremental cost of the call, but will not pay that incremental cost plus a large amount of fixed sunk cost plus a large subsidy for, say, rural service. This problem is that of the bridge crosser who would pay $1.00 but not $1.50 to cross the bridge. To be fair, this problem has nothing at all to do with deregulation; it would exist as long as the regulator is determined to hold local prices down by obtaining a large share of fixed, sunk costs from the long-distance caller. And the only criticism one can make of this is to ask the regulator *why* s/he is doing it. Is there something virtuous about local calling or wicked about long-distance? Is it that those who make local calls are poorer and this is a form of income transfer? How do we know? Who buys the products made by firms that call long-distance? Are they farmers selling food? In the airline industry (some observers believe), regulators for many years charged more for long-distance routes in order to subsidize shorter service. Why, asked Professor Caves, should a grandmother flying from Boston to Los Angeles pay more so that a businessman flying from Utica to Buffalo can pay less?[102] This is not to say that there are not good social reasons for making local service available to every citizen. However, narrower, targeted subsidies, such as the life-line service that has been introduced in some communities,[103] would seem a better way to further this social goal. It is hard to see why affordable local service should come at the expense of permitting long-distance rates to reflect the lower costs that technological progress has made possible.

A second way of dealing with the problem is basically to do nothing. One can simply impose specially cumbersome burdens of proof upon those who would lower the access charge, hence lowering long-distance rates to levels closer to the costs of providing long-distance service. If one requires definite proof that in the absence of a lower charge, there will be sufficient bypassing to impose still greater charges on residential users, the burdens are not likely to be met. Moreover, regulators may accept one or more of several newly hatched economic theories,[104] apparently designed to show that long-distance callers ought to pay more for the local portion of their calls than other local callers. This second approach however, would be tragic, for it will lead to desertion through bypassing and eventually to higher costs for the remaining users.

Third, the regulators might devise an economically -oriented system of charges so as to align more closely the prices of various services with the incremental costs of providing those services. Professor Kahn has provided numerous suggestions regarding such a system.[105] Among other possibilities, local service might be measured and charges assessed accordingly. Charges in older areas of the city (hooked up permanently to local networks in the past) might be lowered while connection charges in newer areas might be raised. These proposals would allow regulators to lower the access charges for long-distance service while at the same time concentrating the costs of local service on those who create most of those costs and who, as a rule, are most able to bear them.[106] To the extent that local rates might still be prohibitive to particularly needy customers, targeted subsidies might best address their concerns.

I favour the third method for dealing with the bypassing problem. Access charges plus a bypass tax threaten to forfeit the benefits both of deregulation and of technological change, while ignoring the problem threatens to hurt the residential consumer. Cost-based charging is consistent with a pro-competitive theory of regulation that sees regulation, at least in part, as an effort to bring to the consumer at least some of the advantages of economic efficiency where the market cannot be relied upon to do the job. I shall leave the reader to find the details of the necessary changes in Professor Kahn's work.[107] Here, I simply point out that the danger of *not* following sound economic principles when regulating segments of otherwise deregulated industries is one of the major risks facing the public in the newly deregulated world.

Risk Four: Antitrust Policy Will Be Unable to Prevent Anti-Competitive Bottlenecks in Partially Deregulated Industries

THE PROBLEM OF BOTTLENECKS

A final risk arising in the newly deregulated industries involves the inability to deal with residual elements of monopoly power, actual or potential. Deregulation, after all, did not come about in the airline or telecommunications industries because anyone thought them perfectly competitive. Rather, those urging deregulation felt that *on balance* the evils of regulation exceeded those of relying upon free markets protected by antitrust. In each industry, there remain residual areas of potential market power, sometimes called 'bottlenecks',[108] which, at least in the short run, threaten significant anti-competitive harm.

A useful example of a bottleneck in the airline industry arises out of the recent controversy about the computerized reservation systems (CRS's), owned and supplied to travel agents by American Airlines and United Airlines.[109] Critics claim that American and United design their CRS screens to favour their own flights, thereby placing competing airlines at a disadvantage.[110] These critics also note that competitors cannot replicate the United or American CRSs because of the prohibitive costs of creating a CRS and a shortage of skilled programmers.[111] In addition, because high fixed costs make a large-scale operation more efficient, new entrants would need to capture a fairly large market share before they could compete with the dominant carriers.[112] Finally, travel agents are most likely to buy the system supplied by the airline that is dominant in their region, and once they buy one system, they are unlikely to switch. These facts, the critics conclude, make the CRS a kind of regional natural monopoly, the control of which allows an airline to injure or destroy competition in the entire airline industry.[113]

A similar argument against integrated operation in adjacent industries is raised against local telephone operating companies. Local companies are still regulated because they possess significant monopoly power in local markets. To what extent should they be allowed to expand into other businesses – either businesses such as telephone equipment, which supply ingredients of the telephone system, or businesses such as information processing, which use local communications extensively as part of the product that they sell? Some fear that the ability of the BOCs to control local telecommunications while offering these other services would give them an unfair advantage, allowing them to distort or destroy competition in these other fields.

What shall we do with these bottlenecks? Should we isolate them, forbidding their owners to enter other related businesses? Or should we regulate them in an effort to control abuses inherent in integrated ownership?

Antitrust law has varied in its treatment of bottlenecks. The different treatments are perhaps best illustrated by comparing a classic Supreme Court case with a hypothetical situation. The original and most famous 'bottleneck control' case is *United States v. Terminal Railroad Association*.[114] A combination of railroads had acquired exclusive control of all railroad terminals in St Louis and imposed discriminatory charges upon their competitors for use of the facilities. The Supreme Court held that the unification was an unlawful combination in restraint of trade and 'an attempt to monopolize commerce among the States which must pass through the gateway at St. Louis'.[115] Because the unified system provided more efficient service than separately managed terminals, however, the Court refused to order immediate dissolution of the combination, and instead ordered the association to admit its competition to the facilities on equal terms.[116]

In contrast, consider the following hypothetical. Suppose that George and Edward invent a better spring for a traditional mousetrap that they produce in competition between themselves and with others. As in the case of the railroads, George and Edward's exclusive control over the spring will hinder

– perhaps decisively – other competitors in the mousetrap market. Antitrust law, however, will not impose equal access requirements upon George and Edward. It will not require them to provide their mousetrap competitors with the spring on 'fair' or 'equal' terms, nor will it require them to set up a separate spring company and divest it.[117]

The reason for this different treatment lies in the need to favour efficiency and encourage innovation. Restraining railroads from excluding their competitors from gateway passage is unlikely to have an adverse effect upon the construction or maintenance of gateways. But requiring an inventor, even of an unpatented invention, to give his secrets away to his competitors discourages innovation and invites unwieldy court supervision in an effort to determine 'fair' terms. That is why courts have struck down or tried to supervise very few bottlenecks – and virtually none where the bottleneck was created by a single firm, rather than by agreement among several competing companies.

To understand one's different intuitive reactions to these two examples, particularly in the present deregulatory context, consider the following pairs of questions. First, compare:

(1)   Should an airline be permitted to provide a computerized reservation service for travel agents? with
(2)   Should an owner of a computerized reservation service be permitted to provide airline service?

Then compare:

(1)   Should a local telephone company be allowed to enter an 'information service' industry? with
(2)   Should a firm that sells an 'information service' be allowed to provide local telephone service?

In the first pair, an affirmative answer to either question approves a single integrated firm offering both CRS and airline service; in the second, an affirmative answer to either question approves a single integrated firm providing both information and local telephone service. In both pairs, however, the second question is phrased so that it seems to call more quickly and more easily for an affirmative response. One's responses to the first and second questions differ because the first questions – like the *Terminal Railroad* case – focus attention upon the likely anti-competitive features of the integration, whereas the second questions – like the mousetrap case – focus attention on potential competitive benefits.

The preceding examples suggest that analyzing these deregulatory 'left-over' bottlenecks may be simpler than it first appears. We need only ask the most basic of antitrust questions: (1) What are the likely anti-competitive effects of the integration? and (2) What are the potential countervailing economic virtues? We might also ask: (3) Which institution – antitrust or regulation – can more effectively identify and weigh the relevant factors and take curative action?

SOME BOTTLENECKS EXAMINED

These basic questions will be considered with respect to both the computerized reservation systems in the airlines and the integrated services in the telecommunications industry.

1 *Computerized airline reservation systems*   Critics identify three serious risks of anti-competitive harm. First, they argue that the CRS-owning airlines bias the programmes and displays in their own favour.[118] Carrier *A*, for example, may use a computer algorithm that lists all of its own connections before it lists any connection with other airlines.[119] Or it may list carriers with which *A* maintains a marketing relationship before it lists other carriers,[120] or it may make up a supposedly neutral order for display – say, 'list carriers in order of elapsed time' – but then use fake elapsed times to make certain the computer displays *A* and its friends first.[121] To address this problem, the CAB issued a rule requiring CRS owners to offer unbiased display screens.[122] But, the critics said, CRS owners circumvented the rule by offering subscribing agents two display screens – the first complying with the CAB regulation and the second biased in their own favour.[123] The owners then offered incentives to agents to use the 'secondary' displays by tailoring fees to the number of bookings made from those screens.[124] The owners also offered a 'lock-in' device that automatically displays the 'secondary' screen when the terminals are turned on in the morning, altogether bypassing the unbiased screens.[125] The combination of financial inducements and the lock-in mechanism, critics said, effectively reversed the priority of the primary and secondary screens, so that travel agents and their customers continued to learn less, or later, about the flights of competitors. The traveller was unlikely to learn enough about what was occurring to punish the travel agents who used 'biased' screens by switching to travel agents who did not. The result was faulty or incomplete information that distorted consumer choice. Recently, however, American Airlines, United, and TWA agreed voluntarily to end the secondary display bias.[126]

Second, a synergy between airline ownership and ownership of a CRS permits the CRS-owning carrier to protect its market position in both the CRS and airline industries. An airline dominant in a particular region can offer powerful inducements to travel agents in that area to use its CRS system.[127] Thus, in Denver, an important United Airlines hub, United's APPOLO system accounted for 72 per cent of the market, and in Dallas, an American Airlines hub, American's SABRE system accounted for 88 per cent of the market.[128]

Once a CRS-owning airline has achieved dominance in a particular regional CRS market, it can use its dominance to protect its market position in the airline industry.[129] Airline market entry is hindered not only by the usual difficulties confronting entrants in a particular airline market, such as finding space at the airports, but also by a biased reservation system.

This problem could be serious because the airline industry is competitive in a special sense: many routes can support only one or two firms, so potential competition from other nearby carriers is important in disciplining the dominant carrier. The higher the entry barriers, the less effective the discipline. For reasons earlier discussed,[130] one should be reluctant to allow any significant additional barrier to entry.

Third, the critics argue that an owner may use information stored in the CRS about each passenger's itinerary, class of service, fare code, and so forth, for anti-competitive purposes. The CRS affords direct, immediate access to the proprietary information of each carrier.[131] This information offers valuable insights into market responses to new fares, routes, or services.[132] Although the CAB requires American and United to share with their competitors any marketing data they generate on computer printouts,[133] this requirement is easily circumvented. The CRS owners can simply display the information on their own terminals without printing it out. They can also secure a competitive advantage by delaying the transfer of, and charging high prices for, any information they do print out.[134]

Moreover, the exchange of information itself poses an anti-competitive threat even if the CRS owners do not use their competitors' proprietary information unfairly. The immediate communication of marketing data made possible through the use of CRSs increases the likelihood of tacit cooperative agreements. The more concentrated regional markets become, the greater the risk that such information-sharing will inhibit competition by encouraging oligopolistic coordination.[135]

Given these apparently significant anti-competitive risks, what are the countervailing economic benefits that favour ownership of CRSs by airlines? The CRS is primarily an information display programme; a separate firm may not be able to gather the necessary information as readily as an airline can gather information about the schedules of its competitors. The airlines and the Department of Justice argue that there are significant efficiencies involved in integrating the computer operations involved in CRS's with the airlines' internal reservations systems.[136] Whether one could preserve these efficiencies while allowing other smaller airlines to participate in the ownership of a CRS, or after requiring divestiture, is a subject of considerable debate.

The need to encourage innovation also justifies allowing integrated ownership to continue. The airline owners of CRSs invested money in developing them. Their investment succeeded. Antitrust courts are reluctant to forbid vertical integration that flows from *internal expansion*, particularly expansion that was successful in the marketplace. It is a little as if one tried to take George and Edward's mousetrap spring away from them. It is no wonder, then, that the Department of Justice and earlier regulatory authorities tried to control the anti-competitive *effects* of the ownership – insisting upon 'unbiased' displays, prohibiting certain price discrimination, and so forth – rather than requiring divestiture.

Nonetheless, certain special circumstances weaken the force of this traditional argument. The CRS-owning airlines have by now presumably made considerable profit from their investment in CRSs. The systems are well enough developed so that a sale would likely reward them with the capitalized value of potential future profit. Further, there is some antitrust precedent that suggests that an initially pro-competitive venture might, after achieving its pro-competitive purposes, become anti-competitive; at that later time, more drastic remedies may become appropriate.[137] Finally, the airlines were regulated when they entered the CRS business. American and United, the largest CRS owners, were also the largest regulated carriers. One might ask to what extent such regulated investment is entitled to a *more* than reasonable return. Is it then more fair (or less unfair) to force divestiture upon such a firm once it has earned a generous profit on its investment if (1) the anti-competitive risks are significant; (2) the other economic justifications for integration seem relatively weak; or (3) the government finds it difficult to regulate effects alone?

The arguments about CRSs may come down to questions about what relief can practically be ordered: divestiture, forced admission of other airlines to ownership, or enforcement of 'anti-bias' rules. To decide what form of relief is practical would require further examination of the facts – particularly those related to efficiencies of integration.[138]

2   *Integrated telephone service*   A similar problem exists in the newly deregulated telecommunications industry, where the local telephone companies are left behind as regulated pockets of monopoly power. Regulators are asking whether they should isolate the Bell Operating Companies (BOCs) or allow them to enter related businesses, such as the provision of various information services or long distance telecommunications.[139]

Several arguments are typically advanced against allowing the BOCs to provide integrated service. Some of them are better than others.

First, there is a simple 'deep pocket' argument. It claims that the BOCs may use the profit from their monopoly communications businesses to subsidize 'below cost' prices in their competitive businesses. In this simple form,[140] the argument suffers the defect of all 'deep pocket' arguments; it proves too much. If taken literally, it would prevent any firm with substantial resources from entering any line of business for fear that it would use its resources to drive competitors from the field and then raise prices. It assumes the anti-trust laws are incapable of dealing with the 'predatory' below-cost prices that are preconditions of this argument. And by preventing competition now, it effectively throws out the baby with the bathwater.

This argument is particularly difficult to make plausible in the context of telecommunications. Several other competitors or potential competitors, such as IBM (which owns a substantial portion of MCI), have resources at least as great as the BOCs.[141] Furthermore, regulation of local monopolies creates, if anything, less reason to fear a 'deep pocket' than usual, because regulation, in so far as it is effective, prevents monopoly profits and therefore means the pocket is not unfairly deep.[142]

Second, critics claim that to allow BOCs to enter related fields will replicate the problem of integration that led to the antitrust suit against AT & T. This argument is simply mistaken, and it is important to understand why.

The problem that led to the AT & T suit was not simply the problem of vertical integration. The government did not claim that a natural monopoly should do *no* business in any competitive sectors. It did not argue, for example, that a natural gas distributor should be forbidden to sell heating system filters, or that a railroad could not sell souvenir menus – or that an airline (when regulated) should not be permitted to offer charter service. Rather, the government claimed that the natural monopoly controlled *a large portion of the market in the competitive sector*.[143] AT & T controlled (through Western Electric) more than 80 per cent of the equipment manufacturing business; it controlled more than 70 per cent of long-distance telecommunications.[144] In this context, the integration was viewed as unlawful because it helped to perpetuate an already existing monopoly share of an important competitively structured industry.

In the case of the BOCs, the circumstance of their integration or internal expansion is critically different. The issue is whether the BOCs should be allowed to enter different markets, or various competitive industries, where they now account for zero per cent, not 70 per cent, of the competitive marketplace. Such entry raises a potential problem only if the BOCs would have both the incentive and the ability to use their local exchange monopolies in those related fields unfairly, in a way that improperly allows them eventually to dominate or to monopolize those fields.

The opponents of BOC entry make the more serious and important claim that the risk of improper or unfair competition, and even eventual BOC dominance, is great. In support, they present two arguments.[145]

The first argument is that firms may misallocate costs from their competitive businesses to their monopoly service. To the extent that this argument simply restates the Averch–Johnson effect,[146] it is weak. A regulated monopoly has an incentive to pad its rate base if it can borrow money at a rate lower than its allowed return on investment. For example, if a regulated telephone company can borrow money at 8 per cent, it will borrow as much as possible, build pyramids with it, and collect a 9 per cent return from the users of telephone service, as long as the regulator allows 9 per cent and doesn't catch the padding. If the rate-base padding consists of investment in a related competitive service, such as some kind of information service, the cost of which is partly and improperly charged to local telephone service, it may be hard to detect. Still, it is not likely that the regulator would allow the local telephone company a higher rate of return than the cost of capital, at least not in the near future when regulators are desperately trying to minimize the increase in local residential rates made necessary by deregulation. If so, the Averch–Johnson problem does not seem likely to have major empirical significance.

Even without the Averch–Johnson effect, however, firms may still be able to profit from misallocation of costs. The Averch–Johnson effect depends upon returns higher than the cost of capital because investment in pyramids is not in itself profitable. A BOC may, however, be able to enter a related business that would itself provide an adequate return on capital. In that case, *any* return which the regulator allows on the investment, even if less than the cost of capital, is supracompetitive – that is, excess profit.[147] The BOC might pocket this profit and get rich on the backs of its ratepayers. Alternatively, it might correspondingly lower its prices in the competitive market and thus gain a decisive advantage over its rivals, despite facing the same real costs that they do.[148] In either event, the public loses.

The plausibility of this scenario depends upon whether the BOCs will be able to slip misallocation by the regulators. Certainly, regulators are unlikely, in this era of concern for local rates, to ignore potential rate-base padding.

Furthermore, to the extent that the BOCs are currently earning less than a fair return on their local investment, padding becomes less attractive and less troublesome, and may to a degree even be viewed as merely compensatory.[149] On the other hand, the similarities of the various telecommunications industries, combined with the real possibility of genuine economies from integration, may make some padding very difficult to detect.[150] While the danger of competitive harm through misallocation may not be great, it cannot simply be dismissed as trivial.

The critics' second fear is that the BOCs might use their local exchange monopolies to obstruct others in competitive sectors, with an eye to gaining for themselves a large enough market share to facilitate future monopoly profits. For instance, a local company might design its exchange services so as to be most compatible with its own information services or equipment.[151] It might also directly hinder competitors who seek necessary local connections.[152] Because of the ease with which much of this behaviour might be defended on grounds of 'efficiency',[153] its prevention on a case-by-case basis might prove especially difficult. In a nutshell, this argument suggests that it is a mistake to let a bridge owner go into the railroad business, lest it use its power over the bridge to obstruct competing railroads. The argument is logically sound, but the question is one of balancing. Are the risks of such undetected conduct great enough to warrant prohibition?

Before we can answer this question (a task that this chapter does not attempt), we must ask about the potential benefits of BOC entry. These benefits appear to be much stronger here than in the case of the CRS. First, there may be economies in having BOCs provide certain information services along with telecommunications. These economies include efficiencies in integrating equipment, avoiding facilities duplication, and increasing the convenience of consumers who would receive a broader range of telecommunications services from a single supplier.[154] In fact, competitors of the BOCs point to these possible economies when they claim that it will be difficult for a regulator to catch anti-competitive abuses. Second, the ability to offer these services may help the regulated BOC attract firms away from bypassing, thereby helping to protect residential customers from increased rates.[155] Third, allowing the BOCs to enter means new competition in competitively structured industries.[156] These benefits tend to neutralize the anticompetitive disadvantages of integration.

RESOLVING BOTTLENECKS

Having identified the anti-competitive dangers and economic benefits of bottlenecks in both the airline and telecommunications industries, our remaining task is to identify which institutions are best suited to resolving the problems posed. Should we deal with these potential anti-competitive problems through antitrust or a regulatory mechanism? Antitrust policy is administered primarily by courts, operating through rule and precedent. Courts find it difficult to reverse direction or to have a change of heart once a case is decided. Courts also have difficulty investigating underlying circumstances – particularly changes in circumstances – because they depend upon a record, produced through an adversarial process, for their information. In addition, courts find it difficult to balance factors tending in opposite directions, for they are uncomfortable in the absence of standards for weighing each factor in the balance.

The regulatory agency is more flexible. It has a staff that can conduct factual investigations. Because it has less need to consider the precedential value of what it does, it can more easily experiment and make exceptions. Finally, perhaps because it can rely more easily upon its expertise to justify its decisions, it hesitates less to balance competing factors to reach a result. Regulation exacts a price, however, in terms of delayed decisions, expensive bureaucracy, diminished predictability, and imperfect replication of the free market.

These institutional considerations, combined with the foregoing substantive analysis, point in the following direction. The telecommunications 'bottleneck' problem seems more amenable to regulatory control. BOCs could enter other lines of business provided an agency supervises their basic local-service pricing behaviour, scrutinizing their conduct to ensure that they do not take unfair advantage of a local telecommunications monopoly to restrict or deny a competitor essential services. Regulatory supervision seems appropriate because there are both economic benefits and competitive risks to allowing entry; continued supervision may help to maximize the benefits while minimizing the risks.

The CRS bottleneck poses a set of practical questions concerning relief. Would the obvious stringent antitrust solution – divestiture – prove too costly? Is it possible to require partial ownership by other airlines, effectively forcing existing owners to become joint venturers? Just how expensive, in terms of efficiency, would these solutions be? Would the only other alternative – some form of continued government supervision or regulation – prove still more costly? Professor Kahn has argued extensively that the antitrust solution – divestiture – is most appropriate here.[157]

To answer the practical questions and resolve the policy considerations would require considerably more detailed analysis. It would also require gathering facts to evaluate my rough empirical judgements. But if the main points raised are roughly correct, the present situation, institutionally speaking, seems ironic. Instead of using regulation to supervise BOC entry into new fields, we are using an antitrust court essentially to forbid it, at least in fields related to telephone service.[158] Instead of searching for ways to change the structure of CRS ownership, we are regulating CRS conduct. Our basic institutional instinct seems backward.

Conclusion

Deregulation, like regulation, will raise a host of difficult analytic problems that traditional antitrust policy cannot resolve. The examples of airlines and telecommunications suggest at least four such risks, which should alert us to four corresponding policy needs:
(1) the need for a strong antitrust policy to maintain competitive market structures;

(2) the need to avoid protecting competitors where doing so is inconsistent with promoting competition;
(3) the need to follow sound economic principles where regulation continues in other segments of the industry or in related industries; and
(4) the need to minimize the potential anti-competitive impact of residual monopoly power in newly deregulated industries.

These needs are, in sense, old ones, but the deregulation of the airline and telecommunications industries increases the importance of our recognizing and satisfying them.

Appendix

Table 1.1   Real revenues and fares adjusted with the Consumer Price Index

Year	Average fare per revenue passenger mile		Revenue passenger miles (Billions)	Total Revenues Constant $
	Current $	Constant $		
1973	.066	.154	129.3	19.912
1974	.075	.158	133.0	21.014
1975	.077	.149	135.2	20.145
1976	.082	.150	149.1	22.365
1977	.086	.147	161.3	23.711
1978	.085	.135	188.2	25.407
1979	.089	.127	209.9	26.657
1980	.116	.146	201.3	29.390
1981	.131	.150	199.9	29.985
1982	.123	.132	212.0	27.984
1983	.121	.126	229.4	28.904
1984	.129	.129	246.2	31.760
1985	.122	.118	270.1	31.817

Notes:
(a) Dollar figures are adjusted to 1984 dollars using the Consumer Price Index.
(b) Total revenue is in billions of 1984 dollars (and is equal to average fare per RPM multiplied by number of RPM).
Source: U.S. General Accounting Office, Deregulation: Increased Competition Is Making Airlines More Efficient and Responsive to Consumers, Appendices III, XXI, and XXII (6 November 1985).

Table 1.2   Passenger savings if Airline fares had increased with the rate of inflation in the Consumer Price Index (1973 base)

Year	Savings in 1973 passenger miles	Savings on additional passenger miles flown	Total
1974	0.517	0.015	0.532
1975	−0.647	−0.030	−0.677
1976	−0.517	−0.079	−0.596
1977	−0.905	−0.224	−1.129
1978	−2.457	−1.119	−3.576
1979	−3.491	−2.176	−5.667
1980	−1.034	−0.576	−1.610
1981	−0.517	−0.282	−0.799
1982	−2.845	−1.819	−4.664
1983	−3.620	−2.803	−6.423
1984	−3.233	−2.923	−6.156
1985	−4.655	−5.069	−9.724
Total	−23.404	−17.085	−40.489

Notes:
(a) All amounts are billions of 1984 dollars, adjusted using the Consumer Price Index.
(b) Column 1 gives the reduction in airline revenues (savings in passenger costs) to fly the same number of miles as flown in 1973; it is the difference between the inflation adjusted average fare per RPM in each year and the 1973 average fare, multiplied by the number of miles flown in 1973. In arithmetic terms, Column 1 equals $(P_t - P_{73}) \times Q_{73}$.
(c) Column 2 gives the additional reduction in airline revenues (savings in passenger costs) realized on additional miles flown; it is the difference between the inflation adjusted average fare per RPM in each year and the 1973 average fare, multiplied by the number of miles flown in each year in excess of total 1973 mileage. In arithmetic terms, Column 2 equals $(Q_t - Q_{73}) \times (P_t - P_{73})$.
(d) Column 3 is the sum of Columns 1 and 2.
Source: Calculated from data in Table 1.1.

Notes

1. The discussion in this section is based upon S. Breyer (1982) Regulation and Its Reform, Harvard Press. Additional discussion and sources can be found in that book.
2. See e.g. T. G. Moore, *Transportation Policy* (1988), 3 Regulation 57, 59–60.
3. Ibid., p. 59.
4. See e.g. W. Haraf (1988), *Bank and Thrift Regulation*, 3 Regulation 50.
5. See e.g. P. Joskow and R. Schmaleansee (1987), An Analysis of Electric Utility Regulation, MIT Press.
6. See e.g. T. Moore, *Transportation Policy*, p. 60.
7. For an up-to-date discussion of the current status of such 'alternative' methods of regulating the environment, see R. Stroup (1988), *Environmental Policy*, 3 Regulation 43.

8. Ibid.

9. For a quick summary of the status quo, see e.g. M. Breger (1988), *Negotiated Rulemaking by Government Agencies*, Washington Legal Foundation Legal Background, 11 Nov.

10. See R. Noel, *Regulation After Reagan* (1988), 3 Regulation 13.

11. This portion of the paper is drawn from Breyer (1987), *Antitrust, Deregulation, and the Newly Liberated Marketplace*, 75 Calif. L. Rev. 1005. It is reprinted with the permission of the editors of the University of California *Law Review*.

12. I do not mean to suggest that competitive markets will promote efficiency under all circumstances. See Elzinga (1977), *The Goals of Antitrust: Other than Competition and Efficiency. What Else Counts?*, 125 U. Pa. L. Rev. 1191, 1191 n.1 (noting that a competitive market will not secure efficiency in an industry with declining long-run average costs).

13. See Part I.

14. See Part I.

15. *Aviation: Hearings on H.R. 5234 and H.R. 4652 Before the House Comm. on Interstate and Foreign Commerce.* 75th Cong., 1st Sess. 76 (1937) (statement of Edgar S. Gorrell, President, Air Transport Association of America).

16. Airline Deregulation Act of 1978, Pub. L. No. 95–504, 92 Stat. 1705 (codified in scattered sections of 18, 26 and 49 U.S.C.; the Act is located primarily at 49 U.S.C. §§ 1301–1384 (1982)).

17. See, e.g. *In re* Use of the Carterfone Device in Message Toll Tel. Serv., 13 F.C.C.2d 420, 423–24 (1968) (declaring illegal an FCC tariff prohibiting attachment of telephone equipment not provided by AT & T); J. Meyer, R. Wilson, M. Baughcum, E. Burton & L. Caouette (1980), *The* Economics of Competition in the Telecommunications Industry 111–53 [hereinafter Charles River Associates] (a Charles River Associates study seriously questioning the existence of natural monopoly in the telecommunications industry).

18. Sudit (1973), 'Additive nonhomogeneous production functions in telecommunications', 4 *Bell J. Econ. & Mgmt. Sci.*, 499; Vinod (1972), 'Nonhomogeneous Production Functions and Applications to Telecommunications', 3 *Bell J. Econ. & Mgmt. Sci.* 531.

19. See Staff of Subcomm. on Admin. Practice and Procedure of the Senate Comm. On the Judiciary, 94th Cong., 1st Sess., Report on Civil Aeronautics Board Practices and Procedures 40–58 (Comm. Print 1975) [hereinafter Kennedy Report].

20. In part, the business community was expected to benefit from the pressure of competition that would reduce or eliminate perceived excess charges that AT & T had imposed upon long distance, commercial, and urban callers. See below p. 35. In addition, business, with their more complex needs, would be more likely than most individual consumers to benefit from service innovation.

21. Senator Kennedy's investigation of the CAB revealed that that agency violated relevant regulatory statutes, used inadequate or improper procedures, inappropriately focused on increasing airline profits rather than reducing fares, followed incoherent route award policies, and skewed its enforcement policies towards stopping charter and other low-fare flights. The investigation produced strong evidence that the Board itself maintained unnecessarily high fares, prevented – sometimes unlawfully – new low-fare airlines from entering the industry, and tried to stop service, as well as price, competition. For a detailed account of these policies. See Kennedy Report, above note[19].

22. The FCC brought about open entry into manufacturing and connecting of telephone equipment. See Proposals for New or Revised Classes of Interstate and Foreign Message Toll Tel. Serv. and Wide Area Tel. Serv., 56 F.C.C.2d 593 (1975) (First Report and Order permitting connection of terminal equipment without carrier-supplied connecting arrangements); 58 F.C.C.2d 736 (1976) (same case) (Second Report and Order extending access to private branch exchanges, key telephone systems, main system telephones, and coin telephones); *Carterfone*, 13 F.C.C.2d at 423–24 (allowing use of telephone interconnecting devices not furnished by AT & T).

 By contrast, competition did not become legal in long distance switched service until effectively ordered by the District of Columbia Circuit Court of Appeals. See MCI Telecommunications Corp. v. F.C.C., 561 F.2d 365 (D.C. Cir. 1977) (holding that the FCC has no general authority to insist on approval of new services without a finding of 'public convenience and necessity'), *cert. denied*, 434 U.S. 1040 (1978), *later proceeding* 580 F.2d 590 (D.C. Cir.) (holding that the previous decision's mandate requires AT & T and the FCC to provide interconnections to MCI), *cert. denied*, 439 U.S. 980 (1978). For an overview of the actions of the FCC and the federal courts from 1959 to 1979, see generally Knieps & Spiller, 'Regulating by partial deregulation: the case of telecommunications', 35 *Admin. L. Rev.* 391, 397–405 (1983).

 Finally, the breakup of AT & T, which was intended to promote competitive conditions in both equipment manufacturing and long-distance service, grew out of a consent decree settling judicial litigation. United States v. American Tel. & Tel. Co., 552 F. Supp. 131, 226–32 (D.D.C. 1982), *aff'd sub nom.* Maryland v. United States, 460 U.S. 1001 (1983). Under the consent decree (also called the 'Modification of Final Judgement' or 'MFJ'), AT & T divested its local service subsidiaries, which now operate independently as regulated local monopolies. AT & T, in competition with other firms, continues to provide equipment and long distance service. See R. Crandall (1988), *Telecommunications Policy in the Reagan Era*, 3 Regulation 28.

23. See e.g. S. Breyer, above note 1, at 292–93 (discussing the debate over natural monopoly and structural competition in the telecommunications industry). For arguments predating deregulation, see Kennedy Report, above note [19], at 38–40; Charles River Associates, above note [17], at 111–53; G. Douglas and J. Miller (1974), *Economic Regulation of Domestic Air Transport: Theory and Policy*; 2 A. Kahn (1971), *The Economics of Regulation: Principles and Institutions* 113–250

24. The number of certificated carriers increased from 33 in 1976 to 114 in 1984. See U.S. General Accounting Office, Deregulation: Increased Competition is Making Airlines more Efficient and Responsive to Consumers 12 (1985) [hereinafter GAO Report]; Moore, 'U.S. Airline deregulation: its effects on passengers, capital, and labor', 29 *J. L. & Econ.* 1, 5 (1986).

25. See Gao Report, above note [24], at 15–16. In the first quarter of 1984, 97% of passengers traveled in markets served by more than three airlines. *Id.* at 16.

26. See below Table 1.1 in Appendix.

27. See below Table 1.2 in Appendix. Dollar figures have been adjusted to 1984 dollars using the Consumer Price Index. These figures were calculated on the basis of Department of Transportation Air Carrier Traffic Statistics. See also Bailey (1986). 'Price and productivity change following deregulation: the US experience', 96 *Econ J. 1*, 5 (providing an index of airline fares in 1983 as a percentage of the CAB formula fare).

28. Testimony of Alfred E. Kahn before the U.S. Senate Committee on Commerce, Science and Transportation, 22 Sept. 1988, at 2. For similar comparison of

50

Stephen Breyer

1978–87, see Testimony of Secretary of Transportation James Burnley before the House Committee on Commerce, Science and Transportation, 22 Sept. 1988 (average fare declined 13% since 1978; savings in 1987 $13 billion).

29. GAO Report, above note 24, at 74.
30. See *New York Times*, 20 March 1988, p. E-3. Figures also based on information reported by Eastern Airlines.
31. Although total employment increased overall roughly 9% between 1976 and 1982, it has been dropping since 1980. See Moore, above note 24, at 25–6. Real airline wages were 1.8% higher in 1983 than in 1977. See S. Morrison & C. Winston, (1986) *The Economic Effects of Airline Deregulation* 44. The apparent stability of the figure, however, conceals the fact that layoffs of lower paid workers artificially increased the average wage. *Id.* at 43–44. Recent trends – such as the increase in nonunion airlines, bargaining agreements calling for wage concessions, and the successful institution of two-tiered wage structures – suggest that deregulation may adversely affect the wage rates of higher paid, unionized employees in the long run. See *id.* at 44.
32. See Moore, above note 24, at 11–4, 26.
33. see GAO Report, above note 24 at 50–2; S. Morrison & C. Winston, above note 31, at 13–42; Bailey, above note 27 at 14.
34. See Greenwald, 'Is there cause for fear of flying?' *Time*, 13, Jan. 1986, at 49.
35. *Id.* (reporting 520 fatalities on Air Japan, 329 on Air India, and 248 on a military charter).
36. See M. Brenner, J. Leet & E. Schott (1985), *Airline Deregulation* 128; Robson, Flying deregulated skies is no greater hazard,' *Wall St. J.*, 24 Jan. 1986, at 20, col. 4.
37. See *New York Times*, 20 March 1988, p. E-3; D. Martindale, 'Ten years of turbulence', *Frequent Flyer*, October 1988, pp. 38, 41. Figures also based on National Transportation Safety Board information as reported by Eastern Airlines.
38. See Kennedy Report, above note 19 at 62–63 & n.127 (referring to testimony of Professor William Jordan that without regulation there would be several hundred competing carriers and to contrary testimony suggesting there could be as few as five).
39. See *id.* at 96–99, 112–30.
40. As of September 1986, even if all the proposed mergers were approved, the top eight firms' collective market share would be no larger than it was in 1974 – approximately 90% of revenue passenger miles. Based on Department of Transportation traffic data for 1974 and the first two quarters of 1986, the Herfindahl-Hirschman Index (HHI) has increased only slightly, from 1272.9 to 1339.6 (calculations on file with the author).
41 Compare Calkins (1983), The new merger guidelines and the Herfindahl-Hirschman Index, 71 *Calif. L. Rev.* 402 (discussing the implications of replacing the concentration ratio with the HHI as a measure of market concentration) with Baker & Blumenthal, 'The 1982 guidelines and preexisting law. 71 *Calif. L. Rev.* 311, 334 & n.87 (1983) (arguing that the switch in measures of market concentration is unlikely to affect the outcome of cases). See also Kauper (1983), The 1982 horizontal merger guidelines: of collusion, efficiency, and failure. 71 *Calif. L. Rev.* 497, 510 & n.30 (discussing the increased levels of concentration tolerated by the Justice Department in 1982 as opposed to 1986).
42. Compare *Merger guidelines of the Department of Justice – 1968*, 2 Trade Reg. Rep. (CCH) 4510 (Aug. 9, 1982), with *Merger Guidelines of the Department of Justice – 1982*, 47 Fed. Reg. 28,493 (1982). The 1982 Merger Guidelines expressly

discuss potential competition only in the context of nonhorizontal mergers. See *id.* at 28,499–500.

43. See, e.g. Y. Brozen (1982), *Concentration, Mergers, and Public Policy*, 12–14, New York, Free Press (arguing that antitrust enforcers' focus on concentration is misguided).
44. See, e.g. *Oversight of Civil Aeronautics Board Practices and Procedures: Hearings Before the Subcomm. on Admin. Practice and Procedure of the Senate Comm. on the Judiciary*, 94th Cong., 1st Sess. 672 (1975) (statement of William Kutzke, Office of General Counsel, Department of Transportation).
45. Market definition may be contested in merger cases. For example, in hearings concerning the merger of Northwest and Republic Airlines, the Department of Justice advocated adoption of a product market definition of non-stop flights between city pairs. Republic countered that the Department's definition was too narrow because it excluded substitute services that might be offered by connecting or one-stop flights. Similarly, in Department of Transportation hearings regarding the merger of Texas Air and Eastern Airlines, witnesses debated whether the appropriate market definition ought to be airport pairs, city pairs, or the complex of services representatives of a hub and spoke network.
46. In the early 1970s, two or more airlines not actually serving a city pair served both endpoints of every major route segment. See Kennedy Report, above note 19, at 63.
47. Ibid., 9.
48. Only one small city lost service altogether between 1976 and 1983, but over 40% of smaller cities lost some service. See Moore, above note 24, at 6, 15. But see GAO Report, above note 24, at 29 (reporting that 114 nonhub communities wholly lost scheduled air service between 1978 and 1984). Professor Kahn reports that the only communities that have lost scheduled service to date are those that were previously served by noncertificated carriers. This is likely due to the fact that the Deregulation Act itself provided for subsidies to ensure that no community enjoying certificated service would lose it within the first ten years of deregulation. Kahn, 'American deregulation lessons for Europe, Wall St. J., 2 Oct. 1986, at 6, col. 2 (European edition).
49. See Civil Aeronautics Board Sunset Act of 1984, Pub. L. No. 99–443, 98 Stat. 1703 (codified as amended at 49 U.S.C. § 1551(b)(1)(C) (Supp. 1986)).
50. See Kennedy Report, above note 19 at 80.
51. Ibid.
52. Ibid., 79–80.
53. Ibid., 118–20
54. Not once did the CAB allow a carrier to go bankrupt. *Id.* at 80. Circumstances are different today. See In re Frontier Airlines, Inc., 74 Bankr. 973 (D. Colo. 1987).
55. See generally 4 P. Areeda & D. Turner, Antitrust Law 939–962 (1980) (discussing the various 'economies' defences).
56. Cf. id. 927–931 (arguing that proof of no 'preferred purchaser' should be required only in cases where the possibilities of harm are substantial).
57. Texas Air's recent merger with Eastern Airlines was conditioned in this manner. Professor Kahn has argued that United should have been allowed to acquire Pan-American's trans-Pacific routes and assets to preserve three competing American carriers. See *Hearings Before the Subcomm. on Monopolies and Commercial Law of the House Comm. on the Judiciary*, 99th Cong., 1st Sess., (26 Feb. 1985) (prepared statement of Alfred Kahn, professor of political economy, Cornell University).

58. See 49 U.S.C. § 1378(b)(1) (Supp. 1986) (even a proposed merger that will substantially reduce competition may be approved if there is no 'less anticompetitive' alternative and if the anti-competitive effects are 'outweighed in the public interest'.).

59. See e.g. Brown Shoe Co. v. United States, 370 U.S. 294, 344 (1962) ('It is competition, not competitors, which the [Clayton] Act protects.').

60. See 2 A. Kahn (1971), *The Economics of Regulation* 127–52. Different versions of this analogy, in other contexts, appear in DuPuit (1844), 'On the measurement of the utility of public works', 8 *Annales des Pont et Chaussées* (2d Ser.) *reprinted in* 2 *International Economic Paper* 83 (1952); Hotelling (1938), 'The general welfare in relation to problems of taxation and of railway and utility rates', 6 *Econometrica* 242.

61. See, e.g. Federal Power Comm'n v. Hope Natural Gas Co., 320 U.S. 591, 603 (1944) (requiring a 'balancing of the investor and the consumer interests' in fixing utility rates); Missouri *ex rel.* Southwestern Bell Tel. Co. v. Public Serv. Comm'n, 262 U.S. 276, 289–312 (1923) (Brandeis, J., concurring) (arguing that utility base rates should allow current income to cover all costs, including capital charges, in order to give investors a stable rate of return).

62. See Ramsey (1927), 'A contribution to the theory of taxation', 37 *Econ. J.* 47.

63. Specifically, the high fixed cost of heavy-duty cable was believed to account for a large portion of AT & T's revenue requirements. See Note (1975), 'Recent federal actions concerning long distance telecommunications: a survey of issues affecting the microwave specialized common carrier industry', 43 *Geo. Wash. L. Rev.* 878, 894; see also General Tel. Co., 17 F.C.C.2d 654, 657 (1969) (stating that users must bear the 'massive capital investments' required to construct and maintain communications routes).

64. By using microwave technology, the competitors avoided AT & T's high capital costs. See Note, above note 63, at 894; see also Establishment of Policies and Procedures for Consideration of Application to Provide Specialized Common Carrier Services, 29 F.C.C.2d 870, 925–26 (1971) (First Report and Order) (noting that the proposed plant investments and revenue requirements of the new market entrants were not anywhere near those of AT & T).

65. See generally Irwin (1964), 'the communication industry and the policy of competition', 14 *Buffalo L. Rev.* 256; Waverman, 'The regulation of intercity telecommunications', in A. Phillips (ed.), 1975, Promoting Competition in Regulated Markets 201; Note, above note 63 at 894–6.

66. This cost breakdown appears in Long-Run Regulation of AT & T's Basic Domestic Interstate Services, F.C.C. No. 83–1147, at 5 (1983) (comments of United Telecom Communications). More recently, AT & T has similarly broken down its own costs as 60% access, 25% general and marketing, 13% network, and 2% operator services. *National Telecommunications & Information Administration (NTIA), U.S. Dep't of Commerce, NTIA Special Pub. No. 85–16, Issues in Domestic Telecommunications: Directions for National Policy* 91 (July 1985) [hereinafter NTIA]. See generally id. at 91–4 (describing the costs that long-distance competitors face).

67. See *Consumer Protection and Finance: Hearings Before the Subcomm on Telecommunications, Consumer Protection, and Finance of the House Comm. on Energy and Commerce*, 99th Cong. 2d Sess. app. at 9, 13 (1986) [hereinafter *Consumer Protection Hearings*] (statement of Alfred Partoll, Vice President, AT & T); Reply Comments of AT & T, above note 66, at 28–31.

68. See above note 22.

69. See generally NTIA, above note 66, at 7–29 (discussing innovations in telecommunications technology).
70. See Investigation of Access and Divestiture Related Tariffs, 97 F.C.C.2d 1082 (1984); MTS and WATS Market Structure, 93 F.C.C.2d 241 (1983).
71. Businesses that primarily call one or a few locations have, in fact, been able to satisfy a large portion of their needs through private systems for some time. See Allocation of Frequencies Above 890 Mc., 27 F.C.C. 359 (1959). More recently, technological advances have broadened the extent of service that private systems can feasibly provide. Merrill Lynch, for example, has constructed a facility to provide long-distance service to the entire New York financial district. MacAvoy & Robinson (1983), 'Winning by losing: the AT & T settlement and its impact on telecommunications', 1 *Yale J. on Reg.* 1, 37 n. 149.
72. United States v. AT & T, 552 F. Supp. 131, 226–32 (D.D.C. 1982).
73. See *id.* at 165–8, 171–3.
74. See MacAvoy & Robinson (1985), 'Losing by judicial policymaking: the first year of the AT & T divestiture, 2 *Yale J. on Reg.* 225, 249.
75. See Kahn (1984), 'The uneasy marriage of regulation and competition', *Telematics,* Sept. at 1, 13 (stating that the higher local access charge paid by AT & T is inefficient because it requires AT & T customers to pay more than the marginal cost of access).
76. Equal interconnection was to have been 'complete' by 1 September 1986. See *AT & T*, 552 F. Supp. at 233. The BOCs have not met this schedule. Furthermore, waivers are permissible in the case of many small offices, which serve up to 40% of the population. MacAvoy & Robinson, above note 74 at 249 n. 96.
77. The FCC has stated that the extra charges on AT & T are just a temporary measure for this purpose. See *Long Distance Competition: Hearings Before the Subcomm. on Communications of the Senate Comm. on Commerce, Science, and Transportation,* 99th Cong., 1st Sess. 126–27 (1985) [hereinafter *Senate Hearings*] (statement of Charles Brown, Chairman, AT & T); MacAvoy & Robinson, above note 74 at 258 (citing Patrick (1984), '*On the road to telephone deregulation. Pub. Util. Fort.*, 6 Dec. at 19). Nonetheless, AT & T and several observers have doubted that the charges have served only this purpose. They assert that the extent of the extra charge has been far greater than necessary to compensate for the difference in service. See *Senate Hearings* above, at 126–7 (statement of Charles Brown, Chairman, AT & T); MacAvoy & Robinson, above note 74, at 249. In addition, at least two observers have feared that the FCC would seize upon the residues of unequal interconnection as a reason to continue the differential charges indefinitely See MacAvoy & Robinson above note 74, at 249. It is worth noting that several of AT & T's competitors have indeed requested such extensions. See *Senate Hearings,* above, at 126–7 (statement of Charles Brown, Chairman, AT & T).
78. The FCC had previously accomplished this end by requiring AT & T to price its services at fully distributed cost; that is, to recover a ratable portion of all common costs out of each relevant service. Although the FCC recently abandoned this pricing practice, see Guidelines for Dominant Carriers' MTS Rates and Rate Structure Plans, 50 Fed. Reg. 42,945 (1985) (to be codified at 47 C.F.R. §1), it has been argued that even the FCC's current standards, while less onerous, still prevent AT & T from lowering its prices to incremental cost. See *Consumer Protection Hearings,* above note 67 at 11–12 (statement of Alfred C. Partoll, Vice President, AT & T).
79. See *Consumer Protection Hearings,* above note 67 at 11–12 (statement of Alfred C. Partoll, Vice President, AT & T); Kahn, above note 75 at 11.

80. A belief that AT & T was engaging in predatory pricing of long-distance service was a major reason that the Department of Justice sought to break up the company in the first place. United States v. AT & T Co., 524 F. Supp. 1331, 1364–70 (D.D.C. 1981); MacAvoy & Robinson, above note 71 at 25–7. Charges of such predatory pricing are less common today, but are not unknown. See MacAvoy & Robinson, above note 75 at 258 (quoting Comments of the Dep't of Justice. In the Matter of Long-Run Regulation of AT & T's Basic Domestic Interstate Services (Apr. 2, 1984), at 2).

81. See U.S. General Accounting Office, Telephone Communications: Bell Operating Company Entry Into New Lines of Business 10 (1986).

82. Markets in which AT & T has been said still to possess monopoly power include intrastate toll service, 800 service, and international voice service. AT & T has strenuously argued that it has no market power in these areas. Reply Comments of AT & T, above note 66 at 50–8. Even if AT & T has monopoly power in these sectors, however, they clearly constitute too small a portion of its business to provide a meaningful subsidy to competitive sectors.

83. 15 U.S.C. § 2 (1982).

84. See Reply Comments of AT & T, above note 66, at 47–8.

85. According to AT & T, MCI's revenues have grown from under $100 million in 1978 to $2.5 billion in 1985. GTE Sprint has increased its revenues from $50 million to over $1 billion in the same period. In 1985, MCI had assets of $3.89 billion, GTE Sprint of over $1 billion. See generally, Consumer Protection Hearings, above note 67, app. at 3–6 (statement of Alfred Partoll, Vice President, AT & T).

86. See Reply Comments of AT & T, above note 66 Attachment 1 at 11 (statement of Kenneth Arrow, Professor of Economics, Stanford University).

87. See id. at 11–12.

88. Of course, given the fact that the income effects of telephone deregulation are perverse, helping the business user at the expense of the residential customer, Congress might never have approved it.

89. This assumption is implicit in the consent decree's equal access requirement. AT & T, 552 F. Supp. at 232–4. The judgment court has recently indicated that it expects most customers to continue to receive long-distance service by this means for some time. United States v. Western Elec. Co., 627 F. Supp. 1090, 1095 n. 16 (D.D.C. 1986).

90. See NTIA, above note 66 at 116. In approving the consent decree, the district court explicitly recognized the existence of this technology and gave AT & T permission to use it. AT & T, 552 F. Supp. at 175–6.

91. See MacAvoy & Robinson, above note 74, at 250–1.

92. See Kahn (1984), 'The road to more intelligent telephone pricing', 1 Yale J. on Reg. 139, 141–4; MacAvoy & Robinson, above note 74, at 4–9; MacAvoy & Robinson, above note 74, at 228–32.

93. See MacAvoy & Robinson, above note 71 at 2–3.

94. Ibid, p. 4.

95. This pricing feature is accomplished through a process known as 'averaging', by which long-distance customers in all parts of the country pay the same rates regardless of the costs of serving them. See Reply Comments of AT & T, above note 66, at 58–59; Kahn, above note 93, at 144; MacAvoy & Robinson, above note 71 at 4.

96. See Kahn, above note 92 at 150–1; MacAvoy & Robinson above note 74, at 241–2.

97. 47 U.S.C. § 151 (1982).

98. This possibility is discussed and deemed 'unworkable' in NTIA, above note 66, at 117–18.
99. See *id.* at 114–15 & 27.
100. See id. at 117–18.
101. See id. at 117.
102. See R. Caves (1962), *Air Transport and Its Regulators: An Industry Study*, 435–6.
103. One proposal, for example, would allow low income users unlimited free calls to five preselected numbers, while charging on a measured basis for all other calls. See NTIA, above note 66, at 122; see also Kahn, above note 92 at 145–58 (suggesting that 'telephone stamps', analogous to food stamps, could be issued to those targeted as genuinely poor). The CAB's change of policy during the 1950s, deemphasizing subsidy of short-haul routes out of trunk line fares in favour of directly subsidizing independent local carriers, is in some sense similar. See R. Caves, above note 102, at 435–6.
104. See Kahn, above note 93, at 142–3, 144–5.
105. See *id.* at 147–8, 155–7; Kahn, 'The next steps in telecommunications regulation and research, *Pub. Util. Fort.*, 19 July at 13; Kahn above note 75, at 14–15.
106. People who make many local calls, for instance, may be wealthier than those who make few such calls. Similarly, there may be a correlation between residence in a newly developed area and ability to bear the additional costs of connection to such an area. Of course, the distribution of wealth may not follow the distribution of costs in all instances. Where there is a correlation, however, the argument for economically based charges is especially strong.
107. See above notes 75, 92 and 105.
108. For an explanation of the term 'bottleneck', see 3 P. Areeda and H. Hovenkamp, *Antitrust Law* ¶ 736.1, at 492 (Supp. 1986).
     Bottlenecks also arise in the form of limited space at certain airports, preventing competing airlines from landing as many planes as they wish.
110. See *Computer Reservation Systems: Hearings Before the Subcomm. on Aviation of the Senate Comm. on Commerce, Science, and Transportation*, 99th Cong., 1st Sess., 4 (1985) [hereinafter 1985 *CRS Hearings*] (statement of Matthew Scocozza, Assistant Secretary, Dep't of Transportation); *Review of Airline Deregulation and Sunset of the Civil Aeronautics Board (Airline Computer Reservations Systems): Hearings Before the Subcomm. on Aviation of the House Comm. on Public Works and Transportation*, 98th Cong., 1st Sess., 71–4 (1983) (CAB report to Congress).
111. In 1984, United claimed to have made expenditures of $500 million on its APOLLO system. See Notice of Proposed Rulemaking, 49 Fed. Reg. 11,644, 11,650 (1984). American reported development costs of $160 million and an investment of $350 million by 1985. *Id.;* see also *1985 CRS Hearings*, above note 110, at 85 (prepared statement of Robert Crandall, President, American Airlines).
112. See Notice of Proposed Rulemaking, 49 Fed. Reg. 11,644, 11,650. Systems owned by other airlines – TWA's PARS system, Delta's DATAS II, and Eastern's SODA – altogether account for only a 19% market share. See *id.* at 11,649.
113. See *1985 CRS Hearings* above note 110, at 35–6 (statement of Lamar Muse, Chairman, Muse Air Corp.).
114. 224 U.S. 383 (1912).
115. Ibid., 409.
116. Ibid., 410–13.
117. See GAF Corp. v. Eastman Kodak Co., 519 F. Supp. 1203 (S.D.N.Y. 1981). Professor Areeda uses an example that I have copied here. See P. Areeda, *Antitrust Analysis* 525–6 (3rd ed., 1981).

118.ᶜ See above note 110.
119. See *1985 CRS Hearings*, above note 110, at 49 (prepared statement of Phil Bakes, President, Continental Airlines); *id.* at 110–11 (statement of Gary Adamson, President Air Midwest).
120. See *id.* at 49 (prepared statement of Phil Bakes, President, Continental Airlines).
121. Third Party Complaint of Delta Air Lines, Inc. at 11–14, Delta Air Lines, Inc. v. American Airlines, Inc., No. 44094 (U.S. Dep't of Transportation, filed 16 June 1986) (arguing that American Airlines' manipulation of 'elapsed times', which are the total times between published departure and arrival times, resulted in CRS displays which favoured American Airlines over other carriers).
122. 14 C.F.R. § 255.4 (1986).
123. See *1985 CRS Hearings*, above note 110, at 30 (statement of Daniel May, President, Republic Airlines). At least one critic claims that the primary screens remain biased, See *id.* at 68 (statement of Phil Bakes, President, Continental Airlines).
124. See *id.* at 132–3 (prepared statement of Alfred Kahn, Professor of Political Economy, Cornell University).
125. See *id.* at 62 (prepared statement of Northwest Airlines).
126. See *id.* at 13 (statement of Matthew Scocozza, Assistant Secretary, Dep't of Transportation).
127. Travel agents will naturally prefer to use the CRS providing the most accurate data about the carrier with whom they place the most bookings. See Notice of Proposed Rulemaking. 49 Fed. Reg. 11,644, 11,652. By providing competitors with inaccurate information about its flights – or no information at all – the CRS-owning carrier can seriously impede its competition in the CRS industry. See *1985 CRS Hearings*, above note 110, at 131 (statement of Alfred Kahn, Professor of Political Economy, Cornell University).
128. See 49 Fed. Reg. at 11,649.
129. See *1985 CRS Hearings*, above note 110, at 32 (statement of Daniel May, President, Republic Airlines).
130. See above text accompanying notes 44–7.
131. See *id.* at 26–7 (statement of Charles Rule, Deputy Assistant Attorney General, Antitrust Division).
132. See *id.* at 31 (statement of Daniel May, President, Republic Airlines).
133. 14 C.F.R. § 255.8 (1986).
134. See *1985 CRS Hearings*, above note 110, at 17 (statement of Charles Rule, Deputy Assistant Attorney General, Antitrust Division); *id.* at 31 (statement of Daniel May, President, Republic Airlines); *id.* at 50 (prepared statement of Phil Bakes, President, Continental Airlines).
135. See United States v. Container Corp. of America, 393 U.S. 333 (1969) (exchange of price information among regional competitors held to encourage changed policies); Sugar Inst. v. United States, 297 U.S. 553 (1936) (collection and dissemination of sales and production statistics by trade association held to be an unreasonable restraint on trade).
136. See *1985 CRS Hearings*, above note 110, at 25 (prepared statement of Charles Rule, Deputy Assistant Attorney General, Antitrust Division).
137. See United States v. Pan Am World Airways, 193 F. Supp. 18 (S.D.N.Y. 1961), rev'd on other grounds, 371 U.S. 296 (1963).
138. Professor Kahn has urged divestiture. See Kahn, above note 28, at 14.
139. The AT & T consent decree, on its face, essentially forbids the BOCs from engaging in any business other than local and intraexchange telephone service. *AT & T*, 552 F. Supp. at 227–8. The decree also provides, however, for removal

of these restrictions 'upon a showing . . . that there is no substantial possibility that [the BOC] could use its monopoly power to impede competition in the market it seeks to enter'. *Id.* at 231; see also *id.* at 186–95 (discussing restrictions on BOCs). The district court subsequently promulgated procedures for granting waivers from the restrictions in individual cases. United States v. Western Elec. Co., 592 F. Supp. 846, 873–4 (D.D.C. 1984), *appeal dismissed*, 777 F.2d 23 (D.C. Cir. 1985). At the same time, it has forbidden BOC expansion into most telecommunications fields. See *id.* at 867–8; United States v. Western Elec. Co., 627 F. Supp. 1090 (D.D.C. 1986).

140. A more sophisticated form of this argument – that the BOCs may persuade the regulators improperly to include costs of the competitive enterprise in the monopoly rate base – is discussed below at text accompanying notes 145–50.

141. In 1984, IBM had assets of $42.8 billion. *Consumer Protection Hearings*, above note 67, at 292 (statement of Alfred C. Partoll, Executive Vice President, AT & T). Bell South, the largest of the BOCs, had assets of $23.7 billion. NTIA. above note 66, at 65 n.31.

142. In enforcing the AT & T consent decree, the judgment court has imposed a variety of restrictions upon BOC entry into fields related and unrelated to telephone service. *Western Electric*, 592 F. Supp. at 868–72. But see Schwartz (1985), 'Diversification and regulated industries – what's next for the telephone holding companies?' 7 *Comm./Ent. L.J.* 195, 216–17 (arguing that these restrictions are of little practical effect). Some of the court's language suggests that it imposed these restrictions in part out of a fear of simple predation. 592 F. Supp. at 853. Other language, however, indicates that the court was focusing on the more plausible danger of misallocation. *Id.* at 863–4; see also United States v. Western Elec. Co., 1986–1 Trade Cas. (CCH) ¶ 66,987, at 62,057–58 (D.D.C. Feb. 26, 1986) (mere size is 'not [a] legitimate obstacle[]' to diversification). It is also interesting that, in approving GTE's acquisition of Sprint long-distance service, the same court considered GTE's 'deep pocket' an argument in *favour* of the merger. See United States v. GTE Corp., 603 F. Supp. 730, 735–6 (D.D.C. 1984).

143. See United States v. AT & T, 524 F. Supp. 1336, 1346 (D.D.C. 1981).

144. See Second Computer Inquiry, 77 F.C.C.2d 384, 471 (1980); United States v. American Tel. & Tel. Co., 552 F. Supp. 131, 171 (D.D.C. 1982); see also MacAvoy & Robinson, above note 71, at 3 (suggesting that AT & T had an even greater share of the telecommunications market).

145. A third argument, heavily relied upon by the court in enforcing the consent decree, is that diversification may distract a BOC from its principal task of providing excellent local service. *Western Electric*, 592 F. Supp. at 858–67; 627 F. Supp. at 1096 n.18 (same case). It is unclear, however, that diversified companies are less efficient or innovative than those that produce a single product. But see Schwartz, above note 142, at 201–14 (pointing out difficulties inherent in diversified operation). Furthermore, new technology, with its accompanying threat of local system bypass, will provide the local BOCs with continued incentive to operate efficiently. See above text accompanying notes 89–107.

146. See Averch & Johnson (1962), 'Behavior of the firm under regulatory constraint'. 52 *Am. Econ. Rev.* 1052.

147. This analysis assumes that the investment is in fact useful *only* in the competitive sector. To the extent that costs are common between the monopoly and competitive enterprises, it may not be inefficient for monopoly customers to bear most or all of these costs. To the extent that investment would be necessary to provide the monopoly service *in any event*, there is no excess profit if customers in the competitive sector receive a free ride. See Reply Comments of AT & T, above

note 66, Attachment 1 at 12–22 (statement of Kenneth J. Arrow, Professor of Economics, Stanford University). The concern of some enforcers about misallocation of *common* costs thus appears somewhat confused. See e.g. *Western Electric*, 592 F. Supp. at 853.

148. See generally T. Brennan (1986), Regulated Firms in Unregulated Markets: Understanding the Divestiture in *U.S. v. AT & T* 17–23 (draft of unpublished manuscript, on file with author) (discussing the risk that a firm operating in both a regulated market and an unregulated market may use profits from the regulated market to gain a competitive advantage in the unregulated market).

149. See MacAvoy & Robinson, above note 74, at 255; NTIA, above note 66, at 45, 75–6 (concluding that BOCs are unlikely to cross-subsidize).

150. See *Western Electric*, 592 F. Supp. at 854–55; T. Brennan, above note 148, at 22; see also NTIA above note 66, at 75 (suggesting that cost accounting and allocation requirements to prevent cross-subsidization would be more efficient than requiring structural separation of services in regulated and unregulated markets); below, p. 000–00 (discussing efficiencies that would result from allowing BOCs to offer a wider range of services).

151. See *AT & T*, 552 F. Supp. at 188–91; T. Brennan, above note 148, at 13–16, 39–40 (arguing that opportunities for this form of discrimination exist even in the markets specifically opened to the BOCs by the Modification of Final Judgment, the settlement that ended the antitrust action against AT & T in 1974).

152. The Justice Department's original case against AT & T was based largely on allegations of such obstruction. See *AT & T*, 524 F. Supp. at 1348–50, 1360–61; MacAvoy & Robinson above note 71, at 14–16.

153. A company might claim, for instance, that its services are most compatible with its own equipment only because this is the cheapest way to construct the services, or that its delay in connecting competitors is due to technical difficulties. See T. Brennan, above 148, at 40.

154. See generally NTIA above 66, at 77–82 (describing inefficiencies resulting from current restrictions on BOC operations); T. Brennan, above note 148, at 24–5 (stating that economies of scope may justify allowing regulated firms to enter unregulated markets); Kahn, above note 75, at 9 (discussing the social costs on several companies to provide different aspects of telephone service, rather than on one integrated telephone service company).

155. See MacAvoy & Robinson, above note 74, at 254.

156. See *id.* at 254–5; Brennan, above note 148, at 25–6.

157. See, Kahn, above note 28.

158. See *Western Electric*, 592 F. Supp. at 867–8 (denying BOC entry into interexchange markets); 627 F. Supp. 1090 (same case) (denying BOC entry into interexchange and information services markets); 1986–1 Trade Cas. (CCH) ¶ 66,987, at 62,060–62 (same case) (denying BOC entry into paging, mobile radio and voice storage and retrieval markets); cf. United States v. GTE Corp., 603 F. Supp. 730 (D.D.C. 1984) (approving consent decree allowing GTE to acquire Sprint, despite objections by Department of Justice under Clayton Act).

2. Entry, Divestiture and the Continuation of Economic Regulation in the United States Telecommunications Sector

Robert W. Crandall

There is a remarkably widespread notion that the United States has 'deregulated' its telecommunications sector. In fact, all of the regulatory institutions that controlled telephone rates twenty-five years ago – the Federal Communications Commission and the fifty state commissions – are alive and well. There have been no deregulatory statutes passed by the US Congress. Interexchange rates are still regulated, as are local rates. There is even a new regulator – the Federal District Court for the District of Columbia – as the result of the AT & T antitrust suit that was settled in 1982.

Nevertheless, it is impossible to deny that major changes have taken place in the US telecommunications sector and that these changes are having major repercussions in virtually all other national telecommunications industries. The American Telephone and Telegraph Company has been broken into eight separate companies. Its former operating companies are forbidden to offer long-distance service outside their franchise areas, to manufacture equipment, or to offer most information services. The equipment business has become extremely competitive. The long-distance market is quite competitive, at least for the moment. And there is a general feeling that regulators are being increasingly constrained by competitive forces.

In this chapter, I shall detail the practical effect of the liberalization of entry and the divestiture of the American Telephone and Telegraph Company upon US telecommunications markets. I shall also attempt to draw some tentative conclusions about the effect of these dramatic changes on the efficacy of regulation. In particular, I shall ask whether regulation can coexist with competition. This is obviously a question that should interest European telecommunication authorities, who (like their US counterparts 30 years ago) generally view competition as an anathema.

The US Telecommunications Sector

As recently as twenty years ago, the United States telecommunications sector comprised only AT & T, a handful of independent telephone companies (Continental, GTE, Rochester, United, etc.), and a large number of very small rural cooperatives. AT & T companies accounted for 80 per cent of local service, virtually all long-distance service, and a very large share of telecommunications equipment produced and sold in the US. A few large companies were allowed to own microwave circuits for private use. In all other respects, the US telephone industry was a monopoly.

Beginning in the 1960's, entrepreneurs began to ask why they should be excluded from the sale of simple terminal equipment or the offering of common-carrier microwave services. No one had a very good answer to these questions; hence, the US federal courts and the Federal Communications Commission slowly admitted new entrants into interstate services and terminal equipment markets, a process fought by the incumbent carriers with every political, legal, and economic weapon at their disposal. The incumbents lost virtually every battle in the courts and at the FCC although they were able to fight some rearguard actions in state regulatory commissions and in the Congress.

By 1978, the legal principle of competitive entry into terminal equipment and interstate long-distance services had been established. AT & T and the independents continued to hold monopoly power in local markets and were able to produce their own equipment, but they were in the difficult position of competing with new entrants in long-distance and terminal equipment while offering the regulated local connections for the new entrants' services and equipment.

It was perhaps inevitable that this mix of competition would result in endless regulatory battles over the incumbent firms' rates and the terms for offering local connections to their new competitors. As early as 1974, the Justice Department was persuaded to bring a massive antitrust suit against AT & T for abusing its local monopoly position to maintain monopoly power in equipment manufacture and interstate services. In more normal times, this suit might not have been won or even filed. However, through a combination of surprising circumstances, in the aftermath of Watergate, AT & T found itself forced to negotiate a settlement to the suit.

In 1982, AT & T agreed to divest itself of all its local operating companies in order to keep its long-distance services, equipment manufacturing, and research division (Bell Laboratories). In addition, AT & T was freed from an earlier antitrust consent decree that limited it to domestic regulated telecommunications markets. AT & T clearly felt that a settlement that allowed it to participate in all high-tech markets at the cost of losing low-growth local operating companies was better than the prospects of fighting the antitrust suit through the US courts for another decade.

The AT & T antitrust settlement and earlier terminal equipment decisions at the FCC have transformed the US telecommunications equipment market into one of the most open and competitive in the world. In addition, the equal-access requirement that is now in the 1982 antitrust decree – requiring all divested AT & T operating companies to offer equivalent connections to all long-distance competitors – is making the US long-distance market highly competitive.

Monopoly remains in local services, aided and abetted by an unfortunate FCC decision in the 1970s that limited competition in cellular services. This monopoly is jealously protected by many state regulatory commissions who see regulation as a means of cross subsidizing politically organized constituencies. However, some states are now beginning to entertain a variety of proposals for liberalization and regulatory flexibility. As a result, not even local service is off limits to competitive carriers in some states.

The divested Bell operating companies are, however, prevented by the 1982 decree from responding to competitive thrusts in their local markets by entering long-distance or information-service markets. In addition, they are barred from equipment manufacture by the decree. As a result, they fear that they will be slowly squeezed by competition and forced into steady decline.

Regulatory Rate Distortions and The Invitation to Entry

Telephone regulation in the United States has been full of ironies. As in other countries, the US telecommunications monopoly was largely the creation of government, which had to assert regulatory control in order to protect the public from the monopoly power it had created. By exempting telephone mergers from antitrust in the 1920s, the US Congress permitted AT & T to achieve a market share that was subsequently to expose the company to anti-trust attack. But for forty years, regulation insulated the telephone monopoly from competitive entry directly while indirectly creating the incentives that would attract entrants in the 1960s.

Surprisingly, regulators and AT & T seem almost to have conspired to attract entry into long-distance services. For decades, local telephone service costs were not defrayed from long-distance calls. In the 1950s, however, state regulators began to argue for a shifting of costs from local to long-distance services, thereby raising long-distance rates above marginal cost. From all appearances, AT & T did not offer any resistance to this gradual shift of the burden of costs to the long-distance service even though the greatest shift occurred in the precise year that MCI entered as a private-line long-distance carrier, 1969. AT & T appears to have been totally unconcerned about a policy that greatly stimulated MCI's (and other entrants') interest in switched message services.

Nor was there any apparent opposition to uniform geographical pricing that developed under the Federal Communication Commission's aegis despite the obvious economies of call density. The defence of such pricing is that it is 'just and reasonable', regardless of how unreasonable and unjust it may seem to rational analysts that persons in dense markets should subsidize those in rural areas. No one suggests that geographical uniformity in the price of housing or of retail foodstuffs is required for justice to be served, but in telephony and other utility services this notion is widespread.

The combination of geographically uniform rates and distorted long-distance/local ratemaking was sure to create entry incentives as technology changed. Real rates on the most dense long routes were rising more rapidly than costs in the 1950s and 1960s, and the minimum efficient scale relative to the size of the market was declining because of the development of microwave technology. Surely, someone would discover that the price of telephone service between Chicago and New York was far too high, and it was equally likely that someone would find a way to offer such service at a much lower price. Only if large users were unusually somnolent or all entrepreneurial energies had been drained from high-technology markets could such distortions be ignored.

It seems equally unlikely that the executives at AT & T did not realize that once entry began in telecommunications, its Western Electric subsidiary would be unaffected. They must have known that Western Electric was not a paragon of efficiency and, therefore, that new vendors would be eager to find new suppliers when launching a competitive assault on AT & T. The FCC also knew this, but it was forced by political pressures in 1938 to suppress a staff report that advocated separation of Western Electric from AT & T. As a result of this decision and the settlement of a 1949 antitrust suit against AT & T, the integrated telephone monopoly continued into the 1960s. Thereafter, the monopolists' political power waned.

Divestiture, Entry, and Private Networks

The development of competition in US interstate telecommunications services dates back to 1959 when the FCC began to admit private non-telco users of microwave frequencies. These predominantly large users had an advantage over smaller firms who could not justify their own microwave systems, but in 1963 a new firm, MCI, appeared, offering to remedy this inequity. In 1969, MCI was granted permission to enter private-line services, an opening it aggressively expanded upon by moving into switched services without FCC approval. By 1977–78, MCI had repulsed all legal challenges to its switched message service, and as a result the interstate interexchange market is totally open to competition today.

Because of the 1984 AT & T divestiture, most local telephone companies in the US, unlike most in Europe, are now independent of the (interstate) long-distance carriers and their equipment suppliers. They are free to purchase equipment from any supplier and may not dictate customers' choices of terminal equipment.

The liberalization of entry into long-distance services was an important event in the recent history of US telecommunications regulation, but far more important was the deregulation of terminal equipment and the development of a competitive equipment industry. Kenneth Flamm has analyzed the slow pace of technical change in telecommunications relative to computers and all but concluded that regulation has been to blame. The 1982 antitrust decree has forced AT & T's equipment manufacturing division to meet a competitive market test, a change which should accelerate technical progress in US telecommunications.

The liberalization of terminal equipment occurred in the late 1970s. AT & T was broken up in 1984, but its operating companies began to act much more independently in the early 1980s. The result of liberalization and competition was a dramatic loss of market share for AT & T in terminal equipment, such as PBXs, and a loss in its share of the central-office switching equipment market, which it has recently recovered. (See Table 2.1)

The independence of telephone service companies from equipment companies is important in understanding the current US telecommunications sector because this independence has provided increased competitive pressure in a crucial market. Private telephone users may now purchase their own equipment, including microwave facilities, fibre optics systems, large switches, PBXs, and key systems.

Beginning in 1975, *sales* of telephone equipment in the US began to grow much more rapidly than telephone-company *purchases* of equipment. There is no record of the identity of the purchasers, but it is a safe bet that most of these purchases were by firms with their own private telecommunications networks. In 1986, approximately $13 billion of a total of $39 billion in US telecommunications investment was accounted for by these private networks and private households.

Further evidence of the substitution of private services for common carriage services may be found in the sharp slowdown in the growth of the measured telecommunications sector in the US despite six years of sustained economic expansion (See Table 2.2). For the two decades ending in 1981, output growth in the regulated telco sector was about 8 per cent per

Table 2.1   Competition in US interexchange, digital switch, and terminal equipment markets

Carrier	Interexchange market shares (%)		
	1978	*1982*	*1987*
AT & T	99.5	94.4	62.5
Local exchange Cos.	—	—	24.1
MCI	0.3	3.1	7.0
SPRINT	0.2	1.5	4.6
Others	0.0	1.0	1.8

Company	Digital switches – market shares (%)	
	1982	*1986*
AT & T	1	49
Northern Telecom	66	35
GTE	3	10
Others	31	6

Company	PBX – market shares (%)		
	1978	*1982*	*1987*
AT & T	48	23	22
Northern Telecom	9	13	20
Rolm (IBM)	7	13	16
Mitel	0	12	10
NEC	3	5	9
Others	33	34	23

Table 2.2 Telephone industry indexes of industry output, 1960–86 (1977 = 100)

Year	(1) Industry data	(2) BLS index	(3) BEA index
1960	27.2	27.4	28.9
1961	28.8	29.1	30.3
1962	30.8	31.2	32.9
1963	33.1	33.5	36.0
1964	35.7	36.1	38.7
1965	38.9	39.4	42.4
1966	43.0	43.5	46.5
1967	46.6	47.2	50.5
1968	50.4	51.0	54.9
1969	55.9	56.6	60.4
1970	59.7	60.4	66.9
1971	62.7	63.4	70.2
1972	68.7	69.2	76.9
1973	75.8	76.2	83.1
1974	81.8	81.8	87.3
1975	85.4	84.8	90.5
1976	91.1	90.8	94.2
1977	100.0	100.0	100.0
1978	111.0	110.8	110.4
1979	123.0	122.2	118.4
1980	134.7	133.2	129.3
1981	142.1	140.7	136.5
1982	145.9	144.2	140.5
1983	149.5	146.6	151.3
1984	154.2	149.1	150.9
1985	162.8	153.8	153.3
1986	168.4	157.2	154.9

Sources:
(1) Author's calculation for 1972–86, based upon data from US Telephone Association; FCC, Statistics of Common Carriers; Annual reports of OCCs and Western Union. For 1960–72, same as (2).
(2) US Bureau of Labor Statistics, Office of Productivity.
(3) US Department of Commerce, Bureau of Economic Analysis, National Income and Product Accounts, Table 6–2.

annum. Since then, it has averaged only 3 per cent despite the continuing growth of telecommunications-consuming service sectors and rapid technical change.

The slow growth of the regulated sector is obviously due to the shift of large users towards private carriage. But why should these large users prefer their own services to those of the telephone companies? There is no evidence of a decline in service quality in the regulated sector. Fibre optics and digital switching have spread very rapidly among the traditional telephone carriers in the past five years. The real cost of interexchange services has fallen dramatically. Unless the economies of scale and scope are negligible in this sector, the impetus for private carriage must derive from the rates set by regulators.

Rate Distortion and Rebalancing

As in many countries, regulators in the US are subject to political pressures to conceal the true cost of a regulated service through various cross subsidies. In telephony, not only are rates set to subsidize local service from long-distance revenues and rural service from revenues on dense routes, but there is a tendency for regulators to set 'business' rates above residential rates in the hope that few consumers will recognize that high business rates contribute to high prices of final consumer goods and services.

These distortions in telephone rates take many forms. Multi-line local business access rates are set above residential access rates (See Table 2.3). The federal subscriber line charge is set much higher for multiline business customers than for single-line customers. Long-distance services are used

Table 2.3   Residential and business monthly telephone rates, 1980 and 1987 ($/month/line)

	24 most urbanized states*		
	December 1980	*December 1987*	*Percentage increase*
Largest exchanges:			
Residential-flat rate (n=25)	9.87	15.93	61.3
Business, measured (n=23)	11.95	21.22	77.5
Business, flat rate (n=19)	25.13	38.14	51.8
Smallest exchanges:			
Residential-flat rate (n=24)	6.63	12.96	95.4
Business, measured (n=20)	10.53	20.77	97.3
Business, flat rate (n=21)	11.32	24.41	115.7
	*24 most rural states**		
Largest exchanges:			
Residential-flat rate (n=24)	9.94	17.60	79.9
Business, measured (n=12)	17.23	31.01	80.0
Business, flat rate (n=24)	26.99	47.10	74.5
Smallest exchanges:			
Residential-flat rate (n=24)	6.87	14.47	113.3
Business, measured (n=12)	12.01	24.14	101.0
Business, flat rate (n=24)	14.97	33.79	128.8

Notes
* 'Urbanized' is measured by the share of a state's population in metropolitan areas.
n =number of states for which data are available for 1980 and 1987.
Source: NARUC and Census Bureau.

heavily by many large businesses; hence, the attempt to cross-subsidize local service from long-distance rates is a penalty on many large business users.

To its credit, the Federal Communications Commission has recognized the dangers inherent in distorted (i.e. non-cost-based) rates in a telecommunications market in which entry has been liberalized. It has moved to reprice service by imposing monthly subscriber line charges (SLCs) on final customers in order to reduce access charges for long-distance carriers. This repricing has raised local rates and reduced long-distance rates substantially, but it cannot offset all of the local/long distance distortion. Even when fully implemented, the SLC will only eliminate about 15 per cent of the difference between monthly subscriber access rates and costs.

US policy-makers have been relatively sanguine about distorted rates because they have not seen the 'bypass' problem develop very rapidly. To them, bypass of the network occurs only when a long-distance carrier uses a non-telephone company circuit to originate or terminate calls. As I have argued above, this is far too narrow a definition. Private networks may bypass the network almost invisibly.

But even the traditional bypass may begin to occur if AT & T loses a substantial share of its interexchange market to new competitors. Under the present regulatory system, access rates for long-distance carriers are set to cover the federally assigned cost of local circuits. If the use of these circuits declines because of bypass, the access charges must rise. Since AT & T still accounts for more than 75 per cent of the interstate interexchange business, its marginal cost of access is very low. (If it had 100 per cent, its marginal costs would be zero.) As a result, it does not find bypass a very attractive alternative. However, if AT & T's market share were to fall to less than 50 per cent of long-distance, it might begin to find bypass more attractive.

Other Problems with Liberalization and Regulation

It is a curious fact that AT & T and the local telephone companies in the US remain highly regulated, but that their new competitors are virtually unregulated. As a result, competitive responses by these large incumbent firms to new competitive thrusts are more often parried in the regulatory arena than in the marketplace. The danger in this approach, of course, is that regulators will protect inefficient new competitors from the competitive responses of existing firms, creating a substantial loss in economic welfare and establishing a large number of new clients who can only survive through regulatory forebearance. The comparison with US banking and savings and loans is all too inviting.

This is not a trivial problem. Regulators are never very good at measuring the costs of regulated services. We all know that accounting measures of costs are not very useful, particularly in industries with rapid technological change and pervasive joint and common costs. The Federal Communications Commission refuses to admit directly that it cannot measure the costs of individual services, but it has yet to succeed in reaching a definitive judgement on any individual rate.

Under the present regime of liberalization *cum* regulation, US regulators typically allow new entrants to set rates without regulatory approval, but they continue to attempt to regulate the 'dominant' carrier rates without being able to measure costs. It is not surprising, therefore, that regulators are now beginning to turn to 'price-cap' regulation or simply selective deregulation in order to escape from the burden of approving individual rates. But such approaches frighten politicians because they fear that the competitive energies of the large incumbent carriers will be devoted to business services and that, as a result, residential rates will have to rise. At present, there is simply no resolution of this problem, but it should serve as a warning to other countries that liberalization and regulation in this sector may not work very well.

The problems of regulating a market in which competitive entry is permitted are currently most severe in interstate services. State regulators have not been as hospitable to competition in intrastate toll or local service markets. These problems will spread to the intrastate markets, however, as state commissions find regulatory boundaries more difficult to police. New cellular or fibre-optics systems will begin to grow more rapidly. Incumbent local telephone monopolists will then attempt to respond by reducing rates to the affected customers. The state commissions will then find themselves in precisely the same predicament as the FCC.

The Benefits of Liberalization

Despite my concerns over the unlikely emulsion of regulation and competition in this industry, the benefits of entry liberalization appear to be substantial. The early evidence suggests that productivity has accelerated in the regulated telecommunications sector since 1970 and has not fallen in the mid 1980s despite all of the problems created by the 1984 divestiture (See Table 2.4). Given that private networks are flourishing despite the improved performance of regulated entities, one may only conclude that productivity is probably increasing even more rapidly in these private carriage systems.

US data on telecommunications equipment prices are very poor, but the available evidence suggests that the rate of decline of equipment prices has accelerated with the detariffing of terminal equipment and the AT & T divestiture. Of course, the US dollar may have been partly responsible through early 1986.

Interstate long-distance rates have fallen dramatically in recent years due to the repricing of access, but intrastate rates have not fallen as quickly (See Table 2.5). The difference is due to the state regulators' desire to continue the subsidies flowing from long distance to local access.

Inexorably, competition will force regulators first to pursue more rational rate-setting strategies and then eventually to give up on detailed supervision

Table 2.4 Annual growth in output, labour, input, capital input and total factor productivity in regulated telephone common carriage, 1961–86 (%)

Year	Value-Added	Labour hours	Capital stock	Total factor productivity
1961	5.8	−3.7	6.4	3.4
1962	6.9	0.9	7.0	2.3
1963	7.1	1.6	6.9	2.3
1964	7.5	3.7	7.4	1.6
1965	8.9	4.4	8.0	2.3
1966	10.1	7.1	8.0	2.4
1967	8.3	−2.0	7.3	4.7
1968	7.8	5.0	6.8	1.7
1969	10.7	9.5	7.1	2.6
1970	6.0	2.7	7.8	0.2
1971	4.9	−2.7	7.4	1.5
1972	10.0	3.8	6.7	4.4
1973	9.9	3.3	6.9	4.4
1974	7.9	−0.8	6.6	4.2
1975	4.1	−0.5	4.4	1.6
1976	6.5	−0.1	3.8	4.3
1977	9.2	3.9	4.2	5.1
1978	10.4	6.1	5.0	5.0
1979	10.8	5.1	5.5	5.5
1980	9.4	1.4	5.4	5.6
1981	4.8	0.6	4.7	1.8
1982	2.3	−8.9	3.4	3.8
1983	2.1	−6.4	2.4	3.2
1984	2.6	−5.0	1.8	3.5
1985	5.2	−1.3	2.1	4.5
1986	3.1	−3.3	1.9	3.3
Average annual growth:				
1961–70	7.9	2.9	7.3	2.4
1971–83	7.1	0.4	5.1	3.9
1984–86	3.6	−3.2	2.0	3.7

Sources:
Output – see text.
Labour – Bureau of Labor Statistics for hours; author's calculation for employment.
Capital – see Table 3–2.

of rates. The federal FCC is pushing very hard for rate caps as an alternative to rate of return regulation, realizing that detailed rate supervision is no longer feasible and is very costly in terms of its effects upon incentives. State regulators generally have not proceeded as far in this direction, but they will be forced to look at similar proposals when they realize that they can no longer prevent entry into intrastate service markets. It is becoming too difficult to separate telecommunications offerings by state boundaries. As long as the federal government continues to permit entry into interstate services and private users can build their own networks, the states will find it

Table 2.5   The trend in real consumer price indexes for telephone service, 1964–87
(1977 = 100)

Year	All telephone service	Local service	Interstate toll	Intrastate toll
1964	152.2	N.A.	N.A.	N.A.
1965	147.4	N.A.	N.A.	N.A.
1966	140.4	N.A.	N.A.	N.A.
1967	138.2	N.A.	N.A.	N.A.
1968	132.7	N.A.	N.A.	N.A.
1969	127.5	N.A.	N.A.	N.A.
1970	121.8	N.A.	N.A.	N.A.
1971	122.5	N.A.	N.A.	N.A.
1972	125.2	N.A.	N.A.	N.A.
1973	121.0	N.A.	N.A.	N.A.
1974	113.6	N.A.	N.A.	N.A.
1975	107.4	N.A.	N.A.	N.A.
1976	105.2	N.A.	N.A.	N.A.
1977	100.0	100.0	100.0	100.0
1978	93.9	94.0	92.1	93.1
1979	84.2	84.0	82.2	84.5
1980	76.0	77.4	73.4	73.4
1981	75.0	78.2	72.1	68.5
1982	77.8	82.1	74.8	69.0
1983	80.3	86.1	74.0	71.5
1984	83.4	94.2	69.4	72.3
1985	83.7	98.1	64.2	70.5
1986	86.1	106.0	58.6	69.1
1987	82.6	107.4	48.1	65.4
Average percentage change:				
1977–83	−3.7	−2.5	−5.0	−5.6
1983–87	+0.7	+5.5	−10.8	−2.2

Note: All indexes are CPI indexes deflated by CPI–U.
Source: Bureau of Labor Statistics.

difficult to maintain artificially high rates for services except for the smallest residential and commercial users.

The Role of The Operating Companies

Competition in US telecommunications came at the expense of protracted antitrust battles and an eventual divestiture of the Bell operating companies (BOCs) from AT & T. But keeping these operating companies confined to the provision of local service is surely only a temporary solution. Over time, it will become increasingly untenable to draw such artificial boundaries around their franchises. Other service providers will be able to offer the last link to their subscribers, but the BOCs will not be able to respond by offering any service that extends a signal outside their franchise areas or transforms that signal. The result will be a slow withering of companies that are the only source of local connections for the last, unfortunate few.

At this juncture, no one has devised a plan for freeing the BOCs from the 'line-of-business' restrictions in the antitrust decree. There are still understandable fears that the BOCs would use their monopoly position in local services to cross-subsidize competitive ventures or to deny downstream services rivals the local connections they need to complete their calls. The judge who oversees the decree appears determined to deny fundamental relaxation of these restrictions until the provision of local service becomes competitive. No one knows when such a condition will exist or if the BOCs will be viable up to such a point. Given the acrimony between the Reagan Administration and the Congress and even the judge, no progress could be made on this issue before 1989.

Trade Issues

One of the unfortunate byproducts of telecommunications liberalization has been the development of a sizeable US trade deficit in communications equipment. Between 1980 and 1987, the US telecommunications equipment sector saw a trade surplus wither and grow into more than a $2 billion deficit. In part, this deficit developed because of US macroeconomic policies and the changes in exchange rates. However, the divestiture and deregulation of terminal equipment have certainly contributed to this deterioration.

US trade officials and even the FCC would like to use the open US market as a bargaining chip in gaining access for US producers to foreign markets. This is a worthy if risky cause, given the marriage of PTTs in other countries to their favoured national suppliers. Nevertheless, it seems unlikely that US politicians will close the US market to competition from foreign firms because of the enormous benefits that competition have in reducing communications costs and diffusing new technology.

Conclusion: Lessons for Europe

The US has always had a private telephone system; Europe, with the exception of the United Kingdom, continues to rely on government-owned PT & Ts. Therefore, liberalization of the US telecommunications sector has occured against a background of public-utility regulation. European countries do not typically have this regulatory heritage.

The US has pursued a remarkably rapid pace of liberalizing its telecommunications markets and attempting to rectify the regulatory errors of the past. However, regulation remains as both an impediment to efficiency and competition and as a source of considerable rate distortions. Over time, US regulators will discover that regulated competition is an undesirable institution and will slowly move towards less detailed supervision of rates. Private market signals, such as the rapid construction of private networks, will eventually force regulators to give up their cherished goal of subsidizing of local service in general and rural residential service in particular. Eventually, they will notice that they are strangling the regulated sector.

The major uncertainties that remain in this slow process of substituting competition for regulation are obvious. If technology continues to move in the direction of increasing the minimum efficient scale of transmission, long-distance competition may be threatened. And if politicians continue to oppose the reduction of inefficient subsidies, future regulators may be reluctant to press for further liberalization or outright deregulation. The availability of private carriage reduces the probability of either outcome, but it would be presumptuous to predict that the proponents of efficiency will totally vanquish the proponents of 'equity' in the near future.

In the US, the threat of private networks is acting as a potent force in disciplining regulators who see business services or long-distance as a source of subsidies for rural service in particular and local access in general. This discipline is important, for it subverts the operation of an inefficient income redistribution mechanism. Obviously, European PTTs recognize this fact and are therefore reluctant to permit private firms to build their own facilities, arguing that it denies society the economies of scope and scale inherent in the PTT network. What is never explained by these PTTs is that their distorted tariffs are also a source of efficiency losses. In the absence of compelling evidence on scale and scope economies, these latter losses are likely to be more important.

The most important lesson from the US experience, however, will be that derived from developing a truly open market for equipment. The US, Japan, and the United Kingdom should find that the combination of a competitive equipment sector and a liberalized services sector will lead to a more rapid pace of technical change inside and outside the network. As long as users must purchase basic services from the PTT and the PTT must buy local equipment, the incentives for innovation may be severely stunted. European PTTs, especially the French system, may respond that they will easily match the rate of progress in North America or Japan in the next decade or two even without these competitive pressures. We may have a nicely controlled experiment to test this proposition in the years leading up to and consequent to 1992.

3. Deregulation in Europe: Telecommunications and Transportation

*Günter Knieps**

Introduction: The Deregulation Debate in Europe

In recent years an increasing debate on the possibility of deregulation and privatization in European countries has been observed. There may be several reasons for this.

Firstly, the policy for achieving the *internal common market* within the European Community by 1992 contains not only steps towards harmonization of government policies between the different European countries (e.g. with respect to standards and value added taxes) but also includes proposals for deregulation (e.g. in telecommunications, transportation and financial markets). The Commission of the European Community is making a lot of effort, especially in the area of new technologies. For example, the Commission has set up several research programmes, such as ESPRIT (European Strategic Programme for Research and Development in Information Technologies), BRITE (Basic Technological Research and the Application of New Technologies) and RACE (R & D in Advanced Communication Technologies for Europe). The 'Green Paper on the Development of the Common Market for Telecommunication Services and Equipment' initiated a wide-ranging discussion on the possibilities of completing the common internal market for telecommunications in the European Community.

Secondly, the European countries are interlinked with the world market and therefore cannot ignore the consequences of foreign deregulation policies, in particular those of the United States and Japan. In the USA an impressive wave of interstate deregulation took place at the end of the 1970s and the

*I would like to thank C. B. Blankart, S. Breyer, R. Crandall and the other participants of the conference on 'Regulatory Reform and the Completion of the Internal Market', European University Institute, Florence, 21 and 22 November 1988, for their constructive criticism. The revised version benefited greatly from the detailed comments and suggestions of S. J. Kamath.

beginning of the 1980s. Thus, Congress passed the Airline Deregulation Act in 1978, the Staggers Rail Act and the Motor Carrier Act in 1980 and the Bus Regulatory Reform Act in 1982. Simultaneously, the Federal Communications Commission deregulated interstate telecommunications (Docket 78–72). In Japan a new telecommunications law liberalizing telecomunications was passed in 1985.

Thirdly, during the Thatcher era, Great Britain, itself a member of the European Community, has taken the *Vorreiterrolle* of privatization and deregulation within Europe. These deregulations may also create impulses for the rest of Europe.

Fourthly, at the same time, there is also increasing debate in the European economics profession on the possibilities of privatization and deregulation; methodological approaches are based either on neoclassical (micro-economic) theory or on the public choice approach. The increasing popularity of the economic issues of deregulation is indicated by the fact that several research institutes in the Federal Republic of Germany have conducted research on this topic (Institut für Weltwirtschaft – Kiel, Soltwedel *et al.* (1986); Walter Eucken Institut – Freiburg, by Windisch (ed.) (1987); HwwA-Institut für Wirtschadftsforschung – Hamburg, by Krakowski (ed.) (1988); Deutsches Insitut für Wirtschaftsforschung – Berlin, by Horn, Knieps, and Müller (1988)).

A Critical Evaluation of The European Commission's Green Paper on Telecommunications Reform

'The Green Paper on the Development of the Common Market for Telecommunication Services and Equipment' – issued by the Commission in June 1987 – proposes that the provision of *terminal equipment* as well as enhanced telecommunication services should be liberalized within and between the member countries[1]. Basic *services* (mainly the telephone service) could still be provided as a monopoly by the national telecommunication administrations in each country; however, the arguments of the public interest being served by such monopolies would periodically be investigated. Moreover, the monopoly arrangement for the provision of the public *network* infrastructure would also be accepted in future.

With these proposals the Commission of the European Community tolerates, at least to some extent, the rather conservative attitude of most of its member countries with respect to deregulating telecommunications. There are, for example, several similarities in the proposals put forward in the report issued by the Government Commission for Telecommunications in Germany in September 1987 (Witte (ed.), 1987), and which currently forms the basis for changing the German telecommunications law which has existed since 1928.

The current reform proposals focus on the transition from the traditional monopoly of national postal, telegraph and telephone administrations (PTTs) towards *limited* competition. In what follows we shall argue that instead of partial deregulation, free entry into all subparts of telecommunications (including network infrastructure) would be desirable in the European telecomunications market on efficiency and equity grounds. In the first section we shall demonstrate that the basic arguments against free entry into all subparts of European telecommunications are no longer justified from the economic point of view. In particular, this includes the argument of economies of scale and infrastructure objectives (e.g. the provision of telecommunications in rural areas or the subsidy of local networks). Due to the increasing rapidity of technical change and the dominance of innovative activities in the telecommunication sector, competition as a process of discovery (von Hayek, 1945, 1968) plays a particularly important role.

In the second section we shall analyze the deregulation experiences in the telecommunication sectors of the USA, Japan and Great Britain in order to evaluate current telecommunications policy in Europe. These countries have undertaken the most progressive steps towards deregulation.

Review of The Arguments Against Free Entry Into Public Networks

COMPETITION NOT FEASIBLE BECAUSE OF ECONOMIES OF SCALE?

In the past, the telecommunications sector has been considered as a classical case of a natural monopoly. Telecommunications systems are characterized by the network effect. With increasing traffic intensity the capacity of the network can be increased without investment costs rising in equal proportion. As a consequence, it was assumed that costs are minimized in each relevant range of production if the total telecommunications supply of a country is concentrated in the hands of only one enterprise. In particular, this argument has led to the institutional justification of legal barriers to entry in order to exhaust economies of scale, as well as to price and rate of return regulation in order to reduce the monopoly power of the active firm, and to the obligation to provide services at uniform tariffs in order to satisfy certain infrastructure objectives.

It is our purpose to demonstrate that the need for regulation due to economies of scale has been strongly overestimated in the past. Firstly, even if economies of scale in a telecommunications system as a whole can be shown to exist, this does not account for which part of the telecommunications system these economies of scale actually occur in. Secondly, we shall see on pp. 92–93, that economies of scale are only a necessary but not a sufficient reason for regulation. Only when economies of scale occur in combination with irreversible costs can they create market power for the incumbent firm, which then perhaps should be regulated by certain government interventions (e.g. rate of return regulation.[2] Thirdly, even this source of monopoly power may disappear due to the perception of new opportunities in innovative sectors. The significance of economies of scale and market shares may be undermined by other aspects of competition such as the rapidity of technological change, the dominance of innovative activities (process and product innovations) and the growth rate of demand.[3]

1 *A more disaggregated search for economies of scale is necessary* During the last decade, the telephone companies in the USA and Canada in particular have made a significant research effort using econometric methods to measure globally the extent of economies of scale in telecommunications systems. They have done this by aggregating the different outputs of a telecommunications network into one output which was measured in net profit units (cf. FCC 1976, Docket 20003). Table 3.1 depicts the essential results of the estimates of scale elasticity, which measures the percentage change in outputs resulting from a 1 per cent change in all inputs.

Table 3.1 provides an overview of the spectrum of point estimates resulting in the different studies (scale elasticities larger than 1 imply increasing economies of scale, scale elasticities smaller than 1 characterize dis-economies of scale).

Table 3.1   Estimations of scale elasticities (%)

Telecommunications systems	Scale elasticities
USA Bell System	0.98 – 1.24
Bell Canada	0.85 – 1.4

Most of the economic studies are based on time series data and their results, therefore, depend upon the specification of technological change over time. The correct specification of technological change in econometric models seems to be a difficult task, particularly if dynamic sectors are under consideration, and no clear solution is currently available. The results of the econometric studies of AT & T and Bell Canada vary greatly, depending upon different specifications of technological progress, from substantial economies of scale to diminishing economies of scale or even diseconomies of scale. In spite of the extensive empirical work conducted in recent years, the actual degree of (dis-)economies of scale in telecommunications systems remains uncertain. In particular, most studies do not sufficiently differentiate between economies of scale on the one hand, and technological progress on the other hand.

The central point of criticism of the investigations of economies of scale in the telecommunications system is their high degree of aggregation. The empirical evidence of economies of scale in the telecommunications system as a whole does not reveal where these economies of scale actually occur. In contrast, the possibility exists that economies of scale only occur in some areas, whereas in the rest of the system a linear technology exists, with all economies of scale (in relation to the relevant range of demand) already exhausted. For the case where the existence of economies of scale is used to support the argument for government intervention (e.g. rate of return regulation), the question has to be asked as to what is the smallest sub-system which can be characterized as a natural monopoly.

2 *Economies of scale in the area of long-distance network infrastructure?* In long-distance networks, economies of scale may occur due to the exploitation of the law of large numbers. Line utilization may be greatly increased if certain lines can be used by many customers. In particular, this creates a reduction of the required reserve capacity. Moreover, the access to a large network is

of more value than access to a small network. Therefore, each additional telecommunications customer tends to create a benefit for other customers. This
is a phenomenon of positive network externalities, and will particularly be
the case for public communications networks. In contrast, it may be the case
that additional users of a computer network (e.g. for special problem-solving
applications), even with only a small number of users, may create negative
externalities, for example, by extending the time of access and processing (or
other disturbances). It can be expected that the economics of bundling as well
as the positive network externalities may become decreasingly important if
a certain network size is reached. Since in many industrialized countries
most households are connected to the telephone network, it can be expected
that the economies of network size are widely exhausted (von Weizsäcker,
1984: p. 121). The construction of competitive network infrastructures in the
high-volume long-distance traffic of the industrialized countries, therefore,
cannot be expected to create a significant waste of cost (cf. Meyer et al.,
1980; p. 181 f.).

In the USA, Great Britain and Japan the question as to whether competition
in the telecommunications infrastructure would cause inefficient cost duplications, has only been discussed under the assumption of entry in the more
lucrative high-density market. As far as newcomers are actually entering the
highest density market areas, it can be expected that, at least in these dense
areas, economies of scale no longer play any significant role. In contrast, the
actual problem which has to be solved is to combine the fulfilment of socially
desired universal service objectives with free market entry.

COMPETITION NOT FEASIBLE DUE TO UNIVERSAL SERVICE OBJECTIVES?

Although efficiency arguments no longer justify traditional government
interventions in long-distance telecommunications (due to technological progress and change in demand), there are still strong opponents of deregulation,
in particular in the European countries. Their major argument is that
cream-skimming activities by entrants would make the traditional cross-
subsidization unstable. Therefore, the introduction of competition would
destroy the traditional universal service objectives (like the universal access
to telephone service). In the following, we shall demonstrate that in fact it
is possible to make competition in telecommunications and certain universal
service objectives compatible.

1 *The instability of internal subsidies under competition* The term 'cream-
skimming' by market entrants is strongly related to cross-subsidization.
If one is interested in the relevance of such cross-subsidization in the telecommunications industry, one immediately runs into a serious problem of
terminology. Public enterprises like PTTs' consider services cross-subsidized
if their prices are below average costs, based on arbitrarily allocated overhead
costs (like the relative usage time, etc.). In particular, this leaves excessive
strategic room for deriving politically accepted cost[oblique]benefit ratios for
socially desired services. As is already well-known from the famous study by
J. M. Clark (1923) on overhead costs, there is no economic reason to do so.

Instead, from an economic point of view, the question arises as to whether the allocation of costs is acceptable in such a way that no incentive is created to separate from an efficient joint production. This immediately leads to the currently well-known incremental cost test developed by Alexander (1887) and extended by Faulhaber (1975) with game theoretical tools.

According to the *incremental cost test*, no cross-subsidization occurs if the revenue of each product (or coalition of products) at least contributes its incremental costs. In other words, overhead costs should not play any role as criteria for cross-subsidization because their specific allocation does not influence the incentive to give up joint production.

As a consequence, the cost/benefit ratios of various services published by public enterprises usually overestimate the degree of cross-subsidization. The larger the size of the overhead (non-separable) costs, the less important are cross-subsidization and universal service arguments. However, if over head costs are not important, the cost/benefit ratios of different services are a useful approximation for the degree of cross-subsidization: for example, the overhead costs between postal and telecommunications services are quite low. Therefore, the cost/benefit ratio of postal services (ca. 88 per cent in West Germany in 1984) is a good approximation of the extent of cross-subsidization between postal and telecommunications services (Annual Report of the German PTT, 1984: p. 80).

Access to the networks is usually subsidized by long-distance calls. The costs of local access are particularly high in areas with low population densities due to the longer access lines. In the past, cross-subsidization between long-distance calls and access to the network steadily increased. Technological progress in transmission technology strongly reduced the costs of long-distance transmissions, whereas similar strong progress in local transmissions has not taken place. It is estimated that in the USA each minute of interstate usage contributed 14.4 cents on average to the non-traffic sensitive access costs (cf. Bell Operating Companies, 1982). According to the Bell Telephone Company, a customer with a 45 minute interstate publicly switched telephone traffic per business day paid approximately $140 per month as a contribution to the usage independent access costs. This is about four times the average costs of the subscriber plants of $36 per month (cf. Bell Operating Companies, 1982). As a consequence, heavy users of interstate telecommunications services contributed much more than the costs of access to the network. On the other hand, local customers with very few long-distance calls did not contribute enough to cover the complete usage independent access costs. A large number of telecommunications customers belong to this category; for example, according to data provided by the Rochester Telephone Company, 38 per cent of their telephone customers make no interstate calls (cf. Rochester Telephone Corporation, 1982) In the past, therefore, an extensive cross-subsidization of local customers at the burden of long-distance interstate customers could be observed in the USA. In the Federal Republic of Germany, telephone tariffs still strongly depend upon distance upon distance. Therefore, there are large profits in the long-distance sector. The traditional tariff structures in the past led to an increasing cross-subsidization of local networks at the burden of customers of long-distance networks (Knieps, 1985: p. 112 ff.). In fact, possibilities of cross-subsidization did not occur because of the theoretical possibility that the set of cross-subsidy free price vectors would be empty, but, instead, because of politically desired cross-subsidization between the services.

The instrument of cross-subsidization has different serious disadvantages: cross-subsidization is not compatible with free entry because there are some products (or product groups) which contribute higher revenues than their separate production would cost. Therefore, incentives arise for entrants to offer these profitable products and leave the unremunerative products to the public or regulated enterprise. As a consequence, in order to stabilize cross-subsidization, legal entry barriers are also required in such economic sectors (including their substitutes), which otherwise would profit from the well-known benefits of competition (incentives to produce efficiently, introduce new products and technologies, etc.).

Furthermore, there is an intrinsic lack of public control, because the extent of cross-subsidy is decided mainly by the public enterprise itself (and not by the political sovereign) and is often not even correctly known to the public (due to intransparent accounting systems). Therefore, cross-subsidization is to a large extent arbitrary and the result of regulation. The extent of cross-subsidization may even increase over time by accident, due to changing cost and demand characteristics (for example, cross-subsidization between long-distance and local calls has rapidly increased during the last decades due to different speeds of technological progress).

2   *Free entry and universal service objectives are compatible*

(a)   *Reduction of subsidies between long-distance networks and local networks*   Opponents of liberalization in telecommunications argue that a reduction of cross-subsidization would exclude the concept of universal services. In particular, the national PTTs justify themselves as guardians of the grail of the universal service objectives, for which their own business policy (e.g. uniform tariffs) would be a necessary precondition.

First of all, it must be made clear that the construction and running of certain infrastructure functions does not necessarily lead to (long-run) losses. Examples are the setting up of private parcel services, chain stores, etc. Furthermore, an explicit order by law to provide unprofitable services in many cases does not exist, for example, uniform tariff principles do not necessarily imply that throughout the whole country the tariffs for access lines should be the same, independent of their underlying costs. Although the subsidy of the postal services by the telecommunications sector has a long tradition, even there an explicit order by law does not exist.

The legal burden to cover total costs can therefore only be considered to provide a sufficient degree of freedom to the PTTs to pursue their own policy of cross-subsidization. As a consequence, the PTTs on their own pursue a traditionally discretionary policy of cross-subsidization between several of their services. The PTTs use these subsidies as a strategic tool for defending their traditional monopolies in telecommunications.

The importance of their infrastructure functions of public enterprises in dynamic, innovative sectors may strongly change over time. The experience of recent years has demonstrated that the application of the universal service concept to new, innovative services may lead to wrong decisions as well as to a considerable waste of money. Investments into services for which even in the long run no demand at cost-based tariffs exists is one example of such developments. On the contrary, in the future there may be a stronger tendency towards more differentiated demand for service variety. In other words, the development of closed user networks in contrast to open, large universal networks may become important, particularly due to the high innovation rate in the Value Added Network Services (VANS) area.

Traditionally, the fulfilment of universal services (e.g. the subsidy of local telephone access, letter and parcel services) was located in the hands of public enterprises. Since the extent of cross-subsidization is often unknown to the public, at least the possibility arises that the transfer to a more open and transparent subsidy mechanism could increase public resistance to traditional subsidies. However, this does not prove the infeasibility of alternative instruments for financing unprofitable universal service objectives. Instead, this would only demonstrate that the subsidy of those objectives are no longer desired by the public.

The most economically efficient way to make competition and universal service objectives compatible is to reduce the traditional cross-subsidization between long-distance and local networks on the one hand, and between long-distance networks and postal services on the other hand. There is no method by which regulators can 'optimally' cross-subsidize different services due to the knowledge problem (von Hayek, 1945) of how a rational allocation of resources can be found in practice. In order to reduce the cross-subsidization between long-distance networks and postal services we propose the organizational separation of postal and telecommunications services. A reduction of cross-subsidization between long-distance and local networks – as has increasingly taken place in the USA since the deregulation of public switched telecommunications services – obviously does not mean that each individual participant must bear his own usage insensitive costs of network access. In contrast, it is possible to apply the process of averaging over several participants in a given area. This, on the one hand, reduces the transaction costs for the collection of a large number of different fixed charges. On the other hand, it facilitates the implementation of what is usually called equal treatment of all participants in a given geographical area.

Although the local networks (in particular the local access lines) traditionally have been subsidized, a possible change might be expected for the future. The introduction of Integrated Service Digital Networks (ISDN) will lead to the situation where even in local networks the principle of multiplexing can be increasingly applied. This means that also in the local networks several circuits of different customers can be combined, and subsequently the law of large numbers can increasingly be exhausted. This development will most certainly lead to reduced access costs. The highest network access costs occur in low-density population areas due to the long-physical access lines. For the future, due to the technical progress in mobile cellular telephone systems, a stronger substitution of conventional copper lines with mobile telephone circuits can be expected (Kahn, 1987). In particular, equipment costs may be expected to drop sharply as in the case of computers. This should also make a significant reduction of (average) access costs to the network possible.

Given that the usage independent costs of network access are covered by fixed (usage independent) tariffs, every competitor in long-distance networks only has to pay the usage-sensitive costs to enter the local networks. As a consequence, the incentives for strategical bypass of local networks (uneconomic bypass) vanish. As long as the long-distance traffic has to pay a usage-sensitive fee in order to cover the usage-insensitive access costs, large consumers of long-distance services may still have an incentive to bypass the local networks (the different possibilities for service bypass are explained in CC Docket 78–72, 3rd Report and Order 1983; CC Docket 80–286, November 1982).

(b)   *Universal service tax*   It is not necessarily the case that the subsidization of certain services, for example, local networks or postal services, is demanded by the public (e.g. by explicit votes). If, however, that is the case, the parliament has to decide on who should provide the subsidized services on the one hand, and how these subsidies should be financed, on the other hand (Knieps, 1987b; Blankart and Knieps, 1989; Knieps, 1988).

Traditionally, the fulfilment of universal service purposes (e.g. the subsidy of local telephone access, letter and parcel services) was located in the hands of public enterprises. A symmetric solution to introduce competition – in the profitable as well as the unprofitable markets – on the one hand, and to continue the fulfilment of unremunerative universal service purposes on the other hand, has to remove the burden of this responsibility from the public enterprises.

The company, regardless of whether it is public or private, should become active in a non-lucrative market which could work with the lowest subsidy. The rate of subsidy would be determined as the difference between the incremental costs and the politically determined price of a service. A larger subsidy is not necessary because production is thus guaranteed, even without obligation to serve. In particular, it is not necessary to contribute to the non-attributable costs of a firm, because they also occur with the production of the non-subsidized products. Each enterprise should be able to reveal its incremental costs for the provision of socially desired products on the basis of its own accounting system. This competition for subsidy would also reveal the actual (incremental) costs of traditionally subsidized services (Knieps, 1987b). For example, in the labour-intensive area of the postal services an extensive potential for rationalization can be expected.

Furthermore, in the area of local telephone networks, the PTTs may not necessarily be the most cost-effective supplier. There might also be the case that alternative networks by communities or private local telephone companies enter the market. Competition for local network monopolies could accelerate the introduction of new technologies like mobile telephone services.

The subsidy could either be financed by the public budget or by a universal service tax in the form of an explicit access charge. The advantage of the subsidy by the public budget would be to avoid the administrative costs of collection as well as price distortions in the strongly taxed markets. The disadvantage of this solution seems to be the strong political resistance nowadays to increasing the public budget.

A universal service tax would have to be raised in such a way that entrants and the national enterprises would have to make the same contribution in order to finance the universal services. The size of this payment should be measured in such a way that an enterprise which is more efficient or more flexible than the national enterprise would, even under the burden of such payments, be able to work profitably. On the other hand, a less efficient enterprise could not enter this market. The payment would, therefore, be raised in correspondence with the value-added tax (Knieps, Müller, and von Weizsäcker, 1981: S. 147ff.; Knieps *et al.*, 1982).

It can be expected that competition in the profitable services, for example, in long-distance telephone services, would very rapidly lead to cost-oriented tariffs. Since the PTTs would no longer have any universal service obligation, they would also have no pressure to continue artificial tariff discrimination (e.g. between public switched telephone service and leased lines). As a consequence, possibilities of tariff arbitrage would vanish. The universal service tax should be raised in such a way that the result would be the same burden for the traditional national public enterprises and for newcomers.

2. Market Entry in Public Networks: The Experience of the USA, Japan and Great Britain

It is well-known that the computer industry has been one of the most dynamic sectors in this century. At the same time, as an efficient method of finding new products, competition in this sector has become increasingly important nationally as well as internationally. There is no doubt that the computer industries in competitively organized countries dominate those in the socialist countries. During the last decades the telecommunications sector has been strongly converging towards the data processing sector. In combination with strong progress in the transmission technologies (e.g. microwaves, satellites, fibre optics), this implies that the telecommunications sector has increasingly developed from an originally stationary industry to a progressive one. The basic characteristic of this development is the increasing innovation potential of the telecommunications services. This rapidly increases the spectrum of terminal equipment, the potential of network usage and the possibility of different network infrastructures. Therefore, it can be expected that competition as a method of developing new products will dominate the centralized process in order to explore the innovation potential more rapidly and more exhaustively (von Hayek, 1968). In fact, this is the major argument for the abolition of all legal entry barriers within the telecommunications sector.

The USA, Japan and Great Britain are the most progressive countries in deregulating telecommunications. Entry became not only possible in the market for terminal equipment and telecommunications services, but also in the area of public networks.

It is interesting to remember that the deregulation of telecommunications in the USA started on the level of interstate networks rather than on the services or equipment level. The 'Above 890' decision of the Federal Communication Commission (FCC) in 1959 granted firms with high communication demand the right to build their own microwave systems. Applications to provide specialized common carrier services with microwave systems in competition to the traditional monopolistic carrier AT & T started to be granted in 1970. Market entry, with the establishment of domestic communication satellites, became possible in 1972. The resale and shared usage of AT & T's private line services only became allowable four years later in 1976. Since 1980, free entry has been possible in all parts of interstate telecommunications, including the construction of network facilities to provide public switched services. In many states local networks are still in monopoly, including such parts of intrastate long-distance telecommunications networks which belong to the same Local Access and Transport Area (LATA)[4] (Knieps, 1983; Knieps, 1985: chap. III. A.; OECD, 1987; Wieland, 1985).

In Japan a new telecommunications law was introduced in 1985. As a consequence, several Japanese firms became active as new network suppliers, in competition to the traditional monopolist, Nippon Telegraph and Telephone (NTT). In the mean time, there exist several suppliers of public telecommunication networks in Japan, including traditional electricity and highway companies. Market entry took place by means of microwave systems, satellites and fibre optic networks.

Already in 1984, Japan National Railways founded the subsidiary, Japan Telecom, to become a network carrier with a fibre optic network. The state-owned highway company together with several automobile firms founded Teleway Japan, which also became active with a fibre optic network. In addition, electricity companies started to found subsidiary companies in order to build their own regional fibre optic telecommunications networks. Market entry with communication satellites took place by three private consortia of firms active in trade, banking and production. Market entry with microwave systems was undertaken by one of the leading producers of ceramic components for integrated circuits. Of course, market entry in the Japanese telecommunications sector took place not only with alternative networks, but also with new services on the basis of public networks (Ito and Iwata, 1986; Müller, 1987; Neumann, 1987; OECD, 1987).

The most progressive country as regards deregulating telecommunications in Europe today is Great Britain. Until 1981 British Telecom operated as part of the Post Office as the monopolistic supplier of the whole British telecommunications sector. With the passing of the Telecommunication Act in October 1981, the statutory monopoly of British Telecom to run the British telecommunications network ended. In February 1982 the Mercury consortium (Cable and Wireless, Barclay's Merchant Bank and British Petroleum) received a licence to operate a private digital network with fibre optic cables for voice and data in competition with British Telecom. Since 1984 Mercury has been wholly owned by Cable and Wireless. In addition, market entry of private suppliers of value added network carriers on the basis of public networks has been allowed (Commission of the European Communities, 1987: Appendix A; Heuermann and Neumann, 1985; Müller, 1986; OECD, 1987).

The major advantage of this extensive entry deregulation is the possibility of exploring rapidly and exhaustively the increasing innovation potential of the telecommunications sector.[5] The development of new transmission technologies (e.g. microwave systems, satellites, fibre optic cables) together with the digital transmission and switching technologies strongly increase the possibilities of different network architectures as well as the potential of new network services and the spectrum of terminal equipment.

The market entrants in the public networks of the USA, Japan and Great Britain typically pursued a strategy of providing new services (product innovations) together with new network architectures. For example, in the USA the firm, DATRAN, was founded in 1973 in order to construct a digital communications network for business users. The introduction of new switching technologies and the optimization of the network for data transmission made a more accurate and high-speed data transmission possible, which traditional telephone companies had not been able to offer until that time. Market entry with satellites was allowed in the USA in 1972, and very recently it has also been permitted in Japan. In these countries the supply of new innovative services plays a central role. This became possible through the different cost characteristics of satellite systems as compared to terrestrial systems. Satellite transmission costs are almost independent of distance, they allow a high speed of transmission, and they also provide the possibility for multiple distribution of communications signals. Thus, satellite systems are particularly suitable for the transmission of large data quantities at high speeds over large distances. One example is the transmission of newspaper articles from one composing room to printing offices located in different places. The construction of a high quality digital fibre optic network by Mercury in Great Britain also led to a better quality of network services. Since the transmission is more accurate and more rapid than those of British Telecom, the service offered by Mercury has been of particular interest for business data communication.

In those countries where market entry in public networks has been allowed (USA, Japan and Great Britain) the question as to whether this would cause inefficient cost duplications does not play a significant role nowadays.[6] Firstly, it is widely recognized that the growing demand for telecommtelecommunications reduces the importance of economies of scale in long-distance telecommunications. Secondly, it becomes obvious that entry may lead to a more efficient utilization of existing network capacities, if networks which were previously reserved for internal usage of train systems, highways or pipeline companies can be used for public telecommunications. Thirdly, the importance of different network qualities, due to different usage characteristics of alternative transmission systems (e.g. terrestrial versus non-terrestrial), becomes increasingly important, especially for business users.

As a consequence of the progressive entry deregulation in the USA, Japan and Great Britain, competition in the international telecommunication markets also increases. For many years AT & T was the only supplier of international voice communications for the USA in cooperation with the PTTs abroad. International message and data transfer was handled by ITT World Communication, RCA Global Communications and Western Union International. In the mean time, other suppliers of international voice and data services (for example, MCI, USA Sprint and Graphnet) entered the market. Since 1986 it has been possible for suppliers of value added network services to be registered as recognized private operating agencies and they are therefore entitled to bargain with foreign telecommunications administrations over the right tow use oversea cables. At the same time, the FCFC granted two USA firms the right to set up private oversea cables. The purpose of this cable system is to sell bulk transmission capacities for non-common carrier users (Commission of the European Communities, 1987: p. 158).

From 1952 till quite recently, KDD (Kokusai Denstrin Denwa) was the only Japanese international network carrier and service supplier. Since the new telecommunications law of 1985, two new firms have applied for licences. International Telecom Japan Inc. (ITJ), a consortium of Japanese firms, applied to offer a world-wide service network for Japanese enterprises on the basis of lines leased from Intelsat or the national telecommunications administrations. The second consortium (International Digital Communications – IDJ), comprises Japanese Warehouse Ito, the British firm Cable and Wireless and the USA regional carriers Nynex and Pacific Telesis as well as Merill Lynch. IDJ applied for a licence as network carrier in order to use a world-wide fibre optics network planned under the direction of Cable and Wireless.

In August 1983, the British government decided that Mercury could also enter the market for international switched services. Mercury now has the licence to provide all telecommunication services, nationally as well as internationally. Several services between Great Britain and the USA have already started. In order to increase international competitiveness, Cable and Wireless, the owner of Mercury, has been allowed to build a transatlantic fibre optics cable.

It is obvious that those countries which are most progressive in deregulating their national telecommunications sectors are also most active in liberalizing international telecommunications. In particular, there is pressure from new firms already active in the national markets in the USA, Japan and Great Britain to enter the international market.

The liberalization of national and international telecommunications markets not only increases the spectrum of available telecommunication services but also reduces the long-distance telecommunications tariffs (especially on 'high-density routes'). Although these reductions in long-distance tariffs are partly due to the rebalancing of tariffs at the burden of local tariffs (see pp. 86–88), they also reveal the increasing efficiency as a result of entry into long-distance telecommunications.

Partial Deregulation Due to Infrastructure Objectives: the Experience of the USA, Japan and Great Britain

THE INSTABILITY OF PARTIAL ENTRY DEREGULATION

Although the USA, Japan and Great Britain are the most progressive countries in deregulating their telecommunications sectors, they pursued a strategy of partial entry deregulation in the past. Even today there exist some regulations for market entry. In the following, we shall demonstrate that the strategies of partial deregulation have become unstable over time because entrants offered services which were highly substitutive to the monopolized services or even masked monopolized services as competitive services.

In the USA during the first two decades of deregulation of interstate telecommunications, entry was only allowed in the area of private line services, and the monopoly of public switched services was reserved for the traditional network carrier, AT & T.[7] This strategy of partial deregulation was only given up by the FCC in 1980 (C.C Docket 78–72) when it became obvious during the 'Execunet Case' that the borderlines between private line and public switched services were becoming blurred.[8] Since the divestiture of AT & T in 1984,[9] free entry into inter-LATA telecommunications has been possible, whereas in many states intra-LATA basic telecommunications is still provided under monopoly (by the newly founded regional holding companies). Nevertheless, one can observe some tendencies towards a weakening of these regional monopolies. Firstly, since the FCC's Computer Inquiry III,[10] competition has been allowed in enhanced local services. As has already been realized on the long-distance level (Computer II Inquiry),[11] technical progress makes it increasingly difficult to differentiate between basic communication and enhanced communication. Secondly, the introduction of microwave systems becomes increasingly attractive, especially in rural areas due to their high cost-saving potential compared with cables (Kahn 1987). Thirdly, the possibilities for bypassing local networks for long-distance telecommunications are increasing due to technical progress in satellite and microwave systems.

In Japan, entrants are classified into different categories according to their activities. The provision of a licence by the Ministry of Posts and Telecommunications (MPT) to set up a network (Type I Telecommunications Business) is dependent on 'economic' criteria such as sufficient demand in the underlying area or the avoidance of overcapacity (Ito and Iwata, 1986). Furthermore, foreign capital investment is restricted to a one-third maximum. Although in general the entry policy seems quite generous, the application of a third satellite enterprise was denied (Müller, 1987: p. 313) and market entry into international telecommunications is hampered by the MPT's intention to restrict the influence of foreign countries. Suppliers of services which rent network capacities from firms of category I either serve the demand of a large number of unspecified users ('Special Type II Telecommunications Business') or small-scale value added network services ('General Type II Telecommunications Business'). General Type II suppliers are almost unregulated. In contrast, Special Type II suppliers have to be registered by the MPT.

The traditional network carrier, NTT, originally tried to exclude resale of leased lines by forbidding access to its public switched network. It soon became obvious that this would inadequately restrict the scope of products of service suppliers. Since 1985 the resale of leased lines has been allowed, but only for data communication (Neumann, 1987: p. 150). The resale of leased lines for voice communication connected with the public switched network is still restricted. Although NTT strongly intends to continue with these restrictions, there is already instability due to the increasing tendency to mix voice and data communications services. In addition, new network carriers are allowed to resell leased lines from NTT to become active in geographical areas where they do not have their own physical networks. Moreover, there exists the alternative of using the network capacities of NTT's competitors (including the local network capacities of the electricity companies) as well as the possibility for large customers to bypass NTT's local networks using microwave systems or CATV networks.

In Great Britain the entry of only one alternative network carrier (Mercury) has been granted. All value added network services (VANS) using leased lines from British Telecom or Mercury have to be licensed by the Department of Industry. These licences run for a period from 10 to 25 years. British Telecom defines VANS as services by which private firms rent circuits, add either special equipment or transform them so that specific services become possible (Beesly, 1981). It is the purpose of the licence procedure for VANS that only more advanced services should be supplied through competition, whereas the resale and shared usage of leased lines should remain prohibited. There are obviously large enforcement problems due to the difficulties of differentiating between pure resale and VANS (similar to the problem in the USA of differentiating between basic and enhanced services). There are, for example, services which, on the one hand, satisfy typical characteristics of value added services but, on the other hand, also include the resale of transmission services. Therefore, the registration procedure has been adopted such that shared use as well as resale for limited user groups is permitted. The prohibition of simple resale shall remain (at least) until July 1989 (Heuermann and Neumann, 1985: p. 123).

Mercury has permission to compete with British Telecom on all levels of telecommunication activities, including the local networks. In the mean time, competition occurs between British Telecom and Mercury in providing data communication in large towns. A further threat to British Telecom's monopoly on the local level may eventuate due to the bypass activities of Mercury's business customers using the services of cellular radio companies or CATV networks.

The experience of the USA, Japan and Great Britain demonstrates that the separation into monopolistic and liberalized submarkets is likely to become unstable over time. As soon as a specific submarket is reserved for a monopoly (for example, public switched services or basic services or voice communications) incentives arise for entrants to extend the borderlines of the competitive submarket. Great Britain and Japan could have learnt this from the deregulation experience in the USA. Nevertheless, they tried the strategy of partial entry deregulation, although with different market split criteria.

THE INSTABILITY OF CROSS-SUBSIDIZATIONS

In the USA the policy of *partial* entry deregulation was justified by infrastructure objectives and equity considerations. As long as a relevant subpart of telecommunications was monopolized, enough revenue could be earned there to cross-subsidize the supply of non-lucrative telecommunication services in rural areas or in local telephone services. For example, AT & T's monopoly in public switched services until 1980 has been justified by the FCC such that 'entry in the Private Line Market . . . will not require any significant adjustments in the rates charged for local telephone services.' (FCC Docket 20003, First Report, 1976: p. 162). In fact, the political aim of the Communications Act of 1934 (section 1), namely 'to make available, so far as possible, to all the people of the United States a rapid, efficient, nationwide, and world-wide wire and radio communication service with adequate facilities at reasonable charges', was still not abandoned.

However, free entry into interstate public switched telecommunications, which had been initiated by the unexpected instability of partial deregulation, initiated a trend away from rate-averaging towards cost-oriented tariffs. The cross-subsidy in favour of rural areas decreased because elements of traffic density became important in telecommunication tariffs as a reaction to price-setting of market entrants.

Furthermore, cross-subsidizations between interstate public switched telecommunications and local networks became unstable.[12] Traditionally, the public switched interstate traffic had to contribute to the non-traffic sensitive network access costs according to its actual usage of the local networks. In the past, the intense (business) users of interstate communications strongly subsidized local networks because they paid much more than the costs of their network access. As a consequence, incentives existed for entrants to bypass local networks, especially in areas with a high concentration of interstate business customers. In order to avoid such 'uneconomic' bypassing, the FCC immediately changed the traditional contribution system so 'that a substantial portion of fixed exchange plant costs . . . assigned to interstate services should ultimately be recovered through flat per line charges that are assessed upon end users' (C.C. Docket, 78–72, p. 3). In the meantime, local tariffs are increasing towards cost-oriented network access and usage charges.

In Japan, too, the principle of nationwide universal service at uniform tariffs has a long tradition. NTT's tariffs for long-distance telecommunications are typically independent of traffic density. Moreover, local networks are heavily subsidized by long-distance traffic (Ozawa, 1984). The new telecommunications law intends to continue these possibilities of cross-subsidization by means of asymmetric regulations between NTT and its competitors. In contrast to its competitors, the NTT has the general obligation to provide a nationwide telephone system, including the responsibility for local networks. In exchange, NTT can forbid the resale of its leased lines, thus implying only partial deregulation. In the mean time, these resale restrictions are becoming increasingly difficult to enforce. It can be expected that the intense market entry at all levels of telecommunication systems in Japan will soon end NTT's possibilities of cross-subsidization within its network by rate-averaging.

It is unlikely that the non cost-oriented access charges to NTT's local networks could avoid the expected increases in local tariffs. On the one hand, the new network carriers owned by electricity companies can rely on their own local networks (e.g. the Tokyo Power Company can use its local network in the area of Tokyo and serve its regional customers by bypassing NTT's local network). On the other hand, some of the new network carriers in particular provide their own local lines to their larger customers. The experience in the USA demonstrates that there exist bypass technologies (e.g. small satellite antenna, shared leased lines) which make the bypassing of local monopolies cost-effective even for smaller users, if access charges are not cost-oriented. Although the access charge debate still continues in Japan, serious doubts exist as to whether, through excessive access charges, entry may be controlled and the traditional subsidy of local networks can be continued as at present. Finally, it remains unclear as to what extent the infrastructure objectives reflected in the traditional NTT tariff structure are still socially or politically desired for the future.

In Great Britain, the principle of a universal nationwide telephone system at uniform tariffs has also played an important role in the past. There has been cross-subsidization between high-density and low-density routes and between long-distance and local networks. The new telecommunications law still assigns some non-lucrative infrastructure obligations to British Telecom. In contrast to Mercury, British Telecom has to provide existing pay-telephones and the emergency call system independent of their rentability, and some services (e.g. telegrams) have to be continued even when they are not economically viable. Furthermore, British Telecom has an obligation to provide a nationwide network.

Although the tariffs of British Telecom are regulated with respect to price increases, they are allowed to vary according to traffic density in order to compete with Mercury. British Telecom's possibilities for cross-subsidization will be further decreased when simple resale becomes allowable in the near future. Although Mercury has to bear their costs of access to British Telecom's local networks, there seems to be no adequate source to finance British Telecom's unlucrative service obligations by excessive access charges. In the past, Mercury's business strategy was to provide services mainly for business customers, who usually have easy access to bypass technologies, for example, with cellular mobile telephone or CATV networks. The quality of British Telecom's local networks is, moreover, not always sufficient for Mercury's digital services. In order to achieve cost-effective, high-quality local network access, Mercury is currently building a fibre optics cable network in the city of London using the old water-pipes from the hydraulic system dating back to Victorian times (Heuermann and Neumann, 1985: p. 133).

Implications for the Liberalization of the European Telecommunications Market

The experiences of the USA, Japan and Great Britain demonstrate that the large innovation potential of the telecommunications sector can only be achieved rapidly, if market entry is possible not only in the area of terminal equipment and VANS, but also in the area of basic services and networks. Although many entrants may only want to compete in the terminal equipment or VANS segments of the market, the possibility of free entry into basic network infrastructure has the additional advantage of disciplining the incumbent carriers. Only then will it be likely that leased lines will be provided at cost-oriented tariffs and a large variety of services will be offered with optimally designed network architectures. Moreover, the need to differentiate between basic networks and VANS, which becomes increasingly difficult with respect to the various switching components, will also disappear as soon as free entry in to the basic network infrastructure market is granted.

Furthermore, it has become obvious that the strategy of partial entry deregulations intended to achieve unprofitable infrastructure objectives does not provide a stable solution. In spite of the costly enforcement and control efforts in the USA, Japan and Great Britain, the split in monopolized subparts and liberalized subparts has become unstable. It is, therefore, unrealistic to expect that the 'split-market' approach of the current European telecommunications policy (i.e. PTT monopoly of public network and telephone services and liberalized VANS and terminal equipment market) will turn out to be stable in the future. As soon as the Integrated Service Digital Networks (ISDN) are introduced in Europe, the differentiation between voice communication and data communication will become even more difficult. The recent proposals (e.g. in Germany) to liberalize non-terrestrial networks (e.g. satellites, cellular mobile telephone) will also challenge the monopoly of terrestrial networks due to the large possibilities of substitution between terrestrial and non-terrestrial communications.

Since one cannot expect that a partial deregulation strategy in Europe will be stable in the future, one can also not expect that the traditional cross-subsidizations for the benefit of local networks or rural areas will be able to continue, even if this were intended. Entrants would simply concentrate on the lucrative subparts and leave the unlucrative subparts to the telecommunications administrations. The process of entry deregulation in the USA demonstrates that the cross-subsidization of local networks by long-distance traffic – depending on the actual usage of the local networks – becomes unstable due to the possibilities of bypassing the local networks.[13] This is the reason why the infrastructure problem in the USA as well as in Japan and Great Britain still remains unsolved.

A more promising approach for the European telecommunications policy seems to be to allow free entry into all subparts (including public networks and basic telephone services). The socially desired universal service objectives should be financed with alternative methods instead of cross-subsidizations, unless future innovations arise which overcome this problem without requiring subsidies. A basic prerequisite would be to move the asymmetric burden of providing unremunerative services from the national PTTs.[14]

All companies, regardless of whether they are public or private, should have the opportunity to supply the non-lucrative socially desired services by competing for a subsidy. The competition for subsidies would also reveal how high the infrastructure burden really is and what the minimal costs of traditionally cross-subsidized services are (Blankart and Knieps, 1989: pp. 20 ff.). For example, in the area of local telephone networks, the PTTs may not necessarily be the most cost-effective suppliers, if new firms with cost-saving technologies like mobile telephone and microwave systems entered the market (Kahn, 1987). This may be of particular importance in rural areas where the frequency spectrum is not so scarce as in towns. It can be expected that the competition for subsidies would strongly reduce the volume of required subsidies.

From an allocative point of view, a superior alternative for financing the required subsidies may be the public budget.[15] In the present context, it would seem that there is a strong political resistance against increasing the burden of the public budget. Therefore, a more realistic approach could be the introduction of an entry tax, which all suppliers of lucrative telecommunications activities (PTTs and their competitors) would have to pay, independent of the actual usage of the local networks (Knieps, 1987b).

The entry tax should be designed in such a way that entrants and the national enterprises would have to make the same contribution in order to finance the required subsidies.

The experiences in the USA, Japan and Great Britain demonstrate that equity considerations in the form of socially desired infrastructure objectives may strongly influence the course of the deregulation processes in the telecommunications sector. Although finally those objectives cannot be stabilized through cross-subsidizations financed by the monopolistic subparts of the system, similar considerations can currently be observed in the rest of Europe. Nevertheless, in order to rapidly reap the benefits of free entry into European telecommunication sectors, it is necessary to find an early political consensus on which unlucrative infrastructure functions (if any) should be provided in the future, and how they should be financed without having to restrict entry into telecommunications. In that context, one would also have to deal with the rentkeeping activities by the telecommunication administrations and the postal unions to maintain the status quo. It would seem to be important for European telecommunications policy to learn from foreign experiences, but not to imitate their errors.[16]

A Critical Evaluation of the European Deregulation Policy on Transportation

In recent years there have been some tendencies towards liberalization in European transportation markets. To cite a prominent example: the Council of Ministers of the European Community has recently decided on a stepwise deregulation of airline markets. In future, the strict bilateral sharing rules of capacity will no longer hold and more than one airline company per country will be designated to serve the international traffic ('multiple designation'). Moreover, the cabotage prohibition on providing inland transportations within foreign countries (with ships, trucks or aircraft) will be liberalized. In addition, tariffs will be less influenced by political tariff commissions and will reflect actual market conditions more closely.

At the same time, it is argued that there exist boundaries of deregulation in the transportation field due to bottlenecks of infrastructure (Sandhäger, 1988). Infrastructure problems (e.g. airport congestions) are considered an important bottleneck problem in the deregulation of the American transportation sector, particularly for airline deregulation. In addition, it is feared that a comprehensive deregulation of the market for transportation services will not lead to increased competition, but instead to cartelization and subsequent excessive prices (Sørensen, 1988: p. 6). The recent concentration wave in the American airline sector has led to the increasing popularity of advocates of reregulation in the USA.[17]

In the first subsection below, it is argued that complete deregulation of the supply of transportation services in Europe is possible and economically beneficial, independently of whether the transportation services are provided on roads, rails, waterways or in the air. A necessary condition, however, is the free and equal access of all (actual and potential) suppliers of transportation services to the infrastructure (airports, railways, highways, etc.). In the second subsection, the deregulation experience within the American transportation sector is described and commented upon. In the third subsection, lessons from this experience are drawn with respect to the liberalization of the national and international European transportation sectors.

No Market Failure in The Market for Transportation Services

The traditional regulation of the transportation sector has been justified by several peculiarities of this sector, mainly: indivisibilities, the network structure, the necessity to provide socially desired universal transportation services below cost, as well as the failure of intermodal competition. In what follows we shall analyze whether these peculiarities justify regulation of the market for transportation services.

INDIVISIBILITIES

The transportation of persons or goods on roads, railways, waterways and in the air seems at first glance very heterogeneous. Nevertheless, the different transportation modes share as a common denominator the existence of an infrastructure (of routes) in order to be able to provide transportation services. Although the infrastructure and the transportation services are complementary, they do require a quite different division of labour between the State and the market.

The construction of the infrastructure is typically characterized by several indivisibilities. If, for example, a canal is built between two towns, at a given point in time more than one ship will be able to use the waterway without disturbing others. As long as usage of the infrastructure is so small that *non-rival* usage exists, market prices do not make sense. Even where bottlenecks exist (for example, in local traffic) it may be very costly to exclude users who do not want to pay. As long as infrastructures of routes have the characteristics of a public good, the State may play a significant role in guaranteeing its financing. On the other hand, externality costs in the usage of infrastructures may lead to optimal congestion tolls, which may significantly contribute to the financing of the infrastructure costs (Mohring and Harwitz, 1962: pp. 80–87).

In contrast, the supply of transportation services (for example, the provision of transport by bus, aeroplane, ship or train) is not characterized by significant indivisibilities, provided the appropriate vehicle size is chosen. Transportation services are, therefore, private goods, characterized by rival usage and excludability. It is obvious that indivisibilities with respect to infrastructure of routes are no argument for restricting competition in the supply of transportation services.

TRANSPORTATION NETWORKS

The markets for transportation services are, however, far from the ideal picture of perfect atomistic markets. An essential characteristic with respect to the supply of transportation services is its *network structure*. If the amount of traffic is not high enough to make a direct connection between two places beneficial, incentives exist for *bundling*, for example, with hub- and spoke systems. Economies of scope in serving several lines jointly (e.g. coordination advantages, more efficient usage of vehicles) may have the effect that in a given region only one supplier of services of a transportation mode is optimal. Economies of scale in bundling the traffic over networks have in the past been a basic argument for justifying government regulations or State-owned enterprises in the transportation sector. Legal entry barriers were created in order to avoid inefficient cost duplications. At the same time, regulations of profit were introduced to restrict the market power of the active firms (e.g. Bailey, 1973; Kahn, 1971).[18]

The basic argument of theory of contestable markets is that economics of scale are a necessary but not a sufficient condition for the existence of market failure. The lack of competition between active firms in the market may be replaced by efficient potential competition (Demsetz, 1968; Baumol, Panzar, and Willig, 1982).

The condition for the functioning of potential competition for disciplining firms already in the market is that the incumbent firms do not have asymmetric cost-advantages with respect to potential entrants. In fact, if economies of scale exist in combination with *irreversibility of costs*, a need for regulation in order to discipline the incumbent firms does exist. It is important to distinguish fixed costs from sunk costs. If K_0 is the ex ante cost of building a plant, and K_1 is the ex post value of the plant (i.e. what it can be sold for), then $k = K_0 - K_1$ represents the sunk costs. Such irreversible, or sunk costs occur, for example, with respect to the construction of infrastructure (e.g. railways). In that case, the resale value of such equipment (given that demand is going down) is very low, because the railways cannot be transferred to another geographically distant market. In contrast, the pure existence of economies of scale or large fixed costs, which are not irreversible, is nevertheless compatible with free exit as shall be demonstrated by the following example. If the demand for traffic connecting several villages is low, there obviously exist strong economies of scale in such markets. Nevertheless, the costs to set up a network of bus traffic are not irreversible because the buses can be used to serve other networks in different locations once demand in the former network has dropped too far to keep up a profitable bus service, that is, buses represent capital on wheels which are not irreversibly bound to a specifically located network. The same 'hit and run' entry may be expected with respect to trains, aeroplanes, trucks, or ships.

Irreversible or sunk costs are not relevant as a decision variable for the old incumbent firms. However, they are relevant for potential entrants, since they have yet to make the decision as to whether to sink these costs in a given market or not. The incumbent firms, therefore, have lower decision-relevant costs than potential entrants. This is a source for strategic behaviour by the incumbent firms, which allows them to produce inefficiently or to make positive profits without necessarily attracting market entry. If, however, irreversible costs do not exist, inefficient allocation of inputs, inefficient production technologies, or excessive capital usage with positive profits automatically lead to market exit of incumbent firms because potential entrants with lower costs are able to enter the market, especially if the latter also have free access to the most efficient technology.

An important condition for the effectiveness of potential competition in disciplining the incumbent transportation firms is the access to the infrastructure under similar conditions for all active and potential competitors. As long as incumbent firms have preferred access to landing rights, railways, bus-stations or other infrastructure they have an asymmetric cost-advantage which they can use as a competitive advantage with respect to newcomers. The conclusion that the market for transportation services therefore would not be contestable, however, does not hold because the asymmetrical access to the infrastructure can be removed.

THE SUPPLY OF UNIVERSAL TRANSPORTATION SERVICES BELOW COST

The necessity of universal transportation services has been a central argument to justify legal entry barriers in the transportation sector. Regulated firms or public enterprises have been deemed to have the obligation to provide universal services, if necessary, below (incremental) cost. One example is local public transportation services. In addition, the provision of regular scheduled services in low-density regions is often considered as a source of deficit. Opponents of deregulations will correctly argue that the finance of deficits from excess profits in other lucrative areas of the enterprise (cross-subsidizations) are not stable under competition (see pp. 76–78). In particular, there exist incentives for newcomers to enter the lucrative areas and leave the deficit areas to the public enterprise ('cream-skimming').

As has been argued on pp. 80–81, the provision of universal services need not necessarily be financed by cross-subsidization. Under free entry, the need for subsidies may strongly decrease, due to more efficient supply of services (e.g. the airline deregulation experience in the USA). The remaining burden of socially desired subsidies need only be borne symmetrically by all suppliers of transportation services, independent of whether they are incumbent or whether they are newcomers (Knieps, 1987b). A first condition may be to oblige all firms to serve a certain area below cost. For example, the right to provide intercity bus services may be combined with the obligation to service deficit areas. A second more flexible possibility is the introduction of a universal service tax by means of a universal service fund (see pp. 80–81). Each supplier – irrespective of whether it is a public or a private transportation firm – would have to pay a positive universal service tax into this fund if it provides profitable transportation services in a region, and it will get a subsidy if it offers a non-lucrative transportation service in another region. If the universal service fund could be financed by the public budget, this could be preferable from an allocative efficiency point of view (Blankart and Knieps, 1989).

INTERMODAL COMPETITION

Until now we have analyzed the possibilities for competition within particular transportation modes but not in relation to competition between different transportation modes. The fact of competition working with respect to the supply of transportation services requires that neither the railways nor their competitors on land, sea or in the air be restricted from exercising their advantages. In the past, restrictions on competition in the motor carrier market, in particular, were (at least to some extent) justified by the special burdens of the railways with their rail network. Lower boundaries for tariffs as well as entry barriers by means of licence-systems in the trucking industry were the consequence. Whether the railways have to contribute more to their infrastructure than other transportation modes is an open question. Nevertheless, the solution should not be to restrict competition with respect to the supply of transportation services. Instead, every transportation mode and its transportation services should symmetrically contribute to the burden of infrastructure by raising optimal congestion tolls.

An efficient intermodal split of the supply of transportation services requires that every supplier of transportation services on a given mode (e.g. railways) is also free to offer services on other modes (e.g. roads, waterways). Only then would it be possible to exhaust economies of scope for providing transportation services with combined modes.

The Deregulation Experience in The Transportation Sector of The USA

In what follows, we shall summarize the effects of deregulation of the American transportation markets, with respect, in particular, to the lessons for Europe.[19]

The deregulation of interstate airline traffic by the *Airline Deregulation Act* of 1978 led to increasing entry and exit of firms. As a consequence (average) tariffs as well as profit rates decreased and price-quality options increased. Although often ignored in studies on the effects of deregulation, part of the price-savings were related to decreasing transportation quality due to higher loading rates or increasing bundling of traffic over hub- and spokes. The possibilities of network optimization due to bundling increased after free entry on routes became possible. This is also one important reason why the supply of airline services in low-density areas could continue, even with partly lower tariffs. Furthermore, an increasing number of commuter-airlines were prepared to serve a large portion of the low-density markets without subsidies. In addition, the need for subsidies decreased due to the introduction of competition for subsidies in order to serve unprofitable lines.[20] The deregulation actually effected in the USA related to market entry and tariffs only, whereas safety regulations (by the Federal Aviation Administration) continued to be supervised.

These and other positive effects of deregulation can be observed, although not all asymmetries between incumbent firms and entrants have been removed. Thus, the experiment of a bidding process for landing rights by the Federal Aviation Association in 1982 was stopped after only six weeks due to the resistance of incumbent airlines (Bailey *et al.*, 1983).

The deregulation of intercity bus transportation by the *Bus Regulatory Reform Act* of 1982 has led to increased competition, in particular to increased market entry by small bus firms. As a consequence, tariffs have decreased on high-density routes and increased on low-density routes. In addition, some routes are no longer being served, although this tendency has been limited by specific open subsidies from local communities. The introduction of a universal service tax as a substitute for the unstable cross-subsidies has, however, not been implemented (United States Senate, 1984; ICC, 1984).

The deregulation of the interstate trucking industry by the *Motor Carrier Act* of 1980 has led to increased market entry. As a consequence, the tariffs have decreased as have the profit margins, and the routing structure has increased. The number of traded licences as well as values has dropped significantly. The trucking service in low-density areas has not deteriorated (Bailey, 1985; OECD, 1985).

The *Staggers Act* of 1980 brought greater tariff flexibility. The lower boundaries for tariffs disappeared so that the railways could gain back customers from the trucking industry. On the other hand, large shippers, which depended on the railways (e.g. coal, iron and other mass products) came under protection by the introduction of upper-tariff boundaries. At the same time, the 'common carrier principle' and subsequent obligations to serve disappeared. As a consequence of this deregulation, the frequency of freight trains has decreased as well as the number of personnel, whereas the length of the trains has increased. Railway companies have become active in offering transportation services on other modes (waterways, roads). These beneficial effects of the Staggers Act could be observed, although the access to the railways of other companies is no longer guaranteed (Boyer, 1987: p. 280).

Lessons for The European Transportation Sector

A tendency towards liberalization of the European transportation markets currently exists. Nevertheless, there are already voices that are critical, pointing out that the deregulation may eventually lead to cartelization and subsequently excessive prices (Sørensen, 1988: S. 44f.). The recent wave of concentration in the USA airline market has raised the demand for reregulation.

We have argued that the market for transportation services is contestable, provided free and equal access exists for all (active and potential) participants to the infrastructure. The USA experience already demonstrates that the administrative, long-run allocation of scarce landing rights may significantly restrict the competitiveness of the market for airline services. This procedure in general benefits the incumbent firms at the disadvantage of potential entrants. This is a major source of possibilities for incumbent carriers to extract rents based on local monopoly positions at hub airports. While the incumbent firms own enough landing rights, entrants may be forced to switch to unfavourable landing times or to other airports. This is the reason why incumbent firms may have advantages in building up optimal network structures. Although the network characteristics in the airline market strengthen the effects of asymmetric access to landing rights, it would be wrong to conclude that the supply of airline services via networks themselves already builds an entry barrier.

As long as landing rights cannot be traded freely, incentives exist to get access to scarce landing rights by means of mergers.[21] Thus, for example, the merger between Eastern Airlines and New York Air was strongly motivated by hoarding of landing rights to obtain a monopoly-like position for flights between Boston and Florida.[22] The solution for obtaining an efficient airline market, therefore, consists in removing the asymmetric access to landing rights and not in the reregulation of the market for airline services.

Another criticism raised is that serious infrastructure shortages may occur if traffic continues to grow, which would then have negative feedback effects on service conditions (Sørensen, 1988: S. 44f.). Such infrastructure problems (e.g. bottlenecks at airports) are also considered a serious shortcoming of deregulation in the USA. So far as deregulation leads to a shortage of airport capacities, the appropriate solution is not to restrict market entry but to increase the price for landing rights so as to allocate existing airport capacities. Moreover, airport capacities of existing airports may be extended and new airports may be built. One should learn in Europe from the experience in the USA, namely, that the liberalization of the transportation markets also requires an equal access to the infrastructure.

The possibility of liberalizing the European transportation markets is without doubt also influenced by pressure from different interest groups. Potential losers on the national level are the incumbent transport firms who are afraid of losing their licence rents. Another problem on the European market is that some countries may lose their 'national flag' status in the airline market, if foreign companies are allowed to enter and public subsidies are no longer granted. Nevertheless, we should hope that the effort in the direction of a common European market by 1992 may lead to an exhaustive liberalization of the European transportation market, and not only to a harmonization of traditional regulations.

Notes

1. In addition, the Commission pleaded for a liberalization of the procurement policy of the national telecommunications administrations as well as for an introduction of European-wide telecommunication standards.
2. The reader is referred to the results of the contestability literature (Baumol and Willig, 1986; Baumol, Panzar and Willig, 1982) as well as Demsetz (1968). It is the concept of competition for a market rather than competition in the market which is important.
3. The recent dynamic theories of monopoly (e.g. Armentano, 1982; Demsetz, 1982; Fisher, 1981) argue that conventional sources of monopoly power, such as economies of scale, do not confer monopoly power. Instead, supply substitutability and entry are the principal competitive constraints on behaviour in allegedly monopolistic markets (Fisher *et al.*, 1983: pp. 20, 25).
4. Local Access and Transport Areas (LATAs) were defined in 1982 during the Antitrust Case between AT & T and the Department of Justice. LATAs are much larger than a local network. The size of a LATA may even cover a whole state (FCC Docket 78–72, phase III, 31 May 1983, p. 12).
5. It is well-known that in a dynamic environment it is more important that competition is a social mechanism by which innovations are stimulated. The competition process can be seen as a 'discovery procedure' (von Hayek, 1968) which dominates the centralized monopolistic process if the purpose is to try out better problem solutions compared to those which have been available in the past.
6. In contrast, the major question is to what extent the distributional objectives could still be fulfilled under competition (see pp. 90–96).
7. 'Only Private Line Service, however, was opened to competition, basic public telephone service (MTS and WATS) remains a telephone monopoly' (FCC Report, 1976: p. 99).
8. For example, electronic private branch exchanges made it possible to route a telephone call automatically either over a private line or a public switched line depending on th available capacities at a given time.
9. United States vs. AT & T Co 552 F. S. . . . 131 D.D.C. 1982, Maryland vs. United States. . . U.S. . . . 51 U.S.L.W. 362& (US 1 March 1983).
10. Third Computer Inquiry, Report and Order, FCC Docket No. 85–229, 1986; p. 252.
11. Second Computer Inquiry, Rules and Regulations, FCC Docket No. 20828, 1980.
12. There still exists the possibility of cross-subsidy between (monopolized) intra-LATA long-distance and local networks.
13. This should not be confused with the requirement that long-distance carriers have to pay the usage-dependent costs of using the local networks. Such necessity is stable and does not create incentives for uneconomic bypass of local networks.
14. A more detailed version of the following proposal can be found in Knieps (1987b) and Blankart and Knieps (1989).
15. Of course, from an efficiency point of view, cost-based tariffs in all subparts of a telecommunications system would be desirable.
16. Another, rather cynical, approach would be to consider the current proposals of the European Commission's Green Paper as a necessary step in an unavoidable dynamic adjustment process. Why should European policy makers be more capable of avoiding the strategy of partial deregulation than their colleagues in the USA and Japan?

98   Günther Knieps

17. See for example *Business Week*, cover story: 'Is Deregulation Working?' 22 December 1986, pp. 48–53.
18. In addition, one could observe obligation to serve and unitary tariffs to guarantee socially desired unitary services (see pp. 93–94).
19. A more detailed explanation can be found, for example, in Windisch (ed.) (1987) and Horn, Knieps, Müller (1988).
20. See Knieps (1987a) and the literature cited therein.
21. The same is still true in the German truck market where access to licences very often can only be acquired by means of buying the whole firm or by mergers.
22. See '*Die Zeit*', No. 24, 28 March 1986, p. 29.

References

Alexander, E. P. (1887), *Railway Practices*, New York.
Armentano, D. T. (1982), *Antitrust and Monopoly, Anatomy of Policy Failure*, John Wiley & Sons, New York.
Bailey, E. E. (1973), *Economic Theory of Regulatory Constraint*, Lexington Books, Lexington, Mass.
Bailey, E. E. (1985), *Economic Deregulation in the United States: Transportation and Communications*, unpublished manuscript.
Bailey, E. E., Graham, D. and Kaplan, D. (1983), *Deregulation the Airlines, An Economic Analysis*, Civil Aeronautics Board, Washington D.C.
Bailey, E. E. and Williams, J. R. (1988), 'Sources of economic rent in the deregulated airline industry', *Journal of Law and Economics*, Vol. 31, pp. 173–202.
Baumol, W. J., J. C. Panzar and R. D. Willig (1982), *Contestable Markets and the Theory of Industry Structure*, Harcourt Brace Javonavich, New York.
Baumol, W. J. and Willig, R. D. (1986), 'Contestability: developments since the book', *Oxford Economic Papers*, 38, pp. 9–36.
Beesly, M. (1981), *Liberalization of the Use of British Telecommunications Network*, London.
Bell Operating Companies (1982), Comments of the Bell System Operating Companies and American Telephone and Telegraph in Response to the Fourth Supplemental Notice of Inquiry and Proposed Rulemaking, CC Documents 78–72, Phase I, Aug. 6.
Blankart, C. B. and G. Knieps (1989), 'Grenzen der Deregulierung, im Telekommunikationsbereich? Die Frage des Netzwettbewerbs', in: H. St. Seidenfus (ed.): *Deregulierung – eine Herausforderung an die Wirtschafts – und Sozialpolitik in der Marktwirtschaft*, Berlin, pp. 149–72.
Boyer, K. D. (1987), 'Privatisierung der Eisenbahnen in den USA und Kanada',' in: R. Windisch (ed.), *Privatisierung natürlicher Monopole im Bereich von Bahn, Post und Telekommunikation*, Tübingen, pp. 245–308.
Clark, J. M. (1923), *Studies in the Economics of Overhead Costs*, University of Chicago Press, Chicago.
Commission of the European Communities (1987), Green Paper on the Development of the Common Market for Telecommunications Services and Equipment, Brüssels.
Demsetz, H. (1968), 'Why regulate utilities?', *Journal of Law and Economics*, Bd. 11, pp. 55–66.
Demsetz, H. (1982), 'Barriers to entry', *American Economic Review*, 72, pp. 47–57.
Demsetz, H. (1982), *Economics, Legal, and Political Dimensions of Competition*, North-Holland Publishing Company, Amsterdam.

Faulhaber, G. R. (1975), 'Cross-Subsidization: pricing in public enterprises', *American Economic Review*, 65, pp. 966–77.
Federal Communications Commission (1976), Docket 20003 Washington.
Fisher, F. M. (1981), 'Stability, disequilibrium awareness, and the perception of new opportunities', *Econometrica*, Vol. 49, No. 2, pp. 279–317.
Fisher, F. M., Mc Gowan, J. J. and Greenwood, J. E. (1983), *Folded, Spindled, and Mutilated, Economic Analysis and USA v. IBM*, MIT Press, Cambridge.
Foreman-Peck, and J. Müller (eds) (1988), *European Telecommunications Organization*, Baden-Baden.
German PTT (1989), *Annual Report – Geschäftsbericht*, Frankfurt.a.m.
Hayek, F. A. von (1945), 'The use of knowledge in society', *American Economic Review*, 35, pp. 519–30.
Hayek, F. A. von (1968), *Der Wettbewerb als Entdeckungsverfahren*, Kieler Vorträge, N. F. 56, Kiel.
Heuermann, A. and K. H. Neumann (1985), *Die Liberalisierung des britischen Telekommunikationsmarktes*, Berlin u.a.
Horn, M., Knieps, G. and Müller, J. (1988), *Die gesamtwirtschaftliche Bedeutung von Deregulierungsmabnahmen in den USA: Schlubfolgerungen für die Bundesrepublik Deutschland*, Nomos Verlag, Baden-Baden.
Interstate Commerce Commission (1984), *The Intercity Bus Industry*, Washington.
Ito, Y. and A. Iwata (1986), *Deregulation and the Change of Telecommunications Market in Japan*, Paper on the Malente Symposium, Max Plank Institute, Hamburg.
Kahn, A. E. (1971), *The Economics of Regulation: Principles and Institution*, John Wiley & Sons Inc., New York.
Kahn, A. E. (1987), *The Future of Local Telephone Service: Technology and Public Policy*, Wharton, Fishman-Davidson Center, D. P. No. 22.
Knieps, G. (1988), 'Reform der Deutschen Bundespost: vom Monopol zum beschränkten Wettvewerb', in: *Orientierungen zur Wirtschafts- und Gesellschaftspolitik*, 37, pp. 18–20.
Knieps, G. (1987a), *Deregulierung im Luftverkehr, Neuere Entwicklungen in der Wettbewerbstheorie und ihre Auswirkungen im Linienverkehr*, J. C. B. Mohr (Siebeck), Tübingen.
Knieps, G. (1985), *Entstaatlichung im Telekommunikationsbereich. Eine theoretische und empirische Analyse der technologischen, ökonomischen und institutionellen Einflubfaktoren*, J. C. B. Mohr (Siebeck), Tübingen.
Knieps, G. (1987b), 'Zur Problematik der internen Subventionierung in öffentlichen Unternehmen', in: *Finanzarchiv*, N. F., Vol. 45, pp. 268–83.
Knieps, G. (1983), 'Is techological revolution a sufficient reason for changing regulations? – the case of telecommunications' in: *Zeitschrift für die gesamten Staatswissenschaften (Journal of Institutional and Theoretical Economics)*, 139, pp. 578–97.
Knieps, G., Müller, J. and Weizsäcker, C. C. von (1981), *Die Rolle des Wettbewerbs im Fernmeldebereich*, Nomos Verlag, Baden-Baden.
Knieps, G., Müller, J. and Weizsäcker, C. C. von (1982), 'Telecommunications policy in West Germany and challenges from technical and market development', *Journal of Economics*, Suppl. 2, pp. 205–22.
Koran, D. and Ogur, J. D. (1983), *Airport Access Problems: Lessons Learned from Slot Regulation by the FAA*, Federal Trade Commission, Washington.
Krakowski (ed.) (1988), *Regulierung in der Bundesrepublik Deutschland*, Verlag Weltarchiv, Hamburg.
Meyer, J.R., Wilson, R.W. and Alan, W. (1980), *The Economics of Competition in the Telecommunications Industry*, Oelschlaeger, Gunn & Hain.
Mohring, H. and Harwitz, M. (1962), *Highway Benefits, An Analytical Framework*, Northwestern University Press.

Müller, J. (1986), *Competition in the British Telecommunications Market: The Impact of Recent Privatization Deregulation Decisions*, Paper on the Malente Symposium, Max Plank Institute, Hamburg.

Müller, J. (1987), 'Liberalisierung des japanischen Fernmeldewesens: Ein mögliches Modell für die Bundesrepublik?', *DIW Wochenbericht* 23/87, pp. 312–17.

Neumann, K. H. (1987), *Die Neuorganisation der Telekommunikation in Japan*, Berlin u.a.

OECD (1985), *Economic Surveys, United States*, Paris.

OECD (ed.) (1987), *Trends of Change in Telecommunications Policy*, North-Holland.

Ozawa, T. (1984), *The Study on Access Charges*, 6th International Congress IDATA: The New Communications Business, 24–6 October, Montpellier.

Sandhäger, H. (1988), 'Praktische Deregulierungs- und Privatisierungsperspektiven für die Bundesrepublik Deutschland', in: O. Vogel (Hrsg.), *Deregulierung und Privatisierung*, Deutscher Instituts-Verlag, Köln, p. 172 ff.

Schulte-Braucks, R. (1986), 'Das "British Telecom"' – Urteil: Eckstein für ein europäisches Fernmelderecht?', *Wirtschaft und Wettbewerb*, 3, pp. 202–15.

Schumpeter, J. (1942), *Capitalism, Socialism, and Democracy*, Harper, New York.

Soltwedel, R. *et al.* (1986), *Deregulierungspotentiale in der Bundesrepublik, Kieler Studien 202*, J. C. B. Mohr (Siebeck), Tübingen.

Sørensen, F. (1988), 'Deregulierung und Privatisierung im Verkehrs- und Nachrichtenwesen – Luftverkehr – Kommission der EG, Brüssel', in: O. Vogel (Hrsg.), *Deregulierung und Privatisierung*, Deutscher Instituts-Verlag, Köln. pp. 38–46.

United States Senate (1984), Hearings before the Subcommittee on Surface Transportation, Oversight of the Bus Regulatory Reform Act of 1982, Washington.

Weizsäcker, C. C. von (1980), 'A welfare analysis of barriers of entry', *Bell Journal of Economics*, Autumn, 11, pp. 399–420.

Weizsäcker, C. C. von (1984), 'Free entry into telecommunications?' in: H. Giersch (Hrsg.), *New Opportunities for Entrepreneurship*, Symposium 1983, Tübingen, pp. 107–28.

Weizsäcker, C. C. von (1987), *The Economics of Value Added Network Services*, Cologne.

Wieland, P. (1985), *Die Entflechtung des amerikanischen Fernmeldemonopols*, Berlin u.a.

Windisch, R. (ed.) (1987), *Privatisierung natürlicher Monopole im Bereich von Bahn, Post und Telekommunikation*, J. C. B. Mohr (Siebeck). Tübingen.

Witte, E. (ed.) (1987), *Neuordnung der Telekommunikation, Bericht der Regierungskommission Fernmeldewesen*, Heidelberg.

4. Comments on Telecommunications Regulatory Reform in the European Community

Herbert Ungerer

Introduction

The previous chapter by *G. Knieps* on deregulation of telecommunications in Europe offers a thorough review of a number of important issues in current European telecommunications. His chapter lays great emphasis on the issue of competition in the provision of the basic network infrastructure.

EC telecommunications policy has emphasized a different aspect: it views telecommunications mainly as a major issue in the general transformation of Europe's economy into a service-based economy. This has led EC telecommunications policy, as set out in the Green Paper on the Development of the Common Market for Telecommunications Services and Equipment, cited by G. Knieps, to emphasize three aspects:

- concentrating on the general economic impact of telecommunications. In a European economy which is shifting from industrial to service-based activities, this means ensuring the full use of telecommunications services for the economy as a whole;
- defining the major objectives of EC telecommunications policy as a function of this concern: liberalization of use of the network; unrestricted connection of terminal equipment to the network; unrestricted provision of services via the network – while accepting national diversity concerning the conditions under which the network infrastructure is itself provided in the Member States of the European Community;
- modifying regulation – or 'deregulating' – essentially with a view to optimizing the role of telecommunications in the wider economy – instead of aiming at the implementation of an abstract economic model for the sector.

Let me go into more detail on these aspects.

The Service Economy and The 1992 Objective

The reform of the Treaty of Rome, the so-called Single European Act, means that achieving a Europe-wide market by the end of 1992 is now a legally binding obligation on all twelve EC Member State governments.

The Europe-wide market in 1992 will mean: free movement of people, capital, goods, *and* services throughout Europe.

1992 therefore requires, among the many profound changes implied by these goals, in particular that the common market be fully implemented for what have hitherto been some of the most regulated sectors of the European economy: financial and insurance markets, transport, and tele-communications. Within this broad range of services which represent a large share of the potential for the future growth of the European service economy, telecommunications plays – in a more and more communications-based society – a key enabling role.

Between 1970 and the mid 1980s, the share of employment in the European Community accounted for by market and non-market services rose from 48 per cent to 59 per cent.

While employment in industry has declined over the past decade, services have been the major job creator compensating for losses in industry, though at present unable in Europe – in contrast to developments in the United States – to create enough jobs to prevent an overall increase in unemployment.

Telecommunications have been a crucial factor in the service sector's role as a job creator.

Information and knowledge have become important factors of production. The ultimate beneficiaries of more and better access to information are consumers. If knowledge is to enter continuously into the production and market processes of locally produced goods and services it must be 'transported' via an efficient conduit at low cost and high speed. Last, but not least, it must be packaged in ways which maximize its utility. This is the task of a growing part of the services industry, whose productivity, again, depends on the size of the market.

Services already account for nearly two-thirds of Community output and employment. By the year 2,000, two-thirds of the wealth of advanced countries will be generated in strongly information-related activities.

Telecommunications will thus be a determining factor for Europe's future role in the world's expanding services market.

Free circulation of services in the European Community will mean more trade. Trade in services means more freedom of choice for the user. More freedom of choice for the user requires the liberalization of structures.

1992 therefore will inevitably expose telecommunications to a new competitive environment – let me call this 'competition for excellence'; and 1992 will introduce new demands for a reorganization of telecommunications. Europe's industrial and service enterprises will depend critically on the Europe-wide telecommunications infrastructure for their international operations in the coming Europe-wide market.

The combined effect of technological change and of 1992 gives the movement towards the reform of the telecommunications sector stability across Europe.

The Basic Principles of European Telecommunications Reform

A broad consensus has developed on the fundamental principles determining the course of the reforms in Europe. In this process the Green Paper has served Europe-wide as a yardstick.

The details of the ten basic regulatory positions put forward in the Green Paper are shown in Figure 4.1. Without going into detail, let me concentrate on three areas which are determining action at EC level, but which are also at the heart of the national reform debate in all European countries:

- *The trend to liberalization*

    Europe-wide – and world-wide – all countries are confronted with the fact that the enormous new technological possibilities offer a broad range of new activities for *both* the users *and* the public telecommunications operators, *both* in the terminal *and* in the services field.

    In regulatory terms, a clear answer must now be given, everywhere, saying whether those involved should be restricted in the use of this vast new potential, or whether they should be allowed to make full use of it for economic and social growth.

    In accordance with the general trend in the European debate, the Green Paper takes a very clear position on this basic issue. In favour of liberalization – EC-wide – of the market for terminal equipment and far-reaching liberalization of the telecommunications services market, in particular for all value-added services.

- *Participation in the new markets*

    The new potential for users *and* public telecommunications operators demands a clear position, as regards access to the new market.

    The Green Paper clearly adopts the position that *both* users *and* PTOs – Telecommunications Administrations – should be able to participate fully in the new growth markets without undue restrictions. The Green Paper aims at the 'creating more freedom of action for the European user, for European industry, *and* for the European Telecommunications Administrations'. Europe has clearly voted against any 'line of business' restrictions. I believed that an important lesson has been learnt here from the United States' deregulation experience of the past years.

    However, a number of charges are implied by the acceptance of this position in the whole Community:

    - regulatory and operational functions must be separated in a more competition-orientated environment. Telecommunications Administrations cannot at the same time be player and referee;
    - there must be clear rules for Open Network Provision. ONP – the European counterpart to the American ONA. Conditions for access to the public network and the most basic public services must be defined in a transparent and open way;

Figure 4.1   **The Green Paper's proposed positions**

The general objective of the positions set out is the development in the Community of a strong telecommunications infrastructure and of efficient services: providing the European user with a broad variety of telecommunications services on the most favourable terms, ensuring coherence of development between Member States, and creating an open competitive environment, taking full account of the dynamic technological developments underway.

A) Acceptance of continued exclusive provision or special rights for the Telecommunications Administrations regarding provision and operation of the network infrastructure. Where a Member State choses a more liberal regime, either for the whole or parts of the network, the short and long term integrity of the general network infrastructure should be safeguarded.

Closely monitored competitive offering of two-way satellite communications systems will need further analysis. It should be allowed on a case-by-case basis, where this is necessary to develop Europe-wide services and where impact on the financial viability of the main provider(s) is not substantial. Common understanding and definition regarding infrastructure provision should be worked out under E) below.

B) Acceptance of continued exclusive provision or special rights for the Telecommunications Administrations regarding provision of a limited number of basic services, where exclusive provision is considered essential at this stage for safeguarding public service goals. Exclusive provision

must be narrowly construed and be subject to review within given time intervals, taking account of technological development and particularly the evolution towards a digital infrastructure. 'Reserved services' may not be defined so as to extend a Telecommunications Administration service monopoly in a way inconsistent with the Treaty. Currently, given general understanding in the Community, voice telephone service seems to be the only obvious candidate.

C) Free (unrestricted) provision of all other services ('competitive services', including in particular 'value-added services') within Member States and between Member States (in competition with the Telecommunications Administrations) for own use, shared use, or provision to third parties, subject to the conditions for use of the network infrastructure to be defined under E).

D) Strict requirements regarding standards for the network infrastructure and services provided by the Telecommunications Administrations or service providers of comparable importance, in order to maintain or create Community-wide interoperability. These requirements must build in particular on Directives 83/189/EEC and 86/361/EEC, Decision 86/95/EEC and Recommendation 86/659/EEC. Member States and the Community should ensure and promote provision by the Telecommunications Administrations of efficient Europe-wide and worldwide communications, in particular regarding those services (be they reserved or competitive)

Figure 4.1 continued

recommended for Community-wide provision, such as according to Recommendation 86/659/EEC.

E) Clear definition by Community Directive of general require- ments imposed by Telecommunications Administrations on providers of competitive services for use of the network, including definitions regarding network infrastructure provision. This must include clear interconnect and access obligations by Telecommunications Administrations for trans-frontier service providers in order to prevent Treaty infringements. Consensus must be achieved on standards, frequencies, and tariff principles, in order to agree on the general conditions imposed for service provision on the competitive sector. Details of this Directive on Open Network Provision (O N P) should be prepared in consultation with the Member States, the Telecommunications Administrations and the other parties concerned, in the framework of the Senior Officials Group on Telecommunications (SOG-T).

F) Free (unrestricted) provision of terminal equipment within Member States and between Member States (in competition with Telecommunications Administrations), subject to type approval as compatible with Treaty obligations and existing Directives. Provision of the first (conventional) telephone set could be excluded from unrestricted provision on a temporary basis. Receive Only Earth Stations (ROES) for satellite down-links should be assimilated with terminal equipment and be subject to type approval only.

G) Separation of regulatory and operational activities of Tele-communications Administrations. Regulatory activities concern in particular licensing, control of type approval and interface specifications, allocations of frequencies, and general sur-veillance of network usage conditions;

H) Strict continuous review of operational (commercial) activities of Telecommunications Admin-istrations according to Articles 85, 86 and 90, EEC Treaty. This applies in particular to practices of cross-subsidization of activities in the competitive services sector and of activities in manufacturing;

I) Strict continuous review of all private providers in the newly opened sectors according to Articles 85 and 86, in order to avoid the abuse of dominant positions;

J) Full application of the Com-munity's common commercial policy to telecommunications. Notification by Telecommuni-cations Administrations under Regulation 17/62 of all ar-rangements between them or with Third Countries which may affect competition within the Community. Provision of information to the extent required for the Community, in order to build up a consistent Community position for GATT negotiations and relations with Third Countries.

Figure 4.2 **Timetable for implementing the Green Paper**

1 Rapid full opening of the terminal equipment market to competition by 31 December 1990.

2 Progressive opening of the telecommunications services market to competition from 1989 onwards, with all services other than voice, telex and data communications to be opened by 31 December 1989. This should concern in particular all value-added services. Special consideration should apply to telex and packet- and circuit-switched data services.

3 Full opening of receive-only antennas as long as they are not connected to the public network, by 31 December 1989.

4 Progressive implementation of the general principle that tariffs should follow overall cost-trends. A review of the situation achieved by 1 January 1992 was announced.

5 Clear separation of regulatory and operational activities.

6 Definition of Open Network Provision (ONP). This was initially to cover access to leased lines, public data networks, and ISDN. Directives to Council to be submitted according to progress of definition work.

7 Establishment of the European Telecommunications Standards Institute.

8 Full mutual recognition of type approval for terminal equipment.

9 Introduction – where this does not yet apply – of value-added tax to telecommunications, by 1 January 1990 at the latest.

10 Guidelines for the application of competition rules to the telecommunications sector, in order to ensure fair market conditions for all market participants.

11 Opening of the procurement of Telecommunications Administrations.

• tariffs must follow overall cost trends, they must be cost-oriented.

• *Organizational change*
All Member States accept that the organization of the Telecommunications Administrations needs to be adapted to the new competitive environment. The Green Paper accepted that, within the framework of the EC Treaty, this major issue in the national debates must be largely a national responsibility. The 'Green Paper proposals concentrate on priority issues which must be resolved at Community level for all Member States'. They leave out 'questions which are important but fall to the national level, such as which status – private or public – is best suited to facing the developing competitive market, and related questions of finance, organization and employment relations'.

This is also true for the issue of network competition which is left to the national level in the Green Paper. The Green Paper accepts the continuation of exclusive rights for the provision of the basic network infrastructure, and the provision of telephone (voice) for the general public.

It also states that a number of infrastructures/services adjacent to the main network infrastructure need special consideration. This concerns in particular satellite communications, mobile radio communications and cable-TV networks. Out of these, satellite communications have been singled out as an area on which a common position must most urgently be reached.

● *Safe-guarding the integrity of the network*
However, the long-term convergence and integrity of the network must be safeguarded – an objective strongly endorsed by the EC Council of Ministers in its Resolution of 30 June. The promotion of a strong Europe-wide network infrastructure, integrating fully also the peripheral regions of the European Community, has been a major goal of EC telecommunications policy since 1984. This goal is at the heart of our initiatives and measures in favour of:

● the co-ordinated introduction of ISDN;
● the measures to develop the new Europe-wide digital mobile system;
● the promotion of a strong European standards system in telecommunications;
● the strengthening of Europe's technology capability in the area, with the RACE programme, focused on Integrated Broadband Communications, with a total contribution from the Community budget of 550 million ECUs up to 1991 (1 ECU = approximately 1 US$).
● the promotion of telecommunications investment in the peripheral regions of the Community, with the STAR programme, financed from the EC's European Regional Development Fund with a total contribution of 780 million ECUs up to 1991 and a roughly equivalent contribution from the countries concerned: Italy, Spain, Portugal, Greece, Ireland, United Kingdom, France.

These general principles sum up the EC's telecommunications policy. Figure 4.2 shows the timetable for implementing the liberalization programme of the Green Paper, as announced in February 1988. Without examining every point, I would just note that all the EC measures announced in February 1988 have now been initiated or will soon be proposed for political decision.

Future Issues

This means that the process is well underway but it also means that a critical period of decision-making is ahead:

● a major issue, at EC level, will be without doubt the discussion of the approach to the common market on telecommunications services;
● another will be the opening of telecommunications equipment markets, i.e. the procurement of Telecommunications Administrations;
● the discussion on the full mutual recognition of type approval for terminal equipment will soon reach a critical stage;
● the reshaping of the European standards system will have to prove itself in real operations;
● as the sky above the equator starts to fill with European satellites, the issue of the future development of satellite communications in Europe can no longer be dodged.

Progress at Community level, and in national debates and reform projects in EC Member States, is encouraging. But a number of signposts will have to be carefully heeded if the new Europe-wide momentum is to be strengthened and to be explained to the general European public.

First, we will have to show that high-quality public service is compatible with a more competitive environment. The European value of public service must be safeguarded along with a European response to the need for more competition and flexibility in both services and equipment.

Second, there must not be and cannot be what has been called 'social dumping'.

The creation of the Europe-wide market by 1992 must maintain – and develop – the social achievements obtained in the EC Member States individually. Rights of employees and requirements of employers mut be combined with the new commercial strategies to form a harmonious global strategy.

Third, Community solidarity with regard to the major international questions in telecommunications. The EC Council has called for common positions on international telecommunications questions, in a world market which is shaken by the deregulation of the major telecommunications markets.

The preparatory work for the ITU's World Administrative Telegraph and Telephone Conference – the WATT-C – has shown that the working out of common positions can be a difficult process.

A further test case will be the treatment of telecommunications services in the current GATT-round. Trade relations with the United States in this area will command constant attention. The global trade deficit of the Community with Japan in telecommunications equipment remains at dangerous levels, demonstrating an unsound imbalance in the opening of markets. To give but one example, imports of facsimile terminals into the Community from Japan stood at 267 million ECU in the year to June 1988 – up 88 per cent on the previous year.

The whole trade area will require careful attention. While the Community continued to enjoy an overall surplus of 1,029 million ECU in its 1987 telecommunications equipment trade, this picture was flawed by deficits of 944 million ECU with Japan and 494 million ECU with the US. European consensus on the liberalization programme would be difficult to maintain if imbalances in trade were to steer the European market into sustained and destabilizing trade deficits.

Some General Conclusions

The agenda for the future is thus packed – and will sometimes prove difficult. Let me add here some general conclusions on telecommunications regulation as they result from the EC's telecommunications programme:

- the EC liberalization programme is founded on the firm belief that the future development of the telecommunications sector and the full use of its economic potential must be based on the interaction of public and private investment – which can take place most effectively in a free market environment;

- deregulation of the telecommunications sector cannot mean the abolition of all rules, but must involve the establishment of reasonable regulation in the best way suited to guaranteeing the future working of an open marketplace for all market participants. Future regulation must conform to certain basic principles; it must be based on objective criteria; it must be transparent; it must guarantee equality of access and non-discrimination;

- regulation in sectors as complex as telecommunications must guarantee stability, in order to allow investment to take place. It must correspond to market trends. It must be based on a realistic assessment of what is politically feasible;

- given the importance and wide ramifications, regulatory changes in telecommunications can only be introduced progressively. Time must be allowed for present structures to adjust. Stability of regulation means that it must be based on a broad consensus of all socio-economic groups: a stable regulatory approach must unite sound economic principles *and* social dynamics.

5. Deregulation of the Telecommunications Sector: A Movement in Line with Recent Technological Advances

P. Koebel

Since the end of the 1970s deregulation of telecommunications has been a very topical subject. At first confined to the United States, the movement spread to Great Britain in the middle of the 1980s and then on to most other European countries. Large-scale work has been started since then in relation to the possibility of introducing new regulatory measures, and massive restructurings of markets have taken place. Attempting a synthesis of this work would be a difficult task, and assessing past experiences would be premature, all the more so since some of the certitudes one could have upheld three or four years ago seem to be far less well-founded in 1988.

This chapter is less ambitious. It sets out to give an interpretation of current regulatory developments, the main theme being technological progress. It is written around the idea that although they come up against all kinds of obstacles, regulatory developments in the telecommunications sector, more than in any other sector of the economy, derive naturally from recent technological advances. This primacy of the technological variable appears under two complementary aspects:

- firstly, it classically affects the economic parameters of supply and the conditions in which demand is brought in to play, and it modifies the behaviour of the actors in a process where the stake is the sharing out of the added value produced by the sector;
- secondly, it leads the authorities to seek to define a new organizational framework: not only must the telecommunications market be optimized, but also the entire economy, as an economy of services in which the main part of productivity gains potentially resides in the processing and transport of information.

Seeking new regulation methods constitutes a long-term task which is not without risks; some of the major difficulties in this quest will accordingly be mentioned. It can even lead in return to influencing, if not the rate, then at least the forms of technological innovation.

The American and British experiences are particularly representative of these mechanisms. The case of France also highlights the essential role of technological progress: but, in contrast, although the French telephone plan – implemented fifteen years ago in order to bring the backward French network up to date – contributed to building a modern, high-performance network, it has, however, checked the movement leading to massive regulatory developments.

The final part of this chapter refers to scenarios and risks both at the national and European level. Since regulatory developments in this sector are governed by an identical, predominant variable in all European countries, they should lead to homogeneous organizational frameworks more easily than in other sectors of the economy; the example of France shows, however, that certain national specificities must be taken into account. Even a project like as the Integrated Services Digital Network (ISDN) is the subject of relatively divergent interpretations in Europe, which makes it all the more crucial to work out long-term common platforms in the telecommunications sector, such as, for example, the 1987 Green Paper of the EEC.

Radical Technical and Economic Transformation of the Telecommunication Sector

It is increasingly clear that one is witnessing the end of the opposition between a compartmentalized telecommunications world and the outside world, resulting from unyielding technical and economic logic; the traditional structure of the telecommunications market – supply of all telecommunications services by monopoly – is being called into question by technological evolution.

Technological Progress and Market Structures

The techniques implemented in the telecommunications sector have undergone a real revolution in recent years. Let us recall that it is mainly a matter of digitalization and emergence of high capacity transmission systems, which allow a very significant fall in the marginal cost of transmission and create a clear convergence of switching and information processing techniques. These technological evolutions clearly show that the telecommunications network is no longer homogeneous. Two different functions appear: the information transportation function and the processing function of this information performed within the network or by the computers located at subscribers.

Interestingly, these two functions have fundamentally opposite economic characteristics. The construction and maintenance of transmission networks have extremely high economies of scale: the expenditure necessary to open a transmission link is hardly dependent on the capacity offered, due to the size of the fixed costs. In contrast, the production of the 'routing' function, formed by all switching exchanges and the logical relations between them, does not enjoy economies of scale: the cost is approximately proportional to the traffic conveyed and it grows more than proportionally to the number of network subscribers.

Consequently, it is increasingly clear that the transmission network is a public good and theoretically cannot be provided – on account of the very great economies of scale – except by a monopoly regulated by the authorities or by potential competition. It seems logical, on the contrary, that routing networks have to be built and sold by competing businesses: switching exchanges and the corresponding routing networks become differenciated (by technique or by levels of service for example) in order to adapt to professional demand. Accordingly, the 'Transpac' network in France – the first large-scale value added network in Europe – possesses its own switching and its own routing, whereas its information transits through the general telephone network.

These characteristics are not easy to demonstrate quantitatively. For instance, since the two functions, transmission and routing, cannot be separated and must be analyzed simultaneously, econometric analysis of the costs of telecommunications networks leads to unutilizable results: the economies of scale of one of the functions are counterbalanced by the diseconomies of the other. However, they ae now widely accepted, in the United States as in Europe.

On the basis of this fundamental observation – the existence of two different functions within telecommunications – one can form an initial idea of the conflicts arising from technical developments in the telecommunications sector.

For example, the above rather theoretical analysis very rapidly became concretized by the reduction of technological barriers to market entry: not only does a given part of the market prove to be of a 'competing nature' as seen, but, in addition, potential competition to the monopoly (public or private) has the means to develop. This element was fundamental in the process which led to the disvestiture of AT & T in the United States in 1984.

In other respects, the question very soon arose as to where the synergies are located in relation to the supply of the new value added telecommunication services: are they located with network operators or with data processing equipment manufacturers? The rapid launching of integrated networks (ISDN, for instance), which are supposed to have very high economies of scale thanks to digitalization, and which apparently increase the links between transmission and routing, can be considered as one of the answers given by network operators to this question.

Technological Progress and Demand

Not only have the characteristics of supply changed; technological progress also plays a decisive role in the sphere of demand.

As seen, the rapid developments of generations of basic equipment lead to a decline in technological barriers to entry or their almost total disappearance, and to the entry of firms which are gradually appearing as a credible alternative to the established monopoly.

Simultaneously, telecommunications occupy an increasingly large place in the intermediate consumptions of firms – in particular by the development of private networks – which, quite naturally, seek the best quality and the most innovative products. Are the traditional operators and the traditional regulatory frameworks able to answer these demands?

For instance, two main problems appear with regard to prices. Firstly, hardware and software developments have led to a considerable fall in costs; however, it is becoming clear for professional users that this fall is not at all reflected in the prices charged by traditional public operators. This impression was confirmed in Europe following the first deregulations in Great Britain and the United States; and voices are, of course, rising against this situation.

Secondly, economic distortions resulting from the traditional tariff structure are gradually appearing. One must not, of course, forget that the public monopolies in Europe have traditionally paid more attention to residential users than to professional ones, and have continued to do so in this recent period. This is particularly true in France, for technical, economic and political reasons at one and the same time. As the outset, network externalities justified a policy with a bias for households: one can mention the cross-subsidization between firms and households concerning tariffs, and the development of commercial services better adapted to managing rapid growth of residential lines rather than advising on the choice of equipment or network planning. However, for political reasons, the tariff redistribution which, by reducing the prices charged to households, enabled the network to develop, cannot be completely called into question today. Even in countries which have deregulated the telecommunications sector, the rebalancing of tariffs comes up against the unwillingness of the authorities who fear the reactions of residential users to a considerable increase in the subscription amount. In the United States, for example, Congress and the local regulation agencies for a long time successfully opposed the FCC (Federal Communications Commission) projects which set out to adjust prices to costs, though this is necessary, all the same, in a competitive environment.

It is not only the prices which create problems to be solved. The commercial organization of the traditional operators is not necessarily adapted to professional demand: for instance, the structures in place can obstruct real commercial contracts, medium-term commitments, levels of service, and so on.

This situation explains a dual behaviour of firms. In a first stage, they exert pressure on the authorities to relax the monopoly policy with more or less success; in a second stage, they may draw the conclusion that it is preferable to depend as little as possible on an infrastructure managed in terms of objectives going far beyond the telecommunications framework. The development of private networks then constitutes a pertinent answer for firms, since they thereby escape unchosen and unpredictable technical solutions. For a sizeable part of their traffic (internal traffic between establishments), they furthermore avoid financing the transfer of revenue towards residential users: these are also the reasons why in the United States important clients 'bypass' the local networks.

The Regulatory Consequences

It would be naive to believe that the primacy of economic considerations – via technology – is naturally going to lead to progressive changes of the regulatory framework. Although technical advances naturally challenge the telecommunications monopoly, this development is at varying stages in different countries, since it encounters various obstacles – economic, fiscal, corporatist, institutional, or even constitutional as in the Federal Republic of Germany. Nevertheless, such advances have played an essential role in the course of events leading to the Anglo-Saxon experiences and in the management of these experiences, but also in the resistance arising in other countries.

The American and British Experiences

THE PREMISES

There is no question here of describing the beginnings of the deregulation movement in the United States (see the chapters by Breyer and Crandall in this volume). It should nevertheless be observed that although the question has become a media topic only during the past ten years or so, with a final phase widely dominated by anti-trust considerations, the process originated neither in the 1980s or in the 1970s. The history of the telephone in the United States, punctuated by a series of key decisions (1879, 1894, 1907, 1934, 1956, 1968), shows that the tension between monopoly and competition is far older than one would be led to believe by the most recent spectacular event; namely, the judicial decision to divest AT & T, the largest firm in the world at the time, which became effective on 1 January 1984. In each period, the process has been more or less the same: technological innovation, potential then effective competition, growth of supply and demand, and then, finally, arbitration by the authorities. This arbitration has mainly been applied in favour of monopoly except, of course, in the most recent period.

The case of Great Britain is somewhat different in so far as there was no history of the pressure of demand and potential competition playing a decisive role. At the beginning of the 1980s it was decided to rapidly carry out considerable restructurings in the telecommunications sector, this choice being dictated mainly by political considerations. There was, however, the additional conviction that better efficiency of telecommunications services – at the time the performances of the British operator were very mediocre – would have positive repercussions on the entire economy and in particular on services, traditionally a strong point in Great Britain. This was a decisive point, which can also be observed in the United States, and which, a posteriori, justifies the interest of the authorities, which goes far beyond the weight of the telecommunications sector in the GDP: technological progress should lead to potential productivity gains, which mainly reside in the processing and circulation of information. As is known, taking account of all the constraints has led to a policy based mainly on two lines: privatization of the former public monopoly on the one hand, and relaxation of entry conditions, on the other hand. The second line is followed in a prudent manner since only one competitor, Mercury has been authorized, for a transitional period, to build and manage network infrastructures.

THE DIFFICULTIES ENCOUNTERED

In all its strictness, deregulating means substituting market mechanisms for administrative coordination, which can mainly be seen in the setting of prices and the structure of supply. From this point of view it is clear that deregulation has not gone very far; the regulatory burden has only slightly diminished in Great Britain and the United States. If, indeed, part of the telecommunications sector has been given over to competition and requires less administrative intervention, the relations between the competitive part and the part under monopoly remain to be regulated. Furthermore, in the case of privatization, an efficient supervisory authority must be set up for private business, which is no easy matter. In other words, managing a new equilibrium in the market and solving problems linked with new forms of regulation are not easy tasks.

- On the first point, and referring back to the opposition between the transmission and switching functions mentioned in the previous section, it is clear that neither the United States nor Great Britain followed the economic logic of their policy to its conclusion. These countries deregulated the routing networks and protected the local transmission monopoly (distribution) but they neglected to take account of the fact that the long-distance transmission network was also a public good and was to be supplied only by a monopoly; whence the difficulties met by the new competitors of the established operators, such as MCI in the United States, or Mercury in Great Britain, which where not large enough to fully benefit from the transmission network economies of scale. These difficulties only increased, moreover, as the authorities allowed the rates of the dominating firm (AT & T or British Telecom) to draw closer to production costs. Furthermore, the limits fixed for the activities of BOC (Bell Operating Companies) seem difficult to sustain in the long-term: in particular they cannot enter either the long-distance or international market, or the value added services market, and therefore cannot benefit from economies of scale. These rules were enacted for fear of unfair competition on behalf of the BOCs which could have subsidized in a hidden manner the services provided in a competitive market by excessive tariffing of the products protected by the monopoly.

- On the second point, Great Britain rediscovered the difficulties experienced in the United States for many years. It is to be recalled that AT & T enjoyed a legal monopoly and was regulated (particularly on the tariff level) by the FCC (Federal Communications Commission) and by the local agencies in each state. This means of control, based in particular on monitoring the profitability rate, was to a large extent inefficient, and was criticized by most economists: it could not be considered as a reliable guarantee of the fact that the operator was managed correctly. Great Britain believed it had freed itself of these difficulties by adopting a price control system of the services under monopoly, called RPI – x per cent; this system is nevertheless highly criticized today, particularly on the grounds of disadvantages of the same order as the means of control in force in the United States. Therefore, OFTEL – the British regulatory watchdog – is currently reviewing British Telecom's whole pricing structure, and a detailed report proposing, notably, a 'price cap' system on leased lines is expected by the end of the year.

Finally, and it is not one of the lesser problems met by countries which have modified their organizational framework, the number of bodies intervening in the regulation process is increasing. This situation leads to great contradictions sometimes in the coherence of decisions, and it is becoming ever more urgent to define the roles played by each of the authorities in charge of the sector.

NON-NEGLIGIBLE INFLUENCE ON TECHNOLOGICAL PROGRESS

Regulatory measures have striven to adapt to the new economic characteristics of the market, and in doing so they have undeniably stimulated supply and technological innovation in return. But this interaction between technology and regulation is stronger than it appears, particularly when the phenomenon of technical standardization is taken into account.

The concern for standardization has existed since the first years of the telephone – the existing various networks had to be interconnected. Although the authorities intervened in the standardization process in the past, it was probably unnecessary intervention: many sectors in the economy have managed to standardize themselves, in particular via their professional federations, without public arbitration. The sense and the nature of this intervention have, however, changed in the recent past.

Firstly, there has been a growing desire to protect not only the consumer, but also the manufacturer upstream who is in a better position when the standards he uses are widely adopted.

Secondly, and above all, on account of the difficulty in managing a telecommunications sector split de facto into two parts manifesting distinct economic characteristics but with vague boundaries, technical development has been modulated, due to the risks of unfair competition, as it were, in terms of the specific constraints of the regulators.

In the case of the United States, the first stage in this process consisted in laying the principle of a separation between the telecommunications sector and the data processing sector (Computer Inquiry I, 1971). Then Computer Inquiry II in 1980 drew a distinction between 'basic' and 'value added' telecommunications services, and the subsidiarization of certain activities was proposed. Finally, Computer Inquiry III takes account in a fundamental manner of the technical dimension with Open Network Architecture (ONA), in which the regulators propose to orientate the structuring of networks and the distribution of added value created by these networks. These networks are, in fact, to be reduced into individual components, which will be the subject of individualized supply and will be submitted to regulated rate-setting. The FCC drafters insist that it is technological progress and economic analysis of markets which quite naturally lead to this policy, which stands apart from the previous one by the concern to:

- make users benefit from greater technical and economic efficiency enabled by integration of these new services in the network;
- and at the same time, maintain the conditions of fair competitive offer by offering the suppliers of the new services, in competition with the network operators, the same technical and economic possibilities as the operators themselves.

In fact, these new regulatory provisions still remain to be implemented concretely; the private sector submitted the ONA plans only at the beginning of 1988. The American situation is neither an exemplary theoretical model nor a pathway determined in advance in an inescapable manner; in its Green Paper, the EEC however proposed to define a set of conditions which undeniably proceed from the same premises.

The Case of France

Two additional parameters are to be taken into account concerning the other countries of Europe: on the one hand, as seen, the direct or indirect pressures of countries which have already made institutional modifications (price of international connections, existence of multi-national operators, etc.), and on the other hand the coherence constraint at European level. It is important to bear in mind that each country has its own industrial policy traditions, and a given industrial structure which influences its choice. In France, it is paradoxically the existence of a modern network which explains to a large extent the policy adopted in the field of regulatory developments.

LATE AWARENESS

In France, nearly all telecommunication services are run by France Telecom, a public operator placed under the control of the French State. The public monopoly has played a key role in the general development of telecommunications in France, the quality of the service and technological innovation; however, certain perverse effects of the tight interweaving between the management constraints of business and the constraints of public monopoly are manifest in France as elsewhere:

- excessive cross subsidization between types of services and categories of users;
- tax levies and correlative rate increases;
- unsuitable status of the operator in a changing environment.

These distortions were, however, recognized only at a late stage in France: to understand this, one must go back a few decades.

Historically, after a first phase of satisfactory development, the French tele-communications fell considerably behind, both with regard to the number of subscriptions and the quality of phone calls. For reasons linked with certain inefficiencies in the management, lack of funds and persistence of the idea that the telephone is a luxury good, it took a very long time to arrive at a mass diffusion phase of the telephone service. When 'remedial telephone plan' was launched at the beginning of the 1970s, the network had fewer than five million subscribers: in other words, three to four times less than countries of a comparable size. Recourse to loans and leasing, after decades of self-financing, finally led to rapid growth and the lost time was almost made up by the beginning of the 1980s.

The development of French telecommunications has thus been character-ized by interventions by the authorities, and correspondingly, by a failure to take account of demand, which has never played a driving role. But the late recovery has had two notable consequences.

Firstly, radical improvement of the management methods of the Dir-ectorate- General for Telecommunications (now France Telecom) faced with a challenge of this order, and the installation on a large scale of digital equip-ment have led to remarkable productivity ratios, notably in comparison with those of British Telecom; the pressures for structural reforms were thus quite naturally weaker in France than in Great Britain.

Secondly, France today has the most modern telecommunications network in the world, as regards both switching and transmission; in particular the digitalization rate is far higher than that of the American BOCs or British Telecom. This technological advance has enabled a policy of big medium or long-term projects (videotex, satellite Telecom 1, electronic directory, etc.); its effect has been to reverse the impact of the technological argument – the public monopoly has managed to master technological innovation – and it has perhaps also hidden cases where demand is not totally satisfied (radiotelephony, in particular).

It has therefore not been a major concern to challenge the institutional framework, in so far as long-term efficiency was the yardstick; the accent was placed on the necessary homogeneity of networks, coordination of large national projects, concentration on the R & D effort and a critical financial size.

RECENT REGULATORY DEVELOPMENTS

It must first of all be observed that the legislative texts regulating the tele-communications sector in France authorized a certain flexibility, since a third party can be authorized by the Ministry of Posts and Telecommunications to supply telecommunications services, as evidenced by the creation of several private law businesses, partially or totally controlled by France Telecom. Furthermore, the marketing of terminal equipment has always been relatively free, and this is worth underlining.

Although it had no immediate consequences on the evolution of the tele-communication sector in France, the law of 30 September 1986 constitutes a turning point in its history, being a first attempt to separate operation and regulation. It transferred part of the regulatory power, held by the Ministry of Posts and Telecommunications (in particular by virtue of article L33 of the PTT Code), to an administrative commission independent in law from the executive power. This commission is about to be replaced by another at the time of writing (September 1988) but the changes under way should mainly concern TV and not telecommunications. At this stage, three main decisions have been taken.

Firstly, deregulation of value added networks (VAN), so that traffic can be sold to third parties on leased telecommunication lines (decree of 24 September 1987). In this decree, VAN networks are characterized by the fact that they are not allowed to transmit vocal signals and the expenses linked with the sole transmission activity must represent a limited share of the turnover (less than 15 per cent). Depending on whether their size (defined as the capacity of all their external accesses) is lower or higher than a fixed threshold, these networks are subject either to a simple declaration system, or an authorization from the Ministry of Post and Telecommunications.

Secondly, deregulation of cable TV networks, since these can now be installed and operated by private investors (Act of 30 September 1986).

Thirdly, deregulation of mobile communications in the fields of public and private radiotelephony, and in the radio messaging sector, both of which are expected to expand rapidly.

Furthermore, concerning the public operator, France Telecom, the value added tax was introduced on 1 November 1987, and important tariff measures have been taken, setting out notably to decrease cross-subsidization: the prices of long-distance and international calls have fallen by 25 to 30 per cent for households and by more than 35 per cent for businesses.

In fact, the change of government on 8 May 1988 revived the idea of a powerful public service, and the idea of changing the French telecommunication administration into a commercial company was dropped. But for the rest, the same line is followed, based on three main ideas:

● move towards cost-based tariffs;
● integration of the French telecommunications policy within a European context;
● separation between operation and regulation of this sector, following the recommendations of the Green Book published by the European Commission.

However, a more complete draft law dealing with all telecommunication services has not been discussed to date.

Conclusion

Although the few points discussed here demonstrate the importance of technological progress – it modifies the economic parameters of supply, creates potential or effective competition, affects the conditions in which demand is brought in to play, and finally challenges the established monopoly and calls into question the regulatory framework – they also reveal an unstable situation in the telecommunication sector. This instability can be found both in countries which have changed their regulatory systems as well as in the others.

In one case, the regulators are faced with a situation of continual transition requiring permanent arbitration between sufficiently flexible rules – to take account of innovation – and minimal stability of these rules – concerning their application duration, for example – so as to grant them an inciting character for the operators and clients. This type of debate is found, for example, in the Open Network Architecture in the United States, and in relation to the price evolution rules (RPI – x per cent) in Great Britain. The main risk of deregulation resides in the complexity of the new rules, a disadvantage which has apparently replaced that of a lack of productivity of the former operators.

In the other, although it is widely recognized that changes in the regulatory structure of the global industry are unavoidable, the question of how far and how fast these changes should occur is proving extremely problematic for the traditional public operators. However, the policy debate is no longer about monopoly versus competition, but rather about who shall have market access, to what degree and by what rules.

The ideological gulf separating the two categories may be narrowing, but it has yet to be bridged. This is perhaps best illustrated by the bilateral deals on international value added network services either agreed upon or under negotiation between the USA, UK and Japan. Thus, one can draw two conclusions from the previous considerations, one centred on national concerns and the other on considerations of a European character.

1 Taking Account of The New Characteristics of The Market and of The Difficulties Met in The Anglo-Saxon Experiences, The Pathway for A Country Such as France or FRG seems narrow

The authorities have many possibilities of intervention within the framework of a more or less elaborate deregulatory process. At the risk of being hasty, these choices can be summarized in three points, concerning tarrifs (move towards costs), regulation, and tasks of the public operator.

According to the previous analysis, economic logic would require the public operators in charge of transmission (and necessarily to be in a position of monopoly) to be distinct from the operator managing routing networks, so as to ensure that competition in this latter market remains fair and to guarantee that public operators do not give themselves more favourable conditions than their competitors. Such a decision in the case of France would be likely to break the dynamism – exceptional for a public service – of an organization which has managed in ten years to make up for considerable lost time in the telephone sphere and to develop successfully new services such as videotex.

However, if the public operators keep their structure, their means and their bargaining power, there are risks of abuse of dominant position because the efficiency of regulation through a public commission is questionable: in the United States, despite wide investigation means, the FCC

(Federal Communications Commission) has never really been able to estimate either the efficiency of the management of AT & T, or the extent of cross-subsidization between the products under monopoly and the products offered in a competitive market.

Thus, between traumatizing disvestiture and control that can be inefficient and lead to an abandonment of responsibilities, the path is tight and narrow. Furthermore, a solution of that type would have a chance of being efficient only if the authorities apply ordinary tax law treatment to the public operators, allow rates to draw closer to costs and reduce transfers between users. In the opposite case, the opening to competition leads to a creaming off of demand and to a deficit of the public operator, while being faced with competition in the few profitable market sectors.

2 Despite the pre-eminence of the technological variable, coordination proves to be essential to make projects of a technical order converge (in particular ISDN) and all the more so the regulatory frameworks in a European perspective

First of all, these perspectives do not take account of the European dimension. Indeed, in the hypothesis in which monopoly is maintained for the infrastructure network, there are no substantial advantages to be expected from a European perspective, in particular if we take the examples of the American BOCs. However, concerning value added services and technical standardization questions, it is clear that the answer is different.

When we wish to refer to the future of telecommunications in Europe, we are of course tempted to deal with the question globally and integrate it into the internal market concept, both from an internal viewpoint (single telecommunications market as part of the global single market, considered as a tool to reach this single market) and from an external viewpoint (creating a comparable force to the United States and Japan in terms of production costs and capacity to impose standardization).

In this context, one could believe that the primacy of technology should lead to similar regulatory solutions almost everywhere in the world, and at least in countries with a comparable level of development. In the great internal market context, it should be easier to achieve homogeneous regulatory situations in the telecommunication sector in the Community countries.

However, at present, the positions adopted in Europe diverge. On one side stand the champions of free market competition, embodied by the United Kingdom; on the other stand the traditional telecommunication administrations which seem to remain more traditional, as in France and in FRG. The Green Paper published in 1987 by the European Commission can therefore be interpreted as an attempt to use the recent technical and economic developments to define ten or so 'positions' which set out to establish a certain convergence between the policies of the Member Countries. More precisely, it defines itself as a common answer to the American demands to set up suppliers of value added services, and it offers comparable conditions to those which will be offered to European suppliers within the framework of the American ONA arrangements.

Given the constraints faced by its drafters, the Green Paper adopts a low profile; it nevertheless strives to cover the entire telecommunications field:

- equipment: opening of public markets, standardization, common approval of terminals;
- regulation: separation between operation and regulation;
- services: opening to competition of services and tariff principles, for the main part.

But many elements are still obscure, such as the difficult question of the interface between providers of services and the monopoly managing the network (Open Network Provision), and the opening of equipment markets to third countries, the harmful effects of which will be felt by European industry well before the fall in costs and prices hoped for with European integration.

However, the action of the European Community is absolutely necessary. In fact, even a question as 'technical' as the introduction of an Integrated Services Digital Network is not approved unanimously among the European states. Two or three options coexist at present, differing mainly in their degree of 'universality': Great Britain considers that it is a matter of one network like another, whereas France and the FRG seem to make it the outcome of a universal network logic. The ISDN is a project offering great potential for the European Community, and looking forward to the year 2000, it does not suffer from dispersion on a European scale. It must, however, be managed in a prudent manner, and not as an ultimate goal, as this would lead the public operators that adopt it to a difficult financial situation in the long term and to an extremely bad position faced with multinational operators at the *dawn* of the great internal market.

References

AIT (1985), Association des ingénieurs des télécommunications, *Des structures nouvelles pour les Télécommunications*, Novembre.

Averch, H., and Johnson L. (1962), 'Behavior of the firm under regulatory constraint', *American Economic Review*, 52, pp. 178–83.

Bailey, E. (1981), 'Contestability and the design of regulatory and anti-trusts policy', *American Economic Review*, 71, pp. 178–83.

Baumol, W. J., Panzar, J. C., and Willig R. D. (1982), *Contestable Markets and the Theory of Industry Structure*, Harcourt Brace Jovanovich, New York.

Beesley, M. (1981), *Liberalization of the Use of the British Telecommunication Network*, Department of Industry, HMSO, London.

Brock G. (1981), *The Telecommunication Industry*: The Dynamics of Market Structure, Harvard University Press, Cambridge.

Brunetière J. de la, and Curien N. (1984), 'Les transferts de révenus induits par la tarification téléphonique entre catégories d'abonnés et entre types d'usage', *Annales des Télécommunications*, 39, pp. 469–89.

Commission des Communautés Européennes (1987), 'Vers une économie européenne dynamique: Livre Vert sur le développement du marché commun des services et équipements des Télécommunications', COM(87), Brussels.

Coustel, J. P. (1986), 'Telecommunications services in France: the regulated monopoly and the challenge of competition', *Telecommunications Policy*, 10 (3), pp. 229–43.

Curien, N. (1986), 'Bilan des études économétriques sur les coûts des télécommunications en Amérique du Nord', communication au séminaire d'économie industrielle, Direction de la Prévision.

Curien, N., and Gensollen, M. (1987), 'De la théorie des structures industrielles à l'économie des réseaux de télécommunication', *Revue Economique*, 38 (2), pp. 521–78.

Curien, N., and Gensollen, M. (1987), 'A functional analysis of the network: a prerequisite for deregulating the telecommunications industry', *Annales des Télécommunications*, 42 (11–12), pp. 629–41.

Dang N'Guyen, G. (1988), 'Scénarios pour le marché de la valeur ajoutée', *Echo des Recherches*, no. 131 (1), pp. 37–44.

Drucker, M. (1984), 'Beyond the Bell break up', *The Public Interest*, 77, pp. 3–27.

Encaoua, D. (1986), 'Réglementation et concurrence, quelques éléments de théorie économique', *Économie et Prévision*, no. 76 (5), pp. 7–46.

Encaoua, D., and Koebel, P. (1987), 'Réglementation et déréglementation des télécommunications: leçons anglo-saxonnes et perspectives d'évolution en France', *Revue Économique*, 38 (2), pp. 475–520.

Egan, B., and Weisman D. (1986), 'The US telecommunication industry in transition', *Telecommunications Policy*, 10 (2), pp. 164–76.

Ergas, H. (1985), 'Regulation, monopoly and competition in the telecommunication infrastructure', OECD, Paris.

Evans, D. S. (1983), 'Breaking Up Bell', Elsevier Science, New York.

Evans, D., and Heckman, J. (1984), 'A test of sub-additivity of the cost function with an application to the Bell system', *American Economic Review*, 74, pp. 615–23.

Huber, P. W. (1987), 'The geodesic network: report on competition in the telephone industry', US Department of Justice.

Irwin, M. (1984), 'The telecommunication industry' in Adams, W., ed., *The Structure of American Industry*, 7th edn, Macmillan, London.

Kay, J. (1984), 'The privatization of British Telecom' in Steel, D., and Heald, D., eds, *Privatizing Public Enterprises*, Royal Institute of Public Administration, London.

Littlechild, S. (1983), *Regulation of British Telecommunication's Profitability*, Department of Industry, HMSO, London.

Loeb, M., and Magat, W. (1979), 'A decentralized method for utility regulation, *Journal of Law and Economics*, 22, pp. 399–404.

Muller, J., *et al.* (1986), *Die Gesamtwirtschaftliche Bedeutung von Deregulierungsmassnahmen in den USA*, Deutsches Institut für Wirtschaftsforschung, Berlin.

Pautrat, C., and Hurez, B. (1986), 'La nouvelle tarification de British Telecom, un jugement, un exemple', DGT-DACT.

Pogorel, G. (1986), 'L'Europe des Télécommunications: un concept pertinent?', communication au séminaire FERE-Plan, Arc et Senan.

Vickers, J., and Yarrow, G. (1985), *Privatization and the Natural Monopolies*, Public Policy Centre, London.

Volle, M. (1986), 'Réseau numérique à intégration de services: arbitrage entre monopole et concurrence', communication au séminaire d'économie industrielle, Direction de la Prévision.

Wenders, J. (1986) 'Throttling competition', *Telecommunications Policy*, 10 (2), pp. 177–80.

Wenders, J. T. (1987), 'On Modifying the MFJ, *Telecommunications Policy*, 11 (3) pp. 243–6.

6. Efficiency and Prices in the European Air Transport Market: Some further Evidence*

Matthias-Wolfgang Stoetzer

1 Introduction

Over the last few years an extensive body of literature on the deregulation of the airline industry has emerged. This is due, of course, to the path-breaking development in the USA resulting in a virtually complete liberalization of the internal air transport market. This deregulation policy marked a turning point for the airline industry which had been dominated by state regulation since 1938.

With reference to the American market, a wide variety of problems have been discussed; for instance, the issues of destructive competition, mergers and the compatibility of competition and safety (Breyer, 1982: p. 29 ff; Chalk, 1987; Knieps, 1987).[1] The experiences and developments in the USA since 1978 also led to a debate at political and scientific levels on a possible deregulation of the air transport market in Europe (Knieps, 1987; Müller, 1983).

Since the situation in the USA may serve as a point of reference, it is possible to identify and compare the consequences of a regulated versus a deregulated air service market. Above all, two aspects deserve further consideration.

Firstly, the internal efficiency of air carriers, and secondly, the external efficiency regarding the consumer, that is the air transport prices he has to pay.

As to the existence of efficiency differences, most of the relevant work is limited to theoretical conclusions. The following study tries to provide some further empirical evidence on this topic and with respect to air transport fares in Europe.

*I would like to thank the participants of the Conference on Regulatory Reform at the European University Institute for helpful comments. The usual caveat applies.

Figure 6.1   The impact of flight stage distance on unit costs for the Airbus A-310
on routes from London

Direct operating costs (in US cents) per seat-kilometer

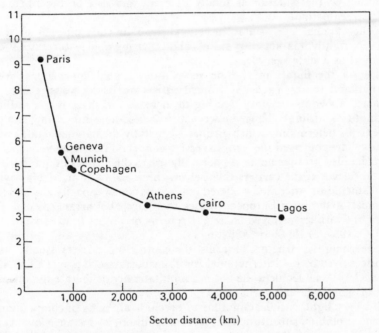

Sector distance (km)

Source: Doganis (1985), S.118.

The remainder of the paper will be organized as follows: section 2 briefly describes the different regulations of air services in Europe and the USA. Section 3 summarizes the main theoretical considerations, suggesting firstly a lack of efficiency and in the second place an increased price level in the European air transport industry. The following section presents an empirical productivity analysis, its results and caveats. Section 5 deals with the analyses of air transport prices. Finally, section 6 contains some concluding remarks.

2   The Regulation of The Air Transport Market in The USA and Europe

By passing the Airline Deregulation Act in 1978, the American Congress decided to deregulate the air service market step by step. As long ago as 1976 the Civil Aeronautics Board (CAB), which was the responsible regulatory agency, took several measures in order to strengthen competition in a market which had been regulated since the thirties.

By 1983 the control of the CAB with regard to market entry and tariffs had been gradually abolished and at the end of 1984 the CAB itself ceased to exist (Kaplan, 1986). As a consequence, since the beginning of the 1980's, prices, quantities and quality in air transport have, in general, been determined competitively (Bailey, Graham and Kaplan, 1985; Ferris, 1984; Eads, 1983).[2]

In Europe the situation is totally different and can be described as a two-step regulation.

At the national level, states, in general, regulate their internal air transport very tightly: market entry, tariffs and other possible features need to be approved by a state agency.

Most of the flights in Europe serve international connections. As to international routes, each government insists on its sovereignty over the air space above its territory, seeking to increase the share in air traffic of its country's airlines. Thus, between the states there are many bilateral agreements determining which airlines – generally the national, state owned airlines – are conferred the right to serve a connection between two airports. More detailed arrangements are normally left to the airlines in question.

At the level of the carriers themselves, these elaborate particular agreements, including prices to be offered and regulation of capacity and services. On most of the intra-European routes there are pool arrangements. This means the airlines involved share the returns or profits from a connection (BEUC, 1985: p. 15; Shaw, 1982: p. 97).

Concerning the structure of tariffs, the contracting carriers usually adopt the prices fixed by the International Air Transport Association (IATA). during the IATA conferences the airlines multilaterally deliberate the prices of air transport for certain tariff zones.

This very tight cartelization aims to preclude all kinds of competition in order to prohibit a substitution of price competition, for instance, by an offer of superior quality. Regulation and collusion of this kind are not limited to Europe, but can also be found on most of the connections to non-European countries (Doganis, 1986: pp. 23–4).

These agreements are only valid for the transportation of passengers and freight by scheduled services. Charter operations are not regulated in this way. Unlike the rights of scheduled flights, non-scheduled traffic allowances have not been regulated by bilateral air service agreements. Some countries have brought charter operations under some form of national control. Such regulations are intended to limit the scope of non-scheduled operations to tourist and holiday markets in order to protect scheduled airlines. But in their area – for example in the Mediterranean tourist market – charter operators are generally unhampered by national controls over route access, capacity or fares.

3 Theoretical Considerations

In the neoclassical theory of the firm, managers are presumed to operate in such a way as to maximize profits accruing to the owners. This is equivalent to a maximization of the present wealth of the firm. The result will be an efficient allocation of the factors of production if the output and input prices are determined by competition and exogenously on the markets. Competition in the air transport market will also ideally lead to prices maximizing social welfare, measured as the sum of consumers' and producers' surplus.[3]

This description seems to be approximately valid for the American airlines, due to the fact that competition regarding prices, quantities and quality of the product and the management performance itself can be assumed to have existed since the beginning of the eighties.

The absence of competition in the scheduled air services in Europe leads to the assumption that there exists a great amount of managerial discretionary behaviour. Theoretical considerations suggest that the result will be, first, an inefficient use of the input resources, capital and labour, and second, that prices will be above their competitive levels.

With regard to inefficiencies, the theory of managerial behaviour puts forward the idea that this discretionary power will lead to economically inefficient decisions for two reasons.[4]

To begin with, the manager, in maximizing his own utility, has an incentive to waste resources. The result will be organizational slack. Several theoretical approaches exist which corroborate this conclusion but differ in detail, for instance, the X-inefficiency hypothesis proposed by Leibenstein, the expense-preference theory of Williamson or Baumol's maximization-of-revenues theory (Scherer, 1980: pp. 34, 464).

Following this line of thought some authors argue that this organizational slack is manifest mainly with regard to the utilization of the input factor labour. The employment of a number of superfluous workers to produce a given output is probable because the reputation and income of managers increase with rising payrolls. Also, conflicts with unions are avoided in this way (Williamson, 1986: pp. 13–18).

Secondly, the European airlines are mostly state-owned. The management of an airline, therefore, may often coincide with the preferences of the owners, who are more or less directly politicians, if it decides to hire more labour than necessary (Hartley and Trengove, 1986: p. 163).

The resulting inefficiency should for this reason be manifest, above all, in a smaller labour productivity of the European airlines.

As to prices, the probable lack of efficiency is a good reason to assume that European air travel tariffs are too high. At the IATA conferences the airlines deliberate and fixe prices which are binding for all the carriers participating. The resulting tariffs are, of course, not those prices the most efficient carrier would like to offer. Instead, they are a compromise, having the features of a cartel-price. Due to the national regulatory agencies not allowing flights at prices below the IATA tariffs on nearly all the intra-European routes, these high cartel-fares can be maintained.[5]

The following sections attempt to give some empirical evidence for both of these questions.

4 Productivity Differences

Previous Studies

The hypothesis to be empirically examined is that the European airlines offering scheduled passenger air services exhibit a smaller output per employee compared to their counterparts in the USA.

In recent years, several studies have been published concerning the efficiency of airlines, but only a few of them deal with a comparison between these two regions.[6]

Forsyth, Hill and Trengove (1986) examine the economic efficiency of seventeen international airlines for the year 1983. As an indicator of efficiency they use the costs per unit of output. The numerator and denominator of this ratio are calculated by aggregating and standardizing the different in– and outputs. Their study shows that the US airlines exhibit a lower cost-intensity than their Europeans counterparts. Unfortunately, however, their sample is limited to 4 US and 8 European carriers.

On the basis of 16 North American and 18 European companies, Barrett compares the labour productivity measured by tonne-kilometre flown per employee. He reveals that in 1982 the labour productivity of the North American airlines was on average 39 per cent above the figure for the European firms (Barrett, 1985).

A very similar result is presented by Ramsden in his study covering the year 1983. He uses different measures of productivity and his sample includes 14 airlines, of which 4 are US and 5 are European air carriers (Ramsden, 1985).

These works are very different as far as the indicators of efficiency used and the methodological approach are concerned. While Forsyth, Hill and Trengove develop a sophisticated method, taking the multiplicity of inputs and outputs into account, Barrett and Ramsden only compute simple averages. A shortcoming of all these efficiency studies is their limited data base. This is confirmed by the fact that often the airline selection process is not motivated.[7] Barrett bases his analysis on thirty-four airlines, but fails to examine whether the differences between the groups are really statistically significant.

So, none of these studies allows a general conclusion concerning the existence of a systematic difference between the USA and Europe.

The Data

In order to come to a reliable conclusion this chapter examines the labour productivity of all airlines reporting the necessary data to the International Civil Aviation Organization (ICAO).

Labour productivity as an indicator of an airline's efficiency can be computed as the tonne-kilometre-performed per employee. The tonne-kilometre-performed will be used as a figure of output instead of the tonne-kilometre-available because an efficient structure of the services offered will lead to a growing number of passengers and freight being transported.

The figure tonnes-performed represents an aggregation of passengers, freight and mail. One passenger is equivalent to 90 kilogrammes in all the ICAO statistics. The tonne-kilometres-performed follow by multiplying this figure by the kilometres flown.

This study relies on data from the year 1983. To choose a more recent period would lead to the problem of having less data available. Also, the efforts of certain European countries to liberalize the air transport market may have had some influence since 1984. Furthermore, the economic situation in Europe and the USA was quite similar in 1983; both industries were facing a time of economic expansion. Finally, this year has the advantage that no exceptional influences like the 1981 air traffic controller strike in the USA are at work.

In order to define the group of scheduled airlines, all firms with a share of more than 20 per cent charter traffic were excluded from the sample. Airlines which specialize in freight transportation were also not taken into consideration because of very different conditions of production between the transportation of passengers and freight. Finally, carriers were dropped from the sample if they used predominantly small aircraft (less than 9 tonnes maximum certificated take-off weight).

After applying these criteria for the year 1983, the data for forty-nine scheduled airlines were available. The figures are provided by the ICAO Statistical Yearbook and the ICAO Statistical Digest (ICAO, 1983; 1984; 1985; 1986).[8]

Out of the scheduled airlines, 21 are European firms and 28 are resident in the USA. The resulting sample comprises all the important national air carriers in Western Europe.[9] With regard to the USA, the sample covers all of the airlines called 'National carriers' according to the classification of the CAB.

The Empirical Results

Table 6.1 provides the main descriptive statistical features of both samples. The average for the European airlines is 97,350 tonne-kilometres (tkm) performed per employee and for the US carriers it is 132,370 tkm on average.

The result of a test as to whether this difference of averages is statistically significant can be found in Table 6.1.

Table 6.1   Comparison of means

X Countries	N	Mean	Std dev	Minimum	Maximum
Europe	21	97.35	37.03	50.00	172.92
USA	28	132.37	61.82	33.52	292.58

Notes
H_O: Variances are equal: $F' = 2.79$ with 27 and 20 DF.
Significance level: 0.021.
H_O: Means are equal: t-value = -2.47.
Significance level: 0.018.

Table 6.2   Regression analysis of the scheduled airlines

PRODUCT = 55.59   −32.80 LAND   +38.38 LENGTH   +2.01 CAPAC

(5.63)**   (−3.49)**   (2.56)*   (2.56)*

F = 23.25   R^{-2} = 0.58   N = 49   Cond: 6.42

White-test: Chisq.-Value: 11.52, Significance level: 0.17

Notes
a   t-statistics in parentheses. Two asterisks show statistical significance at the 99% −,
one asterisk denotes significance at the 95% confidence level, using a two-tailed test.

In order to test the hypothesis of equal variances, a two-sample F-test was used. According to this test the variances in the two groups are different, with a level of significance of 2 per cent. The approximate t-test not assuming equal variances reveals a significant difference of means at the 5 per cent level (two-tailed test). Hence, on the grounds of a sample of forty-nine air carriers it can be concluded that the airlines in the USA work more efficiently than their European counterparts.[10]

But the fact that the labour productivities calculated range from 33.52 to 292.58 thousand tkm in the USA and from 50.00 to 172.92 thousand tkm in Europe indicates that there are other important factors influencing labour productivity. A simple comparison of means, of course, neglects these factors. So the representatives of the European airlines claim that a comparison with the USA is inappropriate, for example due to a different mean of route length (Schoiber, 1987: p. 4). Such a deviation results in a different productivity per employee because the labour intensity per flight is nearly constant with respect to maintenance, flight clearance and crew, but the tonne-kilometres performed are obviously greater on long hauls when compared to short hauls. The same argument holds true concerning the mean capacity of aircraft flown.[11]

For this reason two additional variables are included in the analysis as independent variables: the mean distance per flight of an airline and the mean capacity per aircraft flown.

To carry out a regression analysis the following model is specified: the endogenous variable is the labour productivity of the scheduled airlines, named PRODUCT. By explicitly bringing into the model the exogenous variables − mean distance flown (= LENGTH) and mean aircraft capacity (= CAPAC) − their influence is taken into account. The different regional situations regarding competition is allowed for by using an independent variable: LAND. It is modelled as a dummy variable with a value of one for the European air carriers and zero elsewhere.

The estimation results using weighted least squares are presented irf Table 6.2.[12]

The whole model is highly significant (F = 23.25) and, considering the cross-section nature of the data, a rather large share of the variation of the variable PRODUCT can be explained by the independent variables (R^2 = 0.58). Also, an examination of the assumptions of regression analysis shows a positive result: no interaction effects are present, the White-test points out that the assumption of homoskedasticity cannot be rejected and a condition-number of 6.42 indicates the absence of multicollinearity.[13]

All parameters have the expected sign and are significant at the usual levels. For the problem of efficiency differences the important question is the influence of the variable LAND. This coefficient is negative and highly significant. If different mean distances flown and mean aircraft capacities are eliminated the mean labour productivity of the European scheduled airlines is significantly below the average in the USA. To be more precise, the labour productivity in Europe amounts to 619,200 tkm – about one-third – below the mean of the US carriers (947,200 tkm).[14]

Qualifications

These findings concerning productivity divergences between air carriers can be contested in several ways. The most important methodological short-comings are briefly discussed in this section.

One point of criticism concerns the outputs and inputs chosen.[15] The number of employees was used as an indicator of the labour input. It would be more appropriate, however, to consider a figure taking into account the number of working hours. But the difference between the USA and Europe as to the mean working time per employee during a year is not very large. Therefore, it can hardly be responsible for the productivity gap detected.

More important may be the objection that in comparing productivities it does not make sense to consider a firm with a single product and only one input factor. A more realistic study would have to analyze multi-product firms with several inputs (Sudit and Finger, 1981). First attempts to estimate multi-product production functions in the case of the American airlines can be found in Caves, Christensen and Tretheway (1983) and Good (1985).[16] But these rather sophisticated studies, which often use a translog function to be estimated, are hardly justified in the present context for they must initially assume that all input and output prices are determined competitively, and secondly that air-carrier managers maximize profits. Both assumptions do not apply in the case of the European airlines.

The use of real output indicators is questionable for two reasons. In the first place, the findings depend on the size of the vertical integration of a firm. This will influence the interpretation of the results if a systematic difference exists with respect to the degree of vertical integration between the airlines in the USA and Europe. But there is no evidence in the literature for this to be the case (Doganis, 1986: pp. 73–91; O'Connor, 1985: p. 61).[17]

In the second place, a comparison is only possible under the assumption of homogeneity of products, that is identical quality of transport services. But the mean standard of quality of air services should not be so different to account for the productivity difference proved.[18] [19]

To sum up, the approach adopted should be sufficiently valid with regard to the purpose of this study and in consideration of the similarity of airline operations across countries.[20]

The results confirm the findings of several previous comparative studies. They are further corroborated by the fact that some European airlines, for instance British Airways (Marcom, 1988), have improved their labour productivity substantially during the last years.[21]

5 Air Transport Prices

From the point of view of the consumer, of course, another type of 'external' efficiency – the price charged – is most interesting.

A number of studies have been carried out in order to examine the level of prices of scheduled air services. They adopt rather different approaches to come to a reliable and valid result. One possibility is to compare fares in Europe and the USA (BEUC, 1985; CAA, 1983; IATA, 1984). The cascade-studies, alternatively, derive the cost of a scheduled service from non-scheduled cost data (and vice versa) (CAA, 1977; EC Commission, 1981). Another approach is to analyze the costs that scheduled airlines can control (EC Commission, 1984).

These studies come to different conclusions as to the appropriateness of the European fare level. This lack of conclusiveness is due, above all, to the methodological problems all these works face: comparisons of prices between the USA and Europe depend on the exchange rate chosen. In the same way, the attempt to infer a competitive ticket price from charter operations can

Table 6.3   Analysis of fares[a]

I. *Europe*
TARIF =   73.25 +   0.374 DISTANCE
           $(5.04)^{**}$ $(18.85)^{**}$

$F = 355.27^{**}$ $R^{-2} = 0.86$ $N = 61$

II. *USA*
TARIF =   134.65 + 0.181 DISTANCE
           $(9.76)^{**}$ $(14.37)^{**}$

$F = 206.57^{**}$ $R^{-2} = 0.79$ $N = 57$

Notes
a The figures in parentheses below the parameter estimates denote the respective t-value. Two asterisks indicate statistical significance at the 99%-, one asterisk shows significance at the 95% confidence level, using a two-tailed test.

always be rejected by claiming that relevant differences between charter and scheduled services are neglected.

Finally, relying on the actual costs in order to see if fares are justified implicitly assumes that all current costs are reasonable.

Nevertheless, there are some empirical findings which strongly indicate that European air transport prices deviate from competitive fares.

Firstly, by examining the structure of ticket prices in Europe and the USA some conclusions can be drawn.

For this purpose a univariate linear regression is estimated which explains the fare of a city pair connection (= TARIF) by means of the independent variable route length (= DISTANCE). The prices are the fares to be paid for the coach economy class without any restrictions concerning stopovers, reservations or minimum stay. For Europe the fares are the uniform IATA prices. With regard to the USA where different prices exist, the highest price is used. All fares are published in the *ABC World Airways Guide* in the October 1987 edition.[22] The samples comprise 61 intra-European international city-pair connections and 57 routes within the USA. The results of the OLS estimation are shown in Table 6.3.

The most interesting finding is the very different slopes of the fitted linear regression lines. The marginal price of a statute mile flown in Europe is about twice the figure for the USA (0.374 to 0.181 FCU). Assuming that the US fares due to competition are more cost-based, this indicates that, regardless of the level of prices, the European medium to long-haul coach economy fares are too high and do not follow costs.[23]

This outcome is confirmed by the fact that the types of aircraft flown are the same in the USA and Europe. The technical relationship between cost and distance for the widely used Airbus A-310 is depicted in Figure 6.1 (see page 125). It shows that costs decline sharply with the distance flown and indicates that the ticket price should only moderately rise with the route length.

As to the level of European air transport prices, a valuable approach is simply to look at the tariffs offered by new market entrants. Some examples from the last two years prove the possibility of serving many European routes more cheaply:

- On the Heathrow-Amsterdam route the new carrier British Midland offers flights about 20 per cent cheaper than, for instance, British Airways on similar routes (Marcom, 1988).
- In Germany the airline Aero-Lloyd tried to get government approval for prices which were 20–30 per cent below the existing ones on several scheduled city-pair connections (Interavia, 1988).
- The route London–Dublin has been served since 1986 by the market entrant Virgin Atlantic with a price which is around 30 per cent less than others (Barrett and Purdy, 1988).
- In 1988 American Airlines and TWA wanted to serve several connections from the Federal Republic of Germany to Berlin at prices more than 30 per cent below those previously offered.[24]

These findings and examples strongly support the analytical conclusion concerning the increased cartel price nature of the European air transport fares.

6 Conclusions

Many proponents of a deregulation of the air transport in Europe claim that the scheduled air carriers in Europe are less efficient by comparison with the US airlines. This proposition could be confirmed. By using a sample of 48 airlines mainly working in the field of passenger transportation, significant and important labour productivity differences of about 30 per cent can be detected. This amount is hardly to be explained by methodological deficiencies or specific influences and should lead to cost inefficiencies.[25] Moreover, there is some evidence that the absence of competition in Europe is manifest with regard to the structure and level of air transport prices.

Thus, all these empirical observations and the mentioned studies of productivity, cost efficiency and prices fit very well together. It seems rather evident that the lack of competition in the European air transport market leads to a considerable amount of social costs. Of course, the exact scale of these inefficiencies can only be detected with more detailed studies.

The completion of the internal market of the EEC – intended for 1992 – seems to also give way to changes in the air transport market. First steps in the direction of a moderate liberalization of air transport services may be seen in the decisions adopted by the European Council in December 1987 and the subsequent regulations of the Commission (Dempsey, 1988).[26]

If the transportation of passengers, freight and mail by plane is seen as just one form of service, the competition rules of Article 85 of the Treaty of Rome should apply. But this would mean that European states would have to give up their position of reserving the air space above their territories primarily for their national airlines.

Notes

1. With regard to economic theory, an interesting question is the applicability of the contestable markets theory. This approach points out that even in the case of a natural monopoly – that means strict subadditivity of costs in the relevant output range – potential competition from other airlines should force a carrier to set prices, quantities and quality as in a market with many competitors. The essential problem is, therefore, the absence of barriers to entry. The contestable markets theory argues that it is not the existence of fixed costs but sunk costs – costs due to market entry which cannot be recovered ex post after a commitment to a project has been made – which are a true barrier to entry and therefore hinder the working of potential competition. From this point of view, the air service seems to be the prototype of a contestable market. The transportation of passengers and freight between two geographical points does not involve any irreversible costs. The capital invested in an aeroplane serving a particular

city-pair market is not a sunk cost because it can easily be transferred to other routes (although this capital cost is fixed with regard to additional passengers and freight flown, and sunk in so far as the aeroplane cannot be used for any purpose other than air-transportation).

It has become evident during the last few years that this theory is too simple to correspond with reality. Several studies have shown that many causes weaken the forces of potential competition: slots, computer reservation systems, hub and spoke characteristics and so on. Therefore, today even the advocates of the contestable markets theory no longer claim that air transport is an ideal example for the application of this theory (Bailey and Williams, 1988; Graham, Kaplan and Sibley, 1983; Moore, 1986).

But even if competition does not work perfectly for several reasons, it is quite evident that it performed better in comparison to the regulated industry before 1978 (Morrison and Winston, 1986).

2. This description holds, even taking into consideration the problems of concentration and attenuation of competition on some routes (Kahn, 1988).

3. See Dorman (1983). The problems of externalities, second best and so on are neglected.

4. The differences of technical, allocative and scale inefficiencies are not taken into account. See Sickles (1988).

5. The cartel nature of the IATA tariff conferences is sometimes denied. But none of the arguments used is convincing. See Doganis (1986: p.36).

6. Studies dealing with the efficiency of the US airlines only are rather frequent: Sickles (1985); Sickles, Good and Johnson (1986); Thuong (1986). A comparison of the productive efficiency of the US airlines and a control group of 27 non-US carriers is provided by Caves, Christensen, Tretheway and Windle (1987).

7. Barrett even confounds charter and scheduled airlines.

8. In some cases, where data for 1983 did not exist or were obviously wrong, the figures for 1982 and 1984 respectively were used.

9. Only Jugoslavia was not taken into consideration.

10. A non-parametric procedure leads to the same results. The Wilcoxon rank sum test gives a test criterion of $z = +2.091$ which implies a rejection of the null hypothesis at the 5% level.

11. The influence the mean distance and mean capacity exert on productivity is corroborated by several empirical studies (Ashworth and Forsyth, 1984; Caves, Christensen and Tretheway, 1984).

12. A White-test revealed that OLS estimates are incorrect due to heteroskedasticity.

13. For the interpretation of the White-test and the condition number see Kmenta (1986) and Belsley, Kuh and Welsch (1980).

14. The accuracy of such a conclusion is misleading because of the simplicity of the model. Under this perspective an analysis of multivariate covariance would be more appropriate. But of course this would lead to the same results as to the influence of the variable LAND.

15. Using the tonne-kilometres or passengerkilometres available as an indicator of output instead of the tkm performed does not alter the results.

16. Recent studies indicate that contrary to earlier findings economies of scale, economies of scope and economies of density may be present in the air transport industry. See Bauer (1985), Good (1985).

17. A more theoretical defence for the approach adopted can rely on the assumption of a homothetic production function and an identical ration of input prices. This results in a linear expansion path with a constant input-factor ratio.

18. By using the monetary output indicator, value-added, these problems can be

136   Matthias-Wolfgang Stoetzer

avoided but such an approach engenders other difficulties. Since in Europe the air tariffs are by no means competitive prices, the value of production and consequently the value-added will be overestimated. Furthermore, in the case of monetary output indicators, international comparisons are difficult to make due to the problem of determining an appropriate rate of exchange for the national currencies. See Kravis (1984).

19. This points out the problem that in Europe the price-quality option hardly follows the consumers preferences. The American findings and the Laker airways experiment indicate that many passengers in Europe would prefer a low-price no-frills offer instead of a high-price high-quality service. The substitution of price competition by quality competition is examined in relation to the US air transport market during the sixties by Douglas and Miller (1974).

20. The technology is very similar due to the fact that the types of aircraft used by the firms are the same. Operations and maintenance of aircraft are standardized by international conventions. Furthermore, inputs like fuel and ground equipment are purchased in world markets. Finally, non-flight operations of the carriers are also very similar (e.g. ticketing, insurance requirements, liability for lost baggage and exchange of tickets).

21. In addition, the results are consistent with findings as to the efficiency of the US airlines before and after deregulation. Before 1978, overmanning and high cost levels were widespread phenomena among the US carriers (see Morrison and Winston 1986; Northrup, 1983; Sickles, 1988).

22. The unit is the IATA fare-construction unit, FCU.

23. It is interesting that this fare structure is the same as it was in the USA during the regime of regulation. Before 1978 the CAB adopted a price setting formula which engendered fares that were too high for long haul connections and too low for routes below 400 miles (Bailey, Graham and Kaplan, 1985: pp. 17–20).

24. These prices are very probably not merely dumping tariffs in order to enter the market but are likely to be maintained for a longer period (see e.g. Kieker, 1988).

25. Pearson (1976: p.479) observes a high and positive correlation between a low labour productivity and cost inefficiencies in a sample of 17 West European airlines.

26. Since 1983/84 several European countries, for instance, Great Britain and the Netherlands, have decided to liberalize scheduled air transport.

References

ABC World Airways Guide (October 1987), No.640, Dunstable.
Ashworth, M. and Forsyth, P. (1984), Civil Aviation Policy and the Privatisation of British Airways, Oxford.
Bailey, E. E., Graham, D. R. and Kaplan, D. P. (1985), De-regulating the Airlines, Cambridge (Mass.) London.
Bailey, E. E. and Williams, J.R. (1988), 'Sources of economic rent in the deregulated airline industry', Journal of Law & Economics, Vol. XXXI, No. 1, pp. 173–202.
Barrett, S. D. (1985), Sky High, Airline Price and European Deregulation, London.
Barrett, S. D. and Purdy, M. (1988), 'European air transport – uncabin the consumer', Economic Affairs, Vol. 8, No. 2, pp. 27–30.
Bauer, P. W. (1985), An Analysis of Multiproduct Technology and Efficiency Using the Joint Cost Function and Panel Data: An Application to the U.S. Airline Industry, Unpublished Dissertation, University of North Carolina.

Belsley, D., Kuh, E. and Welsh, R.E. (1980), *Regression Diagnostics*, New York.
BEUC (Bureau Européen de l'Union des Consommateurs) (1985), *Report on Air Fares*, Bruxelles.
Breyer, S. (1982), *Regulation and Its Reform*, Cambridge (Mass.) and London.
CAA (Civil Aviation Authority) (1977), *European Air Fares – a Discussion Document*, London.
——(1983), *A Comparison between European and US Fares*, London.
Caves, D.W., Christensen, L.R. and Tretheway, M.W. (1983), 'Productivity of U.S. trunk and local service airlines in the era of deregulation', *Economic Inquiry*, Vol. XXI, pp. 312–24.
——(1984), 'Economies of density versus economies of scale: why trunk and local service airline costs differ', *Rand Journal of Economics*, Vol. 15, No. 4, pp. 471–89.
Caves, D.W., Christensen, L.R., Tretheway, M.W. and Windle, R.J. (1987), 'An assessment of the efficiency effects of U.S. airline deregulation via an international comparison', in E. Bailey (ed.), *Public Regulation, New Perspectives on Institutions and Policies*, Cambridge (Mass.) and London, pp. 285–320.
Chalk, A. (1987), 'Air travel: safety through the market', *Economic Affairs*, Vol. 8, No. 1, pp. 7–12.
Dempsey, P.S. (1988), 'Aerial dogfights over Europe: the liberalization of EEC air transport', *Journal of Air Law and Commerce*, Vol. 53, No. 3, pp. 615–736.
Doganis, R. (1986), *Flying off Course, The Economics of International Airlines* (2nd edn), London, Boston, and Sydney.
Dorman, G.J. (1983), *A Model of Unregulated Airline Markets, Research in Transportation Economics*, Vol. 1, Greenwich, Connecticut, pp. 131–148.
Douglas, G. W. and Miller, J.C. (1974), *Economic Regulation of Domestic Air Transport: Theory and Policy*, Washington.
Eads, G. C. (1983), 'Airline competitive conduct in a less regulated environment: implications for antitrust', *The Antitrust Bulletin*, Vol. XXVIII, pp. 159–84.
EC Commission (1981), *Report Scheduled Passenger Air Fares in the EEC*, Brussels.
——(1984), *Memorandum Nr.2, Progress towards the Development of a Community Air Transport Policy*, Brussels.
Ferris, R. J. (1984), 'Playing the game after the rules change', *Logistics and Transportation Review*, Vol. 20, No. 1, pp. 77–81.
Forsyth, P., Hill, R. and Trengove, C. (1986), 'Measuring airline efficiency', *Fiscal Studies*, Vol. 7, No. 1, pp. 61–81.
Good, D. H. (1985), *The Impact of Deregulation on the Productive Efficiency and Cost Structure of the Airline Industry*, Unpublished Dissertation, University of Pennsylvania.
Graham, D. R., Kaplan, D. P. and Sibley, D.S. (1983), 'Efficiency and competition in the airline industry', *Bell Journal of Economics*, Vol. 14, No. 1, pp. 118–38.
Hartley, P., and Trengove, C. (1986), 'Who benefits from public utilities', *Economic Record*, Vol. 62, No. 177, pp. 163–179.
IATA (International Air Transport Association) (1984), *International Air Fares in Europe*.
ICAO (International Civil Aviation Organisation) (1983), *Statistical Yearbook, Civil Aviation Statistics of the World* (8th edn), Montreal.
——(1984), *Statistical Yearbook, Civil Aviation Statistics of the World* (9th edn), Montreal.
——(1985), *Statistical Yearbook, Civil Aviation Statistics of the World* (10th edn), Montreal.
——(1986), *Digest of Statistics No. 326, Traffic Commercial Air Carriers 1981–1985*, Montreal.
Interavia (1988), *Der Deutsche Luftverkehr Bereitet sich auf 1992 vor*, No. 7, pp. 2–4.

Kahn, A.E. (1988), 'Surprises of airline deregulation', *American Economic Review*, Papers and Proceedings, Vol. 78 No. 2, pp. 316–22.

Kaplan, D. P. (1986), 'The changing airline industry', M. W. Klass and L. W. Weiss (eds), *Regulatory Reform*, Boston and Toronto, pp. 40–77.

Kieker, B. (1988), 'Wie Geisterflugzeuge', *Die Zeit*, No. 52 23 December, p. 52.

Kmenta, J. (1986), *Elements of Econometrics* (2nd edn), New York and London.

Knieps, G. (1987), *Deregulierung im Luftverkehr*, Walter Eucken Institut, Vorträge and Aufsätze Bd.111, Tübingen.

Kravis, J.B. (1984), 'Comparative studies of national incomes and prices', *Journal of Economic Literature*, Vol. XXII, pp. 1–39.

Marcom, J. (1988), 'British Airways throws its weight around', *Wall Street Journal*, 8 August.

Moore, T. G. (1986), 'U.S. airline deregulation: its effects on passengers, capital and labour', *Journal of Law & Economics*, Vol. XXIX, pp. 1–28.

Morrison, S. and Winston, C. (1986), *The Economics Effects of Airline Deregulation*, Washington D.C.

Müller, J. (1983), 'Air Transport and its regulation in West Germany', *Zeitschrift für die gesamte Staatswissenschaft*, Vol. 139, No. 3, pp. 506–26.

Northrup, H. R. (1983), 'The new employee-relations climate in airlines', *Industrial and Labour Relations Review*, Vol. 36, No. 2, pp. 167–81.

O'Connor, W. E. (1985), *An Introduction to Airline Economics* (3rd edn), New York.

Pearson, R.J. (1976), 'Airline managerial efficiency', *Aeronautical Journal of the Royal Aeronautical Society*, Vol. LXXX, November, pp. 475–82.

Ramsden, J.M. (1985), 'Airline efficiency', *Flight International*, Vol. 128, No. 3984, pp. 32–6.

Scherer, F. M. (1980), *Industrial Market Structure and Economic Performance* (2nd edn), Boston.

Schoiber, F. (1987), *Deregulation in Europe*, Discussion Paper, Airline Industry Seminar.

Shaw, S. (1982), *Air Transport*, London.

Sickles, R. C. (1985), 'A nonlinear multivariate error components analysis of technology and specific factor productivity growth with an application to the U.S. airlines', *Journal of Econometrics*, Vol. 27, pp. 61–78.

——(1988), 'Allocative inefficiency in the airline industry: a case for deregulation', in A. Dogramaci, R. Färe (eds), *Applications of Modern Production Theory: Efficiency and Productivity*, Boston, pp. 149–62.

Sickles, R. C., Good, D. and Johnson, R.L. (1986), 'Allocative distortions and the regulatory transition of the U.S. airline industry', *Journal of Econometrics*, Vol. 33, pp. 143–63.

Sudit, E. F. and Finger, N. (1981), 'Methodological issues in aggregate productivity analysis', in A. Dogramaci, N. R. Adams (eds), *Aggregate and Industry-Level Productivity Analysis*, Boston, The Hague and London, pp. 7–30.

Thuong, L. T. (1986), 'Coping with adverse economic conditions under a regulated versus competitive environment: a study of domestic trunk airlines', *Akron Business & Economic Review*, Spring, pp. 62–7i.

Williamson, O. E. (1986), *Economic Organization: Firms, Markets and Policy Control*, Brighton.

7. Privatization and State Intervention – (An Economic Approach)

Anibal Santos

1 Introduction

Different forms of property of firms and other institutions are usually related to their allocative and internal efficiency levels. This relationship is subject to either economic or political arguments.

In this context private sector supporters usually argue that self interest is the most natural way to motivate each citizen, with competition acting as the main regulatory device. According to this view, the market has the essential mechanisms for generating an efficient allocation of available resources and is usually conceived as a social organization, where freedom of choice, given a legal order, is the crucial element.

In such a system consumers are considered sovereign in their choices. The ultimate aim of production is to satisfy consumers' demand and to produce goods and services at a minimal cost (internal efficiency). The self-regulating nature of competition assures adequate levels of consumer welfare (allocative efficiency).

However, in many countries of the Western world, especially after the Second World War, governments have influenced, for economic or political reasons, the functioning of the productive sector, either through different ways of regulating the private sector or through the creation of firms totally or partially controlled by the State (hereafter referred to as Public Firms). It is obvious that governments and private firms pursue different objectives, but in general this is a strongly controversial point (Sen, 1970).

Then, supporters of public and private sectors made their appearance, and most of the time arguments pro or against seem to be presented more as vague ideological generalizations than in the framework of available economic analysis.

However, interest on the part of the economics profession in the study of the behaviour and performance of public firms and regulated private ones is a relatively recent phenomenon; up to now the results don't seem to be very enlightening. In spite of recent research, comparison of the performance of these two types of firms is an even more delicate subject.

Despite insufficient theoretical knowledge about the realities known as nationalizations and privatizations, and the fact that it is desirable to consider legal, institutional and organizational constraints and also frequent political pressures in order to study the operation of private and public firms, certain groups, representing political or financial interests, do not seem to be inhibited in showing strong support for one or the other of the above-mentioned forms of property.

The economic approach central to this paper has at least the advantage over usual political arguments of offering a rational basis for discussion (even taking into account the simplifying nature of the approach). Theoretical developments in the study of nationalization and deregulation phenomena have mainly made progress during the last decade, but seem to offer a useful framework for analysis.[1]

In this context it is useful to mention two important points which will be present throughout this paper. The first one is that both public and private firms face the same problems of potential conflict of interests between owners and managers – adequate control systems in each case are necessary. The second one is that when there is no competition in the product markets, private property rights should be supplemented by public regulation in order to protect consumers and to avoid the use of private firms' monopoly power as a barrier to the entry of potential competitors into contestable market segments.

In this chapter we assume that there are public firms acting in competitive and monopolist market structures, as a result of a previous nationalization process. On the other hand, the privatization process of both types of firms is assumed to be irreversible, and that process is considered to be different to the liberalization one; in the first case there is a transfer of property, while in the second case a given market segment is opened to competition.

We also accept traditional arguments against public firms: low rate of return on capital, modest productivity, unsatisfied customers, lack of clear objectives and political and bureaucratic meddling in management. Then, among other objectives, greater economic freedom is intended with privatization.[2] A central element of the analysis presented here concerns the objective of efficiency, which is dependent upon competition and, whenever necessary, on regulation.

Section 2 reviews the main approaches to the problem of privatization and one of them – the (normative) economic analysis of regulation and public firms – is selected as the main approach of this paper. Section 3 develops some models of privatization, namely the cases of public monopolies and dominant public firms. Results are presented in the perspective of their usefulness to the decision-maker (the government). Finally, section 4 presents an initial comment on the Portuguese privatization programme, which is now in progress.

2   Approaches to The Problem of Privatization

Trying to classify different approaches to the study of a given phenomenon is generally an exercise with a dubious solution. This becomes even more difficult when available research is based neither upon a sufficiently long period of time nor upon accumulated experience which allows inferences with a somewhat comfortable level of significance.

In spite of these difficulties, it seems quite convenient to classify the different approaches to the problem of privatization into four main groups:

- the pragmatic approach;
- the theory of public choice;
- principal-agent theory;
- the (normative) economic analysis of regulation and public firms.

The pragmatic approach is, beyond any doubt, the one preferred by politicians and several interest groups, who are generally concerned with obtaining meaningful results from the government of privatization programme, and therefore try to influence the rules of the game. It is interesting to verify that, in this case, the main arguments presented are generally of the economic type; in this context, efficiency and economic freedom are quite commonly mentioned to support a reduction in state intervention.

In this case, the role of the State should be limited to establishing and protecting the structure of private property rights. On the other hand, it is implicit in this perspective that a welfare maximum can be obtained in private markets, through the mechanisms of competition.[3]

As to the theory of public choice (Buchanan, 1968; 1975), special emphasis is given to the political process, asserting that the logic of market behaviour extends to political behaviour. In this sense, economic reasons alone do not explain market intervention in the economy, given the fact that it is often the result of political decisions (Blankart, 1983).

The third approach outlined above is based on the principal-agent theory and has been developed mainly by Rees (1985; 1988). It emerges as an adverse selection agency model, where the essential element is the consideration of information asymmetries between the agent (manager) and the principal (the owner) (Guesnerie, 1988).

Finally we may consider the fourth approach – the economic analysis of regulation and public firms. Theoretical developments in this area are generally of a normative type, and are directed to the study of either the economic regulation of private activities or the behaviour and performance of public firms (Rees, 1984; Bös, 1985; 1987; and Santos, 1986). Recently, this approach has been used by Vickers and Yarrow (1988) in their economic approach to the problem of privatization.

Despite the difficulties of practical implementation usually associated with this approach, we believe that it is a rational method of analysis, in which it is still possible to consider the issues of fairness and equity (Baumol, 1986). In spite of the necessarily simplifying nature of most models used, research results in this area seem quite useful to the decision-maker (including the courts), providing a set of principles that allow the analysis of the impact of certain decisions upon performance, both at a firm level and at an industry level.

In the next section this fourth approach will be applied in a comparative study of public and private firms acting in either monopolist or competitive market structures; special emphasis will be given to the study of monopolies with and without fringe competitors.

3   Models of Privatization: The Alternatives

The Situation Before Privatization

The coexistence of public and private firms leads to market structures somewhat different to traditional microeconomic textbook cases. Although there are markets where there is only one firm, be it public or private, in other industries there are oligopolist market structures where these two types of firms compete. Furthermore, there is also the possibility of competition between public firms. In Table 7.1 different market structures are combined, with the two alternative forms of property being considered.

In Western European economies, with relatively large public sectors, the most common market structures are public monopolies and public or hybrid oligopolies. Frequently public monopolies have subadditive cost structures (Sharkey, 1982), in which case they are referred to as natural monopolies.

An alternative market structure, and one which is frequently found in practice, is the case of a dominant firm (either public or private) which faces competition from a fringe of small competitors.

It is common theoretical assumption – and one with a sound empirical basis – that competition improves public and private firms' economic performance,

Table 7.1   Market Structures and Property

	Monopolistic Competition	Monopoly	Oligopoly
Private property	Non-atomistic competition between private firms	Private monopoly (natural or not	Private oligopoly (with or without cooperation
Public property	Non-atomistic competition between public firms	Public monopoly (natural or not)	Public oligopoly (with or without cooperation
Private and public property	Non-atomistic competition between public and private firms	—	Hybrid oligopoly (with or without cooperation)

and in this case private firms are more efficient. When, for technological reasons, it is desirable that only one firm should occupy a market, it is necessary to consider how to control the benefits accruing from (productive) efficiency, so that the firm's monopoly power does not inflict a loss upon consumers. Here, some form of public regulation should be considered.

The above-mentioned alternatives make it possible to stress the competitive and non-competitive cases. In this last case, privatization will not always presuppose an end to state intervention. The relationship between competition and the form of property seems particularly interesting when there are several competing firms in a given market.

Privatization of Public Monopolies

Every privatization process to be implemented will change previous market structures, where there was a given number of public firms in the pre-privatization process. Different situations may arise and several corresponding models may be conceived. At a decision-making level an important point is the comparative analysis of the performance of firms subject to a change in its form of property.

Monopolist structures are, in principle, the more worrisome to the decision-maker who must decide upon the privatization of a public monopoly, namely a natural one. Whenever that monopoly faces small, fringe competitors and is privatized, simple behaviour models allow the researcher to perform some comparative analyses, which are sufficiently interesting given the empirical relevance of such cases.

PRIVATE MONOPOLIES SUBJECT TO REGULATORY CONSTRAINTS

Privatization of a public monopoly ends neither monopoly power nor the possibility of using this power at the consumers' expense.[4] It is obvious that for new shareholders a significant monopoly power is attractive; however, a loss is inflicted upon consumers and a bad allocation of resources follows.

In fact, the absence of competition in natural monopoly industries induces the monopolist to decrease production and so increase prices. This behaviour has at least two consequences. First, taking the competitive case as reference, there is a redistribution from consumers to producers. On the other hand, there is a production loss where value for consumers is higher than its production cost (social cost of monopoly).

Then, higher profits or share prices should not necessarily be seen as the result of higher efficiency levels; instead, they may be the result of the exercise of the monopolist's market power. At stake here is the analysis of the trade-off between shareholders and consumers interest. In such cases privatization should be complemented by greater competition, at least in some market segments (liberalization), or with some kind of public regulation of the private monopoly.[6]

Among the several forms of regulation proposed and developed, we can consider two methods:

1 American type regulation (rate of return regulation);
2 European type regulation (price control).

As to the first type[7] there exists a vast economic literature, beginning with work by Averch and Johnson (1962), later developed by Baumol and Klevorick (1980) and others, among these, Khan (1970) and Breyer (1982) should be mentioned for their work establishing the interaction between economic and institutional arguments. The incentive for overcapitalization of firms subject to rate of return regulation is the most striking aspect of this kind of intervention; however, consideration should be given to the fact that better allocative efficiency might outweigh worse productive allocation. Meanwhile, the possibility that perverse effects might result from this kind of regulation and emergence of the theory of contestable markets (Baumol *et al.*, 1982) had led, in the USA, to the deregulation process of recent years.

In Europe, mainly in the United Kingdom, current privatization processes of natural monopolies have led to the option for price regulation. Differently from the American case, many natural monopolies in Europe are public firms. If monopolies are sustainable, competition will be inefficient; if they are not sustainable, competition is a real possibility and liberalization should be considered.

The shortcomings of the American type of regulation have led to the design of alternative types of regulation in Europe, namely in the country where the greatest experience has been acquired during the last eight years (U.K.). Two forms of control for private natural monopolies have been proposed:

• regulation in the form of an average price constraint;
• regulation in the form of an average revenue constraint.

Table 7.2   Behaviour models of public and private firms

Property Type of regulation	Public (Maximization of global welfare	Private (Maximization of profit)
American (Rate of return regulation)	Greater deviation of price from marginal cost inn comparison to the Ramsey–Boiteux result	Averch–Johnson effect (overcapitalization
European (Average price constraint)	—	Ramsey–Boiteux prices for some cost and demand conditions)
Average revenue constraint	—	Perverse effects in terms of tariff structure

The effect of various forms of regulation on performance levels of monopolist firms after privatization can be summed up in a very simplified way, as in Table 7.2. Here, the case of a public firm is also presented, but a rate of return constraint has been used instead of the traditional break-even constraint (which leads to the Ramsey–Boiteux result).[8]

One characteristic common to all of these regulatory processes becomes apparent through their solutions. They all lead, in one way or another, to situations of inefficiency, only overcome, in some cases, by great amounts of information about costs and demand.

Rate of return regulation is an area in which much research has been done, at both theoretical and empirical levels, and is probably the best studied regulatory rule, mainly in the USA. In Europe it has been rejected on the grounds that is induces suboptimal factor proportions and, according to some authors, it also induces the capture of the regulatory agency by the regulated firm (see e.g. Mitnik, 1980, for an extensive analysis of this problem).

The model of a public firm subject to an allowed rate of return is included here just to point out that a rate of return constraint faced by a welfare maximizing public firm also distorts the firm's behaviour. As a matter of fact, it causes a great divergence between price and marginal cost than the one found when the public firm is subject to a break-even constraint (Ramsey–Boiteux prices).

Models of firms which are subject to an average price constraint or average revenue constraint (European type of regulation) are alternative forms of what is usually known as price control.

This form of regulation of multiproduct monopolies has been suggested by Littlechild (1983) for the U.K. telecommunications industry, and is also applied to gas and airports.[9] Considering their recent application in concrete cases of privatization, and their theoretical interest vis-à-vis the result of Ramsey–Boiteux, it is worthwhile to discuss briefly some of the consequences of these models.

In the case of a firm which maximizes profit subject to an average price constraint, the most interesting feature is that if weights, used in the constraint, are proportional to quantities demanded, given Ramsey–Boiteux prices, then we obtain an identical result to the one derived from the model of a financially viable public firm (Vickers and Yarrow, 1988). However, in practice, such a weighting scheme seems to be rather difficult to implement.

When the firm maximizes profits subject to an average revenue constraint, weights depend on the firm's behaviour. In the case of multiproduct firms, a comparative analysis of cost and demand structures in the relevant markets is necessary to solve the model. Then, one possible approach to this problem is to consider the cases where:

1   markets have similar demand and different cost functions; and
2   markets have similar costs but different demand functions.

This kind of analysis has been followed by Bradley and Price (1987), who have argued that in markets with similar demands and different costs, every price in the average revenue constraint case will be greater than prices in the case of a public firm behaviour model with a constraint giving the same average revenue. When there are similar costs but different demand structures, in markets with inelastic demand, the prices resulting from that model will be greater than prices resulting from a public firm's behaviour model (where the efficient pricing policy is that of Ramsey–Boiteux).

These distortions are due to the aggregate nature of the imposed constraint; several markets are included and the firm is forced to change its relative prices in order to maximize profits, given this aggregate constraint.

PRIVATIZATION OF A DOMINANT PUBLIC FIRM FACING FRINGE COMPETITION

A case deserving some attention is the privatization of a public firm facing competition from a fringe of small private competitors.[10]

The dominant firm has a problem which is not faced by the monopolist; that is, if it increases its prices, some of its customers may decide to switch over to the fringe.[11]

In a dynamic setting, fringe competitors may be seen as regulating the dominant firm's anti-competitive behaviour. However, it should also be noted that the dominant firm may both use its prices as a strategic weapon and cause an increase in fringe competitors' costs.

We shall compare the case of a dominant public firm facing fringe competition with the post – privatization case in which there is competition between private firms of different scales. Meanwhile, it is assumed that the dominant firm being privatized is not 'broken up', at least over a significant period of time.

To model this problem a dynamic approach in the Gaskins (1971) tradition is useful. We shall make use of the results obtained by Encaoua and Jacquemin (1980) concerning a dominant private firm, and the results of Santos (1986) which refer to a dominant public firm. In both situations dominant firms face a competitive fringe, and a policy of irreversible expenses is followed to deter entry.

In the case of a dominant public firm, its objective is the maximization of social welfare, and we consider that the only constraint is that related to the entry rate of potential competitors. This entry rate is the result of current and potential competitors' reactions to the dominant firm's strategy. To model this case in a dynamic context, it is necessary to set a discount rate (opportunity cost of the financial resources used by the firm).

In this case (Santos, 1986), the dominant public firm's profit margins are always negative. This happens, given welfare maximizing behaviour and fringe competition, by small private firms, because if the public firm is to survive, its prices will have to be set below marginal cost (when it has no cost advantages over fringe competitors).

This pricing policy may be seen as predatory, thereby providing an argument for the regulatory agency to interfere to protect the fringe. However, if the public firm's marginal costs are higher than those of the fringe, and if the public firm's losses are not covered, then the fringe will increase their market share and eventually the public firm will be forced out of the market.

If none of the firms has cost advantages and the public firm sets its prices below marginal cost, then fringe competitors have no choice but to upgrade the quality of their goods.[12] In this case, the public firm's pricing policy forces rival firms to increase their costs (Salop and Schaffman, 1983).

If the regulatory agency forces the public firm to be financially viable, another restriction must be added to the model; the public firm is forced to reachat least the break-even point, each year.

This new constraint may decrease the public firm's competitive potential, for it loses some flexibility when using prices as a strategic variable. In this case, if the firm has no cost advantages,[13] entry rate will increase and in the long run the public firm market share will approach zero. Then, the regulatory agency may try to protect the public firm by limiting entry and controlling private firms' prices. However, this policy may well imply a decrease in consumer surplus.

The privatization of a dominant public firm, without breaking it up, leads, in the context of the previous analysis, to a model like the one presented in Encaoua and Jacquemin (1980). Compared with the pre-privatization case, the profit margins are now always positive.

An important result following from this model is that, given price elasticity of demand and concentration levels, the lower the elasticity of the rate of entry is to the pricing policy and the higher this elasticity is (in absolute value) to the non-price policy, the higher the degree of monopoly, is at any moment in time. We have here, once again, the need for regulation by a public agency.

As a matter of fact, the dominant private firm may well try to discourage entry and capacity increases by fringe competitors in order to preserve its market share. In this case, the regulatory agency should carefully follow the exercise of that market power in the long run.

Then, the privatization of a dominant public firm does not eliminate the possibility that the dominant position is used to harm current or potential competition. Where there are various competitors (with asymmetric positions), several possibilities emerge, providing an argument for public intervention. This is, however, a somewhat complex case in terms of analytical treatment.

4 Privatization in Portugal: Some Brief Notes

The creation, of a sizeable public enterprise sector in Portugal has its roots in the political changes of April 1974. Nationalizations began in March 1975 with the banking and insurance sectors and most firms in basic economic sectors were nationalized during the following sixteen months.[14]

These firms have been facing several problems mainly due to the following factors: the principal (regulatory agency) has not set unambiguous objectives to be followed by the agents (firms' management), external borrowing has been extensively used, the nomination of managers has been subject to the influence of several pressure groups, firms have been used as instruments of macroeconomic policy and the lack of incentive systems designed to increase productivity and efficiency has been felt. As a result, many firms have been going through hard times, imposing an unsustainable burden on the government budget.

Several policies have been designed to improve on these problems. In 1983 the law of sector delimitation allowed private firms to enter some industries, which had previously been restricted to public firms, such as the cement and fertilizer industries as well as the banking and insurance sectors.[15] Selling out public firms has also been proposed by business associations, financial groups and, more recently, it has been considered in the programme of government. On the other hand, a privatization process has been underway since 1979 in the United Kingdom and other countries (the French case is also important), which has had some impact in Portugal.

The main difficulty for the take-off of a privatization process in Portugal lies in the concept of nationalization irreversibility according to Article 83 of the Portuguese Republic Constitution. In the EEC, Portugal is the only country where such a notion exists, posing obvious difficulties in the management of the productive system.[16]

In this context, the urgent need to change the forms of property of public firms has been felt. So, given the constraints imposed by the Constitution, it was decided to change the legal status of public firms, permitting the alienation of up to 49 per cent of public firms' capital.[17] This means that a denationalization process is in progress, rather than one of privatization.

As a matter of fact, according to Beesley and Littlechild (1983), the concept of privatization is generally used to mean the selling out of at least 50 per cent of total shares to private shareholders. The basic idea underlying such processes is, as mentioned in section 1, to increase the firms' efficiency levels, ascribing a greater role to market forces.[18]

The situation where future shareholders hold less than 50 per cent of privatized firms ($\Omega < 0,5$) can, in my opinion, result in some confusion, especially on the part of small shareholders who will perceive the control of the firms as remaining mostly in the hands of the State.[19] On the other hand, given the mixed economy characteristics of these firms (the State being the majority shareholder), the capital stock market can react in a deficient way.

According to the formulation presented in section 3, a mixed economy firm, as is the case of the firms resulting from Law no. 84/88, will maximize an objective function (M) which is a linear combination of the objectives of a public and a private firm, that is:

$$\text{Maximize } M = (1-\Omega)\,W + \Omega\pi$$

where W is global welfare and π is profit.

As is mentioned by Bös (1987), this objective function raises several problems, namely those resulting from the bargaining between the two types of owners and from the different results obtained according to each owner group bargaining for power.

According to Article 5 of law no. 84/88, smaller shareholders have the guarantee of holding at least 20 per cent of total shares and emigrants have the right to subscribe to a maximum of 10 per cent. Private entities are subject to some constraints on the amount of the firms' shares they can hold, including foreign entities, whose participation can't exceed 10 per cent of the total shares' alienated. However, there is some possibility that private dominant economic groups (national and international) will be the future owners of denationalized firms; on the other hand, if smaller shareholders do not have access to more than 20 per cent of total shares (Article 5, a)) then one of the basic privatization principles – wider share ownership – will not be accomplished.

In the industrial sector, privatizations began with the public brewery, UNICER, E.P. (Law Decree no. 353/88 of 6 October 1988). I think that this was a commendable decision, for the following reasons:

1   It was a public firm in a sector where neither public goods nor necessities are produced.
2   In Portugal, the brewing sector was a public duopoly (the other public firm being CENTRALCER, E.P.). The least we can say is that this market structure is unseen in Western Europe, thereby raising several theoretical and practical problems.
3   UNICER's rates of return of relatively high, comparing favourably with both the sector and the other public firm.

From the theoretical point of view, this case has been studied in a work that, as far as I can understand, was the first in this area (Silva and Santos, 1983). Several types of strategic behaviour were simulated, with special emphasis being given to the Stakelberg type. As a result of these simulations it seems possible to argue that the public duopoly of breweries is an irrational market structure, especially when it was considered that one of the firms, UNICER, E.P., had a higher productive efficiency level and the other was a monopoly in an essential raw material – malt.

The decision to begin privatizations with public firms having higher levels of performance has been followed in other countries with some success (Kay *et al.*, 1986). In the Portuguese brewing sector there will be, at least for some time, a hybrid duopoly and it is possible that this will improve efficiency in the remaining public firm; in spite of this favourable point, the question remains of the desirability of privatizing simultaneously both public firms.

With regard to public monopolies and dominant public firms facing small private fringe competitors, problems resulting from future privatizations seem to be a much more complex matter.

As examples of public monopolies that seem to be 'attractive' to private investors for future privatization proposals, one can mention ANA (Aeroportos e Navegação Aérea, E.P.; airport facilities), CTT (Correios, Telégrafos e Telefones,E.P.; post office and telecommunications), TLP (Telefones de Lisboa e Porto, E.P.; Telecommunications) and PETROGAL (Petróleos de Portugal, E.P.; oil refining).[20]

As regards dominant public firms (or quasi-monopolies), the appearance of privatization proposals in the transportation sector, seems probable, with likely candidates being R.N. (Rodoviária Nacional,E.P.; road transportation) and TAP (Transportes Aéreos Portugueses, E.P.; airways).

I think that the previous arguments (special account being given to the cases presented), may be helpful to decision-makers and may, in certain cases, provide some clues to the understanding of the regulatory process to be set by the government. Each sector seems to be rather specific, and the decision to be taken should be adequately supported by research on the economic consequences of privatization. Governments should be careful with pressure groups favouring quick privatization, since they may be more concerned with short-term profit than with long-term market efficiency.

Notes

1. Some work in this area has been done by Rees (1984), Bös (1985), Santos (1986), Bös (1987), Vickers and Yarrow (1988). These last two works specifically address the problem of privatizations.
2. For a description and critical appraisal of privatization objectives see, for instance, Kay, Mayer and Thompson (1986).
3. However, reality does not seem to conform to this pattern. As a matter of fact, information asymmetries in the market explain, at least in part, behaviour of the firms aimed at eliminating competition, e.g. mergers, take-overs and other restrictive practices.
4. Financial aspects related to different alternatives of selling public firms are not considered in this paper.
5. We admit the case of total privatization here. If Ω is the percentage of shares to be sold to the private sector, then total privatization means that $\Omega=1$. If privatization is partial, we have $0 < \Omega < 1$.
6. We are concerned here with different regulatory measures aimed at the control of monopoly power. Consequently we will not consider different types of externalities that could demand public intervention.
7. Rate of return regulation affects prices also because profits, taken as a rate of return on capital, are constrained.
8. This is a second best pricing policy where a public firm maximizes a global welfare function, with classical conditions, holding, subject to a break-even constraint. In this case, price-cost margins are higher in markets where demand is less elastic.
9. A comparative analysis of these three sectors, subject to this regulatory rule, may be found in Vickers and Yarrow (1988)
10. The road transportation sector in Portugal offers a good example of this case.
11. It should be clear that markets with dominant firms include the case where an incumbent monopolist faces potential entry.
12. It is obvious that if the public firm always has loss it will go bankrupt. However, statutory provisions may not allow this outcome; this is the case of several European countries, namely Portugal.
13. Sunk costs may provide the dominant firm with sharp cost advantages over potential competitors.
14. The main nationalizations, in non-financial sectors, were in electricity (production, distribution and transportation), refining, petrochemicals, steel, road transportation, airways, cement, paper pulp, tobacco, beer, shipbuilding, chemicals and mining.
15. Law Decree no. 406/83, of 19 November 1983.
16. This situation may change after the foreseeable revision of the Constitution. Then, it will be necessary to consider the advantages of changing the current privatization process.
17. Law no. 84/88, of 20 July 1988.
18. It should be obvious that privatization is not the only process to lead to such results. Allowing for free entry in nationalized industries, creating joint ventures and encouraging competition may well increase industry level performance.

19. About 80% of the investors in British Telecom purchased their shares thinking that they were investing in a low-risk 'project'.
20. Petrogal E.P. only has the monopoly in production.

References

Averch, H. and Johnson, L. (1962), 'Behaviour of the firm under regulatory constraint', *American Economic Review* (Dec.), 1052–69.

Baumol, W. (1986), *Superfairness*. Cambridge: the M.I.T. Press.

Baumol, W. and Klevorick, A. (1980) 'Input choices and rate of return regulation: an overview and discussion', *Bell Journal of Economics and Management Science* (Autumn), 162–90.

Baumol, W., Panzar, J. and Willig, R. (1982), *Contestable Markets and the Theory of Industry Structure*. N.Y.: Harcourt Brace Jovanovich.

Beesley, M. and Littlechild S. (1983), 'Privatisation: principles, problems, and priorities', *Lloyds Bank Review*.

Blankart, C. (1983), 'The contribution of public choice to public utility economics – a survey', in J. Finsinger (ed.), *Public Sector Economics*, London: Macmillan.

Bös, D. (1985), *Public Enterprise Economics: Theory and Application*. Amsterdam: North-Holland.

Bös, D. (1987), 'Privatization of public enterprises', *European Economic Review* (N?. 31), 352–60.

Bradley, I. and Price C. (1987), 'Regulation through an average revenue constraint', University of Leicester.

Breyer, S. (1982) *Regulation and Its Reform*, Cambridge Mas: Harvard University Press.

Buchanan, J. (1968), 'A public choice approach to public utility pricing', *Public Choice*, (vol.5), 1–18.

(1975), 'Consumerism and public utility regulation', in C. Phillips Jr. (edn), *Telecommunications, Regulation and Public Choice*, Washington: Lexington Books.

Encaoua, D. and Jacquemin A. (1980), 'Degree of monopoly, indices of concentration and threat of entry', *International Economic Review* (Feb.) 87–105.

Gaskins, D. (1971), 'Dynamic limit pricing: optimal pricing under threat of entry', *Journal of Economy Theory*, (n? 3), 306–22.

Guesnerie, R. (1988), 'Regulation as an adverse selection problem', *European Economic Review*, (no. 32), 473–81.

Kay, J., Mayer, C. and Thompson, D. (1986), *Privatisation & Regulation – The UK Experience*, Oxford: Clarendon Press.

Khan, A., (1970), *The Economics of Regulation*, vols I and II, N.Y.: John Wiley & Sons.

Littlechild, S. (1983), *Regulation of British Telecommunications Profitability*, London: Department of Industry.

Mitnick, B. (1980), *The Political Economy of Regulation*, N.Y.: Columbia University Press.

Rees, R., (1984), *Public Enterprise Economics*, London, Weidenfeld and Nicholson.

Rees, R., (1985), 'Principal agent theory and public control of production', University College, Cardiff.

Rees, R., (1988), 'Inefficiency, public enterprise and privatisation', *European Economic Review* (no. 32), 422–31.

Salop, S. and Scheffman, D. (1983), 'Raising rivals' costs', *American Economic Review* (Maio), 267–71.

Santos, A. (1986), *Models of Public Firms in Monopoly and Oligopoly Structures*. Lisbon. Portuguese Catholique University (in Portuguese).

Sen, A. (1970), 'Profit maximization and the public sector', *John Metthal Lectures*, 31.3.1970, Kerala University, India.

Sharkey, W., (1982), *The Theory of Natural Monopoly*. Cambridge. Cambridge University Press.

Silva, A. and Santos, A. (1983), 'Modelling a duopoly of public firms: conduct, product differentiation and price regulation', X Conference of EARIE, Bergen, Norway.

Vickers, J., and Yarrow, G. (1988), *Privatization: An Economic Analysis*. London: the M.I.T. Press.

8. The Regulation of New Product Development in the Drug Industry

Erich Kaufer

The Regulation of Medicines: A Historical Sketch of Its Roots

As old as man's search for medicines is his concern about their quality. Because the ingredients of ancient medicines – herbs and spices – were scarce and expensive, adulteration was common practice in the trade. Galen, the famous doctor to the great Roman Emperor Marcus Aurelius Antoninus, even went so far as to hire an adulteror of drugs in order to learn how to protect himself against adulteration.

More than a thousand years later, on 21 May 1297, the Venetian Maggior Consiglio was led by a similar concern in his decision that:

omnes medicine et sirupi et teriaca fiant in duabus vel tribus stationibus vel pluribus pro Communi, et fiant de melioribus rebus, que fieri possunt, et nullus audeat vendere et predictis nisi illi qui positi fuerint per Justicianios pro Communi in illis stationibus (Mandich, 1958: p.105).

And again almost six hundred years later, in April 1848, a select committee of the US Congress proposed legislation for the control of imported drugs for the reason that the US troops had been supplied with adulterated drugs during the war with Mexico. In 1902, following the death of ten children who had received tetanus infected diphtheria vaccines, the US Congress passed the Biologics Control Act, which provided that the manufacture of sera and vaccines be licensed. And four years later Upton Sinclair's book on *The Jungle* of the meat industry in Chicago, where rotten meat together with rats had been packed into cans, brought about the Pure Food and Drug Act. Although mainly concerned with regulations for preserving pure food, the PFD Act was also the first effort to restrain the sale of so-called 'patent medicines' of dubious efficacy.

Then in late July 1937 the chief chemist of the Massengill Company in

Tennessee undertook to find a palatable solvent for the first wonder drug of our times – sulphanilamide, which had saved the life of Franklin Roosevelt's son. He chose an ethylene glycol/water mix flavoured with raspberry extract. On 5 September 240 gallons of a new product – Elixir Sulphanilamide – were shipped to pharmacies. One month later the American Medical Association received two telegrams from physicians in Tulsa, Oklahoma, stating that six people had died after taking the elixir. By 15 October distribution of the product had been stopped, and a frantic search for bottles of the elixir began. By the time the last bottle had been recovered, 107 people had died from poisoning by the elixir. The company had not tested the product on animals prior to marketing. It had relied on the knowledge that ethylene glycol as such was safe at the dosage used, and that sulphanilamide was known to be a safe and potent drug. Unfortunately, the combination of two purportedly safe ingredients turned out to be highly lethal.

Within months Congress had enacted the Food, Drug, and Cosmetics Act, which established the principle that new drugs had to undergo a process of New Drug Approval (NDA) before the Food and Drug Agency (FDA) where the applicant had to prove the safety of his new drug (HuH, 1983). Then in the early 1960s a new sleep-including, drug – thalidomide – appeared which was far superior to the barbiturates. Precisely because it seemed to be so safe – safe also in cases of accidental or intentional suicide – the drug was given to pregnant women. And also precisely because the drug was used so extensively, its tragic side effects on babies were discovered. With a more restrained use these effects probably would never have been traced back to the drug.

At that time Senator kefauver was already investigating the pricing and marketing practices of the drug industry as part of his campaign in the de- bate that 'administered prices' were a main factor contributing to the new experience of inflation cum stagnation (Kaufer, 1976: pp. 58–9). Although thalidomide had not yet been approved for the US market, Kefauver thought that his hearings had uncovered enough evidence of highly defective drug admission and drug testing procedures. In 1962 the Kefauver Amendment to the Food and Drug Act empowered the FDA not only to control the safety but also the efficacy of new drugs, and to impose strict controls on the discovery and testing process eventually leading to an NDA application (Kaufer, 1976: pp. 59–64). However, Kefauver's hearings on the marketing practices of the drug industry also brought the accusation that drug prices were highly monopolistic. While patent royalties of 2.5 per cent of sales were deemed normal in the times prior to the first patented antibiotic, implicit licence fees of 80 per cent of sales were uncovered for the patented antibiot- ics. An apparent 34 fold increase in monopoly power – as measured by the profit – sales ratio – seemed to be outrageously exploitative. Therefore, ever since 1962 the pharmaceutical industry has been subject to various blends of regulation of the drug discovery process and its pricing and marketing behaviour (Comanor 1986: pp. 1181–9). I know of no other industry where the whole process of research, development, testing, pricing, and marketing is subject to as close a scrutiny by governmental agencies.

The Regulation of The Drug Discovery and Development Process

The modern regulatory process for drugs is grounded in the path-breaking progress being in organic chemistry, physiology, pharmacology and in the statistical design of test procedures. The drug discovery process is highly empirical in character.

The laboratory generates a huge number of molecular variants which are tested on animals for therapeutic effects. Of about ten thousand compounds, a thousand turn out to be sufficiently promising to subject them to elaborate toxicological studies on animals, especially tests for mutagenicity, teratogenicity, and long-term carcinogenicity. This whole period takes about three years to complete, and ten out of a thousand initially hopeful products survive all the toxicology tests and are scheduled for further clinical evaluations. Before a company in the United States begins clinical testing, it has to apply to the FDA for permission to start what is called the Investigational New Drug Development. The IND period consists of three phases. In phase I the drug is tested on healthy humans in order to evaluate its relative safety and its pharmacodynamics. In phase II the efficacy of the drug is tested in small groups of patients at various dosage levels. In phase III the drug is evaluated by administering it to large groups of patients in order to search for possible adverse drug reactions when taken with or without other medicines. During phase III, that is about 5.6 years after the first clinical trials began, a New Drug Approval application is filed with the FDA. It takes another 2.5 years before the new drug is finally admitted to the market. From that date on, phase IV research begins because the new drug has to be constantly monitored for as yet undetected adverse drug reactions. Phase IV is called post-marketing surveillance.

Table 8.1   Discontinuations of NCEs during clinical studies (%)

		After IND filing/before phase I begins I	During phase II	During phase III	Total phase
Cardiovascular	(26)	4	12	35	5	55
Anti-infective	(17)	6	24	33	<2	63
Alimentary	(15)	13	7	24	21	65
Respiratory	(13)	15	23	32	<2	72
Neurological	(33)	6	27	31	10	74
Musculoskeletal	(19)	11	11	60	<2	82
Dermatological	(15)	13	33	45	<2	92
All others	(36)	8	22	47	<2	78
Total	(174)	9	20	39	5	73

Source: The Outcome of Research on New Molecular Entities commencing Clinical Research in the Years 1976–1978 FDA, OPE Study 77, May 1988.

The FDA has recently published data on the fate of drugs entering clinical studies. Of 174 NCEs for which IND applications had been submitted in the 1976–79 period, 27 per cent survived until the NDA filling date. However, depending upon the therapeutic field, large variations around the average existed (see Table 8.1).

Looking at the graphic picture of the drug development review process, one gets the impression that drug regulation must be a highly precise and unambiguous scientific undertaking. However, each step in the review process poses serious problems for an effective regulation (Bauke et al., 1984; Iman, 1987; Lasagna, 1976; 1986; Wardell, 1978).

During the screening phase the laboratory produces numerous different chemical compounds, but also a massive number of seemingly minor variations of a basic molecule. The latter discovery method is often derided as 'molecular manipulation'. However, it is a fact of pharmaceutical progress that minor changes in molecular structure have vastly increased the effectiveness of given drugs or have led to the discovery of unsuspected new therapeutic uses. For instance, minor molecular modifications have led to the wide array of antibiotics. And small changes in the configuration of the antihistamine, promethazine generated chlorpromazine (a potent tranquillizer) and impramine (an effective antiderpressant). The list of these cases in long. Thus, even if competition were motivated solely by 'me - too' considerations, it would still have the unintended result of discoveries of highly valuable therapeutic effects being made by serendipity.

Disastrous experiences like the one with the sulphanilamide elixir or with thalidomide stimulated the development of routine studies in animal toxicology. But again these studies pose numerous questions, both of ethical and of scientific evaluation. From a scientific standpoint, a toxicological study should either be induced by an empirical observation or by a hypothesis. In contrast, the routine studies required by regulatory rules are designed to generate a huge mass of data that might be useful in evaluating the potential for harm of the NCE. But in order to collect the mass of data, large numbers of animals are sacrificed. This might be justifiable if the data could be interpreted unambiguously and consistently. But unfortunately, this is not the case (Kessler, 1977; Laurence and Black, 1978; Walker et al., 1984; Zbinden, 1982; Zbinden and Flury Roversi 1981).

First, different species of animals may react differently to a chemical compound, and so too may humans in comparison with animals.

Second, a specific strain of the same species of animal may react quite differently to other strains, for example, some strains of mice may develop breast cancer, others may not.

Third, even for a given strain of an animal species wide variations in results are possible, depending upon age, sex, diet, temperature, caging, season and other experimental procedures.

Fourth, it is false to conclude that a compound is safe for man because no adverse effects have been observed in animals.

Consequently, the regulation of toxicology studies poses several problems. If the rules are rigid and if tests are piled upon tests, for example in order to infer carcinogenicity from long-term animal tests, valuable time will be lost before clinical evaluation can begin and herds of animals will be wasted. Finally, there is a tendency not to permit the initiation of clinical research if the animal studies show severe adverse effects in one species of animal studies show severe adverse effects in one species of animal or even in a strain of a species. However, in the past numerous important drugs were admitted which by today, us standards of toxicology would not have gained IND approval (Lasagna, 1976). Although we do not and cannot know how many valuable new drugs are lost because NCEs do not get IND approval, the potential may be high. At present the danger may still be rather small for countries like Great Britain which do not require a Clinical Trial Certificate before testing on patients begins, and countries like Germany and Switzerland which have no prior restrictions on clinical evaluations.

A serious question is posed by extent to which a regulatory agency should get involved in devising and imposing detailed rules for testing procedures. Since 1979 the FDA has established so-called 'Good Laboratory Practice' rules for the conduct of preclinical research. Although standardization of test procedures is valuable as it tends to make the results more consistent and comparable, the danger is that the introduction of scentific advances in toxicological methods will be retarded. The counterpart to the GLP rules are the Good Clinical Practice rules. Unfounded or even frivolous claims which have been made in the past and continue to be made today for all kinds of 'patent medicines' have led to the introduction of the Randomized, Double-blind, Controlled Clinical Trial (RCCT). Yet RCC trials leave some important questions unanswered (Lasagna, 1986). While an RCC trial may demonstrate that a new drug is superior to a placebo or to another drug, if given to a group of patients, it hardly shows what it does to the individual patient in the naturalistic environment of the general practitioner. General practitioners are trained far less scientifically than clinical researchers; they may be less careful and less informed about certain illnesses. A general practitioner's patients are a much more heterogeneous group than the one selected for controlled trials. The patient taking his medicines at home may not comply with the doctors instructions, or he may take them together with other drugs. Hence, there is also a need for the evaluation of drugs outside the RCCT routine, in the naturalistic environment of the day-to-day general practice (Lasagna, 1986). In addition, there is the ethical concern, namely that withholding a drug room wider use until all the data required to evaluate its efficacy and riskiness have been collected in controlled clinical trial may inflict serious harm or even death upon numerous patients.

For this reason, highly promising new drugs are released early in phase III and given to a select group of physicians to monitor in actual practice. This 'monitored release' of new drugs uses the methods of post-marketing surveillance to allow potent new drugs on to the market more rapidly (Lasagna, 1984). In 1970, for instance, levadopa was admitted to the US market even though not all clinical and toxicological studies had been completed, because people suffering from Parkinson's disease could be treated effectively for the first time. Some 1,500 patients were monitored for adverse drug reactions (ADR) for a period of up to six years. But even this large sample is far too small in the case that rare ADR's are related to the drug. For instance, in order to discover that a drug like chloramphenicol changes the chance of developing aplastic anaemia from 1 in 525,000 to 1 in 40,000, millions of patients would have to be monitored. Hence, phase IV research, that is, post-marketing surveillance, is necessary if the risks of taking medicines are to be controlled within narrow bounds (Kareh and Lasagna, 1976; Lasagna, 1984; Laurence and Black, 1978; Napke, 1983 and Remington 1978).

But establishing a workable system of post-marketing surveillance is a major challenge even for a single country; it is a most difficult task for a huge and diverse market like that of the European Common Market. At present, Great Britain has the best system (Inman, 1987). The Commitee on Safety of Medicines sends out 'yellow cards' with which physicians may report ADRs to a Subcommittee on Adverse Reactions. However, it is generally very difficult to establish a probable or even a causal relationship between a drug and an observed event. There is, therefore, a tendency for ADRs to be under-reported. Great Britain has an alternative system, where the doctor reports prescription-related events on green cards. It is then left to the statistical evaluation of all events related to a medicine to infer whether an adverse drug reaction may exist.

The problem with establishing a European-wide system of post-marketing surveillance rests in the heterogeneity of its population and, above all, its medical practice. British doctors prefer insulin over oral antidiabetics; for German doctors the reverse is true. In comparison to their British counterparts, German physicians are restrictive in prescribing antibiotics. Could this be the reason for the fact that aplastic anaemia is related to chloramphenicol in Great Britain, but not in Germany? In cases of hypertension, British doctors tend to prescribe diuretics, whereas their German colleagues directly attack the heart with highly potent drugs. Besides differences in medical practice, genetic and environmental differences may be important. It is known from studies in Israel that Western Jews tend to be more affected by ADRs than Oriental Jews. And clinical studies in Great Britain have shown that the reactions to drugs of Sudanese people living in Great Britain are more similar to those of the British than to those of the native Sudanese.

A final problem for drug monitoring is related to differences in formulations for a specific drug. Dilantin had been used in New Zealand for years, when it was decided that its formulation should be changed to the one used in the USA. Almost instantly numerous reports of ADRs, ranging from dizziness to coma, turned up. What had made the difference? The active ingredient had not been changed! Investigations turned to the filler, the excipient. In the US case it was lactose, in the New Zealand case it was calcium sulphate. In comparison to lactose, calcium sulphate retards the absorption of the active ingredient. Hence, a change in formulation plus a given practice in prescribing a drug led to big changes in the therapeutic outcome.

The Messingill catastrophe of 1938 should already have been a warning that ADRs may not always be related to the active ingredient. They may also be related to the mix of excipients which embodies the active substance. In 1971 it was reported that a tablet with 1.25 mg of the drug premarin contained a cocktail of 28 different chemicals used as excipient. seven of the 28 chemicals turned out to be potent sensitizers. One patient, who regularly got headaches and prolonged gastrointestinal distress after taking the pill, had no troubles at all once the yellow coating was washed off. Once it is realized that it is not always the active ingredient but the diversity of the mix of excipients, which is responsible for ADRs, the policy towards competition by generics, towards hospital drug committees and towards post-marketing surveillance has to be given more than just second thoughts.

Since we now have a rough understanding of the regulatory problems of drug development, we must consider the following issues.

First, the European Community consists of twelve members, each one pursuing its own regulatory policy. What is to be done if the free movement of goods is to be extended to medicines by 1992? And what is the likely impact of the intended measures on the process of drug development?

Second, ever since the Kefauver hearings drug regulation has extended well beyond laboratory and clinical tests into decisions on pricing and marketing. This has feedback effects on drug development. And these feedback effects differ according to the specific regulatory constraints on pricing and marketing. This raises the danger that country-specific regulatory constraints lead to country-specific non-tariff trade barriers and competitive distortions. What impact will this have on a common European policy toward drugs?

The Regulation of Drug Development in The European Community

For more than two decades beginning in 1965, the Commission of the European Community has tried to harmonize and unify the regulatory rules for the approval of new drugs. This effort is guided by 'Commission Directives', which are binding law for the national authorities (EFPIA, 1988; Poggiolini, 1988; Wardell, 1978). As it stands now, there exist:

• a set of harmonized criteria and procedures for testing and controlling the safety, efficacy, and quality of drugs;
• a definition of the requirements which have to be met by the control and inspection of companies;
• the mutual recognition of toxicological and clinical trials, if they are conducted according to EC directives.

Further harmonizations regarding information and marketing-prescriptions are planned for the next years. All these harmonizations are a precondition for the mutual recognition of the national drug approvals themselves. Since the European High Court has ruled that a product which is admitted for sale in one Member State must in principle be marketable in all other Member States, the mutual recognition of national drug approvals is a necessary step in the direction of a free movement of goods within the EC.

By 1975 the European Commission thought that the harmonization had been developed to such an extent that a major step toward a speedier mutual recognition was justified. A new directive established the 'Committee for Proprietary Medicinal Products' (CPMP). Each country chooses one delegate and one alternate from its senior regulatory personnel. The chairman and one vice-chairman are elected by the delegates, another vice-chairman is nominated by the European Commission. Each delegate may bring up to three special experts with him to the meetings. The CPMP set up working parties to draft guidelines on quality control, and on preclinical and clinical drug evaluation procedures. It was supposed to become the core of the so-called 'multi-state drug application procedure' (MSAP) for the mutual, Community-wide recognition of national drug approvals.

Under the MSA procedure a company which had received a marketing authorization (MA) from the regulatory agency of one Member State could ask for mutual recognition of that approval by at least five other states. The agency which granted the initial drug approval had to send it together with the initial NDA to the regulatory agencies of the countries nominated by the company. Within 120 days each agency had to give approval or raise objections. In the latter case the CPMP had to be notified, and within another 60 days the CPMP had to form an opinion on the matter. It could be overruled by the national agency within 30 days. Table 8.2 summarizes the experience with the multi-state application procedure (MSAP) until its revision by Directive 83/570/EEC became effective in November 1985. EPPIA (1988), p. 22.

Table 8.2   Use of the multi-state application procedure based on Directive 75/319/EEC until November 1985 when Directive 83/570/EEC became effective

Country	Number of cases a country was 1st in granting a MA	Number of cases a country was nominated for an MSAP	Approved	Rejected	Pending
			Fate of MSAP		
Belgium	5	33	24	9	0
Denmark	7	26	16	10	0
France	7	15	10	4	1
Germany	5	25	18	5	2
Greece	0	12	7	4	1
Ireland	1	24	15	6	3
Italy	0	28	14	8	6
Luxembourg	0	37	34	2	1
Netherlands	0	35	27	7	1
United Kingd.	16	20	10	10	0
Total	41	259	175	65	15

Source: EFPIA (1988), p.22.

The United Kingdom leads in the number of cases where a marketing authorization was applied for and granted for the first time. This reflects the high prestige of the British drug evaluation system. The Benelux countries received the largest number of nominations for the multi-state drug application procedure, followed by Italy. All four countries are known for their lengthy processes of granting marketing approvals. Hence, they were very often nominated for a MSAP because companies wished to use their

120 and 60 days' time limits on decision-making as a disciplinary constraint on the drug review process. However, the MSAP hardly had any disciplinary force. Table 8.3 shows that actual decision times were much longer than those specified by Directive 75/318/EEC.

It is also apparent that the national competent authorities did not feel strongly bound either by the marketing authority of another regulatory board or by the opinion of the CPMP, for one-fifth of the MSAPs were rejected by at least one country, the highest number of refusals coming from Great Britain. In only 16 of the 41 MSAPs did all Member States involved grant a marketing authorization; in 6 cases the countries involved came to a decision contrary to the one reached by the competent authority issuing the initial marketing approval.

Table 8.3   Length of time in months needed to reach decisions under the MSAP based on Directive 75/318/EEC

Country	Median time	Mean time	Range of time
Belgium	11	11	9.6–13.9
Denmark	10	10	9.8–14.0
France	13	13	9.5–13.8
Germany	17	17	9.4–21.6
Ireland	12	12	9.6–13.9
Italy	26	n.a.	n.a.
Luxembourg	6	6	2.9–13.9
Netherlands	12	12	9.6–13.9

Source: EFPIA (1988), p. 24.

In view of the long delays in decision-making and the diversity of decisions finally rendered in a multi-state application procedure, the requirement that at least five Member States be involved in the Community approach to drug approval was highly costly. The MSA procedures was, therefore, revised by Directive 83/570/EEC. Now only two additional countries must be nominated in order to be able to apply for an MSA. It is furthermore provided that the agency granting the first drug approval must forward the full dossier on its decision complete with assessment and expert reports and a summary to the other nominated competent authorities. The reason for this is that all regulatory boards should become better informed of and more involved in each other's decision-making. Again within 120 days the agencies have to either grant approval or raise objections. In the latter case, the CPMP receives the full dossier and renders its opinion, which is not binding, within 60 days. The time span for the national competent authorities to deal with the opinion of the CPMP has been increased from 30 to 60 days. However, the CPMP has to be informed of the final decision of the national authority 30 days earlier than the company.

From November 1985, when Directive 83/570/EEC became effective, until February 1988 the new MSA procedure was used for 36 NDAs. The Uk granted the first marketing authorization most frequently that is, in 14 of the 36 cases. France was second with 9, Germany third with 5 cases. After the first marketing authorization had been obtained, the countries received multi-state applications with the following frequencies:

Belgium: 23; Luxembourg: 22; Germany: 21; Greece: 21; Italy: 21; Netherlands: 19; Spain: 18; Denmark: 16; UK: 13; France, Ireland: 12.

Until February 1988, 20 of the 36 cases made their way to the CPMP, and 17 of the 20 resulted in a multi-state approval. The numbers indicate that the MSA procedure is still a lengthy process, with the national competent authorities raising objections against each other almost routinely.

The road to the mutual recognition of national drug approvals is a thorny one. This sobering experience prompted the European Commission to issue a new Directive 87/22/EEC, effective from 1 July 1987. In the early 1980s it could be foreseen that the advances in biotechnology would generate completely new types of drugs. Drugs are normally used to influence the chemistry between the cells of the human body. However, biotechnological drugs influence the intra-cellular processes. Their testing and evaluation poses new problems (Lasagna, 1986), and the Commission wanted to ensure harmonization while drug evaluation procedures were being discussed and developed. So Directive 87/22/EEC established a 'concerted' MSAP for all new drugs derived by

- recombinant DNA technology;
- controlled expression of genes coding for biologically active proteins; and
- hybridoma and monoclonal antibody methods.

A company developing a biotechnological drug has to submit the standard European dossier to the competent authority of a Member State. Ideally, it should apply for registration in all twelve Member States, so that the whole Community would become involved in reaching a decision. In any case, the national authority chosen by the company for the initial approval sends the complete dossier to the CPMP and to the national authorities nominated by the company. It acts as rapporteur on the application to the CPMP and to the other authorities. Authorities of countries not nominated for the concertation procedure receive only summaries of and expert opinions on the drug application.

The NDA is evaluated by the CPMP and national authorities concurrently. Within 90 days, with the possibility of a 90-day extension, the CPMP reaches an opinion on the drug application and sends it to the national authorities. Within 30 days the national authority must decide whether to grant or reject the application. Once the application is approved, the applicant is protected for ten years against imitation, in so far as would-be imitators cannot refer to the registration documentation for their own NDAs. This concerned drug approval procedure, which is obligatory for biotechnological drugs, is optional for

- new drug delivery systems;
- new chemical entities;

- products with entirely new indications;
- radiopharmaceutical products; and
- significant advances in technical processes.

Sufficient experience has not yet been accumulated in order to judge the effectiveness of the concerted MSAP.

Personally, I doubt that the concerted MSAP will be effective. The differences between the national schools of medicine, different attitudes toward the evaluation of risks and benefits, and differently perceived needs for new drugs will lead to diverging interpretations of the NDAs, despite the fact that they have been prepared according to a standardized European format. In my opinion the most likely result is that the European Commission will feel compelled to push for a common European Drug Agency (EDA) to substitute the multi-state application procedure.

The fear is often expressed that a centralized European approach to drug admission will result in a procedure where for every single regulatory measure the most stringent one existing in a Member State will be chosen. This need not be the case for the following reason. If the European Commission asks the Council of Ministers to establish a special commission empowered to decide on the matter, the European Commission must present its proposals for an EDA only to that commission for approval by qualified majority. Procedures within the Council of Ministers tend to be blocked by egoistic and opportunistic national considerations and by all kinds of logrolling on the basis of the principle of unanimity. It has been found that national expert delegates to special commissions behave less opportunistic as they are not so closely bound by partisan considerations and loyalties to specific interest groups. And the principle of qualified majority constrains incentives to logroll.

Thus, the European Commission has a good chance of being able to establish a well-functioning European Drug Agency, with the already existing CPMP prouding a nucleus of experts. Statements on drug regulation tend to invoke the importance of flexibility. But flexibility is difficult to establish and to preserve, above all in a bureaucratic environment. For this reason, drug admission has to rely as much as possible on evaluations by committees of experts brought in from the outside. A regulatory agency using inside expertise has to act in a much more formal and bureaucratic way than an expert committee. This becomes evident from a comparison between the US Food and Drug Administration and the British Committee on the Safety of Medicines. The FDA is plagued by the difficulty of how to attract personnel who, on the one hand, are scientifically so qualified that they are able to evaluate the scientific work of others and yet, on the other hand, are motivated to fulfil administrative duties. In comparison to outside experts, in-house staffs tend to be bound more to yesterday's knowledge and to develop attitudes inimical to novel procedures. It is also easier for the news media to attack an administration than an expert committee. A regulatory administration, therefore, is pushed deeper into an adversary position and has a much higher preference for its own safety. Outside experts may try informal ways of clearing problems in some toxicological or clinical test. But an administration must always prove its carefulness by following routine, well documented methods.

The establishment of a well functioning EDA could make a major contribution toward shortening the whole drug approval process. The typical time taken to complete the development of a NCE by 1985 was about fourteen years. The present value of the total development costs in 1985 was in the order of $100 million. A forward shift in drug admission by one year, even without any reduction in research tasks, would still result in large R & D cost savings because the R & D expenditures would be tied up in the project for a shorter period. The effective patent duration would be lengthened by one year. And for a successful product this could amount to a present value of $50 million or even much more.

However, even if the EDA was modelled not according to the US Food and Drug Administration but according to the British Committee on the Safety of Medicines, serious problems for a European-wide regulation of drugs would arise because phase IV drug research, that is monitored release and post-marketing surveillance, become much more difficult in the heterogeneous context of Europe in comparison to the rather homogeneous one of a single country. The former commissioner of the FDA, Alexander Schmidt, once proposed the following 'equation' for demonstrating the problems of drug regulation:

$$\begin{array}{cccc} \text{Information} & \text{Ability to get} & \text{Ability to} & \text{Ease of} \\ \text{needed to} \quad + & \text{information} \quad + & \text{control use} \quad + & \text{withdrawal of} \quad = C \\ \text{approve} & \text{after marketing} & \text{after marketing} & \text{drug approval} \end{array}$$

where C is a constant.

It says that a given level of 'drug safety' is, in essence, the result of a trade-off between 'pre-marketing' and 'post-marketing' evaluation of drug safety. The more efficient phase IV drug evaluation is – and again Great Britain with its highly regarded PMS and PEM systems is a model to follow – the fewer are the risks that rare side-effects which could not be detected in toxicological and controlled clinical studies will be overlooked. We have seen that drug regulation faces two major problems. First, animal studies are an unreliable model for the effectiveness of drugs in humans. With current standards for animal studies a large number of the important drugs of today would never have been admitted for study in humans, for example: adrenalin, aspirin, cortisone, insulin, penicillin, streptomycin, and tetracyclin are all drugs which are highly teratogenic in at least some species of animals.

The more restrictive the standards for animal studies are, for instance, in order to predict teratogenic and carcinogenic effects in humans, the greater is the number of valuable drugs that will be lost in the discovery process for the reason that the animal studies make wrong predictions. Second, the controlled clinical studies of phase II and III are much better suited for the evaluation of drug efficacy than for drug safety. A double blind test looks for evidence of whether a new drug is superior to a placebo or to other drugs in well-chosen, small groups of patients. The test is scientifically designed and applied in a scientific environment. Drug safety, however, is more a problem of giving a drug in a natural environment to large numbers of patients, who as a population are very heterogeneous: patients may take all kinds of other drugs concurrently, and they comply in various degrees of strictness with the instructions of the physician and pharmacist. It is information collected in this environment which is needed for the evaluation of the benefits and risks of prescribing a certain drug. Furthermore, one has to understand that new drugs are, in essence, a means of finding new fields of medical research, because very often the whole spectrum of physiological processes stimulated by the drug is unknown and is only gradually discovered. This means that no prior knowledge exists for the design of phase I and III studies in order to test for side effects or adverse drug reactions (Laurence and Black, 1978; Maxwell, 1984).

The major challenge for a European-wide drug regulation is the establishment of a reliable and fast system of post-marketing surveillance. This task is all the more easy the smaller the country is and the more homogeneous its medical practice and its population are. But the European Community consists of a diversity of national medical schools with different attitudes toward drug therapies, different drug consumption patterns, and a much more heterogeneous population. It should be easier to run PMS systems on a decentralized national basis. However, what would happen if the competent authority in Greece, say, decided to withdraw a drug, while the Danish one thought the drug should still be available? Is it conceivable that the Danish authority would be able to withstand the pressure to follow the Greek example? The general public does not understand the complexities of drug evaluation.

In the case of oral contraceptives it has been reported that they cause thrombosis in some persons. Although that casualty has never been proven in controlled clinical studies, it could be established that the risk for a young, healthy woman of dying from thrombosis is eight times higher if she takes the pill. That appears to be a tremendous increase in risk. However, what about the risk of dying from unintended pregnancy? With a ratio of one per 100,000 per year the risk of dying from thrombosis after taking the pill is ten times smaller than that of dying in a traffic accident or that of committing suicide. It is also true that women who smoke and take the pill have a somewhat higher risk of dying from thrombosis. Is it really sensible to have these women stop taking the pill, if 2 out of 4–5 are going to die from cancer or heart disease anyhow? Whatever the relative risk of a drug, for example, 1 per 100,000 or one per one million, a drug that becomes associated with some 20 death cases becomes subjected to enormous pressure from the uneducated general public to be withdrawn from the market. A centralized European-wide system of drug monitoring, therefore, poses the problem that reports on adverse drug reactions would be magnified beyond reasonable proportions, because the area over which ADRs are collected becomes so large and because there is the tendency to count the absolute number of ADRs and not their relative incidence. Thus, a unified European market may very well increase the economic risks for companies of marketing their drugs.

The Control of Drug Prices in The European Community

At present a wide variety of approaches to controlling the general level of drug prices exists in the different Member States of the Community. Different methods of price control either impose severe constraints on the free intra-European movement of goods or are responsible for equally severe distortions of competitive processes. But before turning to these issues we should look at national drug price levels and drug consumption differences (Table 8.4). This kind of observation is broadly informative despite the fact that international price comparisons are flawed by numerous methodological problems.

Table 8.4   Selected data on general health and drug expenditures in the European Community.

Country	Health costs as % of GDP (1985)	Drug consumption per capita ECU (1984)	As % of GDP (1984)	As % of total health costs	Prices in 1985 (Eur. Aver. = 100) inclu. taxes	excl taxes
Belgium	6.4	90	0.81	8.6	83	85
Denmark	n.a.	74	0.50	7.0	140	123
France	9.4	102	0.81	8.8	66	66
Germany	8.2	125	0.89	11.0	157	148
Greece	4.6	45	0.95	20.2	n.a.	n.a.
Ireland	n.a.	46	0.67	8.8	116	124
Italy	7.2	78	0.91	12.4	69	68
Netherlands	n.a.	46	0.38	4.1	136	139
Portugal	n.a.	35	1.08	18.9	n.a.	n.a.
Spain	n.a.	48	0.81	12.1	n.a.	n.a.
United Kingdom	6.0	62	0.59	9.6	91	97

Source: Commission of the European Communities, 1988; Eichin, 1988; Hankins, 1988.

A closer inspection of the table shows some similarities and some striking dissimilarities. Thus, there appears to be a close association between GDP per capita and the percentage share of drug expenditures in GDP and total health costs. Both in Greece and Portugal these percentages are much larger than the corresponding ones in more developed countries. Also the share of total health costs in GDP appears to increase with per capita GDP. Taking into account a larger set of country specific data, one concludes that in 1985 a one thousand dollar increase in GDP per capita was associated with a 0.6 per cent increase in the share of total health costs in GDP.

Turning now to the dissimilarities, we see quite opposite relationships between the level of drug prices and the size of the drug bill in Member States. One expects that a country like Germany, which has one of the highest levels of drug prices, would also have one of the highest levels of per capita drug expenditures. But France, with less than half the German price level, expends almost as much on drugs per capita as Germany, and the Netherlands, with almost the same price level as Germany, spends a little more than one-third on drugs (Table 8.5):

Table 8.5   Comparison between Germany's per capita price levels and drug
expenditure and those of other Member States.

Country comparison	Ratio of price levels	Ratio of per capita drug expenditures
Germany/DK	1.12	1.7
Germany/NL	1.15	2.7
Germany/UK	1.7	2.0
Germany/FR	2.4	1.2
Germany/IT	2.3	1.6

Such diversities have numerous causes that cannot be dealt with in this chapter. It is, however, appropriate to again point to striking differences in medical practices. Antibiotics, for instance, make up 20 per cent of all drug expenditures in Greece, but only 3 per cent in Germany. Central nervous system drugs have a share on 7 per cent in Italian drug sales, but one of 22 per cent in the Danish ones. In view of these structural differences in drug expenditures, general across country price level comparisons provide very little information on the impact of price changes on drug expenditures. It should, furthermore, be recalled that these large differences in therapeutic attitudes have an equally large impact on the incidence of reported'adverse drug reactions. Otherwise, what explanation can be given for the finding that the antibiotic chloramphenicol is associated with the ADR, 'aplastic anaemia', in the USA, Great Britain, and Belgium – countries with a wide spread use of antibiotics – but not in Germany – a country with a tradition of restrictive use of antibiotics!

Since we are interested in the typical impact of national price regulations on the free movement of goods in the European Community, only three exemplary kinds of regulatory schemes shall be treated in the following.

Until now the German drug market has been said to be the least restrictive. Some few drugs are excluded from reimbursement by the sickness funds. To increase cost-consciousness on the part of the prescribing physician 'transparency lists' are prepared which give information on the average daily treatment costs for different drugs in the same therapeutic field. There is some experimentation with ways of monitoring the prescribing habits of doctors, and of stimulating the substitution of branded drugs by generics. However, substantial changes may come in the future. Currently under debate in Parliament is a law which would introduce for each therapeutic use a fixed amount of money to be reimbursed. This amount must be set in such a way that patients have access to all drugs necessary for treatment. Drug prices in excess of this amount would have to be paid by the patient.

France controls the prices of those drugs admitted by the Sécurité Sociale for reimbursement. A drug, which has received marketing authorization is not yet automatically admitted for reimbursement. To get on the drug list of the Sécurité Sociale the new drug has to pass through several evaluation steps. In the first step the new drug application is sent to a 'Commission de la Transparence', which gives its opinion on the relative merits of this drug in comparison to existing drugs. It also proposes a rate of reimbursement, which ranges from 100 per cent to 70 per cent to 40 per cent of the drug's price, and gives advice as to dosage, length of treatment, and package sizes. This opinion is forwarded to an 'Economic Group' composed of representatives of the ministries of finance, social security, and public health. This group fixes the price by considering the benefits of the new drug in relation to the benefits and prices of already existing drugs. Once the price is fixed, it may take years before an increase is permitted.

In sharp contrast to France, Great Britain is not concerned with individual drug prices, but only with their general level. The Department of Health and Social Security (DHSS) has the dual responsibility of holding total drug expenditures down to a reasonable level on the one hand, and of protecting the industry's capability to innovate by guaranteeing an acceptable level of profitability on the other hand. The DHSS tries to fulfil these two at least partly conflicting tasks by operating a Pharmaceutical Price Regulation Scheme which sets maximum targets for companies' profitability. If the targets are surpassed, the company has to refund the excess to the DHSS.

What is to be inferred as regards the free movements of drugs in the European Community? The following factors are important.

First, the elasticity of demand for drugs of a given category varies between countries for the reason that different medical practices and consumption patterns exist. Think of the example of the relative use of antibiotics.

Second, depending upon country-specific medical practices, the rates of reimbursement and the price levels or price increases granted by national authorities vary due to different value judgements made on the relative benefits of specific drugs.

Third, differences in the type of price control systems generate different structures of drug prices.

Fourth, in view of the fact that some Member States of the Community have a more or less intense interest in furthering the competitive position of their national pharmaceutical industry, these Member States tend to use their price control systems in such a way that foreign competition is put at a disadvantage. A frequent accusation is that certain cost elements, for example R & D, are not included in the circulation of the prices of imported drugs, although such costs may be reclaimed for domestically produced drugs. Additionally, it is argued that domestically produced drugs get more favourable price levels, price increases, or reimbursement rates.

Fifth, even if all similar drugs carried the same seller prices, the prices to the consumer would vary enormously due to different value added tax rates for drugs, and because of dissimilarities in the wholesale and retail systems of drug distribution (Table 8.6).

Taking all five factors into consideration, it is obvious that there are numerous barriers to the free intra-European movement of drugs and that substantial differences in the prices for the same drug between the individual Member

Table 8.6   Value added tax rates on drugs in the EC (%)

Country	VAT rates on drugs
Belgium	6.0
Denmark	22.0
France	5.5
Germany	14.0
Greece	6.0
Ireland	0.0
Italy	9.0
Luxembourg	3.0
Netherlands	6.0
Spain	6.0
United Kingdom	0.0

States must exist. Such price differences can have important repercussions for the pricing and marketing decision of a company. Suppose a German drug company sells its drug on the Italian market; because of the price controls there, the drug's Italian price will be only a fraction of the one quoted in Germany. But the European High Court and the German Drug Authority have decided that the drug can lawfully be imported from Italy, be repacked according to German standards, and be sold at much lower prices in Germany. In some German states the sickness funds induce doctors to prescribe such imported substitutes. In the case that the loss of revenues therefrom becomes sufficiently large, the German company may decide not to introduce its new drugs in certain Member States, with the consequence that a 'drug lag' between the Member States of the European Community would develop, leading to different qualities of medical treatment.

We finally recognize that harmonization of the regulation of the drug discovery process does not lead to a harmonized policy of drug approval. This will probably be achieved only by a central European Drug Agency.

But even with a central EDA we would not have a uniform availability of drugs in the Community, because an EDA authorization to market a new drug would not imply that the drug is actually admitted for sale on the market. Numerous restrictions on reimbursement and pricing could still prevent it from either becoming available at all or from becoming available on equal conditions.

For this reason the European Commission is working on a new directive which aims at making transparent all measures and criteria by which Member States control their expenditures on drugs. There may be hope that in some future the 'transparency directive' will trigger a movement towards a harmonization of national drug price control systems. But perhaps this can only be achieved if the European Commission decides to eventually develop a common European policy on health.

The Impact of Regulation on New Product Development in The Drug Industry: A European Perspective

A significant characteristic of the drug industry is the fact that deregulation is not an issue. This is true for the regulation of the drug development process and for the regulation of prices and profitability. What is the issue, and it is a most important one, is the question: what kinds of regulation should we have or are we likely to get? From early antiquity until today the adulteration of drugs – or in modern days on would say that the careless production of drugs without proper bioavailability characteristics – has been a major problem of drug therapy. It stimulated state interferences in the supply of drugs. An early example is the decree of the Venetian Maggior Consiglio on the distribution of drugs. Later regulatory measures were almost always introduced in response to drug disasters. In most cases these disasters were not caused by greedy capitalistic profiteering from poor patients.

At the time the Elixir Sulphanilamide catastrophe took its toll of 107 deaths, pharmacological knowledge was poorly developed. Both the active ingredient and the solvent were safe, it taken separately at the appropriate dosages. What was unknown was that their combination was lethal. And evidence has been presented here which illustrates that even today the tendency is to always associate adverse drug reactions with the active substance and not with the cocktail of excipients, and that this tendency of today is still dangerous for individual patients. The obsession that some hospitals have for producing their own formulations of drugs in order to save money is risky for their patients, although these risks, even if lethal, mostly remain undetected.

The MS Food, Drug, and Cosmetics Act of 1938 brought the requirement that only drugs with acceptable safety levels were to be admitted to the market. This provision did not prevent the thalidomide catastrophe. If the drug has not been such a success in Germany for the very reason that it appeared to be so superior to the barbiturates, it would not have been used on so large a scale that its teratogenic effects on babies could have been traced to the drug. Without these tragic repercussions in Europe, the drug would have been admitted, albeit somewhat later, in the United States. In this context it is significant to recall that the Kefauver amendment of 1962 introduced the requirement of efficacy tests to drug regulation. The safety tests had been in the law since 1938. However, one effect of by the thalidomide tragedy was to stimulate changes in the whole procedure of conducting animal toxicology and clinical studies.

But by the 1970s there was a gradual realization that the newly designed regulatory procedures for efficacy and safety testing also had their costs, and some were of a highly unethical nature. It was not only that drug development became costly in terms of investment funds. In addition, the tendency to demand ever new series of tests to determine lethal doses, mutagenicity, teratogenicity and carcinogenicity in various species of animals in long test series proved to be not only wasteful, because animals provide poor models for the behaviour of drugs in humans, but it was ethically questionable. Furthermore the demanding tests carried out during preclinical research had the side-effect that fewer drugs were admitted to the stage of clinical evaluation. Precisely because animals make poor models for drug behaviour, this regulatory measure has resulted in an unknown and unknowable loss of valuable drugs.

For the further evolution of drug development regulation the practolol experience of 1974 was decisive (Laurence and Black, 1978: pp. 79–81). Practolol is a beta-blocker. It was introduced to the British market after a careful review by the Committee on the Safety of Medicines. In practice it proved to be superior to the then existing beta-blockers in the treatment of angina pectoris, high blood pressure and heart rhythm disorders. It became a widely used drug. In 1974 an ophthalmologist saw patients who complained about dry eyes behind the lids. He heard that these patients were all taking practolol. Quite soon an adverse drug reactions necessitating eye surgery, and occasionally leading to blindness, was discovered. Today the use of this drug is highly restricted. It has now been discovered that practolol is responsible for a very rare immunological reaction in a small number of patients. At the time the drug was tested, that effect was unknown; no animal model existed to test it. But even if one had existed, the incidence of the reaction is so rare that 50,000 to 100,000 animals would have been required to detect the effect. Experiences like these have put a damper on the hope that drug safety can be firmly established before drugs are admitted to the market.

First, there needs to be a greater awareness of what Paracelsus wrote more than four hundred years ago: 'All things are poisons and there is nothing that is harmless; the dose alone determines that something is not a poison' (cited in Laurence and Black, 1978: pp. 74–5). Or in other words: 'Drugs are useful poisons', that is, there is no such things as a 'safe' drug!

Second, drug development is an inherently empirical process, in which neither animal nor clinical studies provide reliable ways of ascertaining whether a given drug is safe to an acceptable degree. The assessment of safety is, to a very considerable extent, a task of monitoring the performance of a drug in the natural environment of its actual use.

But this has important implications for a European-wide system of regulating the drug discovery process. The European Commission has gone a long way toward harmonizing the preclinical and clinical tests procedures. However, due to national differences in medical schools, the harmonization of procedures does not ensure that the results of the standardized procedures are similarly evaluated. This experience will probably induce the Commission to give up its efforts to push for a concerted multi-state drug application procedure and to substitute it by a common European Drug Agency. A central drug regulatory agency would evolve either in the direction of the US Food and Drug Administration or in the direction of the British Committee on the Safety of Medicines.

In the first case, the EDA is likely to become even more bureaucratic than the FDA. Then the time to get a new drug approved would be lengthened and R & D costs would increase above the international average, with obvious consequences for the international competitive position of the European Drug industry.

In the second case, the EDA could be a competitive benefit for the European drug industry and the national health services, if two conditions can be fulfilled. New models for preclinical research must be developed so that more new chemical entities can be admitted for phase I and II tests in humans. This would lower the attrition rate of new drug candidates in the early phases of the drug discovery process. And it is, furthermore, of utmost importance that effective ways of monitoring the performance of drugs admitted to the market be developed, because this is the most promising way of shortening the drug approval process without lowering the level of acceptable risks of drug therapy.

A look at part of Alexander Schmidt's 'equation' for the regulation of the drug discovery process helps to derive further implications:

Information	Ability to get	
needed to +	information +	....+ = C
approve	after marketing	

Without an effective European-wide post-marketing surveillance system an EDA would have to rely more heavily on pre-marketing information. But obtaining pre-marketing information is especially costly and time-consuming in the case of drugs for chronic disease, for the treatment of pregnant women and for babies. Drug development costs and times are much lower for short-term therapies. A side-effect of an eventual inability to develop an effective system of post-marketing surveillance would be a shift of R & D efforts away from long-term to short-term therapies. But with the growing age of the population, the incidence of long-term therapies is increasing, thus requiring a shift of R & D efforts in the opposite direction.

The more progress toward a unified European drug approval process is made, the more frustration will arise from the fact that heterogenous national policies of price regulations deny the possibility of gathering the fruits from a unified drug approval process. As drug regulation stands at present, a 'marketing authorization' by a national regulatory agency is no permission to actually market the product. Im most Member States a new drug has to pass through a lengthy evaluation process to determine its economic benefits and costs for the purpose of fixing its price and its reimbursement rate.

In doing this the Member States are guided by national egoistic motives. Some members, not being a home base for a significant domestic pharmaceutical industry, try to act as free riders by not accepting R & D costs in their price controls. Other countries try to attract R & D establishments from their neighbours by a policy of accepting R & D costs as elements of drug prices only if they are expended in the home country. Still others grant higher domestic prices if they are the basis for defending higher prices in export markets. A by-product of certain drug price regulations is a tendency either to distort R & D efforts or to form a drug lag.

In the 1970s France was the only exception to the international tendency for a decline in the number of new chemical entities introduced into the market. But although the French rate of new drug introductions was above the international standard, its share of introductions of important new drugs was below it. The explanation is straightforward. The French price freeze on existing drugs forced firms to withdraw old drugs from the market and to replace them with new ones in order to escape the price freeze for at least some time. 'New' meant any drug which was able to replace an old one in the price control system. If the price regulation authorities try to avoid this bias, they are likely to fall into another one. They may decide to admit only drugs with a 'significant' advance over existing drugs. But in view of the wide interpersonal divergences of reactions to a drug, how does one know what 'significant' means? Is an oral contraceptive which is most compatible with only a small minority of women not a significant advance? Which expert has the scientific authority to pass that value judgement (Lasagna, 1976)? Furthermore, how can experts be certain that a new drug is unimportant, if the natural environment of the market is often the decisive place for really testing drugs? Thus, efforts to avoid admitting trivial modifications of old drugs bear the consequence that at least some important new drugs will be withheld from the market, and this means

1 from health care; and
2 from pharmaceutical research, because so-called 'trivial' molecular modifications have often led to significant new insights into drug effects.

Thus, the European Commission will realize three consequences of the national price regulation schemes.

First national price regulation schemes interfere with efforts to establish a workable system of post-marketing drug monitoring as a means to:

1 reduce the time needed to get a new drug approved;
2 lower the drug development costs or, at least, to lower the rate with at they increase;
3 increase the expected returns from drug development as efforts to increasing the international competitiveness of the European drug industry.

Second, national price regulation schemes are a barrier to the free movement of goods in the Common Market.

Third, national price regulation schemes are characterized by national conflicts over:

1 which Member State is a base to an innovation drug industry;
2 whether there should or should not be an innovative drug industry in Europe, because some members do not care from what part of the world they buy their drugs from as long as they think they can act as free riders on other country's R & D results.

In the end, the European Commission must realize that the logical consequence to a unified approach to the regulation of the drug discovery process is the unified approach to the regulation of the profitability of the drug industry, and maybe even a unified health policy.

References

Baake, O. M. Wardell W. and Lasagna, L. (1984), 'Drug discontinuations in the United Kingdom and the United States, 1964 to 1983: issues of safety', *Clinical Pharmacology and Therapeutics*, Vol. 35, 559–567.

174   Erich Kaufer

Baake, O. M. (1984), 'Drug selection in a regulated society: the Norwegian experience', *Hospital Formulary*, Vol. 19, 411–12, 415, 418, 421.
Commission of the European Communities (1988), *Research on the 'Cost of Non-Europe'*, Basic Findings, Vol. 1.
Comanor, W. S. (1986), 'The political economy of the pharmaceutical industry', *Journal of Economic Literature*, Vol. 24, 1178–1217.
Eichin, K. E. (1988), 'Internationale Perspektiven der Pharma-Industrie', *Pharmazeutische Industrie*, Vol. 50, 277–85.
Emmerich, V. (1980), *Staatliche Interventionen, Arzneimittelmarkt und EWG-Vertrag*, Nomos Verlag, Baden-Baden.
EFPIA (1988), *A Brief Guide to the EEC Directives Concerning Medicines*, Brussels.
Hankin, R. (1988), 'The economic milieu in Europe: view from the Common Market', in: W. van Eimeren, B. Horisberger (eds), *Socioeconomic Evaluation of Drug Therapy*, Springer Verlag, Heidelberg, pp. 15–22.
Hutt, P. B., (1983), Investigations and reports respecting FDA regulation of new drugs, parts I and II, *Clinical Pharmacology and Therapeutics*, Vol. 33: 537–48, 647–87.
Inman, W. H. W. (1987), 'Prescription event monitoring: its strategic role in postmarketing surveillance for drug safety', *PEM News*, March 1987, 16–29.
Kaitin, K. I. (1986), 'Impact of generic drugs on the pharmaceutical market place', *Private Practice*, September 1986, 18–20.
Karch, F. E and Lasagna L, (1976), 'Evaluating adverse drug reactions', *Adverse Drug Reaction Bulletin*, No. 59, 204–7.
Kaufer, E. (1976), *Die Okonomik der Pharmazeutischen Industrie*, Nomos Verlag, Baden-Baden.
Kaufer, E. (1979), *Die Kostendämpfung bei Arzneimitteln*, Nomos Verlag, Baden-Baden.
Kessler, I. (1977), *Putting Reason into Regulation*, Center for the Study of Drug Development, PS 7705, Rochester, N.Y.
Lasagna, L. (1976) *Drug Discovery and Introduction: Regulation and Over-regulation*, Center for the Study of Drug Development, Rochester, N.Y.
Lasagna, L. (1976), 'Consensus among experts: the unholy grail', *Perspectives in Biology and Medicine*, Vol. 19, 537–48.
Lasagna, L. (1984), 'Techniques for ADR reporting', in: Skandia International Symposia, *Detection and Prevention of Adverse Drug Reactions*, Almqvist & Wiksell International, Stockholm, pp. 146–51.
Lasagna, L. (1986), *Clinical Trials in the Natural Environment*, Center for the Study of Drug Development, RS 8695, Boston Mass.
Lasagna, L. (1986), 'Clinical testing of products prepared by biotechnology', *Regulatory Toxicology and Pharmacology*, Vol. 6, 385–90.
Lasagna, L. (1987), *Journal of Clinical Pharmacology*.
Laurence, D. R. and Black J. W. (1978), *The Medicine You Take*, Fontana Paperback, London.
Mandich, G. (1958), 'Primi riconoscimenti Veneziani di un diritto di privativa agli inventori', *Rivista di Diritto Industriale*, Vol. 1, 101–55.
Mattison, N., Thomas, E. Trimble, A. G. and Wardell, W. M. (1984), 'The development of self-originated new drugs by Swiss pharmaceutical firms, 1960–1980', *Regulatory Toxicology and Pharmacology*, Vol. 4, 157–73.
Maxwell, R. A. (1984), 'The state of the art of the science of drug discovery – an opinion', *Drug Development Research*, Vol. 4, 375–89.
Napke, E. (1983), 'Adverse reactions: some pitfalls and postulates', in: M. N. G. Dukes (ed), *Side Effects of Drugs Annual 7*: XV–XXVI.
Poggiolini, D. (1988), 'Perspectives de la libre circulation des médicaments dans la CEE', *Industrie Santé*, No. 133, 15–17.

Remington, R. D. (1978), *Post-marketing Surveillance: A Comparison of Methods*, Center for the Study of Drug Development, PS 7811, Rochester, N.Y.

Walker, S. R. Schuetz, E. Schuppan, D. and Gelzer, J. (1984), 'A comparative retrospective analysis of data from short- and long-term animal toxicity studies', *Archives of Toxicology*, Supplement 7, 485–7.

Wardell, W. M. (1978), *Controlling the Use of Therapeutic Drugs: An International* Comparison', American Enterprise Institute, Washington D.C.

Wardell, W. M. (1979), 'The history of drug discovery, development, and regulation', in: Robert I. Chien (ed.), *Issues in Pharmaceutical Economics, pp. 3–11, D.Heath and Company, Lexington, Mass.*

Zbinden, G. (1982), 'Current trends in safety testings and toxicological research', *Naturwissenchaften*, Vol. 69, 255–9.

Zbinden, G. and Flury-Roversi, M. (1981), 'Significance of the LD (50)-test for the toxicological evaluation of chemical substances', *Archives of Toxicology*, Vol. 47; 77–99.

9. Paradoxes of Deregulatory Strategies at Community level: The Example of Product Safety Policy

Christian Joerges

1 Introduction: The Europeanization of Product Safety Law

The American debate on regulation and deregulation, on the failures of 'economic' regulation and the costs and benefits of 'social' regulation has also concerned Europe for a long time. But it has hardly touched upon the regulatory activities of the European Community. There are many reasons for this apparent gap. Firstly, any effort to apply the conceptual framework of the debate to the achievements and shortcomings of regulation has to take into account the institutional and political differences between full-blown federations or nation states and the Community – for example, the limited legislative and, even more importantly, administrative competency of the Community. Secondly, contrary to the creation of the American Federation, the process of European integration and the efforts to bring about an internal market are faced with 'post-liberal' mixed economies, which have all developed specific regulatory patterns. Thirdly, any regulatory activity on the European level, be it a harmonization of pertinent national regulations or deregulation of such regulations, affects not only the economic interest of more or less powerful societal actors but also the policies of Member States which usually defend their national 'achievements' and tend to identify themselves with the competitive advantages of their industries.

Considering all these differences between national and Community settings, I shall take the liberty of somewhat reinterpreting the agenda of this conference. Instead of addressing directly the pros and cons of the Community's regulatory activities, I shall focus upon the integration process on national policies. I do not, of course, wish to assert that this approach is the only conceivable one. I am trying to show, however, that this perspective is particularly illuminating in the field under scrutiny, namely the regulation of product safety. To state my argument in nutshell: the Community is not facing a simple choice between regulation and deregulation; rather, its present internal market policy is creating regulatory gaps which the Community will have to respond to sooner or later. This argument calls for some additional preliminary explanations.

Product safety policy, which first took on a clearer form in Western industrial states during the 1960s in the context of their various consumer protection movements, has in the mean time, like consumer protection as a whole, lost some of its former attractiveness for political 'go-getters'. However, the safety issue has never disappeared completely from the political agenda. New information on the hazardousness of products used daily in the household and leisure is again attracting the media's attention, alarming the public, and provoking a search for the guilty and demands for remedial measures by public authorities. It is hardly conceivable that either Member States or the Community can afford simply to neglect such demands.

The determination with which the Community and the Member States are moving towards completion of the European internal market has already changed decisively the framework conditions for product safety policy. In this policy area it is no longer sovereign States that are acting; legislative activity is increasingly mediated and coordinated through the Community. Administrative action has to align itself with new forms of cooperation with the Community and among Member States. For the regulatory approaches (the forms of 'legalization' or 'juridification') of product safety policy, the process of Europeanizing them has far-reaching – and, as we shall see, very ambivalent – consequences. The Europeanization of product safety law is not, in fact, determined by genuine safety motivations. The assumption of regulatory tasks by the Community is instead taking place in the context of internal market policy, which is determined economically in the main, and under the institutional conditions specific to Community action.

This theses on the effects of the integration process on product safety regulation will gradually be given more body below by analyses of the most important instruments for action. In line with the logic of internal market integration indicated, the contribution of product liability law to guaranteeing product safety will be covered first (section 2). Preventive legal control of hazards is the 'classical' regulatory pattern in product safety policy. The deregulation debate of the 1980s has effectively discredited this instrument; the second stage in the study will show why the integration process favours regulatory strategies that take the form of 'privatization' of preventive regulatory techniques (section 3). The fourth section will deal with so-called follow-up market controls. These include, on the one hand, powers of intervention whereby the State can in critical situations act on its political responsibility for safety and health, as it were 'ad hoc'; on the other, systematic approaches towards monitoring and influencing the level of product safety as determined by competition mechanisms or under the control of private standardization organizations. It will be argued that this instrument of action must, as the internal market is realized, assume increasing importance (section 5).

2 Product Safety Through Product Liability?

The controversies over product safety policy are to be attributed largely to the fact that, in practice, the guaranteeing of safety by governments tends to be reflected in regulative measures, so that advocates of 'juridification' of the safety issue must expect objections to governmental intervention and paternalism. Such debates are undoubtedly of fundamental importance. But their practical relevance depends on how one defines the limits of the paradigm concerned. On the one hand, advocates of an interventionist safety policy have to take account of numerous bottlenecks that arise. The number and variety of potentially dangerous products, the rate of technical development, the unpredictability of behaviour by product users and the range of their interests in protection *de facto* exclude positive regulation of all product hazards. On the other hand, reservations about governmental measures in no way mean that political responsibility for guaranteeing product safety should be rejected out of hand. What is, instead, asserted is that this task should primarily be approached not by means of not interventionist instruments but 'market-based' regulatory techniques that are indirectly effective, specifically liability law and information policy measures:[1] or that at least, in so far as much techniques are not applicable, self-regulatory mechanisms, specifically product standardization through non-governmental standardization organizations, are 'in principle' to be preferred, since they exploit the professional competence of private individuals, undertakings or organizations, which is in general far superior to that of a government agency. None of this, however, means that the State would lose its function and could completely abandon 'direct' governmental product safety regulation.[2]

The Economic Analysis of Product Liability

If, then, product liability in particular is assigned not mere compensatory functions but regulatory ones, if it is to be employed as an instrument for reaching the 'right' level of product safety, then this sort of 'public-law conception' of product liability law leads to far-reaching requirements regarding its structure.

(a) These consequences have been thought through above all in economic analyses of liability law. On the general assumptions of this approach about rational action by manufacturers and product users and about the function of legal rules, product liability law is (economically) rationally structured if it guides individual profit-maximizing behaviour in such a way as to produce societally optimal welfare, that is if it tends towards making expenditure on accident advoidance correspond to the utility conceptions that members of society have. It is undisputed that this control task cannot simply be left to individual (contractual) negotiation. Firstly, reliance on the rationality of contractual mechanisms, in which safety requirements are 'negotiated' on only implicity for the most part, seems unwarranted. Admitted, the manufacturer can clarify his safety expenditure by corresponding price differentiation. But the purchaser's decision in favour of a more hazardous alternative ought to be considered 'rational' only in so far as he can have any insight at all into the hazards of the products. Secondly, negotiating relationships between manufacturers and users would have to cover all those concerned who are endangered by product risks, including innocent bystanders. But if the transaction costs of individual agreements are prohibitively high, the law itself must determine the optimal welfare allocation of product hazards. Accordingly, it must lay down whether the manufacturer is to be held either not at all responsible for product hazards, or only if negligent, or else 'unconditionally'. The term 'unconditionally' itself is in need of interpretation, and making it specific calls for a further decision about the regulatory functions of liability law. If all 'social' costs arising as a consequence of the production of goods are expressed in product prices, then 'unconditional' liability must take the form of an 'absolute' duty of accountability, extending also to development hazards which are 'objectively' unforeseeable at the time of marketing the product.[3] If instead the sanctions of liability law are to be used to guide the behaviour of manufacturers without punishing them for willingness to innovate, then liability law must be oriented towards manufacturers' possibilities of action, so that 'unconditional' liability takes the form of defect liability, starting at the moment of marketing the product and/or permitting a 'state-of-the art defence'.

(b) Exponents of the economic approach overwhelmingly advocate the last-named alternative.[4] By this alone, they are admitting that there is further political room for decision over and above the structuring of liability law. If development risks manifest themselves in unpredictable fashion, it must be clarified who is ultimately to bear the damage; if innovation is to be encouraged, this does not necessarily mean that experiments with every technology, however risky, must be allowed. But limits are set to liability law as a control mechanism even before these issues of the 'risk society' are reached:[5] since liability law relies on decentralized hazard monitoring by those directly concerned and on the technical problem-solving capacities of the firms bearing the liability, it is not the best thing for hazard situations that can better be determined by central agencies and appropriately limited by universally valid rules; it is equally unsuitable for damage that arises only after a long-time, or only in synergy with other factors. A further problem that questions not only the delimitation of liability vis-à-vis other control instruments, but the control function of liability law altogether arises from the functional shortcomings of the insurance market. If the calculation of risk premiums differentiates by branch of industry or type of product, but the premiums cannot be oriented towards product-specific risk factors,[6] then this restricts the control effectiveness of product liability even in its 'core area'. The list of shortcomings of liability law as a control instrument grows still longer when one comes to check the empirical validity of the assumptions as to conduct that enter into the economic approach, i.e. when account is taken on the one hand of the fact that the 'signals' of strict liability are hard for firms to interpret and leave a wide range of strategic options open to them,[7] and bearing in mind on the other hand the selectivity of the system of private suit, which discourages product users who suffer damage, particularly private final consumers (and their insurers), from recourse to the courts.

Safety Policy and Integration Policy Issues of European Product Liability Law

Analyses of the regulatory performance of product liability law, as developed by economic analysis of law, overlook the real factors governing the political bargaining process; they cannot programme legal decision-making work in detail; and they cannot replace empirical analysis of the implementation of legal intentions. Putting it another way, such analyses do not allow any statements as to what contribution product liability law that really exists in the Community is making towards product safety. In seeking to clarify the Community's need for action in the area of product safety policy, they do nevertheless offer a few aids to orientation.

(a) The state of Europeanization of liability law can be seen from the Directive of 25 July 1985.[8] Article 1 of the Directive plumps for 'strict' liability by the manufacturer in the sense described above. As is well known, the subsequent provisions of the Directive go on to qualify this position in many respects. The narrow definition of product in Article 2 of the Directive limits its sphere of application from the outset; the most important area in the practice of product liability law, namely liability towards commercial users, is, not regulated by Article 9(b). The central problem of the Directive is the specification of 'strict' liability in a 'safety based' concept of defect, introduced in Article 1, fleshed out in Article 6 and further accentuated by the exclusion of liability for development hazards in Article 7(e). The Directive's concept of liability initiated Europe-wide debate on whether the principle of strict liability laid down in Article 1 is compatible with the criteria used in Article 6 to specify the concept of defect. Does recourse to the 'presentation' of the product and the reasonable expectations of users (Article 6 (1)(a) and (b)) constitute a concession to behaviour-oriented negligence criteria?

(b) No end to these debates can be foreseen. Irrespective of this outcome, however, the facts that Europeanization of liability law to date is rather modest, and that the interpretation of the Directive is so hotly debated, are both of significance for integration policy. Firstly, it is indisputable that the Directive, through its manifold limitations, is far from exhausting the control potential that could result from truly 'strict' liability, and thus in particular that even for the Community itself, it does not prejudice the basic dispute between 'market-based' and 'interventionistic' approaches to product safety policy. But even in the limited area of the Directive's scope, controversies over the interpretation of the Community standard for the product safety duty in liability law might develop into a disturbing factor for internal market policy. It is true that different liability criteria in Member States do not constitute barriers to trade within the meaning of Article 30 EEC. But the specification of product safety duties by the courts is relevant over and above private liability law. *De facto*, it means 'content control' over not only the industrial practice of the individual manufacturers concerned, but in some cases also over the standards that these manufacturers have taken as guidelines for their production. Additionally, it cannot be ruled out that national administrations may adopt pronouncements by civil courts as to the level of product safety called for in liability law for the purposes of their administrative practice. To be sure, such considerations are for the moment speculative. Nor are they meant to suggest that harmonization of liability law is an indispensable condition for realization of the single internal market – a glance at divergencies within the product liability law in US States would alone be enough to discredit such a thesis. However, it does not seem too hazardous to assume that the Community, which has only very imperfectly harmonized binding product safety law and is not even aiming at perfect harmonization any longer,[9] will develop interests in a uniform interpretation of standards in liability law, and, for instance, react sensitively to implicit judicial criticism of results of European standardization. Community law even now has mechanisms for preventing disparate interpretation of the Directive. By Article 169 EEC the Commission, and by Article 170 EEC any Member State, can impugn any anti-Community interpretation of the product safety duty under Article 6 of the Directive before the ECJ; national courts may, or must, bring questions of interpretation before the ECJ, pursuant to Article 177 EEC. But these measures are too clumsy to be selective. If there is an interest in uniform legal criteria for the level of product safety, then available legal means are scarcely sufficient to enforce that interest.

3 The Europeanization of Positive Regulation

Expansion of the regulatory techniques for controlling risks has accompanied the history of the industrial mode of production from the beginning. A heterogeneous network of regulatory patterns has emerged, which can hardly be reduced to uniform, systematic legal concepts, but can only be understood historically and in relation to specific issues. Relevant regulations differentiate according to type of product – pharmaceuticals, foodstuffs and cosmetics are treated differently from technical products – according to category of hazard or risk – environmental hazards, hazards of industrial plants, safety at the workplace, traffic accidents and home accidents bring different private and governmental actors into play. My article will concentrate on 'product safety in the narrower sense', dealing with product regulations, particularly for technical products. For the Community, this area is of central importance because the concept of bringing about a single European market is based on mutual penetration of national markets with export goods. This concept is endangered if 'general product safety laws', being prepared or already in force in practically all Community Member States, hinder the import of goods.

Information Systems

A product safety policy needs, if it is to justify its procedures, data on accident figures and information on circumstances surrounding accidents, to derive priorities and develop appropriate strategies to avoid hazards. This statement is anything but trivial. Systematic coverage of product hazards is an extremely complex task, calling for normative decisions that have proved politically controversial (a). For the Community there is the additional factor that its specific legislative acts cannot by any means be oriented exclusively to genuine safety priorities, but instead tend to fit in with objectives of internal market policy, which follows a quite different 'logic' (b).

(a) The US has been the pioneer in developing systematic surveys and assessments of product hazards. The National Electronic Injury Surveillance System (NEISS), set up following enactment of the Consumer Product Safety Act 1972, was the first step internationally towards comprehensive, continuous collection of data, not only about numbers and consequences of accidents, but also about products involved.[10] US experience has been turned to use by Britain with its Home Accident Surveillance System (HASS) since 1976, and by the Netherlands in the Privé Ongevallen Registratie Systeem (PORS) since 1983.[11] However convincing the plan for a systematic accident survey may seem to be, the practical value to attach to data collected still remains controversial. The controversy has a significance in principle, going beyond mere technical difficulties of the data collection. 'Official' data on involvement of products in accidents, at any rate if they are accessible to the public, bring demands for more exact information and for governmental assistance; such consequences inevitably appear to be latently irrational to a safety philosophy that relies primarily on continuing cooperation from experts in the industries concerned and in their methods for analyzing risks.[12] The Community has in no way put these debates on the meaning of accident information behind it. The Council decision of 13 July 1981[13] was restricted, in contrast with the Commission's further-reaching proposals,[14] to carrying out a 'pilot experiment', which left it to Member States to decide the nature of their participation, and was really taken seriously by only three States.[15] The Council's subsequent decision of 23 April 1986 on the 'European Home and Leisure Accident Surveillance System' ('EHLASS')[16] was termed a 'demonstration project'. For a period of five years, data are to be collected throughout the Community – though with the Federal Republic again playing a special role. The project's declared aim is an assessment of the data 'aimed at preventing accidents'.[17] But this assessment is left for the final report on the demonstration project.[18] Whether the Community will ultimately be successful in establishing a European information system on a lasting basis and in making use of it to further its product safety policy is at present hard to predict.

(b) It is undoubtedly difficult in merely technical and organizational terms to set up a Community accident information system. This is not sufficient, however, to explain the Council's dilatory attitude. The difficulties of coming to a decision at Community level should, instead, be seen more in the context of the tension between product safety policy and internal market policy. The safety policy priorities resulting from an assessment of accident information systems and the priorities that determine European harmonization policy and standardization work in the interests of completing the internal market stem from different contexts, and converge only haphazardly. The conditions for a European consensus are equally diverse. The controversies over the significance of national accident information systems involve different 'safety philosophies' and regulatory traditions, which undoubtedly also concern economic interests, but they also bring up the relationship between State and economy in a general, public policy sense. Against this, when it comes to harmonizing national regulations which obstruct internal Community trade or working out European standards, those directly affected always present themselves to state their case. They may fear danger to their market shares at home, or hope that easier access may bring them new advantages on foreign markets.[19] Safety policy decisions are unavoidable even in such bargaining situations. Yet a safety policy consensus cannot resolve economically based conflicting interests, and a compromise formula to reconcile such conflicts of interests may lead to concessions on safety policy questions. These considerations are not intended as a summary, but more as initial pointers to the complexities of the integration process in the area under study here: product safety policy will be able to become established as a European policy area only if it manages to demonstrate its contribution to the realization of the European market. But this is precisely why product safety policy gets enmeshed in a dependency on internal market policy, which is fully occupied with balancing out conflicts of economic interests between economic and governmental actors.[20]

Preventive Product Regulations

Accident information systems are concerned only with the possibilities of rendering product safety policy 'scientific'. Their most important legal instrument to date, which is also supposed to make up for the regulatory shortcomings of liability law, is preventive product safety regulation. By definition such preventive product safety regulations act, unless it has been possible to harmonize them or at least guarantee mutual recognition of national provisions, as non-tariff barriers to trade. This explains why harmonization, deregulation or further development of product safety law has to be a central point of Community endeavours to bring about the internal market. Present legislative developments in Member States confirm the extend' to which the process of European integration is now affecting the forms and contents of national product safety legislation.

(a) If protection of safety interests is recognized as a task for government, then government responsibility must be expressed in corresponding legal acts and competences. In line with this, German foodstuffs law contains a general norm banning foodstuffs hazardous to health (para. 8 LMBG), and empowers government agencies to make this general clause specific through executive orders (para. 9 LMBG). The general ban on 'questionable pharmaceuticals' (para. 5 AMG, together with para. 1 AMG) is supervised by the authorities through a special acceptance procedure (para. 1 ff. AMG). Modern general product safety acts have followed this pattern. Thus, especially when the US Consumer Product Safety Act of 1972 was enacted, it was assumed that safety hazards of consumer goods were to be brought under control primarily through binding standards for specific products,[21] and the French product safety act of 1983 still assigns the task of making the general product safety duty specific to decrees from the *Conseil d'Etat*.[22] Since the early 1980s though, the concept of 'regulation' in all related disciplines has become increasingly associated with negative connotations:

- Economic criticism regards government regulations of the economy as making 'products' subject to the law of supply (by the State) and demand (by interest groups).[23] This criticism is directed primarily against 'economic' regulation of so-called exceptional areas. Verification of product safety is part of 'social' regulation, the justification for which is not disputed in principle. But specifically with product regulation, economic rationality criteria are brought to bear: cost-benefit analyses, which on the one hand quantify the cost-effects of safety requirements on product prices, and on the other calculate the benefits ('savings') brought by safety requirements through their contribution to reducing accidents, ought to decide the extend to which governmental measures are justified.[24]

- Political scientists and legal sociologists have diagnosed shortcomings in the implementation of regulatory programmes, and have explained them by the economic dependency of the competent institutions and through influencing by interest groups. They have analyzed the conditions from which such agencies have emerged, and have recognized in their decision-making procedures the phenomenon of 'regulatory unreasonableness'.[25]

- In legal theory, the rationality of interventionist law has been questioned simultaneously from the differing viewpoints of systems theory and critical theory: governmental influence on law is alleged to overstrain the political system and endanger the normative structure of law; or to destroy the communicative infrastructures of social action contexts.[26]

For legal policy, but also for simple practical dealings with product safety law in force, all these theoretical approaches are of importance.

(i) Regulatory law in the sense described above, of legal replacement of social and economic processes and decisions, has been able to establish itself only in special areas, and even there mostly only in a very formal sense.

Thus, according to German pharmaceuticals law, the licensing procedure is in the sole competence of the Federal Office of Health as the overall federal authority (para. 77 AMG). But the office is obliged to consult a licensing commission on which there are representatives of the medical world, including the pharmaceutical industry (para. 25(6) and (7) AMG); *de facto*, the 'recommendations' of these committees determine official action.[27] Foodstuffs law (para. 26 LMBG) refers to the guidelines of the foodstuffs register, which contains 'substantive' criteria for the manufacturing, the nature and other characteristics of foodstuffs; these criteria are worked out by a commission on which government representatives once again sit together with business people and scientific experts.

Labour protection law has decentralized still further the guaranteeing of safe products at work, through the reference in para. 3 GSG to the 'generally accepted rules of art' and to the labour and accident prevention regulations. The issuing of accident prevention regulations is entrusted by para. 708(1) RVO to the professional associations. The content of the regulations is worked out by expert committees on which, in addition to experts from the professional associations, representatives of trade supervisory bodies and of producers and users of technical products used at work, and from trade unions and employers' associations, also sit; the representative meeting of the professional associations, which has to ratify the outcome of this work, is constituted on a parity basis by para. 708(1) and (2) RVO.

As regards safety design of work materials, the accident prevention regulations usually content themselves with references to the 'generally accepted rules of art'; the division of labour between the professional associations and the German Institute for Standardization (DIN), responsible for standardization work, which this implies, was laid down formally in 1982.[28]

(ii) The reference norm in para. 3(1) GSG is at the same time the key provision in safety law on technical consumer goods. Its regulatory technique may be interpreted as a preemptive answer to criticism of interventionist juridification conceptions – which does not mean that this answer is unproblematic.

By adopting the general product safety duty (products must be of such a nature that when they are properly used, 'users or third parties are protected against risks to life and health of all kinds, as far as the nature of the proper use permits' (para. 3(1) GSG)), the State has established its responsibility in principle for protecting safety interests. At the same time, the fact that this protective task of government is expressed only in the form of a general clause indicates a twofold self-limitation of the governmental regulatory claim. On the one hand, it takes account of the insight that it is not *de facto* possible to guarantee the safety of products comprehensively and in detail through preventive regulations; on the other, it shows a readiness to decentralize specification of the product safety duty as far as seems possible and appropriate, and leave it to non-governmental actors.

This delegation of the work of setting standards to private organizations is not explicitly stated in the wording of the reference in para. 3(1) GSG to the 'generally accepted rules of art' and the 'labour and accident prevention regulations'. It does, however, follow from the facts that the establishment of technical standards that indicate the state of the art is carried out largely by private organizations – the German Institute for Standardization (DIN), the German Electrical Engineering Association (VDE), the German Association of Gas and Water Experts. In addition, it follows that the Federal Republic regulates its relationships with DIN on a contractual basis[29] and, finally, that the professional associations have transferred their powers to enact safety regulations to DIN.[30]

The unburdening of the State consequent upon delegating the production of norms to private agencies is not immediately acceptable either constitutionally or from the viewpoint of legal policy. Two approaches to indirect legal control might be considered: the quality of the standardization process could be influenced by procedural rules on the pluralist composition of standardization bodies and on governmental collaboration in standardization work; and *ex post* verification of resulting standards by authorities or through reports might be considered. In German product safety law, these two approaches are followed together. In the standardization Agreement with the Federal Republic, DIN has undertaken to 'take the public interest into account', to 'give preferential treatment' to requests for standards coming from the Federal Government,[31] and to involve representatives of the Federal Government or of governmental agencies, in its standardization committees. In the new 1974 version of the basic standard, DIN 820, DIN undertook to observe procedural principles aimed at guaranteeing a balanced involvement of 'interested circles'; likewise in 1974, a consumer council was set up as an institution.[32] Whether the norms thus produced meet the safety requirements of para. 3(1) GSG is determined, according to the general administrative provisions under the GSG,[33] by the inclusion of standards in the annexes to those administrative regulations. Inclusion is decided formally by the Federal Minister for Labour and Social Affairs, whose decisions are cooperatively prepared in substantive respects by the Federal Institute for Labour Protection and the DIN's 'Commission on Safety Technology'.[34] Clearer governmental follow-up control arises from the control powers of the Trade Supervisory Offices, competent in *Länder* law, which, pursuant to paras 5–7 GSG, verify observance of para. 3 GSG, call for the submission of expert reports and may issue banning orders.[35]

The trio of general clause in safety law/delegation of specification to private standardization organizations/government rules for standardization work and possibilities of checking the outcome of standardization, taken together, results in a regulatory technique that copes with the bottlenecks arising in preventive government action, but can therefore not be vouched for as guaranteeing perfection by anyone. Critical observers note a structurally based asymmetry in standardization work, which cannot be compensated for by procedural guarantees.[36] It is not disputed either that the Trade Supervisory Offices are able to perform their control tasks only extremely selectively.[37] Despite these shortcomings in the 'post interventionist' regulatory approach of the GSG, the Federal Republic, like other Community Member States, could no longer conceive of alternatives in sovereign terms. The reference technique has gradually become established at European level as the regulatory approach that should in principle prevail – a point we shall return to shortly.[38]

(b) The starting point for our ideas was that the Community cannot let its influence on product safety law in Member States be guided solely by criteria intrinsic to safety policy. Instead, it must, firstly, conceive its own measures in the interest of bringing about a single market, as a policy to break down technical barriers to trade; and secondly, it must in all safety policy initiatives bear in mind its own institutional constraints on action: above all the fact that cooperation by Member States remains indispensable in administering product safety law. The Community's internal market policy objectives and its institutional structures have always determined its policy of approximation of laws in all areas affecting product safety law, though in different ways in the Community's various phases of development. The history cannot be gone into here.[39] The lessons drawn from it all point to the unburdening of the Community's law-making process:

- Community law, as the Cassis de Dijon judgement teaches,[40] allows checking of the content of national provisions against primary Community law (Art. 30 EEC), whereby disproportionate restrictions on free trade need not be accepted by Community law, so that to that extent positive measures of approximation of laws become superfluous.
- Side by side with the Cassis de Dijon doctrine are efforts to replace positive regulation at Community level by mutual recognition of differing national regulatory forms.
- The burden can be expected to be greatly eased by the 'new approach to technical harmonization and standardization',[41] according to which harmonization policy in product safety law will in future be confined to the laying down of 'essential safety requirements', while specification of those safety requirements will be left to the European and national standardization organizations.
- At the same time, the Single European Act has, through the introduction of the (qualified) majority principle in the new Art. 100a(1), increased the Council's capacity for action in all measures that affect the internal market.
- Finally, an easing of the burden on law approximation policy can be expected from the delegating of implementing competence to the Commission, pursuant to Art. 155, 4th indent, EEC. The Commission's efforts to accompany adoption of the SEA with a fundamental strengthening of its position in comparison with existing practice in delegation were, however, not successful.[42]

Altogether, a coherent programme emerges. The difficulties of reaching a European consensus are to be smoothed out by self-restraint on harmonization measures, the move a way from the unanimity principle and the delegation of 'implementing powers' to the Commission; and the Community's limited powers of administrative action are to be compensated for by obligations on mutual recognition of national measures and through cooperation with Member State administrations. This is the context in which European product safety law has to fit.

(i) The trend outlined has not for the moment totally replaced the 'traditional' approaches to harmonization of positive regulations. Especially in pharmaceutical law, but also in foodstuffs law, the Community has pursued a harmonization policy aiming at uniformization of national legislation. Directives 65/65,[43] 75/318[44] and 75/319[45] introduced a Community-wide licensing procedure, aimed at preventing the marketing of unsafe or ineffective pharmaceuticals.[46] The integration policy outcome is ambivalent. The harmonization has certainly brought progress – differing in each Member State – in safety of pharmaceuticals, but it has not produced the intended internal market policy effects. Despite the harmonization of legislation on pharmaceuticals, it has not in the upshot come to uniform safety regulation, because the practice of national authorities is not uniform.[47] In the area of foodstuffs law, as the Commission stressed following adoption of the 'new approach',[48] the technique of reference to standards is not transferable. The Commission's starting point is therefore that, in the light of the Cassis de Dijon doctrine, the Community can in principle do without product regulations in foodstuffs law ('recipe laws') and that Member States will have to content themselves with identification provisions.[49] Additionally, where Community legislation proves unavoidable, directives will unify only the 'basic rules of foodstuffs law', the specification ('implementation') of which is, however, transferred to the Commission.[50]

For the area of labour protection, a two-pronged strategy is being followed. Harmonization of provisions on technical and design safety of work material (machines) is assigned to the sphere of application of the new Art. 100a, so that the principles of the 'new approach' apply.[51] By comparison, protection of the safety and health of workers pursuant to Art. 118a, which allows the adoption by qualified majority of *minimum provisions*, is to deal with organizational measures connected with the workplace. The proposal of 11 March 1988 framework directive,[52] defining in general the spheres of responsibility of employers and workers, is flanked by individual proposals.[53]

(ii) With the 'new approach to technical harmonization and standards'[54] the Community fixed on the reference technique as the regulatory model in product safety for the whole range of technical consumer products and work materials ('machines'). The internal market policy motivation of all the elements of this programme is clear:[55] the information Directive of 28 May 1983[56] on planned legislation or standardization with potentially trade-restricting effect gives the Commission the capability of working towards European solutions for the various areas concerned.[57] In accordance with the so-called Model Directive,[58] approximation of laws in technical safety law is to be confined in future to laying down 'essential' requirements, with specification of legally binding safety objectives being left for European standardization. The requisite intensive cooperation with the European standardization organizations was laid down in 'general guidelines'.[59] Additionally, the Commission is working on a proposal for 'testing and certification in Europe'.[60]

The first directives giving effect to the new approach – namely the Directive on Simple Pressure Vessels,[61] and also the Toy Directive[62] – were able to draw on the preliminary work already done. But with the proposal for a general directive on machinery,[63] the Commission has broken new ground: the range of application of this directive is similar to that of the German GSG, covering both work materials and consumer products (Art. 1). For detailed specification of the 'essential safety requirements' listed in Annex 1, the Commission does not want to wait for European standards to be produced. Instead, it essentially relies on the 'quality' of existing national standards, and on the possibility of quickly verifying that standards comply with the safety objectives of the Machine Directive.[64] The Commission wishes to handle the certification problem through procedures for self-certification by manufacturers (Art. 8).

(c) National debates and controversies on the advantages and drawbacks of national product regulation, on involvement of employers and workers in labour protection, on issues of 'functional' delegation of law-making competence to private organizations and on indirect and/or *ex post* monitoring of these by government have concentrated on the suitability from a safety policy viewpoint of legal regulatory strategies. By contrast, relevant Community documents on Community legislative involvement in product safety have primarily been concerned with the internal market policy implications of a given regulatory approach. In pharmaceuticals law, these are the costs of parallel national licensing procedures, and above all the differences in treatment of the harmonized law. According to Directive 83/571 of 26 October 1983,[65] licensing decisions of other Member States have to be 'duly' taken into account, and differences between Member States discussed at Community level; but there are no legal possibilities of correcting national licensing decisions.[66] The regulations planned under the new harmonization policy are intended to overcome these weaknesses, from the internal market policy viewpoint, of pharmaceuticals law.[67] The relevant directives and draft directives lay a basis for Community-wide rights to market access for goods that meet European or recognized national standards. While they leave untouched the right of Member States to verify the safety of products themselves on the basis of the 'essential safety requirements' laid down in Community law, they do oblige Member States to bring safety objections before the Commission, which alone – after consulting the Standing Committee on Standardization – should take the final decision on whether they are justified.[68] The new approach's primary policy orientation towards the internal market is plain from the asymmetries of the regulations on 'market access' and 'market exclusion'. Member States' legal competencies to take measures against products that in their view do not meet the requirements of Community law have to be notified to the Commission, which then decides whether they are justified.[69] However, difficulties arise when the Commission regards action by one Member State against product hazards as justified. Should a safety defect be attributable to shortcomings in standards the Commission may rescind recognition of these. Whether its further-reaching powers of action, in particular the power to apply Community-wide a ban issued in one Member State that the Commission finds justified, will stand up is at present very uncertain. The Toy Directive does provide that Member States should 'take all expedient measures to withdraw such (hazardous) products from the market or prohibit or restrict their being brought to market' (Art. 7(1)), and the draft Machine Directive has a similar provision (Art. 7(1)). But these provisions can hardly be interpreted as obligations to introduce new possibilities of action within Member States, and even if they were thus interpreted, they would be much too indefinite to guarantee even approximately uniform administrative practice in safety law.

In preventive safety regulation, the trend towards institutionalizing co-operative relationships between governmental and societal actors seems to be making headway generally; and specifically in German technical safety law, the 'functional' delegation of legislative tasks is in line with long-established tradition. From the Community viewpoint, government involvement in product safety law is a major obstacle to achieving the internal market. This alone explains the attractiveness of regulatory techniques that either make 'denationalization' and expanded implementing powers for the Commission possible, as is the trend in foodstuffs law,[70] or otherwise, aim at 'degovernmentalization' of preventive safety regulation as with the reference technique. This means, on the one hand, that the Community must tie legislative activity in Member States down to regulatory forms in line with its objectives – and here it has already been very successful.[71] But 'denationalization' and 'degovernmentalization' of product safety law lead to follow-up problems. The strategy of 'denationalization' aims at unburdening the Council in favour of expanded powers for the Commission. It thus clashes with Member States' interests in not letting responsibility for product safety out of their own hands.[72] The restriction of the majority principle of Art. 100(a) by virtue of para. 4 of this provision and the outcome of the debate on the form of the new version of Art. 145 EEC[73] are general indicators, and the failure of the Commission's original proposal for a directive on additives in foodstuffs[74] a very specific pointer, to resistance to this strategy. The 'degovernmentalization' of product safety law through the technique of reference to standards tends in national law to be balanced by regulations on standardization procedures, and above all, through powers of *ex post* intervention. So far, Community law has not advanced far toward setting up the legal framework conditions for the reference technique. In the 'general guidelines' for Commission cooperation with European standardization organizations, while participation rights for social actors are mentioned, they are in no way definitely clarified.[75] Community law has no influence whatever on procedures of national standardization organizations; only the outcome of standardization procedures can be reviewed at Community level. No powers of positive intervention reflecting public responsibility for product safety are possessed by the Community itself; nor has it been concerned to date to ensure that Member States develop a legal basis for such action.

4 Follow-Up Market Control

The tasks of liability law are not only in the area of compensation, but they also indirectly affect product safety – though these effects are limited and hard to predict.[76] Preventive product safety law necessarily remains imperfect and provisional; imperfect since hazards can never be perfectly calculated in advance; provisional because the risk/benefit assessments reflected in technical safety measures must remain open to reevaluation in changed circumstances or in the light of new knowledge. Still more so, government must stay in a position to assert its responsibility for product safety if it delegates tasks of preventive safety regulation to non-governmental bodies.

Determination of and Response to Product Hazards

However irrefutable the demands for continual adaptation of safety standards and for governmental possibilities of responding to recognized hazards may seem, 'follow-up market control' remains in Europe the poor relation in product safety law.

In determining hazards, reliance is placed, in pharmaceuticals law, on notification by doctors, systematic scientific research or 'duties of report and notification' on the pharmaceutical industry.[77] In foodstuffs law, follow-up market control primarily means application of existing law. But as well as the construction of an effective supervisory system, foodstuffs law also needs procedures for adapting its standards to new findings and requirements. In the area of 'technical work materials', Germany relies on the continual adaptation of technical standards and on monitoring activities by the Trade Supervisory Administration (*Gewerbeaufsichtsämter*). This does not involve systematic determination of hazards. The Administration is not capable of 'directed' monitoring activity; it can, however, follow instructions from other agencies, and also benefit from the work of the *Stiftung Warentest*.

The regulatory functions of follow-up market control differ from one product area to another. In pharmaceuticals law, which in principle provides for preventive controls, the point is essentially to verify the justification of predictions incorporated in the licensing decisions, taking new knowledge into account. By contrast, in the law of technical work materials, it is more to make up for the lacunae in protection through preventive standard setting, and where there are no standards, to lay down initial specifications of the general safety clause. But the practical conditions for effective response to hazards of marketed products also differ considerably. In the pharmaceuticals sector, the number of procedures is limited and channels of distribution easy to follow; the medical profession can be approached and through them often those affected as well. In the foodstuffs sector, on the other hand, those products causing health risks are enormously harder to identify; distribution channels can hardly be controlled, and consumers involved can be reached at most via more or less spectacular alarm notices. The area of technical work materials and consumer products is enormously heterogeneous. Action on medical equipment, complicated plants or high-value consumer goods, which, like cars, are sold through closed distribution systems and in any case are subject to regular official checking, is relatively simple. This is not true for the enormous range of technical consumer products as a whole. Even if manufacturers can be identified, it is hard to trace distribution channels, and determination of all product users involved is inconceivable.

German law does not have effective instruments for action even in severe cases of hazard. The Trade Supervisory Administration's strongest weapon is a ban under para. 5 GSG, directed against manufacturers, and only under special conditions against exhibitors or traders. The product user immediately at risk has to study the federal worksheet if s/he wants information on public supervisory activities.[78]

At the same time, German case law on manufacturer liability has developed the institution of a duty to monitor products.[79] The duty to monitor products is a substitute for liability for development hazards.[80] It cannot become a substitute for administrative follow-up market controls, if only because the courts are not capable of action oriented towards safety policy priorities.

Follow-Up Market Controls and Internal Market Policy

The safety policy shortcomings of German law on follow-up market controls are typical of Member States' law as a whole.[81] But all this does not mean, for instance, that there is no acute need for action at European level. There are two arguments in favour of European initiatives to anticipate national developments: firstly, the Community must be aware that it will be regarded as having responsibility for hazards to the extent that it is successful in imposing its policy on opening up national markets; secondly, it must expect that the freedoms of action at present open to national authorities will lead to new (subsequent) market segmentation because the competent authorities in Member States will interpret the general safety clauses in the new type directives differently, and will respond with different action.

For medical specialities within the meaning of Directives 75/319/EEC[82] and 83/570/EEC,[83] for animal diseases and residues in foodstuffs and fresh meat within the meaning of Directive 81/851/EEC,[84] for foodstuffs and – since the Council decision of 2 March 1984[85] – for consumer goods as a whole, Community information systems exist. The obligation on competent authorities in Member States to notify measures directed against 'serious and immediate' health risks means only that information is passed on by the Commission, not that there will be a uniform Community-wide response.[86] The need for action at European level seems most urgent in the area of application of the new approach to technical harmonization and standards. The safety objectives of the new directives all affect very broadly defined product categories, and have been kept correspondingly vague. The various 'general' product safety duties differ in emphasis[87] and are hardly sufficient for the formation of a consistent European 'safety philosophy'. The new draft Directive on Machinery,[88] with its comprehensive scope, thus represents considerable progress. Admittedly, the wording of this draft presents interpretation difficulties that go beyond even those usually encountered with general clauses.[89]

To be sure, the capacity of general safety clauses to provide orientation remains limited, however well the wording may have been thought out. But that makes their regulatory function all the more important. General clauses guarantee powers to act that have to compensate for the absence of direct, detailed product regulations. Follow-up market control is the most obvious expression of this form of governmental guaranteeing of the safety and health of citizens. If the assumption is true that follow-up market controls will acquire increasing importance as the new harmonization policy takes hold, then the Community must, by providing for anticipatory harmonization of law on follow-up market controls, guarantee Europeanization of decisions in this area.[90]

5 Concluding Remarks: Paradoxes of The Strategy of Deregulation

The conclusions of the foregoing considerations on the effects of Europeanizing product safety law are not to be regarded as legally binding, or as predictions on the further course of European legal policy. They presuppose that the Community's initiatives to complete the internal market, 'deregulate' preventive product safety law and Europeanize standardization will be successful. They further suppose that issues of product safety will long continue to be so pressing that Member States and the Community will not be able to avoid calls for guarantees of safety and health. On these two assumptions, the conclusion seems unavoidable that the Community's very successes in opening up national markets to safety-aware products and the move to the reference technique as the regulatory instrument for technical work materials and consumer goods will produce a 'regulatory gap': market integration requires a positive European product safety policy and new instruments of action in order to adapt safety standards and coordinate response to product hazards. These consequences of the 'anti-interventionist' internal market policy and the 'anti-interventionist' reference technique may at first sight seems paradoxical. However, they are in line with the logic of an integration process that cannot allow the achievements of a single internal market to be brought into question again by unilateral measures by Member States to protect safety interests.

Notes

1. The area of so called information policy has been ignored below. This does not mean that it is unimportant or unproblematic. In information policy too, the question of whether governmental or independent agencies should prescribe and control the content of information is extremely controversial; and the effects of information policy measures depend to a substantial degree on how they are structured and how the public is sensitized to product hazards.
2. The political science analysis by Voelzkow *et al.* (1987), pp. 93 ff and section 3, pp. 183–90, below.
3. See the exhaustive account in the LL.M. thesis by R. Wiehe, forthcoming, ch. 2.
4. For the German literature, see Schäfer and Ott (1986), p. 110 f; Brüggemeier, (1988), pp. 511 ff., 514 ff. with further references.
   On the following see e.g. St Shavell (1984), pp. 368 ff.
5. Cf. Pierce (1980); Sugarman, (1985).
6. Cf. Eads and Reuter (1983).
7. O.J. L 210, 7 August 1985, 29.
8. For details see section 3 (pp. 183–190) below.
9. On development of the NEISS, see the documentation from the Consumer Product Safety Commission, *The National Electronic Injury Surveillance System: A Description of its Role in the U.S. Consumer Product Safety Commission*, April 1986; and Joerges *et al.* (1988), pp. 211–14, and references.
10. On the British HASS system, see the references in Joerges *et al.* (1988), pp. 119–120; on the Dutch PORS cf. Bruggers and Rogmans (1982); see also the two OECD reports (1978; 1979).
11. See the criticisms of the Community's efforts toward an accident information system in Mertens, *BArbBl.* (1986), pp. 32 ff., 34 f.
12. OJ No. L 229, 13 August 1981, 1.
13. OJ No. C 252, 14 October 1978, 2.
14. See Joerges *et al.* (1988), pp. 289–90.
15. OJ No. L 109, 26 April 1986, 23.
16. In the words of the sixth recital in the Council Decision of 22 April 1986 (note 16).
17. Cf. by contrast Art. 7 of the Commission's proposal of 7 January 1985 for a Council Decision introducing a Community system of information on accidents in which

consumer products are involved, OJ No. C 117, 11 May 1985, 4.
18. See Joerges *et al.* (1988), pp. 243 ff.
19. Cf. Section 3, pp. 188–190 (below) and section 5 (below).
20. See Joerges *et al.* (1988), p. 205, with references.
21. Ibid., p. 74 ff.
22. A fundamental work here is Stigler (1971).
23. See e.g. Viscusi (1984), p. 88 ff.
24. Bardach and Keagan (1982).
25. See Teubner *et al.* (1987), pp. 3 ff., 24 ff.
26. See *et al.* (1988), p. 30 ff.
27. See Joerges *et al.* (1988), p. 150.
28. See Joerges *et al.* (1988), p. 150.
29. Cf. esp. para. 1(2) of the Standardization Agreement between the Federal Republic and DIN, 5 June 1975 (reprinted in *DIN-Mitt.* 54 (1975), 359.
30. Cf. (i) (pp. 184–185 above, and for more detail Joerges *et al.* (1988), 150, 172.
31. Cf. paras 1 (2) and 4 (1) of the Standards Agreement (note 29).
32. For more details on all this see Joerges *et al.* (1988), pp. 178–88.
33. Bundesanzeiger No. 205, 3.11.1970, amended by AVV v. 11 June 1979, Bundesanzeiger No. 108, 13 June 1979. ·
34. Joerges *et al.* (1988), pp. 152–58 with references.
35. Ibid., pp. 161–68 with references.
36. Gusy, (1986), p. 241 ff.
37. See Joerges *et al.* (1988), pp. 161, 164–8.
38. b(ii) (pp. 188) below.
39. Details in Joerges *et al.* (1988), pp. 240–98.
40. ECJ, Judgement of 20 February 1979, Case 120/78, ECJ (1979) 649.
41. Council Resolution of 7 May 1985, OJ No. C 136, 4 June 1985, 2.
42. See Council Decision of 13 July 1987, OJ No. L 197, 18 July 1987, 33.
43. OJ No. 369/65, 9 February 1965.
44. OJ No. L 147, 9 June 1975, 1.
45. OJ No. L 147, 9 June 1975, 13.
46. For more details see Reich (1987), p. 229 ff.; Glaeske *et al.* (1988), pp. 13 ff., 16 ff.
47. Reich(1987), p. 235 ff.; Glaeske *et al.* (1988), p. 13 ff.
48. Cf. The Commission Communication to the Council and the European Parliament on Completion of the Internal Market, COM (85) 603 final, 8 November 1985.
49. Ibid., para. 16.
50. Ibid., para. 35 ff.; the Commission did not initially downgrade the Standing Committee for Foodstuffs, which acts as a 'Regulatory Committee', to an 'Advisory Committee' (ibid., para. 46). It has since changed its position; see Commission document COM (86) 87 final, 22 April 1986 on a proposal for a Council directive on the harmonization of Member States' legal provisions on permitted additives in Foodstuffs (Art. 8 and 9 of the proposed directive (OJ No. C 116, 16 May 1986, 2), unchanged in the amended proposal of 26 May 1987 (OJ No. C 154, 12 June 1987, 11)).
51. See (ii) below (p. 188).
52. OJ No. C 141, 30 May 1988, 1.
53. On the equipment of 'workplaces', see the proposal for a first specific Directive, OJ No. C 141, 30 May 1988, 6; for the 'employment' of work materials the second specific Directive, OJ No. C 114 of 30 April 1988, 3; on the use of personal protective equipment of third specific Directive, OJ No. C 161, 20 June 1988, 1; on VDU work, OJ No. C 113, 29 April 1988, 7; on the 'handling' of heavy loads,

the fifth specific Directive, OJ No. C 117, 4 May 1988, 8. The regulatory approach in labour protection law pursuant to Art. 118a, which sets binding framework provisions for employers and workers, is significantly not retained in the case of protection against hazards of biological work materials; here the Commission calls for prior risk analysis, the evaluation of which it in principle wishes to leave up to Member States (see Art. 3(2) of the proposal for a directive of 19 April 1988, OJ No. C 150, 8 June 1988, 6).

54. See note 41.
55. Cf. esp. the Commission's 'White Paper', 'Completion of the Internal Market', COM (85) 310 final, 14 June 1985, and in detail Joerges *et al.* (1988), pp., 341–365.
56. OJ No. L 109, 26 April 1983, 8.
57. The amendment of 22 March 1988 (OJ No. L 81, 26 March 1988, 75) considerably expanded the range of application of the Information Directive. By the new Art. 1(1), it now also covers agricultural products, foodstuffs, fodder and medicaments.
58. See Note 41.
59. Reprinted in DIN-Mitt. 64 (1985), 78 f.
60. Consultative documents III/B/4, 19 January 1988.
61. OJ No. L 220, 8 August 1987, 48.
62. OJ No. L 187, 16 July 1988, 1.
63. OJ No. C 29, 3 February 1988, 1.
64. See Art. 5(4), along with Art. 6 and the 14th recital.
65. OJ No. L 332, 28 April 1983, 1 (Art. 9 (1)).
66. Cf. Glaeske *et al.* (1988), 27.
67. In foodstuffs law, acccording to the proposal for a directive on additives (OJ No. C 116, 16 May 1986, 2), it should be ultimately the Commission alone that should decide on specific directives and on Member States' objections to these (Arts. 3 and 4) – while the Standing Committee on Foodstuffs is to be consulted, it has no vote (Art. 9). The Commission now no longer wishes to claim these far-reaching powers (see the amended proposal of 26 May 1987, OJ No. C 154, 12 June 1987, 11).
68. See the general section VI of the 'Model Directive' (note 41), and e.g. Art. 6 of the Toy Directive (note 62) and Art. 6 of the draft Machine Directive (note 63).
69. Cf. section 7 of the Model Directive (note 41); art. 7 of the Toy Directive (note 62); Art. 7 of the draft Machine Directive (note 64).
70. Cf. note 50 above.
71. Cf. Joerges *et al.* (1988), p. 433 f.
72. Restriction of the majority principle of Art. 100(a) by para. 4 of this provision and the outcome of the debates on implementation of the reworded Art. 145 (see note 42 above); the EP began proceedings against the new arrangements on 2 October 1987 (case 302/87, OJ No. C 321, 1 December 1987, 4).
73. See the Council Decision of 13 July 1987 laying down the procedures for the exercise of implementing powers conferred on the Commission, OJ No. L 197, 18 July 1987, 33.
74. Cf. note 50 above.
75. For more details see Joerges *et al.* (1988), pp. 401–29.
76. Cf. section 2 above.
77. For the German law, see Hart (note 27), *et al.* (1988), p. 115 ff.
78. For more details on all this, see Jeorges *et al.* (1988), pp. 163–8.
79. Most recently, see BGHNJW 1987, 1009 – and BGUNJW 1988, 2611.
80. See Brüggemeier (1986), p. 561 ff.
81. For a comparative survey see Micklitz *et al.* (1988).

82. OJ No. L 147, 9 June 1975, 13.
83. OJ No. L 332, 28 November 1983, 1.
84. OJ No. L 317, 6 November 1981, 1.
85. OJ No. L 70, 13 March 1984, 16; OJ No. L 17, 21 January 1989, 51.
86. For more details see Joerges et al. (1988), pp. 293–8, and the Commission's report of 12 March 1986, OJ No. C 146, 3 June 1988, 8, 10. For more details on the situation in the medicaments market, see Glaeske *et al.* (1988), pp. 26–8.
87. Cf. e.g. Art. 2 of the Directive on Simple Pressure Vessels (note 61) and Art. 2 of the Toy Directive (note 62).
88. Note 63.
89. Art. 2(1): Machinery may not 'endanger the health or safety of persons, and, where necessary, domestic animals or property, when properly installed, and maintained and used for its intended purpose'. Annex I, 1.1.2. d: 'The manufacturer must envisage the hazards present during the normal use of the machine and also those due to a foreseeable abnormal situation'. On the corresponding ambiguities in German law, cf. Joerges *et al.* (1988), pp. 43 f., 145–47.
90. On 8 May, 1989, the Commission published a (preliminary) proposal for a directive on the harmonization of the laws, regulations and administrative provisions of the Member States concerning product safety (COM (89) 162–SYN 192). This proposal includes both a general safety duty and provisions on post-market control and its recitals confirms many of the arguments put forward in this chapter. At present (June 1989) it would be premature to comment upon details of this proposal. It is important enough that the Commission recognizes the need to take further action in the field of product safety policy.

References

Bardach, E. and Keagan, R. A. (1982), *Going by the Book: The Problem of Regulatory Unreasonableness*, Philadelphia.
Brüggemeier, G. (1986), *Deliktsrecht*, Baden-Baden.
Brüggemeier, G. (1988), *Produkthaftung und Produktsicherheit*, ZHR 152, 511 ff.
Bruggers, J. H. A. and Rogmans, W. H. J. (1982), *Registratie van ongevallen in de privésfeer – een inventarisatie van relevante registratie systeemen*, Veiligheidsinstituut, Amsterdam.
Commission of the European Commities (1985), Completing the Internal Market. White Paper from the Commission to the European Council, COM (85) final, Brussels, 14 June.
Eads, G. and Reuter, P. (1983), *Designing Safer Products: Corporate Responses to Product Liability Law and Regulation*, Santa Monica, Cal.
Glaeske, G., Hart, D. and Merkel, H. (1988), 'Regulierung des europäischen Arzneimittelmarktes durch nationales und europäisches Zulassungs- und Nachmarktkontrollrecht', in N. Reich (ed.), *Die Europäisierung des Arzneimittelmarktes – Chancen und Risiken*, Baden-Baden.
Gusy, Ch. (1986), 'Wertungen und Interessen in der technischen Normung', *Umwelt- und Planungsrecht*, 241 ff.
Hart, D., Hilken, A., Merkel, H., Woggan, O. and Glaeske, G. (1988), *Das Recht des Arzneimittelmarktes in der Bundesrepublik Deutschland*, Baden-Baden.
Joerges, Ch., Falke, J. Micklitz, H.-W., and Brüggemeier, G.(1988), *Die Sicherheit von Konsumgütern und die Entwicklung der Europäischen Gemeinschaft*, Baden-Baden.
Joerges, Ch. (1988), Le *'Consumer Product Safety Act',* américain et sa mise en oevre par la *'Consumer Product Safety Commissioner'*, R.I.D.C., 7 ff.
Mertens, A. (1986), *Heim- und Freizeitunfälle: Aufklärung intensivieren*, BArbBl., 32 ff., 34 f.

Micklitz, H. -W., Falke, J., Harland, D., Méloire, M., Hummels, B.M., Joerges, Ch., Ringstedt, N., Snijders, G.M.F., Weatherill, St. and Woodroffe, G. (1988), *Nachmarktkontrolle technischer Konsumgüter*, Study for the Commission of the EC, Bremen.

OECD (1978), *Data Collection Systems Related to Accidents Involving Consumer Products, Paris 1978*. (1979), *Severity Weighting of Data on Accidents Involving Consumer Products*, Paris.

Pierce, R. J. (1980), 'Encouraging safety: the limits of tort law and government regulation, 33 *Vanderbilt L. Rev.* 1281.

Reich, N. (1987), *Förderung und Schutz diffuser Interessen durch die Europäischen Gemeinschaften*, Baden-Baden.

Schäfer, H. -B. and Ott, C.(1986), *Lehrbuch der ökonomischen Analyse des Zivilrechts*, Berlin, Heidelberg and New York.

Shavell, St. (1984), 'Liability for harm versus regulation of safety', 13 *J. Leg. Stud.* 357.

Stigler, G. J. (1971), 'The theory of economic regulation', 2 *The Bell J. of Economics and Management Science* 3.

Sugarman, S. D. (1985), 'Doing away with tort law', 73 *Cal.L. Rev.* 558.

Teubner, G.(1987), 'Juridification – concepts, aspects, limits, solutions', in: Teubner (ed.), *Juridification of Social Spheres*, Berlin and New York, 3 ff.

U.S. Consumer Product Safety Commission (1986), *The National Electronic Injury Surveillance System: A Description of its Role in the U.S. Consumer Product Safety Commission*, April.

Viscusi, W.K. (1984), *Regulating Consumer Product Safety*, Washington, D.C. and London.

Voelzkow, H., Hilbert, J. and Bolenz, E.(1987), 'Wettbewerb durch Kooperation – Kooperation durch Wettbewerb. Zur Funktion und Funktionsweise der Normungsverbände', in Glagow, M. and Willke, H. (eds), *Dezentrale Gesellschaftssteuerung. Probleme der Integration polyzentrischer Gesellschaft*, Pfaffenweiler, 93 ff.

Wiehe, R. (forthcoming), *Nachmarktkontrolle durch privatrechtlich-indirekte Steuerung. Eine ökonomisch orientierte Betrachtung*, EUI Working Paper 1990.

10. Regulatory Reform and the Environment: The Cause for Environmental Taxes

Ernst Ulrich von Weizsäcker

Introduction

Many experts on environmental policy in the European Community would see no reason for any major reform in environmental regulation. The main emphasis in the EEC's Fourth Action Programme for the Environment (1988–92) is on implementation and enforcement of existing legislation. In fact, it is to some extent to the credit of the Institute for European Environmental Policy (IEEP) that the EEC has stepped up its efforts to monitor and enforce its own legislation.[1] In early 1989 the Commission even announced the creation of a European Environment Agency, which is meant to support, in a decentralized fashion, national efforts in implementing EEC legislation. I fully acknowledge the importance and merits of this existing legislation.

If this chapter addresses some obvious weaknesses of the present regulatory approach and offers a few thoughts on major amendments, it should be quite clear that no existing regulation should be sacrificed unless and until one has assurance that the new instruments reach at least the same level of environmental protection.

On the other hand, one should face the fact that environmental degradation is going on at an alarming pace and that the present type of environmental policy seems to be insufficient in dealing with some of the problems. This will be the starting point for my chapter.

Signs of Crisis

Environmental Crisis

We are in the midst of a global environmental crisis. We are losing:

- a thousand tons of topsoil every second;
- three thousand square metres of forests every second;

● more than a thousand, possibly more than ten thousand, animal or plant species every year.

Air pollution is still on the rise worldwide, notwithstanding certain effective abatement measures taken in the affluent countries. Water pollution is horrendous in virtually all countries in the East and the Third World, but is also still a major problem in OECD countries. We definitely produce more waste, including hazardous waste, worldwide than we can safely handle. Resource depletion is going on at an alarming pace. And finally, pollution from human activity has reached the oceans and the outer atmosphere and is threatening our climate.[2]

Even in EEC countries which are considered rich and well organized, the trend of environmental degradation has not been broken. Perhaps the biggest contribution by West Europeans to environmental degradation (worldwide) stems from their far above world average resource consumption. They thereby indirectly but massively contribute to the destruction of the tropical forests, to resource depletion and to the global warming. Inside Europe the severest environmental problems are perhaps the extinction (or nearly) of many wildlife species resulting mostly from habitat destruction – acid rain and the death of forests, the groundwater crisis resulting inter alia from nitrates and pesticide use, the eutrophication of regional seas, and the unsolved solid and hazardous waste problems.

It should be noted that existing European environmental regulation has hardly touched Europe's contribution to the world environmental crisis and has only begun to touch the problems listed above as the severest.

Energy Crisis

The three biggest environmental debates of the past few years are all closely related to energy production: acid rain, Chernobyl and the greenhouse effect. The conventional (acid rain) problems were far from being solved when the threats to the global climate began to overshadow the whole environmental debate. Sea-level rise scenarios are creating a sense of alarm in coastal areas[3] and fears of desertification of Mediterranean and certain North American areas are of no lesser concern. The limitation of greenhouse gases is becoming a top priority on the international environmental policy agenda.[4]

Out of global warming fears, nuclear energy is experiencing a certain upswing in a number of countries. On the other hand, several reasons speak against the assumption that nuclear energy is a long-term solution. Reactor safety under non-war conditions still poses major problems, if only problems of cost and of reliability of personnel, in many countries. Much more disquieting is the vulnerability to terrorism, civil war and war actions. Moreover, the problems of nuclear waste, the aging and decommissioning problems of reactors, and the hazards lying in the handling of fissionable material will inevitably drive costs far beyond present levels. Breeder reactors and reprocessing plants are making things worse and not better. The plutonium cycle and the liquid sodium cooling system contain major additional risks.

Anyway it seems neither technologically nor economically reasonable to use nuclear energy as the main answer to the climate challenge. Under rather moderate energy demand assumptions it has been calculated that one would have to build a reactor every 2.4 days worldwide to substitute all coal power stations within the next 38 years.[5]

Hydroenergy is not a satisfactory answer either. All major dam projects in tropical countries are considered as ecological disasters, and there is little hope for hydropower to reach significantly more than the present 10 per cent of the world energy pie. And other renewables are not readily available on a sufficiently large scale and are still rather expensive in most forms.

Hence it is necessary, so it seems, to seriously think of strategies demanding much less energy than today's production and consumption patterns. The challenge is dramatized by the fact that developing countries will undoubtedly need growing amounts of energy, so that a reduction in energy-linked environmental problems can only be achieved by more than proportional reductions in energy consumption in industrialized countries; but the imperative of energy savings and energy efficiency is not limited to the affluent societies.

The energy-environment crisis is real, despite the temporary fall in oil prices. It is somewhat astonishing how long this reality escaped the attention of the broader public. The calmness is unstable. Any major event can trigger a worldwide awakening which may then suddenly alter the conditions for both industrial production and private consumption. Sudden changes, on the other hand, cause damages that are avoidable.

Worldwide there is a massive and scandalous lack of regulation to tackle the energy crisis. Existing environmental and safety regulations are obviously quite insufficient instruments if the reduction of unnecessary energy demand is to be made a major policy objective. Only a few countries including Denmark and Japan have made some attempts to cope with the challenge. The prevailing attitude is still to treat energy demand as an almost natural phenomenon and to see to it that any energy 'demand', existing or forecast, must be satisfied. In reality, energy demand depends heavily on energy prices and on several other factors which are subject to political decisions. Given the fact that even under today's price regime (in the United States) 'each dollar invested in electric efficiency displaces nearly seven times more carbon (dioxide) than a dollar invested in nuclear power',[6] the inactivity of most nations with regard to energy efficiency seems also economically very unreasonable.

New Challenges From the Internal Market

The completion of the Internal Market is likely to further exacerbate environmental problems. Try to imagine what the 200 billion ECU of additional wealth in the EEC countries, as projected in the Cecchini Report[7] actually mean. They essentially mean more production and more than proportionally greater transport of goods and probably of people. It seems not unreasonable to expect an overproportional increase of pollution with the increase of economic activity.

The chilly winds of competition which will blow after the completion of the Internal Market are likely to make it difficult for local authorities and for governments in the less prosperous countries to accept stringent environmental standards. Eventually, a new period of environmental negligence (as in the late 1970s) may result in all EEC countries if public attention becomes preoccupied with small businesses going bankrupt under the competitive pressures.

More specifically, the deregulation of the transport sector causes headaches with environmentalists. Deregulation leads to higher capacities and lower prices of freight transport in Europe, so that lorries will gain a still further increased market share from railways. A 40 per cent increase in international lorry traffic by the year 2000 has been forecast.[8] This would have disastrous consequences for the environment.

Airline deregulation will also have negative effects on the environment, but these will be quantitatively much less significant than those of road traffic.

Another sector of deregulation which may be of significance to the environment is the unrestricted service market (Art. 8a of the revised Treaty). German electricity utilities, which are required to invest large sums in environmental protection (or in nuclear safety), feel threatened by the prospect of French nuclear electricity being sold at marginal prices to German customers. Cheap French electricity will also jeopardize all attempts to artificially raise energy prices (to encourage energy savings).

There may be many more environmental effects associated with the Internal Market. Waste traffic is likely to increase. Illegal trades in endangered species will be more difficult to control. And the trend to ecologically damaging large field sizes in agriculture may be reinforced.

On the other hand, the new opportunity given by the Single European Act to create a genuinely European environmental policy should not be underestimated. Article 130 R, par. 2 makes the polluter pays principle quasi constitutional in all EEC countries and in addition carries a surprisingly strong mandate to integrate environmental policy into other Community policies. If properly used, this mandate may outweigh all the negative environmental aspects that can be associated with the Internal Market.

In the next section some conventional policy responses to environmental degradation will be briefly discussed.

Environmental Regulation

Standards

For the first fifteen years environmental policy worldwide and in particular in the EEC consisted chiefly of setting environmental standards: quality or immission standards, emission standards and product standards. Complying with these standards involved costs for the polluter (or for the manufacturer of products). Under the accepted *polluter pays principle* (*ppp*) the polluter had to accept this additional cost burden, but was not prevented from passing them on to his customers if the market allowed him to do so.

The setting of standards was the obvious choice for the initial phase of environmental policy. Standards are easy to understand and easy to negotiate and they don't involve direct costs for the State. But they have numerous shortcomings.

Quality standards tend to induce industry to move from highly polluted to less polluted areas. Pollution may travel from one medium to another. And environmental quality standards are of little use for the fight against vehicle emissions – they lead at best to driving restrictions under certain weather conditions – or they lead to emission standards for vehicles.

Emission standards have a great disadvantage in international negotiations. They are clearly favoured by highly industrialized, affluent and pollution-importing countries, but they involve high costs with low environmental benefits for pollution-exporting countries and for less industrialized countries and are therefore less favoured by them. It is not surprising that the EEC Environment Council became an arena of intense fighting the moment that Germany and Holland began insisting on emission standards.

Another shortcoming of standards is that they tend to be static. Once a given standard is reached there is little incentive left for polluters to go further in emission reduction. And if standards are coupled with a 'best available technology' stipulation, polluters often have little interest in progress in pollution prevention technologies because such progress leads to additional costs and no benefits to the firm.

Most importantly in the context of regulatory reform, the standards philosophy involves high administrative costs both on the side of the State and of the polluters. The loose-leaf manuals for the practitioner on only three German laws, the Water Management Act, the Waste Act and the Technical Instruction Air comprise not less than ten volumes of a thousand pages each[9], and of the USA it is reported that twenty years of environmental law-making have created no less than 13,000 pieces of legislation, often at state or district council level. Industry representatives often speak of an asphyxiating effect of the swelling environmental regulation. On the other hand it is quite unfeasible for local authorities to control and enforce all environmental regulations, notably in poorer countries where the authorities lack personnel and equipment. Thus the standards philosophy also reinforces the widespread prejudice that environmental protection is something only the rich can afford.

Other Legal Instruments

Instead of ever stricter legislation one may also resort to environmental liability, as in the USA and Japan. This would make pollution and accidents riskier and more expensive for the producer. From the point of view of environmental protection this is certainly desirable, but the 'asphyxiating' effects may be rather stronger than with straightforward regulation.

Another legal instrument is the environmental impact assessment (EIA), which is an important tool of environmental planning. The EIA is a child of the era of heavy regulation and is certainly not welcomed by industry. But as long as industrial planning is not steered into an environmentally acceptable direction by other signals, the EIA will remain and become more important in Europe as the EC Directive on EIA (85/337/EEC) is being implemented in all Member states.

Finally, laws on the free access to environmental information will receive ever higher significance. But even these create great concerns with industry, this time rather because it fears – or pretends to fear – the watching eye of commercial competitors.

Economic Instruments

In view of widespread dissatisfaction with existing legal instruments and apprehensions of additional ones, economic instruments have attracted considerable attention in recent years. Pollution charges were introduced in Germany (Abwasserabgabe), France (waste water and SO_2 charges) and other countries. Also, tax privileges (e.g. accelerated depreciation) were awarded to environmental investments of companies. In addition, the idea of tradable emission permits, for example, within 'bubbles' of geographically defined total emissions, emerged. Deposits for bottles, tax privileges for clean cars, a superfund fed by the chemical industry are other examples of economic instruments.

Although pollution charges and other economic instruments conform with the ppp, one cannot, from today's experience, escape the conclusion that these economic instruments have had a rather limited effect so far. Perhaps they came too late into an already regulated landscape, or the charges and benefits were too small to make a major difference. In fact, it seems that in no country has the total of environmental charges exceeded one tenth of a per cent of the GNP. In addition, there is very little enthusiasm from the industrial side to have charges introduced which would not *replace* existing laws but only add to already existing costs; and for subventions the climate is not favourable either. The trading of permits, finally, appears to be more difficult to administer than originally thought, and has, at least in Europe, failed to convince people outside academia.

To summarize this section: under present environmental policy trends, industry will have to face ever growing regulation and steadily rising costs and commercial risks. At the same time, it appears highly questionable whether a continuation of the present legislation trends will really lead to the necessary relief for the environment.

Environmental Taxes

Taxes Reconsidered

Taxes are something quite different from charges. Taxes are meant to produce revenues for the State. They are not normally intended to steer the economy or the society. They should have a good yield and they should be fair in terms of social justice. Typically, therefore, it is the rich people who pay the highest (direct) taxes. But as the rich in modern societies tend to be the most productive, taxes tend to work as a deadweight on productivity, as a discouragement for the active people and as an incentive for clandestine work.

It should be noted that the indirect cost burden on human labour consists not only of income taxes. It is also pension funds, health insurances and in many countries solidarity payments for the unemployed. In Germany, net earnings are roughly half the gross salary costs, with income taxes making up roughly another quarter and the sum of the other costs the remaining quarter. In Italy it is even a factor three between net earnings and gross salary costs.

Indirect taxes are taken from goods or services, not directly from people. The most important indirect tax is the VAT which again works as a deadweight on productivity. Only a few taxes have a (very moderate) steering intention in addition to their function of yielding revenues, for example taxes on alcohol, tobacco or fuels. Their original intention was, however, not steering but the taxing of luxury or of consumption.

A host of small taxes still exist in many countries, some of them absolutely insignificant for state revenues and yet quite unjust and nonsensical, such as the tea and the salt taxes.

Tax evasion has become a widespread phenomenon in our societies. Increasing tax bureaucracies are struggling with it less and less successfully. Notably in Mediterranean countries high taxes are an important reason for an enormous shadow economy. For Italy it is estimated that the unreported economy equals the official economy.

It is not the intention of this paper to give a full account of the needs for a fundamental tax reform under the criterion of the steering functions of taxes. But when discussing the introduction of a new type of tax, it will be helpful to remember that not all is fine with the present tax system.

Criteria and Proposals

It is already sixty years ago that Arthur Pigou asked for environmental taxes to internalize external environmental costs into all economic activities. But it took several decades until workable models for environmental taxes were developed. Mostly, environmental tax ideas sprung up in connection with certain environmental financing needs. To finance sewage treatment, waste disposal, flue gas desulphurization or, as in Japan, compensation payments to victims of pollution, the attention always turned to the polluters and to ways and means of making them pay.

Although I sympathize with such proposals, I would not call them taxes. They are charges for a specific purpose. Charges almost invariably create and stabilize state bureaucracies to handle and spend the money according to the purpose. Hence, one would expect environmental bureaucracies to be in favour of such charges while industry will typically be against, for the reasons given in the previous section.

Environmental taxes, as I see them, are of a different nature. They are 'merely' meant to change the frame conditions for production and consumption. Revenues from environmental taxes can be used for whichever purpose, as is the case for revenues from VAT, corporate or income taxes. Therefore they can also be used for financing environmentally undesirable things such as roads or warplanes.

Counterintuitively, this complete openness of their use is where the explosive strength of environmental taxes lies. If governments and parliaments are completely free to use the revenues from environmental taxes, they have the option – and can by law be forced – to return the total amount of environmental taxes to the taxpayer by lowering other taxes, for example income taxes, VAT or corporate taxes. This means that the overall average tax burden may remain unchanged. Hence, you can have environmental taxes totalling 10 per cent of the GNP and still have not the slightest increase of the average tax burden. Ten per cent of the GNP is a hundred times more than the present charges, meaning also a hundredfold steering power. No doubt this amounts to a revolution in both environmental and tax policy. How can this ambitious goal be reached, what are the effects in terms of regulatory reform and what are the possible objections against the project?[10]

To begin with: the goal must not be achieved in one big jump. A big jump in the tax system would be a disruptive disaster for the economy. What I can imagine is a twenty or thirty-year period during which the total of all environmental taxes goes up by a foreseeable 0.3 or 0.5 per cent of the GNP each year. There could even be a period of announcement of several years before the first step is considered, as was the case with the German waste water charges.

The following *criteria* should be observed for all environmental taxes:

1   Taxes should be charged on factors on which there is a *broad consensus* that they are damaging the environment.
2   Environmental taxes should be *just* in terms of distribution. In case of need, social policy compensations should be given.
3   The *administrative costs* of collecting environmental taxes should be small.
4   Environmental taxes should be introduced slowly and *stepwise* to give the economy and technology development time to adjust.
5   Environmental taxes should be introduced *EC wide*, if possible.

Observing these criteria I could imagine the following taxes being reached after twenty or thirty years (1988 prices):

1   *Energy*: ECU 10 per gigajoule of fossil and nuclear energy (one gigajoule is roughly 30 litres of oil, or 280 kWh);
2   *Ground coverage*: ECU 100 per square metre of ground *newly* covered by buildings, concrete or macadam; ECU 2 annually per square metre already covered – as a steady incentive to restore unused ground;
3   *Water*: ECU 10 per cubic metre of polluted waste water of ECU 3 per cubic metre of water used;
4   *Waste*: ECU 50 per ton of unsorted solid waste, ECU 500 per ton of hazardous waste;
5   *Air*: ECU 1000 per ton of SO_2, NO_x, CO or hydro-chlorocarbons, ECU 100 per ton of methane, ECU 50 per ton of CO_2.

It should be made clear that these figures are *not* the result of scientific calculations. They are first approximations to what may be considered a fair and just taxation of natural resources and pollution, all fairly easy to control and all producing considerable income for the State. Tax rates, contrary to charges, can never be justified in scientific terms. The VAT is 3 per cent in Japan, 14 per cent in Germany, 25 per cent in Ireland. None of these values results from scientific calculations. If people find it unfair to charge coal burning twice, via fossil energy taxes and via air pollution, the air pollution tax may be dropped.

Eight Objections and Answers

Any proposal of significant impact will most naturally meet objections. Perhaps the most important are the following:

1 *'Environmental taxes are unnecessary'*
This is essentially an argument in defence of the standards setting or command and control approach.
Answer: I think I have indicated that environmental degradation by land use, energy consumption, water overuse, waste production and the production of greenhouse gases is quite insufficiently affected by conventional environmental policy. Also, pollution control is not satisfactorily achieved by existing policies and it may be at least worth trying out an additional instrument.

2 *'Environmental taxes don't produce funds for environmental policy'*
Huge clean-up costs, debt swaps for developing countries, or the financing of a clean technology revolution seem to create the need for extra state money, hence for environmental charges, not taxes.
Answer: This is not denied. But the financial needs of environmental policy should be clearly distinguished from the steering power of taxes. If taxes produce an incentive structure in which industry creates the clean technology revolution by itself and takes care of much of the clean-up, the whole economy will be better off than with voluminous public clean-up programmes. (But one should not expect environmental bureaucrats to subscribe to this statement.) The financial contributions needed to help developing countries save their forests should be treated apart; it is quite possible that an increase in the fiscal burden for this particular purpose is unavoidable.

3 *'Environmental taxes will never be agreed on (or else: whatever can be agreed will have little effect)'*
Greens who believe nothing leading to significant reductions in pollution can be achieved in a capitalist economy often argue this way. Certain industrialists, on the other hand, have indeed a tendency to resist drastic change.
Answer: Environmental taxes are meant to be compatible with further industrial development. They hit *some* industries but make *others* all the more profitable. Hence, these taxes could be more palatable than many other

environmental policy measures to the industrial world; and hence they are more likely to find broad acceptance.

4 'Environmental taxes are unjust or immoral'

Most indirect taxes have indeed socially undesirable distribution effects. They hit the poor comparatively harder than the rich. The immorality may be seen in such taxes making pollution something you can compensate with money. *Answer*: Social policy should be made using the means of social policy instruments, not by foregoing effective environmental policy aims. The average extra burden from new environmental taxes for the poor may be calculated and may be returned to them directly so that they have the choice either of continuing their old life style at a little extra cost or of shifting to more resource saving life styles and having a little extra money in their pockets. Similarly, it could be argued that commuters should receive a certain gasoline tax compensation payment regardless of what means of transportation they use. As to the morality of environmental taxes, it should be said that if they actually lead to drastically lowered pollution and resource destruction, they serve a very moral purpose.

5 'Environmental taxes put additional burdens on the economy and distort the conditions of competition'

Answer: This argument can be heard from representatives of industrial branches which contribute a disproportionally large share to pollution or energy consumption. And for their companies the argument is likely to be correct. They may have to change, to emigrate or to close. But there are other industries which would actually benefit from any shift of the tax burden from corporate and income taxes to resources and pollution taxes. These industries will become growth industries and should be able to absorb all people losing their jobs in shrinking sectors, provided all goes slowly and smoothly.

There is, however, a more justified fear: Will it be realistic to return the total amount of environmental tax revenues back to industry and the other taxpayers? Is there not an inbuilt momentum of ever increasing state expenditures? That fear is difficult to answer except by saying that the fear is not specific to environmental taxes.

6 'Environmental taxes have an inbuilt tendency to decrease'

It is true that the intended effect of environmental taxes is to reduce their own basis, namely pollution and the consumption of energy, land and other resources.

Answer: During the build-up period of twenty or thirty years, the total revenues are bound to increase even if the taxes steer very successfully. Even in the long run the environmental taxes are never going to come close to zero because there will always be some energy consumption, waste production, etc. Finally, the State may always compensate revenue losses by resorting to traditional taxes.

7 'Taxes are not meant to steer but to have high yields and to be just'

This is the standard objection from the theory of public finances. Historically, the statement is correct. And for the State it is extremely convenient to receive revenues that grow faster than the GNP. It enables politicians to declare from time to time that they are 'reducing' taxes.

Answer: In recent years, the steering effects, unwanted or wanted, of taxation got into the limelight of current fiscal debates. The steering effects of the favourite taxes – income taxes and VAT – which automatically grow faster than the GNP, were discovered to be unwanted. Both taxes work to make human labour and productivity gains artificially more expensive and seem to contribute to unemployment. Hence, it is a weighing of the yield advantage on the side of these existing taxes against the desired steering effect on the side of environmental taxes. As the latter are meant to grow slowly, a political compromise may be within reach.

8   *'Environmental taxes are incompatible with realities in the EEC'*
The concept is new, and it remains to be seen if all EEC Member States will agree on environmental taxes.

Answer: Up until 1992 it would be possible to introduce environmental taxes at a national level. In the process of tax harmonization, according to Article 99 of the EEC Treaty, such national environmental taxes could be used as a bargain chip to negotiate EEC wide environmental taxes. For the Mediterranean countries environmental taxes seem highly attractive in that they rather facilitate revenue collection for the State. Resource consumption and heavy pollution is far more visible and much easier to measure and control than human labour. Also environmental taxes should have a more sweeping effect on environmental protection than the present day standards (which should, of course, be maintained).

If the strategy of harmonized environmental taxes fails, it is still possible, according to Article 95 of the EEC Treaty, to introduce national charges. If the political will is there not to increase the average cost burden for industry, it should be possible to return even the revenues from charges into the economy.

Effects of Environmental Taxes

The effects of environmental taxes are multifold. The Japanese SO_2 levy has worked so well that the still existing strict SO_2 emission standards are never exhausted. They have in effect become completely ornamental. This is one striking example for my expectation that environmental taxes of an appropriate height can eventually substitute a very large part of existing environmental legislation. That would be extremely good news for both the environment and industry. Environmental taxes should figure prominently in every debate about regulatory reform and deregulation in environmental policy.

It should be worth our while to ask what kind of effects they would have. Assuming rational reactions by our economy perhaps the following statements can be made:

● At ECU 10 taxes per gigajoule of fossil and nuclear energy, the renewables would boom and energy efficiency would become a high priority for managers, households and planners. Combined heat and power would become an obvious choice for all power generation. Equally, the Swedish standards for house insulation, the fuel efficient car (3 litres per 100 km), energy efficient light bulbs and appliances and low energy food production and processing would win over their present day energy wasting competitors. Rails and ships would take shares from road and air transport. Railways would thrive by developing high speed systems and quick terminals. Some industries, such as aluminium from bauxite, would be forced to emigrate. No new fossil or nuclear power stations would be built in Europe for many decades, possibly forever.

• At ECU 500 per ton of hazardous waste – in addition to the disposal costs – major changes would be prompted in product design, in production processes, in internal recycling and in detoxification. A close watch should be given to illicit disposal and to methods to control it.

• Waste water and water use taxes would induce water savings, water recycling and internal purification. The lowering of the ground water table could be stopped and rivers would have good prospects of being restored.

• Heavy taxes on land sealing would make it more profitable to clean up derelict industrial land than to use virgin land. The sprawling of agglomerations would be slowed down or even reversed, diminishing the mobility advantage of cars.

• Generally, information intensive production would gain. So would resource efficient services, crafts, repair, science and technology. The clumsy, the dirty and the highly centralized productions would lose.

• Industry and capital would benefit from a strong, clear and predictable sense of direction, which is the prerequisite of a healthy investment climate. And managers would have an easier time justifying to their grown-up children what they are doing and why.

Notes

1. The Institute was the first in the field with comprehensive studies of the legal and practical implementation of EEC environmental directives. e.g. Nigel Haigh (1984), *EEC Environmental Policy and Britain* (2nd edn, 1987): Longman, Harlow. European Community Environmental Policy in Practice (1986), *Comparative Report: Water and Waste in Four Countries – A Study of the Implementation of the EEC Directives in France, Germany, Netherlands and United Kingdom, Vol. 1. Nigel Haugh, United Kingdom: Water and Waste, Vol. 2. Graham Bennett, Netherlands: Water and Waste, Vol. 3. Thierry Lavoux, France: Water and Waste, Vol. 4. Pascale Kromarek, Federal Republic of Germany: Water and Waste*, Graham & Trotman, London. More volumes in preparation.
2. See e.g. *State of the World* 88, Worldwatch Institute, W.W. Norton, New York.
3. Gjerrit P. Hekstra (1989), 'Global Warming and rising sea levels: the policy implications', *The Ecologist*, Vol 19, No. 1, pp. 4–15.
4. An impressive interim report was published by the Committee of Enquiry on the Protection of the Earth's Atmosphere of the German Bundestag, Nov. 1988. The report chiefly addresses the ozone protection issues but devotes one third of the volume to global warming issues.
5. Bill Keepin (1988), *Greenhouse Warming Efficient Solution of Nuclear Nemesis*, paper submitted at a Global Warming Hearing by the US House of Representatives, 29 June; available from Rocky Mountain Institute, Snowmass, CO 81654 – 9199, USA.
6. Ibid., p.3

7. The Costs of Non-Europe; (see P. Cecchini, ed (1988), *Research into the Costs of Non-Europe*, Commission of the European Communities, Brussels.)
8. Study of PROGNOS, Basel, quoted in *VDI-Nachrichten*, 30 Sept. 1988. See also Winfried Wolf (1987), *Eisenbahn und Autowahn*, Hamburg: Rasch und Röhring, p. 355–77.
9. *Die neue TA Luft*, (1987), 3 vols.; *Das neue Wasserrecht für die betriebliche Praxis*, (1987), 4 vols; *Abfallbeseitigungsrecht für die betriebliche Praxis*, (1989), 3 vols. Kissing: WEKA Fachverlag.
10. The remaining part of this paper is adapted from a German article by the author, published in Wirtschaftswoche, Düsseldorf, 10 Feb. 1989, under the title 'Mit Steuern steuern'.

11. Strategies of Regulatory Reform
An Economic Analysis with Some Remarks on Germany

Charles B. Blankart

1 Justification versus Explanation of Regulation

Deregulation has become a very popular slogan in everyday discussions. Regulation reductions are being requested in all parts of the economy, for example, in air and surface transport, in health services, in mass media and in banking and insurance. Proposals have been made for deregulation even in the traditional state monopolies such as the railroads, postal services and telecommunications. Many studies have been made and published showing the advantages of deregulation. But when these proposals come to politics, the previous impetus suddenly vanishes. Programmes are curtailed and eventually shelved. Such is the destiny of the initially pioneering ideas on the deregulation of telecommunications. The demanding proposals made in a special report by the German Monopoly Commission (1981) were later curtailed by the Government Commission for Telecommunications (1987). The Federal Government's following proposal for a Telecommunications Act (1988) made further reductions in the deregulation programme, and the finally proposed Act was again restructured by the parliament, so that the version eventually adopted represents only a very minor step towards deregulation.

As a rule it can be said that there is a large gap between theory and policy in the field of deregulation. This is so because today economic theories of deregulation suffer from a considerable *normative bias*. Their basis is an *economic justification theory* of regulation rather than a *theory of regulatory policy* which would be needed for evaluating reform proposals. Justifications for regulation are given by the traditional arguments of market failure, such as natural monopoly, public goods or consumer misinformation. These norms are then compared with reality and serve as a basis for recommending the introduction or abolition of regulations.

The justification theory of regulation has, however, little predictive power. Whether or not a regulatory measure is justified in the context of a market economy is, in general, of little relevance for political decision-makers' behaviour. They may reject the regulatory measure though it is economically justified, or they may approve or continue regulation though economic justification is not given. The latter case is nicely illustrated by the example of the telecommunications system cited above.

The gap between economic theory of regulation and the policy measures observed can only be overcome if the former is amended by a positive theory of regulation explaining political decisions. Such a theory may serve as a basis for a realistic consideration of deregulation proposals. The intention of this chapter, therefore, is to analyze deregulation from a politico-economic point of view. In section 2 elements of such a positive theory of regulation will be developed. In section 3 these results will be applied to regulation in the Federal Republic of Germany. Section 4 will propose ways towards deregulation in a political environment and section 5 brings some conclusions.

2 Explaining Regulation in the Political Process

Our point of departure is that the justification theory of regulation (natural monopolies, public goods and consumer misinformation) is of little help in explaining regulation. When regulation is politically decided upon, other reasons must be responsible. In an individualistic world, human self-interest is likely to be a leading principle underlying regulatory decision. Individuals or groups endeavour to attain *special treatment* on the market, and *regulation* is, as we shall see, a particularly well suited institutional arrangement for realizing this goal. It serves as a compromise formula to unify competing goals of various interest groups.

Consider a competitive enterprise or industry and the goals of the groups which have vested interests in it: each of these groups wants to change the result of the market process in its favour.
- Capital owners strive for higher product prices.
- Organized consumer groups plead for *selective* price cuts or even for below cost prices for the goods and services they consume.
- Workers and employees of the firm or industry in question fight for higher wages, salaries and improved working conditions.
- Capital good and raw material suppliers demand higher prices for their procurements to the firm or industry.

Each of these groups acting individually is, in general, too small to gain special treatment, for example by launching and enforcing a subsidy programme on its own. But a *coalition* among them (possibly together with groups of other industries) may be strong enough to create the necessary political pressure. A coalition does not, however, emerge automatically. Its members have to agree first of all to a common programme. Their competing goals have to be brought under one roof. The point I would like to make here is that regulation is likely to be a very attractive coalition programme for all participating groups.

The reasons why regulation is so attractive are easily explained when we consider the groups mentioned above. Regulation will consist, *firstly*, in the erection of entry barriers allowing an increase in prices of those goods and services which are in high demand on the market place, but little supported in the political area. The monopoly profits thus created primarily serve capital owners' interests. But, *secondly*, they fulfil the interests of special consumer groups by cross-subsidizing some prices selectively. *Finally*, monopoly profits also serve the labour force and the other input suppliers in their striving for higher wages, salaries and procurement prices. They get their share of the monopoly rents too.

Thus, regulation seems to be a magic formula for improving the position of all groups which are members of the coalition, whereas the position of those who are outside because they are not organized is damaged by the arrangement. The costs to the outsiders do not, however, matter politically because they cannot mobilize political power through organized voting, etc. The whole regulatory deal will be equipped with the label of a 'public service', and will therefore receive an ethical foundation which makes it immune to political attacks.

From a purely economic point of view, such a regulation is clearly a negative sum game: in general, every departure from competitive resource allocation leads to an economic loss (provided that no apparent market failure is present). Moreover, the interest groups involved use resources to enforce regulation in the political process. These are rent-seeking costs representing an additional economic loss.

I have so far avoided answering the question of who the groups are that are able to attain organization and are therefore able to express their wants in politics. Olson suggests in his well known book, *The Logic of Collective Action* (1965), that small groups will succeed in getting organized first of all because they are less paralyzed by the free rider problem. They have smaller organization costs. Therefore regulation is likely to be introduced primarily for small special interest groups. Olson, however, shows in his more recent book *The Rise and Decline of Nations* (1982), that large groups do not necessarily fail to overcome the problem of organization costs, but they need more time. When institutions age, the number and percentage of organized interest groups will rise and the amount of regulation will increase. The problem to be treated in section 4 of this chapter is the way in which attempts to move towards deregulation have to be evaluated in view of this trend of increasing regulation.

The *interest group theory of regulation* developed here may be criticized for being of only restricted value in European countries. It may be said that it is not able to explain socializations or nationalizations, which are so typical for European public utilities in particular. This critique is, however, unjustified. For socializations or nationalizations are just different forms of regulation, and the interest group theory can also be applied to them. We only have to conceive the state treasury and its politicians as particular interest groups. They both support regulation through government takeover where government revenue or government power can be increased. The practical relevance of fiscal arguments can be seen in the German communalization movement

214   Charles B. Blankart

around the end of the nineteenth century (relating mostly to local utilities) as well as to the nationalization of railroads, postal services, telecommunications and the partial nationalization of electricity in Germany (see Blankart, 1984; 1987). The phenomenon of socialization being more frequent in European countries than in the USA probably has to do with the fact that the state treasury was and still is more highly developed as a revenue raising institution in the Old World than in the New world which has a shorter history of a public bureaucracy.

3   The Actual State of Regulation and Socialization in The West German Economy

In this section I shall compare the actual state of regulation and socialization in West Germany with the *interest group theory of regulation* developed in section 2. The turned of increasing regulation is a secular one, which is difficult to identity in a time-series analysis. But there is some empirical evidence of it in a cross-section view over industries. This can be seen in Figure 11.1. This figure has two dimensions. The degree of regulation is tentatively measured on the *vertical axis*. Industries with free market entry are classified as non regulated. Therefore, no interest group attached to the industry (either on the output or the input side) has the power to enforce a political manipulation of prices in

Figure 11.1   Regulation and socialization/nationalization in the Federal Republic of Germany (about 1980)

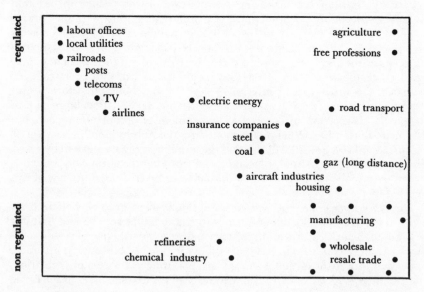

Sources: CEEP (1987); Bundesministerium der Finanzen (1987)

its favour. There is neither *output* nor *input regulation*. At the other end of the regulation scale are industries where market entry is protected. Intermediate cases are placed correspondingly. The horizontal axis measures the degree of *private or public ownership* of capital.

There may be some dispute about the exact location of particular industries. The points indicated in the figure rely on publications of the CEEP (1987) and the Ministry of Finance (1987). An exact location of the industries is not, however, possible (in particular on the regulation scale). The idea behind the graph is only to give an illustration of the situation in Germany, which is likely to contrast considerably with the distribution of industries in other countries, such as the United States and the United Kingdom.

The growing trend toward regulation is revealed by the fact that more and more industries are moving from the lower right hand corner to the upper right and left hand corners. The particular characteristics of the industries marked here are, however, quite different, as we shall see in the remainder of this section of the chapter.

1. The dots in the lower right-hand corner indicate that the bulk of the West German economy is still fairly competitive and not very highly regulated. Here we find most *manufacturing* as well as services such as *the whosesale* and *retail trades*. After all, Germany still adheres to the doctrine of a market economy laid down in the 1930s and 40s by economists of the Freiburg School such as *Franz Böhm* and *Walter Eucken*. After World War II these ideas found support among the Western Allies and were executed to a large extent by *Ludwig Erhard*, the Minister of Economic Affairs during the first and decisive years of the Federal Republic of Germany.

It would be wrong, however, to believe that Germany literally became a free market economy after World War II, and that it has remained one since then. In some industries previous regulation was maintained, and some became regulated later on. In this sense, the figure in the paper represents a historical account dating back much further, to the nineteenth century.

2. The firms and industries in the upper left hand corner are regulated and socialized. (I have omitted regulation of public good supply and environment regulation.) Here, we have to mention, first the *railroads*. Regulation in this sector is particularly strong because it relates to outputs as well as to inputs. Outputs are regulated in the sense that the *Deutsche Bundesbahn* (the state-owned railroad corporation) has to maintain an enormous overcapacity of branch lines. On these lines revenues do not cover costs by far. However, cross-subsidization from highly frequented main lines to branch lines is not, or no longer, feasible, since the *Bundesbahn* has lost its earlier monopoly over long-distance transportation and has had to face competition from road, air and waterway services.

Input regulation exists because the *Bundesbahn* is required by law to hire employees with civil servant status for most of the more qualified jobs. This makes it difficult to redefine jobs and to reallocate manpower when structural changes occur. Therefore, given a competitive labour market outside the railroads, those who are underpaid will have an incentive to quit and those who are overpaid will remain. The effect is that a considerable proportion of railroad employees is overpaid.

Another aspect of input regulation is the *procurement policy* which has to be followed by the *Bundesbahn*. Most of the rolling and fixed stocks have to be furnished exclusively by national suppliers. The *Bundesbahn* and its procurement firms are engaged in a sort of 'liaison' allowing the latter to set prices within a large range and independently of foreign suppliers. These policies are defended for the most part with the argument of protecting domestic jobs.

Given the fact that so many groups ask for special treatment by the *Bundesbahn*, and that competition by other means of transport cannot be prohibited, it is not astonishing to observe an enormous deficit. It amounts to 126 billion DM (equal to about 7 billion US dollars, 1986) or one half of the total federal budget deficit.

Another example of a regulated public industry are the *postal* and *telecommunications* services which are united in one single enterprise, the *Deutsche Bundespost*. Postal and telecommunications services are monopolized and characterized, therefore, by output and input regulation. *Outputs are regulated* in the sense that postal services as well as telecommunications must provide their basic services on a nationwide network at more or less uniform prices. This results in some cross-subsidization between high- and low-density service areas. There is, moreover, a substantial flow of subsidies from telecommunications to postal services, the reason for which can be found in *input regulation*. The *Deutsche Bundespost* is required (like the *Deutsche Bundesbahn*) to hire most of its labour force under civil service contracts. Moreover, an active labour union strongly resists rationalizations, particularly in the labour-intensive postal sector. The unions' claims are supported by some local politicians who fear that they will lose votes in their districts if the unions' assertions, namely that rural service quality will decline if regulation is lifted, turn out to be true. Union power, however, also relies on the fact claims can be easily accommodated by profits in telecommunications.

A final industry in the upper corner to be mentioned is the *airlines industry* or more correctly, *Lufthansa*, the most important German air carrier. *Lufthansa* is a private law company, the majority of whose shares are in government ownership. It is well-known that outputs and prices of European airlines are still heavily regulated by means of country by country contracts and by the *IATA*. It is less well-known, however, that input procurement is also regulated to some extent. *Lufthansa* has an unwritten obligation to buy its aircraft, as far as is technically feasible, from the German aircraft industry. At present, *Lufthansa* can easily fulfil these obligations because of its monopoly position.

3.   Next, we have to analyze the combination of socialization and competition in the lower left-hand corner. It is not astonishing to find this corner empty: for if an enterprise is socialized, the decision rights of the management become public property and special interest groups will try to obtain possession of these rights and to enforce regulation. So we would expect an upward shift of these firms and industries from the lower left to the upper left-hand corner.

Sometimes the German 'Law Against Abuse of Competition' may put a barrier against such upward moves which are clearly anti-competitive. This may be a reason why refineries and chemical industries (as far as they were publicly owned) remained on the lower left hand-side of the above figure. But the constraints posed by the 'Law Against Abuse of Competition' are not always binding. Coal and steel industries, for example, are also partially government owned, but are nevertheless regulated by governmentally organized cartels. Here the Common Market revealed itself as a suitable institution for regulation.

4.   The last group is formed by those industries which are regulated without government participation in capital. They are situated in the upper right-hand corner. First of all, there is *agriculture* which is thoroughly regulated in the interests of producers or of some producers. Here the State has not acquired ownership of capital as there were no profits to be collected for the Public Treasury.

Another group that is probably too heterogeneous for socialization is formed by the *free and self-employed professions*: *lawyers, physicians, architects, pharmacists, craftsmen*, etc. They have successfully managed to maintain or to reintroduce a regulation system similar to that which they possessed under the guild system of the *ancien régime*. For these professions two types of regulation can be distinguished. Firstly, entry barriers are erected in the sense that those who want to practise a free profession must possess a particular degree or licence. A car repair shop, for example, can only be established by someone who has acquired a 'master' qualification in car repairs. Similar regulations hold for all other crafts, such as painters, plumbers, roofers, typesetters, printers and builders. Secondly, highly qualified free professions such as those of notaries, lawyers, physicians and pharmacists maintain analogous entry barriers, but, in addition, the professional associations to which they mandatorily adhere impose price regulations.

Finally some remarks on *insurance*. This sector was regulated at the turn of the century with the idea of consumer protection. Initially, regulation was intended to guarantee that only serious suppliers were admitted to the market. This regulation was regarded as useful, particularly in the life insurance branch characterized by its long-term contracts. Over time, however, this loose form of regulation has been increasingly extended by the initiatives of insurance companies for they soon realized that regulation was an ideal institutional instrument for establishing and enforcing price cartels. The official argument for these manoeuvres was always that solvency required higher prices. Such regulated cartels were particularly successful where uniform contracts could be achieved, such as in motor car liability insurance and in life insurance. As a rule, it can be said that insurance regulation started as an instrument of consumer protection, but then increasingly turned into a tool to protect the suppliers. The effect is that net life insurance premiums are substantially higher in Germany than in other countries such as the United Kingdom where less regulation and more competition prevail (see Finsinger and Pauly, 1986, and for a further discussion, Finsinger, 1988).

To sum up: there are two basic trends in regulation in the Federal Republic of Germany. Starting from a basically competitive economy under private ownership, one trend goes towards regulation, the other towards regulation combined with state ownership, thus corroborating Olson's hypothesis that interest groups become increasingly able to organize themselves and to enforce regulation. The problem to be tackled now is how deregulation should be attained in such a regulatory environment. This problem will be dealt with in the next section.

4 Roads Towards Deregulation

It has become clear by now that little is achieved by only demanding deregulation because of its allocative superiority. Rather, a theory of deregulation has to show ways which lead political decision-makers from a regulated world of public enterprises into a competitive world of private enterprise. The economist as an adviser has to propose arrangements of deregulation and privatization to the politicians that appear to them to offer greater advantages than the status quo. New compromises must be found which may serve as a basis for political decisions. In the remainder of this paper we shall consider three such formulas:

1 general compensation with an application to the project of an Internal Common Market of the EC countries;
2 establishment of off-budget funds;
3 reform through crises.

General Compensation

It has been shown in section 2 that regulation is a negative sum game which reduces the welfare of all participants. It is only enforced because each interest group strives separately to attain a distributive gain at the others' costs. If all interest groups could somehow come together they would realize the costs of their behaviour and decide on multilateral deregulation. Each group would lose in the market regulated in its favour, but it would be compensated by no longer being harmed by regulations benefiting others. Such a game would clearly be a positive sum game. It is similar to a general disarmament of interest groups. Such a package deal whose single pieces are no longer subjected to negotiations is called a *general compensation* (see von Weizsäcker, 1984).

The more groups there are and the more diffuse the distributive effects of previous regulation were, the higher the probability is that the participants will agree to the deal. More groups should not impair the probability of attaining an arrangement in principle; for there are no negotiations on particular topics. It must be conceded, however, that larger arrangements are more heterogeneous and, therefore, become riskier to the participants.

A practical application of the general compensation principle may be found in the proposal to achieve the *Internal Common Market* within the EC by 1992. Each member country is regarded as an interest group in the sense considered here. It agrees to give up regulations in its favour if all other countries do likewise. Perhaps such a general compensation is the only method by which the large number of regulations still in existence can be overcome. Nevertheless, the chances of achieving the Internal Common

Market in one leap should not be overestimated. Four reasons give rise to some scepticism:

1 The European Council decided in June 1985 to approach the Internal Common Market along the path set out in the Commission's *White Paper*. The decision of the Council is not, however, a binding agreement, but rather a declaration of common *intention*. Therefore step-by-step negotiations are still needed, implying a danger that the parties will get stuck on the details.

2 The *White Book* does not propose a general deregulation, but only a *harmonization* of existing regulations or the mutual *recognition* of existing national regulations. This does not exclude the possibility that the new regulations may be even tighter than existing ones for some countries. The common rules agreed on for the regulation of the European agricultural market provide a good illustration of such a harmonization policy.

3 Harmonization, and not deregulation, is also intended in the *fiscal treatment* of individuals by the State. This clearly has the advantage of allowing competition under equal conditions among firms in different member countries. But the harmonization proposed in the *White Book* is in essence a tax cartel among the fiscal authorities of each country. Individuals will lose their choice of taxation, and the State will have fewer incentives to spend public money carefully. The alternative of fiscal deregulation or fiscal competition should at least be considered from these viewpoints.

4 Let me finally briefly review the markets which are likely to be deregulated in the coming years. These are the banking, insurance, airlines and, to some extent, the telecommunications sectors.[1] In all these activities markets have merged within the last few years as a result of the use of computers. It can be argued, therefore, that the basic reason for integration is technical progress (realized through the achievements in microelectronics) and not the attempts of negotiators to achieve the Internal Common Market. The old regulatory rules are simply less and less enforceable because business emigrates to zones without regulation. In this sense, integration policy is more of a creative type than of an initiating one.

Deregulation By Off-Budget Fund Creation

Consider cross-subsidization between services. This core piece of regulation will only work as long as entry barriers are maintained. Under a regime of competition cream skimmers would compete away the profits needed to cross-subsidized politically important services. Thus, competition does not seem to be compatible with special treatment of interest groups. This is so because production and marketing are combined with cross-subsidization under the roof of the firm. If cross-subsidization could somehow be separated from the firm, the problem of cream-skimming would not arise and competition might become feasible. This is the idea underlying the creation of *off-budget funds* (see Blankart and Knieps, 1989).

An off-budget fund is fed by an excise tax of the value-added type paid by all enterprises supplying to hitherto monopolized markets. This implies that the established firm has to pay the tax too when it supplies to such markets. The taxes paid to the fund will be used to subsidize those goods and services to be supplied at below cost prices for political reasons. These goods and services too may be supplied by the established firm or by its competitors.

Let me illustrate the working of off-budget funds with the example of telecommunications. Under the present monopoly system local networks are cross-subsidized by profits on long-distance networks which are incompatible with free entry. An alternative would be to levy a value-added tax on all supplies of long-distance telecommunications, the proceeds would be put in a fund and used to subsidize supplies of local telecommunications. Thus, market entry would be taxed, but not prohibited.

The off-budget fund solution has an important politico-economic implication. Consider telecommunications again: under a cross-subsidization regime a coalition of interest groups would emerge between the local interest groups on the one hand, and the *Bundespost* and its unions on the other. Both groups would fight for the maintainance of the network and service monopoly; the former because they want the local networks to be cross-subsidized, the latter because they expect emoluments and discretionary power through the monopoly. The special fund solution would, however, benefit local interest groups even more. They could participate in the fund management and would no longer be dependent on the benevolence of the *Bundespost*. Thus, the special fund solution is a way of splitting the actual coalition of the opponents to deregulation. The great advantage of the special fund solution is, therefore, to give political support to those groups which favour deregulation.

Reform Through Crises

It is the traditional view that deregulation policy should serve to prevent decline and crises in the economy. But this preventive aspect of deregulation is often little understood in politics; for interest groups will not support measures of regulatory reform as long as the economic situation is good or satisfactory. Even during most of a period of decline, deregulation proposals are not popular. The argument used is: if jobs are in danger, why expose them to the additional risk of competition? Entry barriers and regulation are much more popular policy measures than deregulation during a decline. A change of the actual policy can be expected only when the economic situation has eventually deteriorated so much that it becomes obvious that nobody can gain any longer by maintaining regulation. Thus, a substantial deterioration of the economic situation or even a crisis is a precondition for the enforceability of a regulatory reform.

I should like to illustrate this point with a little piece of German railroad history I studied some years ago (cf. Blankart, 1987). After World War I, German railroads were characterized by strong output and input regulation. Prices were frozen and labour inputs were held at an excessive level in order to provide last-resort employment to many unemployed soldiers returning from the battlefields. This policy, which led to enormous budget deficits, was accommodated by the government by means of the money printing press, as was also the case for most other parts of the public administrations. As a consequence, inflation increased. But no fundamental change in this policy was feasible until inflation reached such astronomic levels that the monetary order broke down in the autumn of 1923, and something had to be done. The government instituted a currency reform, and in order to guarantee stability of the new monetary order, the minister of the treasury simply refused to pay any more subsidies to the railroads to cover their deficit. (Similar reforms were made for the other parts of the federal administration.) Simultaneously, input and output regulation on railroads were lifted. In response the railroad administration to that adjusted its factors of production and achieved a stable and continuing profit a few months later.

5 Conclusions

Simple market analysis is, in general, not enough to explain regulation. Rather, to understand the nature of regulation it is necessary to understand interest group activity. Interest groups strive for economic advantages for their members. But they are often too small to succeed in politics alone. Therefore, they have to form coalitions. A coalition, however, requires a compromise in goals, and the question is: what form of compromise is likely to emerge? It has been shown that regulation has many attractive features of a compromise. It is an ideal institutional vehicle to accommodate a large number of diverging goals.

Regulation has the tendency to increase over time, because interest groups become increasingly capable of establishing formal organizations through which they can promote their goals in the political process.

It is not astonishing that deregulation and regulatory reform are difficult to achieve under these conditions. Deregulation can only occur if it is possible to find arrangements which give greater benefits than those offered by regulation to a sufficient number of the relevant interest groups. I have analyzed three such arrangements: general compensation, off-budget funds and deregulation through crises. My overall evaluation is rather sceptical. A general compensation encompassing regulation of many markets may often be too risky to the participants. Such a conclusion derives from the current attempts to attain a competitive Internal Common Market within the EC by 1992. Off-budget funds are very popular in politics at the moment. However, most of them are not designed to replace existing regulations, but rather to allow new forms of special treatment of interest groups by means which are more or less consistent with the rules of the market. Examples are the 'coal penny', the 'water penny' and numerous funds within the agricultural sector. A final road to deregulation is a general crisis. It is a last-resort alternative which is not very encouraging, but is perhaps realistic. The economist still has an important task in such a politico-economic environment. He has to design alternative regulatory rules and to analyze their advantages and disadvantages. This knowledge will serve as a menu of choice for political decision-makers when it is eventually time for regulatory reform.

Notes

1. For qualifications on the national level see section 1 above.

References

Blankart, Ch. B., (1984), 'Das Wachstum des Postmonopols, Ein wirtschaftshistor-
ischer Beitrag zur ökonomischen Theorie der Verwaltung', *Jahrbuch für Neue Politische Ökonomie*, Vol. 3, pp. 172–97.

Blankart, Ch. B. (1987), 'Stabilität und Wechselhaftigkeit politischer Entscheidungen, Eine Fallstudie zur preußisch-deutschen Eisenbahnpolitik von ihren Anfängen bis zum Zweiten Weltkrieg', *Jahrbuch für Neue Politische Ökonomie*, Vol. 6, pp. 74–92.

Blankart, Ch. B. and Knieps, G. (1989), 'Grenzen der Deregulierung im Telekommunikationsbereich – Die Frage des Netzwettbewerbs', in: H. St. Seidenfus, (ed.), *Deregulierung – Eine Herausforderung an die Wirtschafts- und Sozialpolitik, Schriften des Vereins für Socialpolitik*, Vol. 184, Berlin, Duncker und Humblot, S. 149–72.

Bundesministerium der Finanzen (Ministry of Finance) (1987), *Beteiligungen des Bundes im Jahre 1986*, Bonn.

CEEP (1987), *Die öffentliche Wirtschaft in der Europäischen Gemeinschaft* CEEP – Jahrbuch; Brussels and Berlin.

Finsinger, J. (1988), *Verbraucherschutz auf Versichereungsmärkten, Wettbewerbsbeschränkungen, staatliche Eingriffe und ihre Folgen*, Munich (VVF).

Finsinger, J. and Pauly, M. V. (1986), *The Economics of Insurance Regulation*, Houndmills, Basingstoke and London, Macmillan.

Gesetz zur Neustrukturierung des Post- und Fernmeldewesens und der Deutschen Bundespost (Poststrukturgesetz – PostStruktG) vom 8. Juni 1989', in: *Bundesgesetzblatt* I vom 14 June 1989, Nr. 25, S. 1026–51.

Kommission der Europäischen Gemeinschaften (1985), *Vollendung des Binnenmarktes*, Milano, 28/29 June.

Monopolkommission (German Monopoly Commission) (1981), Sondergutachten 9, *Die Rolle der Deutschen Bundespost im Fernmeldewesen*, Baden-Baden, Nomos.

Olson, M. (1965), *The Logic of Collective Action, Public Goods and the Theory of Groups*, Cambrige, Mass. Harvard Univ. Press, 1965.

——, (1982), *The Rise and Decline of Nations: Economic Growth, Stagflation and Social Rigidities*, New Haven and London, Yale Univ. Press.

Weizsäcker, C. C. von, (1984), *Effizienz und Gerechtigkeit – Was leistet die Property-Rights-Theorie für wirtschaftspolitische Fragen? Schriften des Vereins für Socialpolitik*, N. F., Bd. 140, Berlin, Duncker und Humblot, p. 123.

Witte, E. Neuordnung der Telekommunikation (Government Commission for Telecommunications) (1987), *Bericht der Regierungskommission Fernmeldewesen*, Heidelberg, R.v. Decker's Verlag, G. Schenck.

12. Regulatory Reform: An Appraisal*

John Kay and
John Vickers

1 Introduction

Britain is at the centre of an international process of regulatory reform. The frameworks of competition and regulation faced by existing and potential participants in the telecommunications, energy, transport, water, financial services, and some professional services industries are being transformed. Older, informal structures have been breaking down under the pressure of powerful economic, technological, and ideological forces, and they are being officially dismantled. This is sometimes called 'deregulation', but that is a misleading term because, as often as not, new and generally more explicit regulatory structures are simultaneously erected in place of what went before. The apparently paradoxical combination of deregulation and reregulation, which is most clearly evident in the financial services industry, is what we mean by 'regulatory reform'.

The aim of this chapter is to give an economic assessment of these new developments, drawing several lessons from recent experience. Our prime concern is with the economic performance of the industries in question – the productive, allocative, and dynamic efficiency with which they meet consumers' changing demands. This is our central criterion, and we believe that other objectives – for example, income distribution – are usually better promoted by instruments other than regulation. Nevertheless distributional considerations may exert a major influence on regulatory policy in practice.

Our approach is to identify the market failures that regulation seeks to remedy, and to examine the incentive structures of alternative regulatory schemes. We compare the properties of public regulation and self-regulation, and hybrids such as 'self-regulation within a statutory framework'. Since

*This is a revised and edited version of J. Kay and J. Vickers (1988), 'Regulatory reform in Britain', *Economic Policy*, October 1988.

regulatory constraint is only one of the influences that affect the decisions of economic agents, the analysis of regulation is closely bound up with questions of *ownership* and *competition*.

Competition and regulation are often regarded as substitutes, and the simple maxim '*Competition where possible, regulation where necessary*' indeed has merit as a first approximation for industries in which the source of market failure is the possible abuse of market power. But even in such industries, the connections between competition and regulation, and the ways of combining them, are numerous and complex. In multiproduct industries (or in industries where there are several stages in the vertical chain of production), it can be difficult to regulate one part of the business without affecting the nature of competition in other parts. One purpose of regulation may be to promote and maintain conditions for effective competition: liberalization may then alter the kind of regulation that is needed, not the need for regulation. Regulation may seek to use competitive incentives, for example, in the form of 'yardstick regulation', which seeks to encourage regional monopolists to compete with each other in cost reduction. There are some areas in which franchising ('competition for monopoly') can be used, but that still requires regulation in the form of contract administration and enforcement and franchising may be more appropriately viewed as a means of regulation than an alternative to it.

Where market failure has causes other than market power, regulation can be a prerequisite for there to be effective competition (or indeed a market at all). Without requirements of capital adequacy, the vulnerability of the banking system to bank runs would tend to have an adverse effect on competition in the market for bank deposits. Where product quality is uncertain, asymmetries of information may deter many consumers from entering the market. But, even in cases such as these regulation is not the only way of seeking to remedy market failure. Market participants themselves may be able to surmount the problem by means of reputation, brand names, warranties, and so on.

Finally, competition between the regulators themselves can have a role to play. For example, the exposure of financial fraud is likely to be carried out more energetically if 'self-regulators' within the industry compete with public regulatory bodies. Moreover, financial regulators in one jurisdiction 'compete' with regulators in other countries, in so far as investors direct their business to the most efficient financial market. Similarly, different professional bodies in the same industry (e.g. accountancy) can indirectly compete in terms of standards. These possibilities for beneficial competition between regulators in many ways mirror what happens in competition between firms in markets with asymmetric information. Indeed, the individual firm, with its mechanisms of internal regulation, is perhaps the best example of a self-regulatory organization.

In emphasizing properties of the incentives which exist under alternative regulatory regimes, we stress the distinction between the regulation of structure and the regulation of conduct. Regulators may be concerned with the way in which a market is organized (structural regulation), or with behaviour within the market (conduct regulation). Structural regulation may be preferable to conduct regulation where there is asymmetry of information between the regulator and the regulated. This arises in many contexts. Since it is impossible to determine whether a professional, faced with a conflict of interest, is acting in the best interests of his client, a sensible solution (if the possible conflict is important) may be to say that he can not act in such a case. Since we cannot judge whether a utility that controls the transmission network is offering fair terms of access to independent suppliers, a natural solution is to separate the functions of supply and transmission. Since we cannot know whether a firm is operating at maximum efficiency, the better approach is to impose a market structure (usually a competitive one) which gives incentives to maximum efficiency.

Structural regulation is often concerned with the extent to which firms operating in one regulated market are permitted to enter others. This is the issue of functional separation, often described as single capacity. Where single capacity regulation exists, there is generally pressure to dismantle it. But, at the same time, there are many cases of measures to introduce single capacity rules where dual or multiple capacity already exists. We consider why these conflicting movements exist.

These themes of regulation, ownership, competition, and information will recur throughout the chapter. Section 2 considers the rationale for regulation – the sources of market failure that it seeks to remedy – under three main headings: externalities, competition and monopoly, and information issues. Sections 3 and 4 deal, respectively, with the institutions and mechanisms of regulation. Sections 5 and 6 deal with two specific issues which appear to arise in a variety of regulatory contexts: functional separation of activities as a regulatory technique, and regulation to govern quality of service. Section 7 considers some international aspects of regulatory reform.

Our assessment of regulatory practice reveals many difficulties. In section 8 we examine mechanisms for escaping or minimizing the need for regulation, while section 9 draws some general conclusions.

2   Reasons for Regulation

The primary rationale for regulation, along with other elements of public policy towards industry, is to remedy various kinds of market failure. Traditional analysis distinguishes between *externalities* and *market power* as sources of welfare loss (see, for example, Bator's (1958) classic anatomy of market failure). More recent analysis has greatly illuminated a third major source of market failure: *asymmetric information*. Information problems feature prominently in what follows. They provide the chief rationale for much regulation – particularly in the financial system – and are essential to understanding the relationship between a regulatory agency and the firm or firms that it regulates.

The distribution of income and wealth generated by the market system is sometimes considered as another type of market failure. This is an important issue, but we do not pursue it further here. Industrial policies generally, and regulation in particular, are usually ill-suited to wider distributional ends, which are better accomplished by other instruments of public policy, particularly the tax and benefit system. Regulatory policy should be directed, in an industry-specific manner, at what it does best.

Externalities

Externalities arise when the well-being of one economic agent (consumer or firm) is directly affected by the actions of another. The textbook example is pollution: the effluent from chemical plants has an adverse effect on fishermen, which the chemical companies do not take into account.[1] The regulation of the discharge of effluent is a possible remedy; tax policy might be another. In a partial equilibrium setting, externalities are often expressed in terms of divergences between private and social costs (or benefits). At a deeper level, externalities can be viewed as an example of *missing markets*. In our illustration, if fishermen and chemical companies could trade in contracts for the water to be of given cleanliness, the externality problem could, in principle, be overcome. Of course, problems of transactions costs, contract specification, and enforcement, etc. make this a hopeless idea in practice, but it is important to understand the underlying causes of market failure. As we explain below, information asymmetries are another class of missing markets.

Externalities do feature in some of the industries that are undergoing regulatory reform. In telecommunications there are externalities arising from network effects. The benefit obtained by a subscriber depends upon who else subscribes to the same network. This externality may justify some subsidy to access charges (lines rentals, etc.) from other parts of the business, but their appropriate extent is debatable. It also gives some rationale for the requirement to provide 'universal service'. More importantly, universal service requirements are also justified by public good considerations relating to emergency services (another kind of externality) and social factors. Furthermore, network externalities call for regulation in so far as they distort competition (Katz and Shapiro, 1985; Farrell and Saloner, 1985).

An important kind of externality in financial services has to do with capital adequacy. If a large number of depositors simultaneously attempted to withdraw their funds from a bank or building society, there is a risk that there would be insufficient funds to honour their claims. The resulting negative externality between depositors is clear, and in the limit there is zero sum game between them, in which each is scrambling for a slice of the available assets. One of the purposes of capital adequacy requirements (and related provisions such as insurance schemes) is to ensure that enough liquid funds are available to cover every reasonable eventuality. Such measures themselves give confidence to depositors and, therefore, minimize the chance that there will be a bank run in the first place. Capital adequacy requirements are also important for financial institutions dealing in contracts for future delivery, including options and insurance contracts. If there are doubts as to their ability to honour contracts if prices or circumstances move against them, the market is undermined.

Monopoly and Competition

Market power is detrimental to economic efficiency in several ways, aside from its undesirability in non-economic respects. Allocative efficiency is undermined by the incentive for dominant firms to charge prices significantly in excess of marginal costs of supply; and the lack of competitive stimulus further blunts incentives for dynamic and productive efficiency. On the other hand, despite its general advantages, competition is not always for the best. In a natural monopoly, for example, economies of scale or scope imply that (actual) competition would raise costs or involve wasteful duplication. (Potential competition – the threat of entry – may have advantages even so: see Baumol, 1982 on contestability theory).

In addition to the question of the desirability of competition, there is also the issue of whether it is feasible (in the absence of Government intervention). Figure 12.1 distinguishes these two questions.

	IS COMPETITION DESIRABLE?	
	YES	NO
YES	TYPICAL CASE	CREAM SKIMMING
IS COMPETITION FEASIBLE?		
NO	DOMINANT INCUMBENT(S) PREVENTS ENTRY	SEVERE NATURAL MONOPOLY

Figure 12.1   Desirability and feasibility of competition

This simple picture suggests that there are three kinds of market failure to consider. First, there is the case in which competition is neither feasible nor desirable, which holds under conditions of severe natural monopoly.[2] Anti-monopoly regulation is then the only check on the firm's behaviour.

Second, there is the case in which competition is not desirable, but is feasible. It is possible to construct examples with scale economies in which single firm production is desirable (because the loss of allocative efficiency is outweighed by the gain in cost efficiency), but in which more than one firm enters the industry at equilibrium (see Mankiw and Whinston, 1986; and Suzumura and Kiyono, 1987 for an analysis of the relationship between the optimal and equilibrium numbers of firms).

This could not happen in a contestable market, where it is the threat of entry that disciplines incumbent firms, but the contestable markets theory has illuminated another kind of possible market failure to do with the non-existence of equilibrium: non-sustainability. A natural monopoly is said to be sustainable if prices exist that earn enough revenue to cover the monopolist's costs, but which do not attract entry by rival firms. In multiproduct industries, non-sustainability is often associated with the notion of 'cream-skimming', which is said to occur when entrants undercut the incumbent's profitable business segments and leave him with a loss on the rest of his activities. Such behaviour might seem a rather good antidote to cross-subsidization, in which case it should normally be welcomed, but it can occur when there is no cross-subsidization. In that event, it undermines the stability of equilibrium and has shades of 'destructive competition'.

Where competition is feasible but undesirable, the key policy question is whether there should be regulatory measures to restrict competition, e.g. by prohibiting entry into the market. In general, we would be very wary of making such a step. It may be hard even to determine whether or not natural monopoly conditions prevail. We believe that where competition would be undesirable, it will generally not come about anyway. However, the theoretical possibility exists. But the models which display the property of undesirable competition usually do not allow for the beneficial effects of competition on incentives for internal efficiency, which are important in the overall welfare evaluation. Although the case for regulation to restrict undesirable or destructive competition cannot always be dismissed out of hand, the private interest in it is almost invariably far greater than the public interest. There is a very heavy burden of proof on those who seek to advance this case, and they should be treated with great suspicion.

Finally we come to the case in which competition is desirable but in danger of being thwarted by anti-competitive behaviour by the incumbent firm(s). The threat of predatory behaviour – by price or other means – is the clearest example of such behaviour (see Vickers, 1985 for a brief account). Many regulatory measures for privatized utility companies aim to check anti-competitive behaviour by dominant firms, and we shall consider this problem further below.

To summarize, we have distinguished between three kinds of market failure involving monopoly and competition, and, correspondingly, three types of regulation, namely regulation:

1   to contain monopolistic behaviour;
2   to limit competition; and
3   to promote competition.

Information Problems

Our third category of market failure concerns information problems, which include:

1   failures in markets for information;
2   problems arising from imperfect price information; and
3   asymmetric information about product quality.

It has long been appreciated that markets for information are prone to failure. One difficulty is that the buyer of a piece of information does not know the value of what she is buying unless she knows what the information is, in which case there is no point in buying it. Trust between buyer and seller is important here, as is illustrated in many professional services, which frequently involve the supply of information by specialists. Another difficulty is the appropriability problem: once discovered, a piece of information can be sold and resold at very little cost, but incentives for discovery require that the originator of the information be rewarded at a much higher level than the marginal cost of dissemination. The appropriability problem is central to the welfare economics of innovation (see e.g. Spence, 1984), and arises in markets for professional services as well.

It can also occur in financial markets. Efficient allocation of investment resources is enhanced if financial asset prices reflect information about the available economic opportunities. But if such information is rapidly reflected in prices, there is little incentive to gather it, because a superior strategy may be to sit back and deduce information from prices (see Grossman and Stiglitz, 1980).

A quite distinct information problem occurs when consumers are badly informed about the prices being charged by various suppliers. Under these circumstances, price dispersion can occur even for homogeneous goods of known quality. Some consumers are likely to engage in a search to discover low prices, while others are in danger of being ripped off (see Salop and Stiglitz, 1977). More generally, poor price information for consumers assists collusion between suppliers, because a price cut by any single supplier is unlikely to increase his demand greatly. An obvious solution is for suppliers to advertise their prices, since it is much cheaper for firms to inform consumers than for consumers to inform themselves. However, restrictions on advertising have been common in many of the professions. The pros and cons of such restrictions are discussed further below.

Our third information problem – asymmetric information about product quality – deserves most attention. Information asymmetries pervade markets for professional services. Indeed, demand for many professional services stems entirely from the asymmetry of information: the amateur consumer is essentially buying advice from a better informed professional. Since the consumer cannot directly judge the quality of the service that he or she is buying, indirect assurances as to quality are necessary for the effective functioning of the market. The situation is similar in respect of financial services. It is very hard for many consumers to tell directly whether their broker is offering honest advice (or whether he is 'talking his own book', e.g. by recommending clients to sell shares that his firm wishes to buy on its own account), whether their trades were executed on the best available terms, or whether a bank or insurance company with whom the customer is contemplating doing business maintains adequate margins of solvency.

The seminal article on asymmetric information about product quality is Akerlof's (1970) paper on the market for 'lemons' (American terminology for dud second-hand cars). Consumers cannot tell by inspection what is the quality of a used car, but they can draw inferences about average quality from prices. In particular, average quality will decline as price declines, because potential sellers of better cars have higher reservation prices (below which they prefer not to sell) than potential sellers of duds. Mutually advantageous trades between sellers and buyers of better quality cars are stymied, and the market may be undermined altogether if there are no willing buyers at any price, given their (rational) beliefs about quality.

Insurance markets are prone to asymmetric information problems, with sellers this time being *less* well informed than buyers. If an insurance company cannot distinguish between low- and high-risk individuals, it faces an *adverse selection* problem since at any given price the high-risk people are keener to take out insurance than low-risk people. If an insurance contract was offered on terms that both types found acceptable, a competitor would find it profitable to offer a rival contract tailored to the low-risk individuals (e.g. involving less extensive cover but with a lower premium). By skimming the cream in this way, the first firm is left with the undesirable risks, and competitive equilibrium may fail to be sustained (see Rothschild and Stiglitz 1976). Insurance companies also face a *moral hazard* problem when they cannot monitor, and hence cannot condition the insurance contract upon, the risk-affecting behaviour of the insured. A contract which specifies risk-minimizing behaviour by the insured and a correspondingly low premium is then unenforceable. The worst must be assumed, and the insurance premium must be set accordingly.

In reality there are, of course, numerous ways of attempting to overcome problems of asymmetric information, many of which involve no intervention in the market by external regulatory agencies. Warranties and guarantees can act as a signal of the seller's product quality as well as giving the buyer some insurance against the risk of the product being defective (Grossman, 1981). Liability rules can perform a similar function. The seller's reputation will also be of central importance.

These mechanisms are neither perfect nor costless, but in many circumstances they work tolerably well, and no external intervention (beyond general consumer protection legislation) is needed. However, under some conditions, market mechanisms are not enough. This is especially so when – as in financial and professional services – quality cannot be detected even *ex post*.[3] The forms that external regulation may take in those circumstances are discussed in the next section.

3   Regulation: Institutions and Problems

The Institutions of Regulation

The general economic framework for the analysis of regulation is the class of principal/agent problems. A principal/agent problem generally takes the following form. A (the principal) has objectives which can only be achieved by B (the agent), because B has immediate responsibility for the decisions, or better information, or commonly both. Given that B will typically have different incentives and superior knowledge, how does A construct a framework that ensures that the desired outcome is achieved? Attempted solutions to this problem may be characterized by differences in the degree to which the principal directs the actions of the agent.

We review the institutions of regulation in a descending hierarchy of state involvement, beginning with nationalization and ending with the internal regulation undertaken by firms themselves.

Nationalization is an extreme form of regulation and often seen as removing the need for regulation. The principal/agent problem is resolved by inviting the agent to adopt the objectives of the principal and freezing him from other constraints and obligations. But it is not apparent that nationalized boards are well equipped to determine what the public interest is, or that even if it were clear to them what it is, that they would then have incentive to pursue it; in any event such a loose definition of managerial objectives may not be conducive to efficient management and operation of the industries concerned. It follows that nationalization does not remove the principal/agent problem: it merely puts it within the context of a particular institutional structure.

In the simplest characterization of the process of regulation, A is the government and B the management of the regulated industry. This is, however, an unduly simple characterization. Commonly, there may be four interest groups involved – the voters, the government, a regulatory organization, and an industry – and a principal/agent problem involved at each link of the chain. Politicians, regulators and managers each have objectives of their own, none of the which can be presumed invariably to accord with the public good, and it must be expected that these objectives will influence their behaviour.

It is difficult to assess the extent to which the evident deficiencies of the mechanisms of nationalized industry control are intrinsic to the institution of nationalization as such and to what extent they arise from failure to specify objectives and incentive mechanisms but, given that dissatisfaction with the performance of nationalization is more acute in Britain than elsewhere, we incline to the latter explanation.

The commonest form of explicit regulation is by means of the public agency. There are many such agencies. Some have specific responsibilities for particular industries. Others are defined functionally: the powers of the agency extend across most industries, but only in respect of particular areas of behaviour. In other cases public regulation is the direct responsibility of a government department.

Self-regulation is common among the professions. In some cases the self-regulatory body may receive statutory authority analogous to that which public agencies enjoy: it is usually illegal for unqualified persons to describe themselves as doctors. Buy anyone is free to call himself an accountant, and many people without formal qualifications do. The powers of the accountancy bodies derive in part from the legal status of the audit and partly from the prestige which attaches to the accountancy qualification itself.

An important means of regulation is internal regulation by private firms. This is of obvious significance in financial services, where reputation is central to attracting business. Since reputation is valuable, firms devote resources to maintaining it. Internal regulation is of growing importance in professional services, particularly in accountancy. Here the major international firms promise their customers higher standard (and more expensive) service than the minimum assured by professional bodies and attempt to maintain standards by common procedures and internal quality control. We discuss in greater detail in Section 6 the variety of ways in which regulatory mechanisms can influence product quality.

Regulatory Inefficiency and Regulatory Capture

The principal/agent problem results from differences in the incentives of principal and agent, and in the information available to principal and agent, and it is essentially the interaction between these issues that gives rise to difficulty. If principal and agent had identical objectives, then the fact that the agent had superior information would not be a matter of any practical significance. Equally, if the principal had access to all the information available to the agent, the objectives of the agent would not matter because monitoring his behaviour would be straightforward.

If there is a divergence of objectives between principal and agent, this divergence will remain whatever structures or mechanisms of regulation are put in place. The agent can be required to observe the regulation, but not to adopt its objectives – we can require firms to observe health and safety at work regulations, but not to reduce the incidence of accidents. The pursuit of divergent objectives within the framework of regulation may lead to inefficiency. Thus American utilities have typically been subject to price control based on a 'fair rate' of return on capital employed. If this rate of return exceeds the cost of capital to such utilities, then they can increase profits by expanding their capital base. This effect, first described by Averch and Johnson (1962) may be an explanation for the relatively high cost levels of such utilities observed by, for example, Pescatrice and Timpani (1980). Similarly, German insurance companies subject to premium regulation have, it is claimed, responded by excessive levels of marketing expenditure (Finsinger, Hammond and Tapp, 1985).

Regulatory capture occurs when a regulatory agency comes to equate the public good with the interests of the industry it regulates. The most closely documented case is that of civil aviation in the United States, where it was argued that a regulatory body established to protect consumer interests had in time come to operate a cartel on behalf of established carrier (Miller and Douglas, 1974). This analysis was influential in promoting the deregulation of the industry; but it is apparent that similar tendencies exist in transport industries throughout the world. This tendency to regulatory capture is hardly surprising. The very information asymmetry which creates the need for regulation makes the agency dependent on those it regulates from the beginning, while producer lobbies are commonly better organized and better resourced than those serving consumer interests. It is a striking feature of regulatory history that industries are generally opposed both to the introduction of new regulation and to the dismantling of old regulation. Industries dislike the prospect of regulation but frequently find comfortable ways of living with it in practice.

This creates in turn several kinds of inefficiency. One reflects the costs which may result from the recasting of regulatory objectives. Quality control is, for example, a prime objective of professional services regulation: but it has been widely observed (and will be noted at several points in this paper) that such quality control has been almost entirely concentrated on pre-entry requirements with very little attention given to post-entry performance or education. This may impose high prices on consumers while giving them little substantive assurance of quality.

The possibility that regulatory structures may be turned to an industry's advantage may lead the industry to invest resources in seeking particular kinds of regulation or in influencing the behaviour of regulatory authorities. Since such rent-seeking behaviour may be very profitable, the sums which may be invested in it may correspondingly be high. Such behaviour is capable not only of leading to mistaken regulatory outcomes, but also of distorting the structure of incentives and objectives within the regulated firm.

4 Modes of Regulation

There are two basic means by which a regulator can influence the behaviour of an industry with whose performances he is concerned. She can regulate the structure of the industry and she/he can regulate its behaviour. The distinction between the two categories is not always clear cut, and they are not mutually exclusive; but the general distinction is a useful one. The informational requirements needed to impose structural regulation are generally much less demanding and we will suggest that this is an important reason why it often has advantages.

These are broad categories, and a word of clarification is in order at the outset. By 'structural regulation' we mean the determination of which firms or individuals (or types thereof) are allowed to engage in which activities. By 'conduct regulation' we refer to measures concerned with how firms behave in their chosen activity or activities.

Examples of structural regulation include:

- restrictions on entry;
- statutory monopoly;
- single capacity rules;
- rules against individuals supplying professional services without recognized qualifications.

Examples of conduct regulation include:

- measures to guard against anti-competitive behaviour by dominant incumbent firms;
- price control;
- rules against advertising and other restrictions on competitive activity.

In a number of cases structural regulation and conduct are alternatives to one another. The former aims to create a situation in which the incentives or opportunities for undesirable behaviour are removed, while the latter addresses not the undesirable underlying incentives, but the behaviour that they would otherwise induce.

The recent combinations of deregulation with reregulation are less paradoxical if it is remembered that there are these two broad types of regulation. What has happened in several industries recently is a shift of emphasis between structure and conduct regulation (as in financial services), or a policy

choice between the two (as with the issue of vertical separation in network
industries). The choice is not so much about whether to regulate, but about
which mode of regulation to adopt.

The simplest form of conduct regulation is the directive: the regulator tells
the regulated what to do. Directives raise the twin problems of information
and incentives in their acute form. The directive may simply instruct the
regulated to adopt the regulator's objective: 'run an efficient and economical
telecommunications service', in which case it is difficult or impossible for
the regulator to establish whether, within the limits of what is possible, the
industry has complied with the directive. The alternative is to issue more
specific instructions: 'install exchange equipment of type X'. However, the
regulator, less well informed than the industry about the structure of costs,
the available alternatives, and the problems of day-to-day management, is
in a poor position to judge whether type X is or is not the most efficient and
economical means supply. The regulator is at an informational disadvantage
either in composing his instruction or in monitoring compliance with it, and
there is no escape from at least one of these difficulties.

Thus the weakness of conduct regulation is that to be effective it must be
concerned with aspects of service provision that are readily measured; and
these may be only loosely related to the issues of underlying concern. We
are concerned that the monopoly enjoyed by utilities may lead to excessive
profits: we therefore control the level of profits they may earn. While the
level of profits is (to a degree) observable, the level of profit on particular
services is difficult for an external observer to assess. In any event, profit
regulation neither reassures the consumer that the costs of supplying a
service are reasonable nor gives the industry an incentive to reduce them.
Price regulation appears to tackle the latter problem. However, it gives the
regulator no additional information about the appropriate level of costs; and
if the only guide he has is the actual level of costs the practical difference
between price and profit control may turn out to be slight. The general
weakness of regulating outcomes is that the process generating these outcomes may prove to be inefficient. This was illustrated on pp. 232–233 the
tendency of rate of return regulation to produce high costs and levels of
investment which, depending on the form of regulation, may be excessive
or inadequate, and the likelihood that price control will generate excessive
marketing expenditures.

5 Functional Separation as Regulatory Mechanism

An important kind of structural regulation is functional separation – in which
agents are prohibited from undertaking different activities simultaneously. In
utilities, the issue is whether the operator of a naturally monopolistic network
should be allowed also to operate in potentially competitive business segments
of its industry. In financial services there are the questions of single versus
dual capacity (broking and jobbing), and of polarization (whether financial
advisers may also sell their own financial services). In the professions the best
example is the solicitor/barrister distinction.

It is worth stressing from the beginning that the mere fact that two functions require distinct skills does not in itself justify regulatory intervention to require functional separation. Consumers can decide for themselves which type of firm offered better value for money in relation of their own particular needs. If there are economies of scope in combining two activities, one might expect a relatively high proportion of dual capacity firms. On the other hand, if economies of scope were small or even negative, and if independent services had sufficient value added, then single-capacity firms would tend to prosper. Competitions has the advantages of being flexible and economical of information. If competitive market forces are able to operative effectively, there is no need for outside regulators to prejudge what is the most efficient form or organization, and the claims of would-be self-regulators can be treated with caution. Matters may be different when investors are less sophisticated: for example, if they lack the information necessary to judge the risk of conflict of interest.

Alternative arguments for functional separation concern effects on competition. Let us begin with an example in which one activity is a natural monopoly and another is potentially competitive. The question of functional separation is whether to bar the firm which enjoys the natural monopoly from the competitive activity. An obvious instance occurs in telecommunications where local network operation is a natural monopoly but long-distance connections may be offered by competing services. Recent American policy has favoured functional separation; following the settlement of its antitrust case in 1982, AT & T was required to divest itself of its local operating companies (the 'Baby Bells'). British policy has followed the opposite course: BT was privatized intact without any restructuring. Instead, British Policy has relied on conduct regulation in the form of OFTEL's 1985 ruling on the terms of interconnection between the networks of BT and its long-distance rival Mercury. Very similar issues arise in other industries, notably the gas and electricity utilities, where network activities tend to be naturally monopolistic, but other activities (e.g. power generation) do not. The issue is whether the common carrier who provides the network should be allowed into those other businesses.

The basic problem in these cases is that a firm with a monopoly in one part of the industry has an incentive to exclude competitors from associated competitive activities by denying them access to the output from its monopoly, except perhaps on unattractive terms. By excluding them and duplicating what they were doing, it can obtain for itself the profits that competitors were making in addition to its own. Moreover, once free from constraints imposed by the presence of competitors, a firm would, in general, revise its behaviour so as to boost industry profits yet further. Exclusion therefore has the double advantage of enlarging industry profits and the share of them obtained by the monopoly.[4]

The problem for conduct regulation in these circumstances stems from the informational disadvantages facing the regulatory authorities. First, there is the difficulty of detecting anti-competitive behaviour, and of enforcing measures intended to combat it. (It is hard enough to reach an acceptable definition of 'predatory behaviour', let alone detect and deter it.) Second, even when the instrument of possible anti-competitive conduct is easily observable (as with network interconnection charges, for example), there is the question of how to regulate it. If the interconnection charge is set at too high a level, the regulator partly assists exclusion. But if it is fixed too low, there is a danger of encouraging inefficient fragmentation of the industry. In the face of asymmetries of information, conduct regulation is prone to error and evasion. On these scores, regulation of structure – by means of functional separation – has significant advantages.

6   Regulation of Product Quality

Much regulation is concerned with product quality. Regulation is supported, or defended, because it will raise standards. It must be recognized, however, that raising the quality of good and services provided is not, in itself, necessarily a desirable objective. This does not mean that we are not in favour of reliable electricity, safe aircraft, competent doctors, or solvent banks. Ever more stringent quality standards do, however, have a price. It is most unlikely that it makes sense to provide such a margin of excess generating capacity that the probability of power cuts is reduced to zero. Improvements in airline safety can be taken to the point at which scheduling is seriously disrupted, or costs make services uneconomic. If medical practitioners throughout the world were required to meet US standards, the result would be to deprive most of the population of the world of any access to medical treatment whatever. And if the demands imposed on financial institutions are too great, it will become impossible for new firms to enter the industry.

If consumers are themselves readily able to observe product quality, there is little case for any public intervention. Quality regulation in such a case limits consumer choice. It is likely that different consumers will make different decisions about the combination of price and quality that suits them best, and that the balance favoured by the average consumer will change over time. If telephone users wish to plug inexpensive equipment of low speech quality into the system, and are prepared to tolerate the results, and this can be done without damage to the integrity of the network, then they should be allowed to do so. Best practice is, by definition, better than the average consumer is prepared to buy.

The case for regulation arises where the consumers are poorly informed about product quality. Indeed this motivated some of the first instances of government economic regulation, when the state intervened to restrict adulteration and short measure. The problem is particularly serious when purchasers know little about product quality even after they have bought. After receiving medical treatment, I may (or may not) know whether I have recovered, but do not know how much, if anything, the treatment contributed to that recovery. The inefficiencies which may result from such a process are discussed on pp. 228–230.

Three principal mechanisms are available for relieving them. *Reputation* is the market's own device. When consumers are not themselves able to observe product quality directly, they will prefer to purchase from sellers who are known in the market place to dispense goods or services of high quality. Two public regulatory devices are *licensing* and *certification*. By licensing, the public agency seeks to impose a minimum standard on the market: commodities which do not meet the licensing requirements may not be sold. Certification occurs where the regulatory authority provides consumers with information about the levels of competence of suppliers.

Reputation

Reputation mechanisms operate when future purchasing is affected by the level of quality supplied today. If buyer and seller meet once only (as is common in the used car market), there is less room for reputation to play a part, but in a dynamic setting, the seller must consider how his current behaviour affects future business. As Heal (1976) noted, the situation is analogous to a repeated prisoner's dilemma game. In a one-shot or finitely repeated game, the mutually advantageous outcome is undermined by the incentive to 'cheat' (i.e. supply poor quality in our context), but in an indefinitely long-lived relationship, the incentive to cheat may be outweighed by the desire not to lose future cooperation (i.e. business). See further Allen (1984), Klein and Leffler (1981), and Shapiro (1982).

Four factors that determine the strength of reputation mechanisms are the speed of learning, information exchange between consumers, the degree to which the seller's costs are sunk, and the range of his/her business that would be hit by a loss of reputation. The incentive to cheat by supplying poor quality is greater if consumers are slow to realize that quality is poor. Imperfect learning is indeed a feature of many professional and financial services. It is hard to judge the quality of expert advice without being an expert, and it is difficult to discern whether a broker has been talking his own book. Rapid spread of information between consumers adds to the force of reputation mechanism, because the future custom of many is then affected by the quality supplied to each. Sunk costs matter because they influence how much a supplier has to lose if his reputation is damaged. A 'fly-by-night' with low sunk costs has little to lose: a mobile hamburger van can easily be moved to new territory, but things are different for McDonald's.

The range of a supplier's business that would be hit by a loss of reputation is affected by the use of brand names. If one product type within the brand were exposed as being of low quality, demand for other product types would suffer too. By visibly increasing how much the supplier is staking on his reputation, brand names enhance the credibility of the promise of good quality. If a single practitioner provides a service of poor quality, he jeopardizes only his own business; if he joins in partnership with others he, to some degree, jeopardizes their business also. Because a large firm is better known than a small, the cost to it of being known to be poor and the benefit to it of being known to be good, is correspondingly high. Realizing this, the consumer may expect a large firm to provide better service than a small. For this reason, even if there are no economies of scope or scale resulting from size or conglomeration of activities, there may be marketing advantages from an association of size with quality. This seems to us the essence of the evolution of the accountancy market.

Advertising is sometimes regarded as a signal of good quality, even if it has no directly informative content (see Nelson, 1974, and Milgrom and Roberts, 1986). The basic idea is as follows. There will be repeat purchases of a good only if it is found by customer's experience to be of good quality. A manifestly expensive advertising campaign would not be undertaken by a supplier who had a poor quality product, because he would not get repeat purchases in any event. Therefore, such a campaign is a sign of the supplier's confidence in his product's quality.

The building and maintenance of a reputation for good quality is a vital part of successful competitive strategies in many markets. The need for a good reputation is strengthened when consumers have rival sources of supply available to them. This competition in reputation, which we observe at work in the marketplace, is a kind of competition in regulation, because firms employ methods of internal regulation to ensure that their methods and personnel maintain quality. We believe that this principle extends to external regulation, as we discuss further below.

Constructing a reputation for a large group or profession is an activity with substantial public good aspects and real dangers of ineffectiveness if others 'free ride' on the activities of a few. Examples of recently created professions are those of chartered secretary or corporate treasurer, where it has been important that large firms have been willing to put resources behind public-spirited individuals seeking to build reputation for their professions. But there is no professional body of economists, and little prospect of bringing one about.

Some professional bodies – such as actuaries – have achieved high public esteem without any legal support. Where the activities of a profession have achieved popular regard for a particular title – as with doctor or reverend, for example – there is a case for legal restriction on who may call themselves doctor or reverend, to prevent free riding on the reputation which has been created. The case for restriction relates, however, to the use of the title, not to the performance of the function. The purpose of public intervention is not to stop people seeking medical or spiritual advice from unqualified personnel (and indeed there is no practicable means of stopping them); it is to stop people seeking medical or spiritual advice from unqualified personnel in the belief that they are receiving it from qualified personnel.

A regulatory body without statutory authority has a stronger incentive to ensure the competence and good conduct of its members than one which has a legal functional monopoly. Attempts to promote self-regulation among insurance brokers have enjoyed only limited success perhaps because the public does not regard the title of registered insurance broker as an accolade of much significance. While the interest of registered insurance brokers in promoting statutory restriction on who may sell insurance is obvious, the effect of such a rule may well be to diminish rather than to increase their incentive to ensure high standards among their membership. For this reason attempts to restrict functions to members of self-regulatory bodies should normally be resisted, except where the service provided is a public rather than a private one (audit of limited companies or issue of notes of entitlement to statutory sick pay). These arguments do not apply to conveyancing or the purchase of securities and we do not see why customers who (perhaps foolishly) wish to entrust their conveyancing to their building society or seek investment advice from their barber should not be free to do so.

Parallel regulation

If we could be sure that regulatory organizations were benevolent and well-informed pursuers of the public interest, there would be little to gain from competition between regulators.[5] However, no such assumptions can safely be made. First, the public interest is not the objective of many regulatory organizations, especially SROs. They may claim that their objectives are in line with the public interest, but whether or not this is so will depend on the frameworks in which they operate. Second, even where the public interest objective is given high priority by a regulatory organization, there is the question of how actively it is pursued. It is possible for regulators to slack just as it is for managers of firms to slack. Again, the frameworks of monitoring and competition in which the regulators operate are important. We cannot avoid the old question: *Quis custodiet ipsos custodies?* Competition between regulators may relieve these problems.

Competition between alternative regimes is an everyday occurrence in many markets, including those for professional services. As we argued above, *internal* regulation within firms – quality control and so on – is a very important part of the total of regulatory activity: the firm is the ultimate SRO. Competition between accountancy firms, or law firms, is therefore partly competition between alternative regulatory regimes in so far as the quality of the service provided by a firm depends on the effectiveness of its methods of internal regulation.

In view of its prevalence in the form of competition between firms, it is perhaps surprising that competition between alternative regulatory regimes is relatively rare otherwise (except in financial markets, where globalization has extended its scope). It is true that there are several accountancy bodies – in Britain there are chartered (Scottish and English), certified, cost and management, and public finance accountants – but competition between them is probably only marginal. Likewise, there are separate bodies for solicitors and barristers, but competition between practitioners from the two branches is restricted by regulation.

The general tendency is for there to be functional specialization and compartmentalization between regulatory regimes, with little scope for consumer choice between alternative regimes. The new structure for the financial services industry in Britain, with its five compartmentalized SROs, is a clear case in point. Whether this pattern is to be explained by considerations of efficiency (scale economies in regulation) or by self-interested desires to avoid competition is an interesting matter for debate in individual cases. However, the possibly substantial wider advantages of competition between alternative regimes may not accord with the anti-competitive interests of the

SROs themselves. That is all the more reason why they should not be over-looked when frameworks for SROs are devised.

The advantage of entrusting regulation to an SRO is that practitioners are likely to be better informed than the public authorities about what is happening in their industry: their *ability* to discover and expose malpractice is superior. The disadvantage is that the willingness of an SRO to unearth wrongdoing is likely to be less than that of a public regulator. The revelation of malpractice would be in the interests of a self-regulating club in so far as potential customers read it as a sign that regulation was effective, but against the club's interests if customers drew the inference that wrongdoing was more prevalent. Without some external stimulus these mixed motives may tend to blunt the vigour with which an SRO pursues its regulatory task, and cause it to favour dealing quietly with any wrongdoers that were discovered. This would weaken the discouragement to potential malefactors.

The idea of parallel regulation is to have public regulation in tandem with self-regulation. Against the drawback of duplication (see above) must be balanced two advantages of parallel regulation. The first is that, for a given level of effort by the SRO, the addition of public regulation would lead to the detection and exposure of some instances of wrongdoing that would otherwise have gone unpunished. How much is hard to judge, especially in view of the ambiguity in the motives of the SRO discussed above, but the additional presence of public regulation would at least provide some insurance against self-regulation being ineffective.

Second, and in our opinion more important, the presence of a public regulatory body would have a significant effect on the incentives facing the SRO, and consequently on its regulatory efforts. Potential consumers of the industry's services would be able to compare the results of the SRO's activities with those of the public regulator. If the comparisons were unfavourable to the SRO it would be apparent that the SRO was not doing its job properly, despite its superior information, and consumers would draw appropriate inferences. In seeking to avoid this outcome, the SRO would have every incentive to enhance its regulatory vigilance.

Parallel regulation is most common where regulation by private firms exists in conjunction with the activities of SROs or public agencies. Public regulation of airline safety, or restaurant hygiene, operates principally by promoting internal regulation, since the damage done to reputation if the public agency is forced to act is very great. The principle extends more widely. We have noted that in both financial and professional services, major firms provide, in effect, brand names to which good reputation is attracted, and they protect the value of their brands through internal monitoring.

Such regulation is particularly effective in conjunction with external regulation. The growth of regulation in the financial services industry has led all major financial institutions to appoint compliance officers with a view to ensuring that their regulation is not damaged by outside demonstration of malpractice. If the possibility of such exposure did not exist, many firms might feel it possible to countenance, or desirable to conceal such misbehaviour rather than root out and expose it. Certainly we observe that accountancy firms in competition with each other, have adopted measures to promote internal quality control, that financial institutions, faced with external regulation, have introduced compliance procedures: and contrast that with the notorious unwillingness of doctors, faced neither with competition nor external regulation, to identify incompetence in other doctors.

Licensing and Certification

Statutory licensing is a public regulatory alternative to the private promotion of reputation (Leland, 1979). It is one with greatest merit where there are relatively few differences in consumer tastes and/or a general demand for high quality services. If appropriately informed, few would want to buy financial services from crooks, be operated on by unqualifed medical practitioners, or to purchase incompatible telephones, and there is therefore little cost to preventing consumers from choosing these things. But where there is a demand for a range of qualities of services, licensing tends to raise the average quality of service and causes losses for some consumers who are unwilling to pay what this costs: while incumbent practitioners may use the licensing regime to limit access to the industry by new entrants.

Certification may avoid these difficulties, in that consumers are informed of the qualifications of those who serve them while being free to secure less costly services if they so prefer. Even though training provides no assurance of product quality, it reduces the marginal cost of product quality and thus consumers are correct in associating better qualities of services with higher levels of service. The weakness of the mechanism is that it encourages investment in training, rather than in product quality *per se*: and so certification may lead to excessive pre-qualification expenditure at the expense of post-qualification activity (Shapiro, 1986).

It will be apparent that there are two elements in the distinction between licensing and certification, which need to be distinguished. The first is whether the regulatory authority monitors inputs to the supply process or outputs from it. Often, it is hardly less difficult for the regulator to monitor product quality than it is for the consumer. The regulator is therefore concerned with inputs. The fact that a doctor is qualified is principally a statement that he has successfully completed a prescribed course of training. It is not evidence that he is good, or even a competent doctor (although he may be deprived of his qualification if he demonstrates gross incompetence). The same is true of most professional licensing and of much quality regulation generally.

The second issue is whether the regulator specifies product quality or provides consumer information. Accountancy illustrates both possibilities. The auditing of company accounts may be undertaken only by members of an appropriate professional body. On the other hand, anyone is free to draw up accounts: the public may wish to use the services of a member of one of the several accounting institutes, or to hire an unqualified or semi-qualified practitioner. Regulation provides information, but no more.

Such certification may extend to para-professionals. A para-profession is a profession in the same industry that has a lower ability level than the first

Para - professional.

profession as its entry requirement. Consumers preferring a lower price and lower quality than the first profession offers would benefit from the presence of the para profession. Thus, as well as increasing competitive pressure, the para-profession allows a wider range of prices and qualities to be available. Nurses and pharmacists can be seen as medical para-professionals.

7   The International Context of Regulation

The removal of barriers to international trade raises a variety of new regulatory issues. In the absence of other specific changes, firms which have in the past developed their activities under different regulatory structures come into competition with each other. This puts all forms of regulation under pressure. We have already noted that regulatory reform in financial services is largely the product of the internationalization of capital markets, an similar developments are in process in other industries, such as telecommunications. Differences in regulatory requirements are frequently used as non-tariff barriers to trade – as, for example where alleged health or safety risks are used to exclude foreign products. This is familiar in many industries, most particularly agricultural products. Because national patterns of organization of production have usually reflected their own internal regulatory structures, it may often be the case that regulatory differences which are wholly innocent in motivation nevertheless have the effect of trade business. Often these two factors are combined in practice – regulatory differences which have arisen because of differences in history or national conditions are supported or maintained because this offers advantages to domestic producers. We are not concerned here, however, either with the use of regulation to derive competition advantages or with how the structure of regulation should be conceived in an international economy.

There are two basic ways in which international differences in regulation may be reconciled. One is to promote the harmonization of regulation across different jurisdictions. The second is to permit competition between rules and between regulators, in much the same way as economic integration promotes competition between products and producers. Such competition between rules may, in turn, be governed by reference to the country in which the product is sold (host regulation) or alternatively relate to the country of origin (home regulation). We shall argue that each of these may be appropriate in particular cases. The issue hinges on the nature of the market failure which regulation is designed to relieve.

The financial services industry illustrates the need for harmonization and also both types of competition between rules. As wholesale banking has become an international market, there is a generally perceived need to homogenize principles and standards of banking supervision. At the same time, the Eurobond market developed in London because American regulatory structures were seen as excessively restrictive. That development in turn prompted deregulation in the United States. Recent changes in financial services regulation in Britain have, in part, been promoted by new entry and in part by a sense that business might otherwise be lose to other jurisdictions.

It is sometimes thought that competition between rules leads to a bidding town of standards of regulation everywhere. But if an investor is deciding whether to execute a transaction in London or New York, one consideration is which of the two affords better investor protection. If a financial market was thought to have inadequate regulation, its members would soon suffer if investors could take their business elsewhere. Most transactions occur in markets where there is a degree of prudential supervision, a well developed system of contract law, a balance between the rights of nationals and foreigners and a concern for the reputation of the market and those who trade in it.

This contrast between harmonization and competition between rules is illustrated in the evolution of regulation within the European Community. For most of its life, the attack on regulation as a non-tariff barrier to trade has been directed towards harmonization of the relevant regulations at the Community level. Such measures have, in the main, enjoyed only limited success. In parallel with the drive to complete the internal market, however, the Commission has been concerned to pursue a 'new approach' to these issues.

The new approach rests on the principle, established by the European Court in the now famous Cassis de Dijon judgment, that goods legally on sale in one community state would be refused admittance to another only on grounds of consumer safety or protection. If follows from this that if there are agreed standards on these matters, members states may impose such additional restrictions on their producers as they wish, but cannot use these restrictions to limit trade. The 'new approach' therefore concentrates on safety and consumer protection issues and, moreover, seeks to define these objectives in general terms and to leave detailed specification to European or national standard setting bodies. Thus the thrust of community policy may be said to have moved from harmonization to competition between rules.

The choice between these approaches rests on the underlying economic problem which provides the initial rationale for regulation. Where regulation is justified by reference to *externalities,* the appropriate geographical scope of regulation is the geographical scope of the externality. If aerosol propellants damage the ozone layer, the problem is a global one and the desirable – indeed the essential – level at which the problem should be tackled is by international agreement. Competition rules is wholly inappropriate: everyone has an individual incentive to move to lower levels to regulation and the outcome is damaging to all. Acid rain, or pollution of the Rhine, equally requires international (although not global) cooperation.

Externalities such as these are unusually wide in scope. Most externalities are local in nature. Water pollution, for example, is, in the main, a local issue. It is difficult to see why the European community should wish, or need, to become involved in prescribing drinking water standards and probably undesirable that it should. It is likely, given the difference in incomes and preferences between Denmark and Greece, that they would choose different tradeoffs between price and quality and undesirable that these differences in choice should be suppressed.

Where regulation is made necessary by natural monopoly, the proper scope of regulation is the scope of the monopoly. In reality, international issues rarely arise when regulation is justified under these headings. The

main area in which they do is where natural monopoly is defended by entry restrictions which excludes, among others, foreign suppliers. Transport
and telecommunication systems are common examples here. The general
principle is straightforward. If there is truly a national monopoly, then it will
not normally need the support of statutory entry barriers and, if viable entry
is possible, there is probably no natural monopoly. The issue is not quite as
simple as this, but it is nearly as simple. It follows that a trading community
should routinely seek to remove entry barriers defended on natural monopoly
grounds. Since arguments of this type are very commonly used – in transport
and telecommunications among other industries – to defend national producers who are inefficient or slow to innovate the issue is an important one.
It is when regulation is justified by *information asymmetry* that competition
between rules will often have most to offer. We have described how the
creation of regulation by firms in a competitive environment can often be
an effective mechanism for overriding information asymmetry and similar
opportunities exist for competition between the regulation of different countries. Such competition raises the standard of all regulation, and drives out
otiose rules which offer protection which consumers do not, in fact require.

Thus it is central to distinguish the possible motivations for regulation in
examining its international ramifications. If it is externalities that provide
the rationale, then competition is undesirable. If regulation is to protect the
public from airline hijackers, the hijackers will migrate to whichever regime
offers the least public protection. Cooperation and coordination between
regulators is then indispensable to effective regulation. The same is true
of safety rules, or audit requirements, or rules to maintain confidence in
the financial system. Where regulation is to maintain consumer protection
or quality standards in the face of asymmetric information, however, then
competition is an appropriate vehicle for ensuring that the costs and benefits
of regulation are properly assessed.

Competition in regulation is not a panacea for regulatory failure, just as
product market competition is a not a universal remedy for market failure,
but we suggest its benefits and costs are well appraising. In particular, the
common anxiety to eliminate overlapping jurisdictions, or to standardize
regulatory requirements internationally, often owes more to concern for
administrative tidiness than to an analysis of the weaknesses of regulation
in practice. We would particularly resist the view that the harmonization of
regulation is a necessary preliminary to the development of free in services.
In the contrary: it is free trade in services which is likely to lead to the evolution of a common regime adapted to consumer requirements and sensitive
to changing needs.

8   Minimising The Need For Regulation

It will be apparent from the preceding discussion that no regulatory
mechanism is free from problems and inefficiencies. A central objective is
therefore to develop structures which minimise the need for regulation.

Privatization and Competition

The simplest cases are those where there is no evident market failure to suggest that regulation is required. The most obvious cases are peripheral areas of the public sector. The state has no advantage in running hotels, or ferries, or trucks, or laundries, and these activities suffer only disadvantages in being subject to constraints on their financing and organization structures which are appropriate or necessary where there is no commercial output or where there is political accountability for the results. It is in areas such as these that privatization has enjoyed its most conspicuously successful results.

Attention should then turn to those areas where markets do not work perfectly, but where the market failure is a relatively trivial one. A good example is the demand for universal service. There are arguments for extending the provision of basic utilities beyond the areas where that might be strictly economically justified, but there are means of ensuring this which fall a long way short of nationalization. A simple regulatory condition can deal with the problem (an alternative is contracting out the uncommercial activity – see pp. 245–247 below). Indeed it is likely that private firms will see public relations and advantages, or social obligations, in such behaviour in any event.

The more difficult areas arise where the market failure is by no means trivial. We have identified three main issues – monopoly, externalities, and information. In each of these cases, there is a trade-off between an underlying market failure and the inevitable weaknesses of any regulatory intervention designed to tackle it. The answer, whenever possible, is to find mechanisms for making markets work – to lean with market forces rather than against them.

Where monopoly is the result of statutory restriction, the obvious response is to repeal the statute. But experience has shown that this is by no means enough. The endowment which incumbent firms have built up during a period of statutory monopol – an endowment of marketing presence, and financial and technical advantages – is not easily challenged. UK experience in such varied industries as coaches and telecommunications has demonstrated that these advantages severely inhibit new competitors.

Even where monopoly is unavoidable, there are devices which harness some of the advantages of competition to reduce the need for regulation. They include franchising and yardstick competition.

Franchising

Franchising involves a competition for the market, even where competition in the market is infeasible or undesirable. Potential monopoly power in the market is held in check by the competitively determined terms of the franchise contract. Thus in theory, the problem of asymmetric information faced by the regulator can be effectively bypassed by the use of competition between informed potential franchisees: competition acts as a kind of discovery mechanism.

Our discussion of franchising can be brief, for its pros and cons have been much debated elsewhere: see, for example, Demsetz (1968), Domberger *et al.* (1986), Sharpe (1982), Vickers and Yarrow (1988, section 4.6), and Williamson (1976). The simplest method of franchising is to hold an auction for the right to the monopoly, in which the winner is the bidder who offers the franchiser the largest monetary sum. Such a system helps to transfer the (capitalized) value of the monopoly to the franchiser but fails to deal with the underlying problems of market power and allocative inefficiency. Assuming that the public authorities wish to tackle those problems, we shall focus on the form of franchising sometimes known as the Chadwick–Demsetz proposal, in which the natural monopoly franchise is awarded for a period of time to the competitor offering to supply the product or service at the lowest price(s).

On the face of it, franchising appears to provide a very attractive way of combining competition and efficiency without any great burden on the regulators. This competition for monopoly seems to destroy the undesirable monopoly of information that hinders traditional regulation, and price is set by competition, not administrative decision. Franchising has also met with practical success in a number of areas, including competitive tendering in refuse collection, hospital cleaning and catering, and uncommercial bus services, not to mention its widespread use in the private sector.

But franchising is prone to a number of difficulties in some circumstances, and unfortunately the industries where regulatory problems are greatest (e.g. energy, telecommunications and water) are especially prone to such problems. They include the following:

1 The bidding for the franchise might fail to be competitive, because there may be very few competitors, due to scarcity of requisite skills, collusion between bidders, or strategic advantages possessed by the incumbent franchisee, which deter challenges to him. These could arise from experience effects or superior information over potential bidders.

2 Problems associated with asset handover in the event of an incumbent franchisee being displaced may distort incentives to invest (and indeed the nature of competition for the franchise). Valuation of sunk assets is both difficult and costly. If the incumbent expects that there value in the event of handover would be set too low (high), and if there is a chance of his/her being displaced, then his/her incentive to invest will be correspondingly too low (high). This problem is diminished if the sunk assets are under independent ownership and the franchise is simply an operating franchise, but this raises questions of how the franchiser determines the level of facilities to be provided: as usual the choice is between information or incentive problems.

3 If there is technological or market uncertainty in relation to the product or service in question, then the specification of the franchise contract will be a very complex task (especially if its duration is long, e.g. to minimize asset handover problems), and the need to monitor and administer the contract during its life is certain to arise. In the privatized utility industries, for example, it would be impossible to cater for every eventuality

that might occur in the life of even a short-term contract. Thus, we are left with incompletely specified contracts, but they require continuing contract administration.

Two conclusions are implied by the considerations above. First, the attractiveness of franchising depends on the circumstances at hand. It works best where there are numerous potential competitors with the requisite skills, where sunk costs are not high, and where technological and market uncertainty is not great. Second, franchising involves an implicit regulatory arrangement for all but the simplest products and services. As Goldberg (1976) writes: 'Many of the problems associated with regulation lie in what is being regulated, not in the act of regulation itself.' Franchising should be seen not as alternative to regulation, but a form of it that seeks to use some of the desirable incentive properties of competition.

Yardstick competition

One of the main themes in this chapter has been the importance of information for effective regulation. If the regulator is relatively uninformed about industry conditions, and especially if the regulated firm has a virtual monopoly of relevant information, then the regulatory system is liable to become insensitive to cost and demand conditions. For example, if the regulator can observe actual costs but does not know the potential for cost reduction, s/he faces a dilemma. Setting prices in line with actual costs achieves allocative efficiency but provides poor incentives for cost reduction, while fixing prices for a long time ahead may create good incentives for internal efficiency but is liable to lead to serious losses in allocative efficiency as costs move out of line with prices.

Yardstick competition attempts to resolve the dilemma by bringing regulated firms in distinct markets indirectly into competition with each other in respect of cost reduction. Suppose that a national monopolist was divided into separately owned Northern and Southern units, each with a natural monopoly in its geographical region. Suppose that they face symmetric cost and demand conditions, that the regulator can observe actual unit costs, but that s/he does not know the potential for cost reduction. By making the price that North can charge depend on the unit cost level achieved by South (and vice versa), the regulator gives North incentives for internal efficiency, because North reaps the entire benefit of any cost reduction that it achieves. Given symmetry and the strong incentives to cost reduction built into the system, North's costs provide a good indication of what South may be expected to achieve, and vice versa, and since North's price is linked to South's unit cost, North's price will, in turn, be linked to North's own unit cost level. Thus, allocative efficiency becomes compatible with internal efficiency.

This illustrative argument is based on several important assumptions, which may not hold in practice. First, the firms might seek to collude to act as one, thereby undermining the indirect competition that regulation sought to promote. Second, symmetry between regions is highly improbable, but this does not affect the basic argument provided that the main differences between regions are observable and reasonably stable. Yardstick competition does not work so well, however, when they have unobservable characteristics that are uncorrelated between regions. The danger then is that North's price would be unduly affected by distinctive features of South's situation. Such 'noise' would distort allocative efficiency and would not encourage North to behave as his circumstances warranted.

Nevertheless, it is a general proposition in the theory of incentives that when a principal (in our case the regulator) has several agents (firms) under his control, it is invariably the case that the optimal incentive scheme (regulatory mechanism) involves the reward of each agent being contingent upon the performance of the other agents as well as his own. We therefore know that the best regulatory mechanisms will exploit information from comparative performance (if it is available) in some form, but the question remains of *how* to do so in any particular case. On this it would be foolish to attempt generalization, since the degree of homogeneity between regional units varies from industry to industry.

However, yardstick competition obviously relies on the existence of independent sources of information. Since the ability to make performance comparisons can greatly enhance the effectiveness of incentives, integrated industry structures that leave a firm with a monopoly of information have a major disadvantage. In short, the benefit of having a good information base for effective regulation provides a strong argument for ensuring that industry structure is such as to provide data on comparative performance. That cannot happen in the face of nationwide monopoly, but it is quite consistent with natural monopoly at the regional level. This fact has clear implications for the appropriate structure of regulated natural monopoly industries.

9 The Future of Regulation

General principles

We have argued that regulation is required – and only required – in the face of some market failure. It follows immediately that each regulatory regime should be targeted on the relevant failure or failures. This point seems almost too obvious to be worth making, but the reality of regulation has proved very different. The normal pattern is that market failure provides the rationale for the introduction oof regulation, but the scope of regulation is then extended to a wide range of matters which are the subject of general or sectional interest, regardless of whether there is any element of market failure or not.

In devising any regulatory framework it is therefore necessary to begin by asking how markets have failed. The nature of the market will then determine the design of regulation. Of the three industries with which we have been concerned, monopoly is the principal issue in utilities and asymmetry of information in financial and professional services: externalities are a limited cause of market failure in all three activities. Where the need for regulation is the product of *monopoly*, the first requirement is to see whether structural remedies are feasible without substantial loss of economies of sale or scope. Can competition be promoted? Where it cannot be, the objective should be to 'ring-fence' the area of natural monopoly as far as possible, to ensure that unavoidable monopoly does not lead to unnecessary monopoly in other, naturally competitive markets. Within the ring-fence, regulation will be necessary to restrain prices with minimum detriment to efficiency.

Where *externalities* create the need for regulation, the objective should be to achieve solutions that lean with market forces rather than replace them. Structural remedies can again be contrasted with measures that bear directly on conduct. For example, an activity (e.g. pollution or the supply of unsafe products) that potentially generates negative externalities can be tackled either by liability rules that give aggrieved parties the right to sue for damages, or by conduct regulation. In some circumstances the former method can give good incentives to curb or modify the activity to an optimal extent, and there is no need for public intervention (and associated public information) beyond the provision of a legal framework. But where – as often with safety issues – there is limited scope for different opinions about appropriate levels of quality, and (more importantly) there are free rider problems for individuals seeking to uphold standards, then public monitoring may well be the most effective device. We would also like to see measures to bring into being the 'missing markets' which lead to over-exploitation of under-priced resources.

The most obvious remedy for market failures which result from *information asymmetry* is information disclosure, and this may often be sufficient remedy. It is perhaps, difficult for public agencies to publish information on product quality. But it is possible to subsidize the private production of such information, and it is impossible not to be impressed by the contrast between by the very small expenditure on the public good of impartial information on the qualities of goods and services available and the very large expenditures incurred by those who provide such goods and services on the private goods of advertising and public relations. Measures which seek to suppress communication of information altogether – as with the restrictions on advertising and promotional activity within the professions – seem to us particularly undesirable. Their effect, and to a degree their intention, is to inhibit the development of the market's own mechanisms for monitoring product quality – the establishment of good reputations for products and brands, relative to other products or brands. The task of policy should instead to be promote these. It is these areas that regulatory reform is most urgently required.

Notes

1. Assuming that it has the right to discharge the effluent. If, on the other hand, the fishermen possess and exercise rights to clean water, there is a sense in which they impose a cost on the chemical company, see Coase (1960).
2. In natural monopoly conditions that are not severe, competition may be desirable. Even though single firm production is the most cost-effective, rivalry can enhance allocative efficiency more than it diminishes cost-efficiency.

3. There is a well-known distinction between search goods, whose quality is apparent before purchase, and experience goods, whose quality is apparent only after consumption. Perhaps 'trust goods' could be used as a term to describe goods whose quality is not apparent even after consumption.
4. The basic argument needs modifying, and might not be valid, if competitors have a cost advantage in activity B, or if there are substantial diseconomies of scale. If there is perfect competition (and hence zero profits) in activity B, and if there is no substitutionality between the outputs of A and B, then firm F is indifferent between excluding competitors and not doing so, because it can extract all the monopoly profits either way.
5. Assuming, as is reasonable, that there are no serious diseconomies of scale in the activity of regulation.

References

Akerlof, G. (1970), 'The Market for lemons: qualitative uncertainty and the market mechanism', *Quarterly Journal of Economics*.
Allen, F. (1984). 'Reputation and product quality', *Rand Journal of Economics*.
Averch, H. and Johnson, L. (1962), 'Behaviour of the firm under regulatory constraint', *American Economic Review*.
Baron, D.P. and Myerson, R.B. (1982), 'Regulating a monopolist with unknown costs', *Econometrica*.
Bator, F. (1958). 'The anatomy of market failure', *Quarterly Journal of Economics*.
Baumol, W.J. (1982), 'Contestable markets: an uprising in the theory of industrial structure', *American Economic Review*.
Coase, R.H. (1960), 'The problem of social cost', *Journal of Law and Economics*.
Demsetz, H. (1968), 'Why regulate utilities?', *Journal of Law and Economics*.
Department of Trade and Industry (1988), *Review of Restrictive Trade Practices Policy*, Cm. 331, London, HMSO.
Domberger, S., Meadowcroft, J. and Thompson, D. (1986) 'Competitive tendering and efficiency', *Fiscal Studies*.
Farrell, J. and Saloner, G. (1985). 'Standardization, compatibility and innovation', *Rand Journal of Economics*.
Finsinger, J., Hammond E. M. and Tapp, J. (1985), 'Insurance: competition or regulation? A comparative study of the insurance market in the United Kingdom and the Federal Republic of Germany', *IFS Report Series* 19. London, Institute for Fiscal Studies.
Goldberg, V. P. (1976), 'Regulation and Administered Contracts', *Bell Journal of Economics*.
Grossman, S. (1981), 'The information role of warranties and private disclosure about product quality', *Journal of Laws and Economics*.
Grossman, S. and Stiglitz, J.E. (1980), 'On the impossibility of informationally efficient markets', *American Economic Review*.
Heal, G. (1976), 'Do bad products drive out good?' *Quarterly Journal of Economics*.
Katz, M. and Shapiro, C. (1985), 'Network externalities, 'competition and compatibility', *American Economic Review*.
Kay, J.A., Mayer, C. and Thompson, D. (eds) (1986), *Privatisation and Regulation: The UK experience*, Oxford; Oxford University Press.
Klein, B. and Leffler, K. (1981), 'The role of market forces in assuring contractual performance', *Journal of Political Economy*.
Laffont, J.J. and Tirole, J. (1986), 'Using cost observation to regulate firms', *Journal of Political Economy*.

Leland, H. (1979), 'Quacks, lemons, and licensing: a theory of minimum, quality standard', *Journal of Political Economy*.
Mankiw, N.G. and Whinston, M.D. (1986), 'Free entry and social inefficiency', *Rand Journal of Economics*.
Milgrom, P. and Roberts, J. (1986), 'Price and advertising signals of product quality', *Journal of Political Economy*.
Miller, J. and Douglas, G. (1974) 'Economic regulation of domestic air transport: theory and policy', *Journal of Economic Literature*.
Nelson, P. (1974), 'Advertising as information', *Journal of Political Economy*.
Pescatrice, D.R., and Timpani, J.M. (1980), 'The performance and objective of public and private utilities operating in the United States', *Journal of Public Economics*.
Rothschild, M. and Stiglitz, J. (1976). 'Equilibrium in competitive insurance markets: the economics of markets with incomplete information', *Quarterly Journal of Economics*.
Salop, S. and Stiglitz, J. (1977), 'Bargains and ripoffs: a model of monopolistically competitive price dispersion'. *Review of Economic Studies*.
Shaked, A. and Sutton, J. (1981). 'The self-regulating profession', *Review of Economic Studies*.
Shapiro, C. (1982). 'Consumer information, product quality and seller reputation', *Bell Journal of Economics*.
Shapiro, C. (1986). 'Investment, moral hazard and occupational licensing', *Review of Economic Studies*.
Sharpe, T. (1982), 'The control of natural monopoly by franchising', mimeo, Wolfson College, Oxford.
Shliefer, A. (1985), 'A theory of yardstick competition', *Rand Journal of Economics*.
Spence, A.M. (1984), 'Cost reduction, competition and industry performance', *Econometrica*.
Suzumura, K. and Kiyono, K. (1987). 'Entry barriers and economic welfare,' *Review of Economics Studies*.
Vickers, J.S. (1985). 'The economics of predatory practices', *Fiscal Studies*.
Vickers, J.S. and Yarrow, G. (1988). *Privatization – An Economic Analysis*, MIT Press.
Williamson, O.E. (1976). 'Franchising bidding for natural monopolies – in general and with respect to CATIV', *Bell Journal of Economics*.

Index

accountancy 239, 240–1
  see also financial services
acid rain 199
  see also environmental policies
actual competition 25
  see also competition
administrative deregulation 16
  see also deregulation
ADRs 154, 157, 158–9, 166,168, 170–1
adverse drug reaction *see* ADRs
advertising 233, 28
aggregation:
  telecommunications 75
agricultural industry 217, 221
air traffic control *see* ATC
air transport
  and anti-trust laws 24–6
  computerized reservations 38, 39,
    40–2, 45
  deregulation 21–8, 38, 90–1, 94–5,
    124–34
  domestic 15–16, 23
  efficiency 124–34
  in Europe 90, 91–4, 95–6, 124–34
  in United States 3, 5–6, 11, 15–16,
    20, 23-8, 38, 45, 90–1, 94–6,
    124–6
  in West Germany 216
  indivisibilities 91–2
  landing rights 96
  mergers 20–8
  models of 129–31
  prices 16, 23, 26–7, 94–5, 124–34
  productivity 128–32
  regulation 3, 5–6
  safety 23, 95
  theoretical studies 126–34
  see also transportation
allocation standards 14

  see also regulatory methods
allocative efficiency 10
America *see* United States
American Medical Association 154
American Telephone and Telegraph
  Company *see* AT&T
animal species:
  drug testing 157, 165
antibiotics 157
anti-competitive threats 41–2
  see also competition
anti-trust laws
  and air transport 24–6
  and bottlenecks 38–9
  and regulation 20–1, 22
  enforcement 25–6
  in United States 3, 19–26, 44–5, 114
asset handover 246
AT&T 17, 30–4, 36, 42–3, 59–63, 75,
  82, 83, 85, 87, 114–15
ATC 5
Averch-Johnson effect 42

banking system 224
  see also financial services
bargaining 19
  see also regulatory methods
bargaining powers 11–12
  Bell Canada 75
  Bell Operating Companies *see*
    BOCs
below cost prices 42, 93–4
  see also prices
below cost services 93–4
  see also costs
Benelux countries:
  drug testing 161
  see also European Community
biotechnological drugs 162–3

Index